Two five-year-olds, Jane Ray (Richmond) and Bertha Manter (Arnold) inspect their toes at the beach, 1935. Jane said, "It was Mr. Pollack who took the picture...he used to go around and take good pictures of the people in Madaket."

Nantucket Voices
Volume Two

Katherine Hatch (Dunham) and Florence Ingall (Clifford), dressed as sailor-boys, are dancing to "March of the Wooden Soldiers" for Austin Strong's Follies at the Nantucket Yacht Club, in the late 1920s.

Nantucket

Volume Two

Voices

More
Stories of
Nantucket's
People

by Mary Miles

Trimtab Publications, Nantucket Island, Massachusetts

DEDICATION

This book is dedicated to my big family of Nantucket friends, acquaintances, and especially those people—friends old and new—who trusted me to listen to and record the stories of their lives.

ACKNOWLEDGMENTS

Again, thanks to good friends Suzanne and Jerry Daub, in whose publication *Yesterday's Island* these stories have appeared over the years; to Melody Olbrych, who "tuned up" the book with her layout and design expertise; to Mimi Beman, for unfailing support; to the Nantucket Historical Association, for help in locating pictures and facts; and to my friend Geraldine Gardiner Salisbury, whose mother, Bertha Chase Gardiner, was one of my very first interviews—"GG" has once again provided consistently wise editorial advice.

Trimtab Publications
Nantucket Island, Massachusetts

Layout & Design: Melody Olbrych

© 2004 Mary Miles

ISBN 1-59457-414-6
Library of Congress Control Number: 2003093078

5 4 3 2 1

Manufactured in the USA

First Edition, Volume Two

FOREWORD

We are the lives we live. What we do, where we do it, and the people with whom we do it, provides us with our identity. The deepest sorrow of memory loss is that those who have forgotten the who, what, and where of their past no longer know themselves. In forgetting the past, we forget who we are and lose our sense of self.

This is true of communities as well as individuals. A community that has no memory has no sense of its own identity.

Nantucketers have an especially keen appreciation of the people, the place, and the doings that make the island community what it is. Memory of these things is often expressed in stories. We love to hear, tell, and relive in the imagination, stories about life as it has been lived on island. Dorcas Honorable and Abram Quarry are gone with all their people, but we still tell the legends their people told about the Poot Ponds and the puckwudgies. And so, in a sense, we keep the long vanished Nantucket Indian in our communal memory. We would probably enjoy stories about things that have not happened yet just as much, if they could be told. But remembering can only involve what is past.

Most Nantucketers will confess that more than a few of our favorite tales contain a somewhat gossipy element. It is well to acknowledge that this is one of the ingredients that make oral tradition fragile. We are reluctant to put into print things that smack of gossip. Similarly, some past events reveal rather unflattering aspects of island life. We would just as soon some things about Nantucket's past not be told, just as we would rather certain teen-age escapades of our own not be verbally passed along to our grandchildren even though they may well be as hilariously entertaining as they are revealing.

I became aware of just what a treasure Nantucket's memories are some years ago in, of all places, Florida City. I was with a group of 32 volunteers who had flown there to help rebuild after Hurricane Andrew's devastating assault. We were assigned two tents among the hundreds providing shelter to people whose homes had been destroyed. They were a mixed lot, mostly agricultural workers. We were a mixed lot too, mostly Nantucketers.

We quickly fell into a daily routine that ended just like summer camp, with a cook-out and gathering around the fire to tell stories. Someone would start with an anecdote about a well-known island character. This would be followed by another about the same eccentric, and on and on for an hour or two filling the void left by the lack of electricity in the camp with the power of memory. The next night the focus might be on a place, an old watering hole like The Upper Deck, or crossings on the steamer in ice, in storm, and in victorious aftermath of a Vineyard game.

By the third night I noticed we were not alone. Around the circle of familiar Nantucket faces another circle of faces was assembled. Faces from other tents in the camp. Hispanic faces. Haitian faces. Worn faces of those we heard called "poor white trash" and less complimentary racial epithets. Tired faces of people who understand it is the most vulnerable who suffer longest from "natural disasters." Had they gathered around our lively gam because their sense of community had been swept away with their homes? Could it be that the stories we were sharing about life on a far-away island were helping heal their lost sense of belonging to a community?

I wondered how much they understood. Many spoke halting English. Some none at all. I wondered even longer what they made of that little off-shore community that seemed to be populated by an unusual cast of characters engaged in rather peculiar behaviors. Did they recognize in our stories some islands of their own?

It is true that the past never entirely passes away. What Mary Miles has done is draw us around the fire to savor with our friends and neighbors not just some of the life that is Nantucket, but some of the life that is life.

Reverend Ted Anderson
January 2004

INTRODUCTION

As I wrote in the introduction to Volume One of *Nantucket Voices,* in every life a book…and I might add, in many lives, a whole series of books! I'm so grateful to the many Nantucket people who have shared their stories with me. It was extremely difficult to choose which individuals should be included in Volume One and now Volume Two, as it will be in any forthcoming volumes.

The short glimpses into people's lives in the following pages are only snapshots, in a way—is it possible to even begin to capture in a few pages the essence of a life—especially, in many cases, a very long and rich life? The reader must imagine behind every anecdote an immeasurable collection of other events, memories, thoughts, and experiences. This is the frustrating knowledge with which every oral history interviewer lives: the interview must stop at some point; the tape must be turned off; and the painful awareness sets in that there is so much more to hear and talk about.

Once again, the date of the interview is given at the beginning of each story, so in many cases readers will realize that between that time and now, people have moved on, changes have taken place, and more life chapters have been added. Also, something a little different; this volume includes writings of two people I didn't know, shared with me by their relatives: Charlotte Gibbs Ruley's touching high-school essay about Nantucket, which opens the book, and Esther Gibbs' comments in a small pamphlet about her popular North Shore Restaurant. As well, there's a nonbiographical interview with Edith Andrews—strictly about her bird lore. But Nantucket voices they all are.

There's a term that writer Susan Vreeland used in her book *Girl in Hyacinth Blue* that describes quite well the value of recording oral histories: "how love builds itself unconsciously…out of the momentous ordinary…" Substitute the word "life" for "love," if you want, and that's what, in the long run, matters most—the deep drama and meaning in the day-to-day. I believe it's important for people of the future to know what made people tick in the past. Every now becomes a then all too quickly. And what makes us tick is the momentous ordinary.

Mary Miles
March 2004

TABLE OF CONTENTS

Our Swiftest Season
by Charlotte Gibbs

Class of 1923, Nantucket High School
[Published in the *Inquirer and Mirror,* October 28, 1922.]

Charlotte Gibbs [Ruley] wrote this beautiful and thoughtful little essay while she was a Nantucket High School student in 1922; her daughter, Frances Ruley Karttunen, gave permission to reprint it here.

The busy season has gone, the crowded inns are closed, the summer houses are shut up for the winter, and the summer visitors have at last left our island to the Nantucketers. Even the commons have changed their browns and greens and put on bright reds and yellows, as if to wave the home banners.

If only the summer visitors knew the witching charm of Nantucket when the colors are all flying and the air is just frosty enough to bite cheeks and nip fingers, then they would spend not only the summer but part of the winter here. Some of the best of them, however, have found it out, and we are glad to have them linger. They seem to belong in a way. Our name for them is "On-from-Off." Some of the others think that Nantucket is dull in the winter. Perhaps in the following paragraphs I can change this notion.

School usually opens about the second week in September. The pupils all dress in their best school clothes and gather in chattering, excited groups in the schoolyard until the door is unlocked. Some tell how they spent the summer here, and how much they earned, others of their first trip to America. The new Seniors assume their dignity and try to impress the lower classes with their importance.

After the first day we begin to get settled. The usual routine of studies is followed, but school is not all work. A little later the good times begin. Class parties and dances are looked forward to. For the young folks, school is indeed a lively place during the winter.

"A hiding candy frolic!" "Oh, what fun!" "Where shall we hide?" "Where are we going to meet to decide upon the hiding place?" Such exclamations and questions follow the announcement of the event. The girls all gather stealthily at an appointed place. The boys keep a sharp lookout, but are usually outwitted. On the evening appointed, much disguised maidens take to back streets and round-about ways to reach the hiding place. On our last candy frolic we hid in the police station. Such times we had getting there! Marcella was tracked by five eagle-eyed boys, who blocked her in every possible way, but the interested editor of the "Mirror" aided with his automobile.

Marjorie was invited out to supper, but as one of the boys came to her house, she had her repast served under the bed. One of our teachers broke through her neighbor's hedge to escape the boys picketing in front of her house. Indeed, nearly all had similar thrilling experiences, and when we were all collected at the police station, we were breathless, indeed.

The boys found us, after considerable search. We in turn discovered them, so the expense of the following party was shared by both boys and girls. No island winter is complete without one of these old time candy frolics, and they are looked forward to with glee.

The Nantucket winds have a way of their own, just as we islanders do. They come driving in, cool and salt from the ocean, early in October. All winter they rush along over our island, sometimes at the rate of ninety miles an hour. At night when we lie in bed, we can feel the house rock, and hear the wolves and bears howling around the windows and roaring down the open fire-places. The Weather Bureau puts up signals when a storm is coming, and upon request will tell you the velocity of the wind. We feel the full strength of it, as there is nothing to stop the mad gallop, like troops of horses, across the island. Trees are blown down and vessels driven ashore by nor'easters. Our little stubby pines out on the commons are all flat-headed in the spring. The prevailing winds are southeast, and this accounts in part for our mild climate.

Such winds as these keep the surfmen at Nantucket busy. Treacherous shoals guard our little island; and these, with the frequent nor'east blows, make our waters a place to be dreaded. Over five hundred wrecks have occurred here since the settlement in 1659. Since the writer is a surfman's daughter, she knows more about the life-saving stations than some, and will try to tell you about them.

There are four Coast Guard Stations situated at dangerous, exposed parts of the shore, besides a few Humane houses. The last contain necessary apparatus, so in case of a wreck a long distance off, the life-savers will not have to drag their apparatus from the station along the beach and thereby lose time.

Our Coast Guard Stations are located on Coskata, about two miles from Great Point; at Madaket, on the southwestern corner; on the island of Muskeget; and at Surfside, on the south shore. The last is now officially closed, and all the government furnishings have been distributed among other Coast Guard Stations. The Radio Compass Station takes the place of Surfside to such an extent that most boats in trouble, especially in thick weather, are directed on their routes.

The Coast Guard Stations are much alike, and are all painted white. Each has a barn and a workshop, besides the main building. In this is a kitchen, a captain's room, and two or three boat and beach cart rooms. On the roof is a cupola, where the men stand watches. In the daytime these are four hours long; at night, three.

From five o'clock in the evening until seven in the morning, through fair or stormy weather, the sturdy coast guards patrol the beaches, peering out across the dark waters in search of distress signals. These patrols are divided into eastern and western beats and last three hours. The coast guards also have boat drills, which consist of the launching, manning, and landing of the surf-boat in the surf; and gun drills, or practice in shooting the breeches buoy. Besides these are drills in wigwagging, semaphore, and the international code.

Furthermore, each guard learns the use of the medicine chest and what to do in case of accidents. These hardy, well trained men take part in many a thrilling rescue, and more than one has a medal to show for his bravery.

One of the joys of this same surfman's daughter is a walk across the beaches or commons. A favorite hike is to Miacomet, across the commons and back to Surfside along the beach, with the big rollers piling in. Everything is quiet, save for the harsh cawing of the crows and the pound of the sea against the bluff. The grass is all dried and brown, and the grove of pine trees in the distance looms up in tall dark blots.

A group of red farm buildings stand out against the brown hummocks. Low sand dunes shut out the sea and surf to the left; to the right and ahead is a grassy stretch of ground, both level and rolling. Usually a small hound capers along for company, and noses through the grass in hopes of scaring up a rabbit.

We soon reach Miacomet Pond, a narrow, wavy length of water about two miles long. It was named by Autopscot's Indians, whose village was located near the head of the pond and means meeting place. On one side I see the stiff fingers of the broom, the seeds of which were brought from Ireland many years ago, and planted on the Barrett farm. Since then it has migrated over the island, and finds a welcome at 'Sconset, Polpis, and along many roads.

In June the commons are ablaze with its bright yellow flowers. Looking down from a sand dune, higher than the rest, I see where the pond is opened nearly every year, in the spring, to let the herring and perch run in, and in the fall to let them into the open sea. At Miacomet I usually turn back and walk along the beach, where the dog and I play tag with the waves. We run down daringly near the breakers, but rush back when they tumble over and chase us up the sand. Many dead birds, such as coots, grebes, loons, eider ducks, whistlers, shell drakes, old squaws, and little auks are washed ashore by the waves, and I often come upon a group of crows feasting.

Along the smooth, wet shore lie the pretty periwinkles, marsh clams, penny shells, round winkle shells, dried shark's cradles, and pieces of sponge. By the time I have reached Surfside I have my pockets full. The salt air usually gives one a keen appetite. After one of these walks I feel as if I could eat a mountain.

Who would find Nantucket dull in the winter, with all the wonderful places to walk to? This is only one of many. Capaum Pond is another place; Hummock Pond another; and along the north beach, just on the edge of the chasing surf, almost the best of all.

Spring is usually late on our purple island; but when at last it comes, with its warm and sunny days, every house-keeper gets the house-cleaning fever. The lines in the yards are filled with winter clothing and blankets, hurry-up dinners are eaten at noon, so no time will be lost, the clean smell of soap suds and varnish fill the air, and everything that can be scrubbed is washed until it shines.

Houses to be rented receive an extra spring polish. If you are unlucky enough to be living in one, you know how renters always come to look it over at the wrong time; and how they insist on seeing the room where you are dressing, or the kitchen at dinner time.

After house cleaning is over we have a little peace. Soon they arrive, and we move into cramped quarters until September. Then we are free again, and our village, our commons, and the whole of our island are ours until another visiting season begins.

4

Left to right—
(1) Charlotte Hamblen Gibbs as a young girl; (2) Charlotte Hamblen Gibbs, Nantucket High School graduation, June, 1923; (3) Charlotte Gibbs Ruley on Kite Hill with a pheasant she's shot, circa 1940.

Photo on opposite page—Standing: Surfman Maurice Gibbs, his sons Arthur (in Coast Guard uniform) and John Gibbs. Seated: Charlotte Gibbs, Hilda Österberg Gibbs, Esther Gibbs.

6

The Roots of Their Souls
Are in Nantucket

Maurice & Millie Gibbs, 2003

MILLIE & MAURICE AUG 1948

*I*n early February of 2003, I interviewed two people who have proved that maybe it is, after all, possible to go home again. After four decades and very different lives, Millie (née Norcross) and Maurice Gibbs rediscovered each other a dozen years ago, and are now in the process of living happily ever after. When asked if they are both natives, Millie—who doesn't talk much—said emphatically, "Yes, definitely!" Maurice responded (ever-so-slightly unchivalrously), "She's an older native than I am." Well, he said that because of course there's a story connected to it.

But first, about the Nantucket ancestors: Maurice said, "That's tough to put into a few words. We both go back to Tristram Coffin, so we're distantly related…our families came at the beginning and we're still trying to get it right. The Gibbs part of the family appears to have hailed out of the Barnstable area around 1800, and I'm named after my grandfather, Maurice Gibbs." He chuckled, and added, "Every now and then in the I&M's 'Looking Backward' column there's something about him; it was mentioned at one time that he'd been hailed into court for starting a fire. He was burning his old cranberry bog and it got away from him. So I've made the headlines, in a way."

How about the Gibbs' growing-up years on the island? Millie said, "We spent twelve years of school at Academy Hill." Maurice added, "Millie's father was a builder here on the island, and her grandfather was also a builder, as well as Nantucket's first fire chief, in around 1913. Arthur Augustus Norcross. Everyone knew Millie's father James as 'Red' Norcross. The family lived on Twin Street—I used to beat a path down there when we were in high school, when Millie and I were going steady. In those days," he went on, "you had to do Coffin School time as well as high school, even if you were in the college prep course, which I was; I still had to take woodworking and metalworking, and Millie was learning cooking and sewing and so on." I wondered if Maurice had ever wished to learn to cook, or Millie to create with wood, hammer, and nails, and Millie said, "All I had to do was go down to my father's shop, right next to our house. He was a carpenter, so I could go in and play there any time I wanted."

Did Maurice and Millie have favorite teachers? Millie said, "Oh, Laura Pease—I had her in the sixth grade. She was Fran Pease's mother. There was one teacher I didn't care too much for—she was our fourth-grade teacher, and when we finished that year, goody goody, she went to the fifth grade, so we had her for two years and then I had her again in high school! Let's see, the Hulls were nice—we had Rita in the second grade and Marjorie in the third." Maurice said, "I was sitting in the third grade in Marjorie's class when Tony Dias, who was in high school, came running in the door and said 'Dismiss school!'—that was the day after the Pearl Harbor attack. To a third-grader, that didn't really mean that much other than leaving a vivid image—I can still see the look on Tony's excited face—the superintendent had sent him around to tell each class to send everybody home. And home we went, not quite knowing what was going on."

WHACKO! HELEN BARTLETT GETS MAURICE

Maurice laughed as he recalled being knocked "upside the head" with a ruler in the fourth grade. "I was sitting almost where I'm sitting right now in your living room [at Academy Hill]. I was probably chatting when I should've been listening, and Helen Bartlett had apparently told me to be quiet, but I kept right on talking, and the next thing I knew I had a ruler right alongside of my temple…WHACKO! And it's the only memory I have of corporal punishment in this school. But it worked, and I didn't hold it against her. She was a great teacher. Millie was one year ahead of me, and we had the same teachers. She was Class of 1950 and I was Class of 1951. There were three high school teachers who influenced my life: Arthur Baker in history, which was really my first love; and John Shaw, the science teacher, who was really in his prime then; he got me interested in science and as a result I eventually became a meteorologist. And then I think everybody in our generation was influenced by Mary P. Walker, who will be 96 years old February 17th, 2003. What a sharp woman!"

Young people all had jobs, said Maurice. Millie worked at Cliffside Beach for H. Murray Conrad for five years. She said, "I liked working there. I also helped my father with his bookkeeping. No, I wasn't keeping books at Cliffside—I gave out keys and folded towels," she laughed. "There was always something to do. I don't think I was ever bored as a child." After high school she married and had two daughters. "One daughter has six sons and a daughter," she said, "and the other has two daughters. My oldest grandson, Christian Ray, has two children, so now I'm a great-grandmother. After I was married I did bookkeeping for the Barrett Sightseeing office…and after that…hmmm…Marine Home Center for a couple of years and then Brock's for thirteen years, and then I went to Educational Management Network as bookkeeper."

During high school, Maurice had various odd jobs: "I caddied as a youngster, and mowed a few lawns. I remember a few of the real old-time Nantucketers on Centre Street—I'd take the ashes out of their coal-burning furnaces. I remember Whitty Riddell at the top of Centre Street. He was probably 90 and for a few pennies I was taking his ashes out and getting his coal in. There were a lot of elderly historic people there—of course at the time I didn't recognize them as 'historic' or appreciate that. I also worked for my Aunt Esther Gibbs at the North Shore Restaurant, running errands. When I

Maurice Gibbs at 6 months. He says he still remembers bumping along in that carriage on the unpaved Hummock Pond Road.

Millicent Norcross as a 9-month-old.

turned 14, I went down to the First National Store on Main Street, where Wilson's Gallery is now, and saw Al Fee, and he signed me on; I ended up working in the vegetable and fruit department there for Charlie Ferrara. Until I joined the Navy, it was essentially my only steady job. So I was working after school, and in the summer I worked fulltime, from 1947 until I went off into the service in 1953."

What did kids do for fun then? Millie said, "Oh, we went to the movies, went skating, sliding, dancing. We always had a lot of school dances." Maurice fondly remembers the dance classes, "held at the No. 4's with Al Fee and Charlie Stackpole and Helen Winslow (Chase) as our instructors. The No. 4's? You mean you haven't noticed that engine-company sign over the Hub? They made their space available to us because they had an appropriate little dance floor. Our generation all went to dance classes. We did square dances, line dances, the fox trot, ballroom waltzes, and so on. The sewing place is there now, but the No. 4's club still exists there—it's mainly a social club. But those dancing classes—oh, my goodness, was Helen Winslow ever light on her feet! I always remind her of that when I go down to the Island Home on Tuesday mornings to play the piano. I go down about an hour before the church service and play oldies but goodies, and then when Georgia Snell or whoever comes to conduct the church service, I swing into hymns with them." Maurice is quite musical, and sings tenor in the Congregational Church choir; Millie, he says, has a great voice, but he can't convince her to sing.

When Maurice got out of high school, he aspired to be a ball player. He said, "I went down to Florida and went through Joe Stripp's Baseball School in December of 1951, and then stayed on with the Washington Senators through spring training. But about halfway through, I developed a terrible sore arm, and at about the same time my dad called from Nantucket saying, 'You know, you're number 3 on the draft.' The guy who was ahead of me clearly wasn't going, because he'd broken both knees in football, and so I really was number 2. I knew they weren't going to exempt me because I

10

Left—Maurice, all ready for the Navy, 1952. Right— Millie Norcross in 1948.

was a baseball player…so I came home, and not long after that enlisted in the Navy. I intended to do four years, but I stayed for 34. I became a weather observer, and then gradually worked my training up until I became an enlisted forecaster. And I ultimately got a commission, and continued on. The Navy eventually merged the meteorology discipline with oceanography, and I actually became both. So at the end of my career, I had this fancy title behind my name. During the Vietnam War I was involved in doing forecasts for people going into combat—clearing flights out of the Philippines into Vietnam—but I never went in there myself. My last actual forecast was for the Libyan air strike. So I jokingly say that I went out of the Navy with a bang. And every now and then somebody says, 'But you didn't get him,' and I say, 'Well, I didn't fly the mission—I just did the forecast.'"

FORTY-TWO YEARS BETWEEN DATES

Millie and Maurice were married on October 11th, 1991. Millie had been divorced for some time; Maurice, who has a daughter living on the island and a son in Maui, had retired five years earlier, and then his marriage came apart, so, he said, "I came home to Nantucket. I'd been coming back a lot—I mean, I have 100-plus relatives on the island. I can't come downtown without seeing a relative." It didn't take long for the couple to rediscover each other. Maurice said, "We were steadies when we were young, but there was a little hiatus—something like 42 years between dates. I never missed a day down at Twin Street for almost two years… And when I was 14 and going steady with a 15-year-old girl, I heard about it from my Aunt Esther Gibbs! And just before she passed away, I teased her a little: 'Don't you remember, you told me I shouldn't go with an older girl?' I don't think there was a day when Millie and I didn't see each other. And then we went our separate ways and had our separate lives and our separate families, and our separate divorces…and then I came back to Nantucket. And we started over again. I jokingly say I was a slow learner."

How, exactly, did Millie and Maurice rediscover each other? Maurice said, "Well, you can't hide from each other on this island!" Millie explained, "We went to the same church." And when, I asked, did the light go on again? Maurice admitted that he didn't know exactly when—"It's hard to say how things sneak up on you." This time, he said, he didn't have to go "chasing down to Twin Street," but they just saw each other a lot, went out to dinner, talked. They agree that they knew pretty quickly what was going to happen. Maurice said, "It didn't seem like 42 years had passed."

In 1990, Maurice became assistant to the director of the Nantucket Historical Association: "Little did I know," he said, "that four months later he would leave and I would be the director. I held that position until February of '93, when I resigned. And then I moved over to a volunteer job as president and executive director of the Lifesaving Museum. So essentially, my work on Nantucket has been strictly museum business ever since I returned. Millie has been looking after the books at the Lifesaving Museum. There's been a lot going on—we have HDC approval for an expansion; we haven't got a plan as to when we're going to do it, but we do have the approval, and that's the key."

We kept going back to the good old days. Maurice said that he wasn't into sailing as a young person, but "did a lot of rowing around the harbor in a dory. One of my pals was Jim Gardner—we'd row over to Coatue and fish off Brant Point, the Jetties, or off the beach. Finally, when I was old enough to drive a Model A Ford with the big tires, we'd go out to Great Point and fish up there. And that's in the days when if there were four cars up there it was a crowd…it was being 'ruined' when the fifth car showed up. Now it's crowded all the time." He shook his head, then said, "I didn't take up sailing until I was back up here on leave during my Navy career, and I bought a Flying Dutchman from Alan Mills, and that was when I first sailed. In the Navy, from 1972 until I retired, I was a volunteer sailing instructor for the Navy. We had sailing clubs at all our naval bases; the Navy encourages young sailors and officers to learn to sail…then when they go out on that destroyer they'll have a better appreciation for Mother Nature. And you can't get out of boot camp unless you can swim. It's a little-known fact that in World War II, more sailors died of drowning than enemy action. I had an uncle, Ed Roy, who was on the Grand Banks for forty years, and when he finally retired, that's when I learned he didn't know how to swim!"

DOING PUZZLES, SAVING LIFESAVING STATIONS

What do Maurice and Millie Gibbs do when they're not working? Millie said she likes gardening and doing puzzles. "She's a great puzzle-pusher, and the dining room table is full up right now," said Maurice, whose two favorite pastimes are reading (he's recently finished Beckschloss' *The Conquerers: Roosevelt, Truman, and the Destruction of Hitler's Germany*) and music. He also admits to "some involvement with other nonprofits." In 1995, he became interested in preserving lifesaving stations around the country and was instrumental in forming the U.S. Lifesaving Service Heritage Association, of which he is now president. "We've saved quite a few stations," he said. "We have a distressed list of about 35; and with the National Park Service we're inventorying what's left—to find out condition, owners, and future viability. There are about 140 of the old historic stations built before 1950, some as far back as the 1870s, on the East and West Coast and on the Great Lakes, and even the Gulf Coast."

Maurice and Millie have some concerns about today's Nantucket. Maurice objects to the "huge rambling houses," and Millie grumbled a bit about people who come here because they love the island, "and then they want to change it!" Maurice said, "When we were kids growing up, it was in a lot of ways a super-extended family. Adults would make it their business to get kids out of trouble, or correct them if it was necessary…and that was accepted. You don't see that now. Talking with all those old people for whom I was emptying ashes—they all were mentors in a way, and I'm not sure that that process is alive and well any more. And the taxing structure is forcing people who have family homes or property to sell because there's no way to meet the taxes, forcing them off the island. A large spec house was built next door to us, and as soon as it changed hands twice, our taxes doubled…and that's happening all over the island. I don't think our citizenry and our Town Meetings are paying enough attention to that."

But despite some contemporary island problems, Nantucket is still home to this couple. Maurice and Millie reflected for a few moments on changes to their island in the past few years. Yet Millie can't stand the thought of living in a city: "There are still a lot of people I know, and most are friendly…when you grew up here, everybody knew everybody else." Maurice laughed: "Which had its good and bad sides. Growing up here, by 8 o'clock the next morning, my father knew everywhere I'd been and everybody I'd been with! And it was good for me…but I didn't like it. Still, compared to the mainland today, look at the security we still have. This is home—my roots are here, and I'm not going to live elsewhere unless the taxes force us to. It's still a lovely place to live. It's the roots of our souls, really, right here. We have our family here, we have our ancestors over there in the cemetery; we have our home, everything ties us to this place."

The interview ended with a question: What do you love most about life? Millie quickly answered, "Being healthy." Maurice said, "Still being here!"

Left—Maurice says this photo, c. 1991, is entitled "Slow-Learner Gibbs and Millie—only took 42 years to get it right!"

Above—Maurice and Ellen Gibbs at 12 Cliff Road, June 1937.

13

MAURICE & MILLIE GIBBS

Above—Maurice Gibbs, all dressed up for his NHS senior class trip to Washington in 1951. The building in the back is his aunt Esther Gibbs' North Shore Restaurant.

Right—Millie Norcross in August 1948. Maurice Gibbs in August 1948.

Below—A very young Maurice Gibbs with his parents in 1934, at John Ring's farm.

MILLIE & MAURICE AUG 1948

14

Over the Land & Far Out to Sea

Ellen Gibbs Holdgate, 2003

The title is from a poem Ellen Gibbs Holdgate wrote while she was living in Ohio and longing for her native island. She's an amazingly multitalented individual, one who not only remembers well her growing-up days on Nantucket but also writes warm, touching, and often humorous memoirs about those times for herself, her family, and her friends. She paints (but doesn't exhibit); knits, crochets, and does prodigious needlepoint; she's been a fishing buff of renown, with 31 plaques to her credit; she's raised five children and cared for many dozens of others; she's maintained lifelong friendships with many islanders, no mean feat in a busy, sometimes difficult lifetime. And she's part of a family whose members today claim "countless cousins," many of whom still live on the island, the others coming back regularly whenever they can. "At one time," she said, "I wrote them all down, and found I had something like 43 first cousins and over 70 second cousins. And many of them come down every summer and visit. How many are still on the island? Oh, golly—loads! And we're all close…"

A Long History at 12 Cliff Road

"I am a native," she went on. "Most of my ancestors were born at 12 Cliff Road, which was originally North Street—my father and his brother and sisters and his father, and before that his grandmother Rebecca, who is my great-grandmother. Sarah Pinkham Bunker, my great-great grandmother, moved in there when she was 16 months old, and lived there forever after. She was born over on North Liberty Street. I've never mentioned this to my brother, Maurice Gibbs, because I'm afraid he'd laugh at me, but I believe the old homestead was haunted. I told my cousin Fran Karttunen, and thought she might laugh too, but she didn't. She said her mom [Charlotte Gibbs Ruley] told her about it. My mother rented rooms in the summertime, and would put me in the north room, where the ghost lived. I was scared to death. I'd undress and dress in the bathroom, and then jump into bed and pull the covers over my head. I never saw the ghost, but even if it was 95 degrees outside, that room was very cold. I wonder if the ghost is still there…"

Were Ellen and her brother Maurice taught the family history as children? Ellen answered, "Yes—actually, my aunt Esther Gibbs told me more about it than anybody. I had a great childhood. We could go anywhere; we used to go out in the woods and chop down trees and branches to build little cabins…we had a ball. And of course there was plenty of ice-skating. Fran Pease's mom, who taught kindergarten (and had the best pear trees which she used to let us climb to pick the fruit), once went skating with us on the mill pond, and fell and broke her wrist. She was such a sweet lady. Once, my girlfriend and I went to Hummock Pond and we couldn't find Maurice. His shoes and his bike were there, but he wasn't, and there was an air hole in the ice—we thought he went in. We ran all the way back to the police station, where my dad was working, and he was like a madman; he jumped in the car and went out there with us… And what Maurice had done was skate down to the other end of the pond, but you really couldn't see him, because of the bushes across there. So I guess he got a good lecture. It was scary, though, because we just figured he was gone." Ellen added with a smile, "You know, Maurice was not as much of an angel as everyone thinks…I wasn't, either. I fought with him all the time—in fact, Aunt Esther gave me a nickname, Tuffy, because I'd chase him with dead rats or snakes or that sort of stuff. He'd run…and that made me feel powerful! He's 15 months older, my only sibling. My father always said he wanted twins, and that's the closest he could get. I always wanted a sister…but I had so many close girlfriends who were like sisters, and then one thing about living here with your cousins and aunts and uncles and all that—the cousins were as close as siblings. In fact, we still are, to this day. I used to take my cousin Fran out in the field behind the Oldest House and pose her—stick her up in a tree, or put flowers around her and take pictures. So I guess I was always artistically inclined. I don't know where the writing part came from. Fran's mother, Charlotte, taught me to sew…she was an excellent seamstress. My other grandmother, Grandma Jewett, taught me to crochet when I was five years old. When I joined the Brownies, Mrs. Kay Gardner, up on Sunset Hill, had us knitting squares and she'd put them together for blankets for poor people…and during the war, my mother knitted hats and gloves and mittens for the servicemen. She died seven years ago…she lived with me for the last few years of her life.

"Mom worked a lot, mostly in the summertime, and when my parents were still together—they eventually separated—she rented rooms. After that, she waited on tables and was an accountant, and did all kinds of different things. My father didn't remarry until after I'd left the island, and I left when I was 17. I quit school, I'm ashamed to say, and went down to Florida to be with my mom, who by then had moved there. I got a job in a hotel…and then I met a young man and got married, which was a dumb thing to do, but I did it. We lived in Ohio, and I had six babies—one, Dale, died when he was a week old. He was my third boy; that was really tough. Five boys and one girl. Lots of kids—but I'm glad I've got 'em. In 1969 I was divorced and just brought the kids home. And they tell me it's the best thing I ever did for them. I'd been gone for seventeen years. And oh, I missed this place…that's partly why I wrote all this stuff down, because I was so homesick. There was a period of seven years when I couldn't afford to come home. That's when I

Young Maurice and his sister Ellen Gibbs posed for a formal portrait at a photo studio over what is now Mitchell's Book Corner.

Ellen and Maurice Gibbs pose with little cousin Judy Bailey. Note the dog in background with ears "at the ready."

really started writing my memories.

"Luckily for me, Maurice, who was still in the service traveling all over the world, let us use his house. I don't know what I would've done… Four of the children, whose last name is Charnes—David, Ellen, Jimmy, and Scott—are all here; Danny lives in Ohio. David has a garage and a tackle shop next door that he leases. Jimmy works for the Water Company, out in 'Sconset. Scotty has his own automotive business. And Ellen works for the airport, in maintenance…she's been there for years. She started there when my husband Kenny was still the manager. I love having my children around me. I have seven grandchildren and nine greats…the greats are all in Ohio.

WORKING PRACTICALLY AROUND THE CLOCK

"When we got back to Nantucket, I worked three jobs. I was supposed to get support, of course, but that didn't happen for long. I worked for Henry's Grinder Shop, which started out in the lower section of the JC, where the Taproom is now. That was Henry Fee's first place—he was a wonderful boss. I also cleaned houses on weekends, and worked at the laundry; when I got through there I'd go to work for Henry at 6; in the hour or so in between I'd run home and make supper for the kids. My oldest son who came with me was 15, so thank God he stayed with the little ones…I'd get through at midnight, tally up all the money and take it to the auditor upstairs, and then fly home and go to bed and get up the next morning and go to work again. I'd throw a load of laundry in every night before I went to bed. And you know, I was so busy I didn't have time to be resentful!" Ellen laughed. "So it was wonderful to meet Kenny—by then my kids were older; my youngest son was about 7, and he just fell in love with Kenny. Kenny taught him all about the boats, how to run them, how to fix them. And he had ten years on fancy yachts down in Florida because of that knowledge. Kenny gave them all their first car…it wasn't a new one, but it ran! As a teenager, I didn't have a car…I walked. I'm amazed at how little the kids walk today, because I lived with Dad out by the MSPCA, and walked to Academy Hill to school and back home to lunch and back again. I used to love to go rollerskating, out where the Muse is now—Manny Dias' father had a skating rink built there, with a little hamburger stand next door—and I thought nothing of walking down Crooked Lane, over to the Muse. I walked everywhere, didn't think a thing about it. You were lucky if your parents had a car, and most of them probably didn't, if they lived in town. And most kids had to work; my brother worked in the produce department for the First National Stores. At 16 I worked as a telephone operator in the summer; that was my first big-time job, or that's what I thought. Number ple-ase?" she added with a laugh.

How about your school years? I asked. "Well, I remember Miss Esther Johnson, first grade; she was a very strong lady, and there was a boy in class who said a bad word, so she called the school nurse, and they stuck soap in his mouth. So we always behaved ourselves in her class! Miss Johnson lived on India Street. We liked her…and then we had Miss Rita Hull in the second grade, and Miss Marjorie Hull (her sister) in the third grade…and in my adult years I ended up looking after and cleaning house for her. There were actually three Hull sisters. One of them didn't teach; she was married to Parker Gray. Maurice and I were very well behaved in school, because if we were naughty and our parents found out, we got it twice as bad at home. The whole town was your family, really. I really didn't like junior high much, because my aunt, Eleanor True, was the music teacher, and her husband, my uncle Roy True, ran the Coffin School, where I went for homemaking classes, so he could see me over there. And my Uncle Harry Jewett was the truant officer, and my father was a policeman! So we really couldn't do anything bad, because there was always somebody looking at us. I'll never forget in high school one time, I went with a couple of boys out to the dump to shoot rats. They were shining their flashlight around…and then they saw the State Trooper coming, and like an idiot, I put the gun under my coat—I could've blown my head off! He asked what we were doing there, and the boys said, 'Oh, just spottin' rats.' He told us we'd better go home. I really sweat bullets—I thought he was going to tell my father. He never did. I was probably 15 then.

JOYRIDING, THE CONFESSION CAPER, & PLAYING POST OFFICE

"My dad was a policeman in 'Sconset, and my 'angel' brother Maurice used to disconnect the mileage thing on his car, and we would 'borrow' it and go joy-riding all over the island. Once, we had a girlfriend with us; she'd just broken up with her boyfriend, and someone was following us; we thought it was this boy. So she gave him a hand signal that wasn't very ladylike, and come to find out it was the State Trooper! So we sweat bullets for that one, too…but he never told our dad. I think I loved that man till he died! When we'd get home, Maurice would hook the mileage thing up again and make sure the right amount of gas was in the car. I don't think my father ever knew what we were up to—I never heard anything about it.

"When I was about 8, we lived on a farm on Old South Road, and Maurice and I took turns bringing the cows in, gathering the eggs…it was my job to make the butter—a big old mayonnaise jar and a wooden spoon was my churn. I enjoyed that. Mrs. Gibson, up on Quarter Mile Hill, owned the house, and she said to Dad, 'Well, if you raise the potatoes, I'll let you live there.' And she did. So we had the house for potatoes! There was a little shack with a generator, and an underground room outside, and Maurice and I took turns at dusk going into one and clicking something and running over to the other and clicking something else, and then BOOM! the lights came on. That was fun. And special—nobody else had that. Out there we had a woodpecker that was trying to get in, and my brother went out there with a broom, to kill it, and my best friend Diane Holdgate [Legg] and I knocked him for a loop so the bird could fly away—we didn't want him to kill it! Of course he whacked me, but he didn't hit Diane. It was wonderful being on a farm—I saw calves being born, puppies…it was nice.

"Oh," Ellen laughed, the memories coming thick and fast, "I'll tell you a funny story. When I was about 11, I went with Diane and her friend Audrey Duce to the Catholic Church; she was going to confession, and I had no idea what that was about. There were two little booths in the back, so she went to one, but came right back and said, 'There's a man in there.' Well, I thought she'd walked in on a man in the bathroom, and I started to laugh! And of course she and Audrey were telling me to hush, but I thought that was so funny!"

Did Ellen have jobs when she was in school? "The biggest thing I did was babysit. The day Wayne Holmes went away to college, I was pushing a baby carriage, and the day he came back I was still pushing a baby carriage. He said, 'Is that all you do?' and I said, 'Just about.' I must have taken care of about 120 children from the time I was 9 till I was 17. But I love children, always have, so to me that was a good way to make money. What did we do for fun? Well, we went to the beach…my brother and I used to meet Diane and tell our parents we were going to the movies, and we'd go swimming. At night, down at the Jetties. And when we could, a whole gang of us, the North Liberty

Street crowd, would go to what they call Cliffside Beach now—we called it Conrad's then. There was a raft out there, and we'd swim underneath it, and of course there were air pockets, and we'd play Post Office…we thought that was terrific! Diane was always there; I cannot remember not knowing Diane. She still lives here. I wrote a long story about our childhood memories for her, because she couldn't remember all that stuff, and I could…and it just made her day! Things like throwing potatoes down Gibby Wyer's chimney…" Ellen laughed: "It was Halloween and a bunch of us kids found a bushel of potatoes, I don't know who had 'em, and we decided to up on Gibby's house and drop them down the chimney…and then we took off running, of course. He was a nice man—he started the Boys Club here, and Maurice and Ricky Lewis were the first to sign up to join.

CRAZY OVER HORSES

"More childhood memories? I loved going to Mr. Wyer's barns and brushing the horses. That was fun, because he kept some machinery way down in the back alley, and he'd walk his workhorses down there to hook up to a plow or a wagon, so he'd just let us ride on their backs down there—that was a treat and a half. The stables were right across from Ellen Ramsdell's cottage on Centre Street, where my cousin, Fran Karttunen, lives now…that big barn was his. And we were just up the hill, so we played there a lot when we were little kids. He was good to us; he'd let us polish the saddles or whatever, and we thought we were such a big help. His wife was awfully nice, too…she'd give us cookies. I loved horses—I rode until I left the island. Out at the Hunt Club I was in a horse show one time, and I was too late going out to Clara McGrady's Hilltop Stables to pick out Lady, the horse I wanted; she was already spoken for, and the only one left was Snowflake, a great big white horse, very headstrong. So I took Snowflake and went over to the Hunt Club and was in the show, and suddenly that horse decided it was going home, whether I wanted to or not. And we went flying down the road, hellbent for leather…everybody thought I was going to fall. A horse can tell when someone's afraid, and I was just a little kid then. So we were barreling down the road and I managed to stay on, but one of the fellows who worked for Mrs. McGrady came galloping up and grabbed the reins to stop the horse…because he would've taken me right back to the barn.

20

Left to right— (1) Ellen, holding her doll, with brother Maurice Gibbs. (2) Ellen enjoying a ride on Irving Wyer's pony, 1940. (3) Clowning at the beach: from top, Ellen, Mary "Deedle" Glidden, Judy Brownell (Collatz), and Mona Glidden. (4) Ellen as a young woman.

"Clara McGrady's stables were out past the cemetery, on Vesper Lane. Her horses were named Barmaid, Lady, Little Man, Texas, Snowflake…and Midnight, who was mean! My dad was a very good horseman, and used to help Mrs. McGrady teach horseback riding, so Maurice and I got to ride free. But Maurice fell off a horse and was dragged…he was lucky he didn't get clipped in the head; after that, he gave it up. The Hunt Club was a big place, shaped kind of like a U, and just loaded with horses. Mr. Wahl, who lived off island, would come every year and bring fifty or sixty horses, and the people had fox hunts, all dressed up…it was really nice. Actually, I think what they chased were jackrabbits.

"Other childhood adventures? Well, the farmhand at Mr. Wyer's stable, Manny Sylvia, used to chew tobacco, so one time when he set it down, Richard tore a hunk off and gave me some, and we both were really sick…my parents said we were green. Who was Richard? He was one of my best childhood friends; we remained in touch for all our adult life, until he died about ten years ago. He was like a second brother to me. We called him Joe, I don't know why; the family came here when he was three—his father, Claude, was the minister of the Congregational Church. Reverend Bond was very popular and active in town, refereeing for many sports. He was also an excellent boxer. Once he took Joe and me way up into the old attic of the vestry, which had been the original church in Sherburne, and we saw the huge timbers, held together with pegs…I don't know how they moved that building. I've painted a picture of Joe as a small boy, sitting on the church steps in the snow, listening to the Christmas music—both my father and his mother were in the choir. Joe and I became close friends—never sweethearts—and he was my brother's friend, too. We played baseball and football and built camps and all that sort of stuff. His family left Nantucket when he was maybe 14, and then he went into the service, later married and had a family, but we stayed in touch, and I still correspond with his widow, Eloise."

What about memories of World War II, when Ellen was quite young? She showed me a story she'd written and illustrated about those times: *Will the Planes Come Tonight?* "That was a scary time," she said. "Joe's mother and the two boys and my mother and the lady we rented from used to go and sit in her house during air raids…we were so frightened. And once, a pilot flew quite low over his wife's house to say goodbye before he went overseas, and it scared me to death! I thought the plane was coming through the house…and I was alone, so frightened I was rooted to the floor. One time when we were at school, some strange planes were sighted overhead, and the little kids had to be taken home…scary, because they didn't know if we'd be bombed or what was going on. Jack Gardner was the one who rushed me and my brother home—we were so frightened!

"But you know, I have lots of very good memories, too. Maurice used to make me press his pants…see, when my parents separated, I was 16, and Maurice was dating Millie, and he'd be getting ready for a date…I'd say, 'Press 'em yourself!' And he said, 'If you don't, I'm gonna tell Dad you smoke.' So of course I always pressed his pants…they always had a good crease. It may have been down the sides, but it was a good crease!"

ABOUT AUNT ESTHER

"I'd always told Aunt Esther that if I ever got home to Nantucket, I'd never leave. After I came back, while she was still living, I'd take her riding over the moors, and she loved that. And she always said to me, 'I don't know anybody else who loves Nantucket as much as you do.' I'd say, 'Yes, so why should I leave?' Aunt Esther was a very interesting person; she had quit school too, and worked at the Roberts

House and saved her money and bought what had been a country market, Cathcart's, and turned it into the North Shore Restaurant." Ellen chuckled, "I remember going into Cathcart's once to buy some candy; I paid him with Monopoly money. I had no idea it wasn't real money, but he took it. He was such a nice man.

"Anyway, Aunt Esther was always good to me; she bought me my first set of oil paints; she bought me my first bra, my first slip when I was just a teenybopper...I really loved her. When I was married and in Ohio, she sent me, believe it or not, steamed clams in a can—I don't know where she found them—and they were delicious! She'd also send me Indian Puddings, because you couldn't get them out there; and she sent me a beautiful table with all Nantucket tiles; it was gorgeous, and the ex-husband busted it, but I saved what tiles I could and sent them to my girlfriend on Nantucket to keep for me. Just recently I dug them all out because my son was remodeling his house, and he put a bay window in, and they went perfectly right there. So Aunt Esther is still with us.

"In her later years, she got cancer—the doctors operated and gave her six months to live, but she lived for two years. She was a fighter, and I think that's where I get it from. In those two years she went to Colorado to see a nephew, to Florida, Alaska, and she took me to Finland, and Norway on a cruise ship. It was very hard for her, because she wasn't well, but she would not give up...I actually moved in with her for a month, toward the end...this was after my marriage to Ken. It was hard, but she didn't have anybody... A lot of people thought Esther was kind of a mean person, but she wasn't—she had a heart as big as all outdoors; she'd worked at the Roberts House with a woman who had umpteen kids, and lots of times they didn't have anything, so Esther would come by with Christmas presents. She didn't tell anybody, she just did it. And she did that for a lot of people. She got me out of my shell; when I was young, I was quite shy, and she told me, 'You've got to stand on your own two feet!' She'd say, 'Speak up! You're no dummy!' So she was a very big influence on me."

HAPPY TO BE ON NANTUCKET

How and when did Ellen meet Ken Holdgate? "Well," she said, smiling, "he's known me since I was born. He and his first wife were friends of my parents...so it's kind of strange, but after he divorced, we found we had kind of the same interests—fishing, digging clams, all that. So we just fell in love. That was back in 1974."

Despite some tough times in her life and a major health problem now, Ellen says, "I've always been

upbeat. I'm a happy person...I really can't do much now, except for knitting and crocheting and painting. I used to be an avid fishing person, and I really miss it, but I just don't have the wind power to do it any more. I guess my major life accomplishment has been to make my children happy. I'm writing a lot about my memories so they can know what life on the island was like. I think that's important. They're happy to be on Nantucket.

Ellen Holdgate with her Charnes children: at left Dan, David, and Ellen; at right Jimmy and Scott. 2001.

And so am I!" she concluded. "I wouldn't want to live anywhere else. I feel safe here."

The following is from a little pamphlet prepared by Esther U. Gibbs, its contents used with permission of her niece, Ellen Gibbs Holdgate.

THE NORTH SHORE RESTAURANT, 80 CENTRE STREET NANTUCKET, MASS.

In the early days of Nantucket, the section of the town where the "NORTH SHORE RESTAURANT" is located was called "North Shore."

The restaurant is located on the site where Benjamin Franklin's Grandfather's mill stood. Along here was once an opening to the sea known as BARZILLAI'S CREEK which was broad enough to sail boats to GULL ISLAND. Nowadays, the approach to the house known as GULL ISLAND is from a lane which leads off to the left, just beyond the Restaurant.

The "LILY POND" once surrounded GULL ISLAND—and there was an earthen dam to control the water until a little girl, "LOVE SWAIN" on her way home from play, with a shell or stick in her hand-made a small hole in the dam and let the water out. She told no one, but went to bed early to be awakened by her father's voice saying "that some one had let the water out of the Lily Pond—and all the boats in the Creek had gone out to sea."

The little girl never told anyone what had happened—until in her 80's—she called a few people around her while she lay on her death bed—and confessed the story as told above.

After the pond was drained, and there was no water to run the mill, the land was filled in, and a grocery store was built and operated by various owners and called "NORTH SHORE GROCERY." In 1943, I purchased the building and converted it into a restaurant. While digging the cellar I found the base of the old mill and brick drains.

The dining room is decorated in the era of whaling days with authentic relics, many of which were in my family-others I have obtained.

At breakfast you may help yourself to a cup of coffee to drink while waiting for your breakfast to be served.

A different menu is served daily of home cooked food—specializing in Quahaug Chowder, Garlic Shrimp, Fish in season, Steaks, Chops, and a variety of home made breads and pastries, at moderate prices.

I have had many compliments on the cleanliness of my kitchen.

ESTHER U. GIBBS
OWNER - MANAGER

Left—Winner of more than 30 fishing awards from the Angler's Club, Ellen Holdgate poses with a recent catch—a huge bass. 1997. Right—Aunt Esther Gibbs, dressed for hunting. Note the 1935 license plate on the car behind her.

24

As "Nantucket" as Scallopin'
Alfred Orpin, 1989

ot many women get to come into the Pacific Club," Alfred Orpin remarked with a twinkle in his eye as he opened the door to that estimable institution for me. But that was where we'd decided to have our conversation.

We sat down at a little table where heaven knows how many cribbage contests have been won and lost over the last century and a quarter. There was a little old-fashioned, green-shaded gooseneck lamp on the table, as if ready for a game. Mr. Orpin turned out to be a good bit more shy than when he'd given a fascinating talk at the Whaling Museum the week before. I had taken two old friends from New Jersey there, wanting them to experience early in their visit the aura of whaling that pervades this island even today. "Gosh," one of them remarked after the talk; "And I thought *you* had a broad Yankee accent!" (Of course, Alfred Orpin looked surprised when asked about partic'lar ways of saying words, and Nantucket expressions. Like most people, he thinks everyone else has the accent!) My friends were charmed, of course, and while the museum had been full of visitors that morning, at 1:00 we were the only three present.

Tailoring his reg'lar talk just for us, he gave a wonderful history of the whaling industry, and a good definition of the different types of whales, as well. Plus an accurate description of exactly how whales had been "landed" and cut up. If the three of us were heartstruck at the demise of so many of these huge mammals at the hands of the human creature in days gone by, we were also cheered to hear of measures being taken today to save the whale.

How did Alfred Orpin get started at the museum? Well, he said, he retired in 1971 from his 43-year career at the Wannacomet Water Company, and along about 1978, Frank Paterson, a retired Methodist minister who was managing the Whaling Museum at the time, asked if he didn't want to give some of the talks. "What kind of talks would you want?" inquired Orpin. "Well," said Paterson, "here are two talks, for example. I give one of them." "So," said Alfred, "I said, 'All right, I'll do yours.' I did it that year, on a part-time basis, and eventually I worked into the ones I do now. This is my eleventh year."

THE EARLY DAYS

Alfred was born at home, on New Street, in 1906, the son of Herbert and Marietta Orpin, also natives. "My father's people go back to the middle of the century on Nantucket," he said. "They came from Nova Scotia in 1747. My mother's parents came later, from England." Asked about his early memories, this just-turned-83-year-old told of going to a small school almost opposite Lyons Street, on Orange: "That's where we went for the first four grades. We always lived in the New Town, as they called it. The kids in the south part of town went to the Orange Street School, then the fifth grade went to Academy Hill, through the end of high school. I graduated in 1925."

Mr. Orpin remembered his boyhood, saying it wasn't a time of a lot of fun and games—most youngsters worked pretty hard then. But lest I think it was an altogether serious life, he confessed that "we were all scoundrels in those days," when I told him of another Nantucketer of about the same vintage who'd confessed to pestering the horses at the Pease Stable, on the corner of South Water and Broad Streets. He also, like this other fellow (man-about-town Gibby Wyer), remembers the lure of the railroad yards, down by Steamship Wharf. "There was a locomotive turntable there," he said. "It had tracks on it, and was quite lahge—it was used to turn the locomotive. And we used to get on it and spin it 'round and 'round. We weren't supposed to do that, but it was fun, and that's why we did it. Once I caught my foot under it…oboy! Don't think I went back. There was all sorts of antics in relation to that railroad," he remembered. "They had a pump car, you know, had handles on both sides…we used to get that and run it back and forth on the tracks. Never got caught, but eventually they hid it behind the locomotive so that you'd have to push it out all the way around, so that ended that."

Did he remember any other high-jinks connected with the railroad? "Oh," he answered, "that's rather vague. I rode on the train now and then. 'Course, I remember when they tore up the tracks…I went out with my uncle when they were doing that—it was during the first World War, you know….they took all the tracks and used them in the war effort." That story elicited another early memory—of the very first "aeroplanes" that came to Nantucket. "They landed in the harbor—I remember one landed out near the jetties, and was disabled…we all remember the first one. It came right down here on Washington Street, in the water. They had the hydroplanes in those days. Oh, they let the schools out, you know, let all the kids out to watch the plane. That was quite an event…"

OPENING SCALLOPS AFTER SCHOOL

What kinds of jobs did you do as a youngster? I asked. "We were all more or less engaged in scallopin', in season. Every fall, that was a must. Whole families would do it. After school, we went and opened scallops—yes, I could still do it. Nowadays they use gloves; in the old days, they didn't. Going to school, it was difficult to hold the pencil, because our hands would be so tender. The money we earned went right into the family… My father died very young, when he was 35," he went on. "He followed the sea-fishin', scallopin'—right around these waters. There were six children, four still living. One brother, the youngest, was lost at sea, on a scalloper; another brother was manager of the water company for many years.

"In the summers," he continued, "I worked for my uncle; he had a fish market on Main Street, right where the Erica Wilson shop is now. In those days, they had hosses—they were used mostly for transportation, not so much for pleasure. I'd harness 'em up in the morning—people would order fish, and we'd go out with these boxes…I was prob'ly 15 or 16… And then of course came the automobile…went about 12 miles per hour then. The first car that we operated was the old Model T—my uncle had one of those, and we used to deliver the orders with that. My first car? Oh gosh, I don't know—that's quite a while ago. I was quite well along before I got an automobile…not too many had them.

"Some of the other stores on Main Street were the First National, right about where Patton's Jewelry Store is…then it moved across the street to…let's see, 'twas right this side' the old Sweet Shop on the left…and then J.B. Ashley was up on the corner—he ran the meat department of the First National—the grocery store was separate. Other stores? In the very early years there was a man by the name of Rosen, I think, right where Murray's Liquor Store is now…had all kinds of boots and shoes, and fisherman's goods, you know. There was a Mr. Kaplan, who was on the left-hand side of the street, where the art shop is now…he sold shoes and suits, men's suits. Murray's has been on Main Street a long time; that used to be Emil Janesky's—Phil Murray's father worked for him, and took over the store when Janesky moved to New Bedford…"

After he got out of high school, Alfred Orpin left the island briefly to work in Baltimore—but "we got caught up in the Great Depression, so I came back to Nantucket to work…there was plenty of work here. I went to work for the Wannacomet Water Co. and never left—43 years. I was running the engines down in Wyer's Valley—and during the war the winders were all covered, so as not to shed any light at night on account' the submarine danger. That was a very difficult time. Food, such as meat, and sugar, and things of that nature, were hard to get."

ODD AS HUCKLEBERRY CHOWDAH

That elicited a couple of moments of silence; then I asked Mr. Orpin if he could cite any "Nantucketisms." "No...can't think of any—I'm rather vague on that." But he chuckled suddenly, and recalled that "one of the historians used to refer to someone in Nantucket as being 'odd as huckleberry chowdah.' I think that was Dr. Will Gardner, who was a retired Episcopal minister, said that."

Alfred Orpin recalled other times and events: blueberryin' out' the airport ("no poison ivy out theyuh, but you'd run into it out Madaket way," and the best thing to do was to wash your hands with strong yellow soap); stories of groundhogs that got so pesky they had to be disposed of a few years before he was born; hahd winters; a recent perambulation to look at all the swans at Hummock Pond; singing for years in church choirs; and gahd'ning at the Kimball estate in the years after his retirement, where he grew flowers, vegetables, everything.

Finally, it was time to leave the Pacific Club and Alfred Orpin's gentle company. Has it been a good life on Nantucket? I asked. "Well," he answered with a smile. "It's been all right. I mean, we can't complain...I hope I've helped some."

Good memories, good stories; good man, Alfred Orpin.

28

❧

Alfred Orpin passed away in the early 1990s.

This famous compass rose was placed on the building by H. Marshall Gardiner, who owned a photography shop that in recent years was Nantucket Looms.

30

Living on Easy Street
Florence Clifford, 1999

lorence Clifford, a native Nantucketer, is just about the youngest person in her eighties you can find. She's wonderful news for anyone who thinks there's such a thing as "old." Her fame extends beyond her baking, but yes, she's well known for her blueberry pies and other goodies at the annual Congregational Church Fair. I met with her in her neat and picturesque house facing out onto the Nantucket harbor, and she expressed doubt that she'd have much to tell me, but that was dead wrong. Her memories of the island of the past will stir nostalgia in natives and long-time islanders and regret in others that they didn't know yesterday's Nantucket.

MOOING BOATS & FUNNY SIGNS

The house has a nautical theme, with old lanterns hanging from the rafters, ocean scenes, ships' quarterboards here and there, and a beautiful large ship model hanging in the picture window, through which you can see the harbor basin with all its floating beauties. "Oh, I keep track of things going on in this basin, you bet!" she said after a boat horn had mooed—and indeed those beeps punctuated our conversation several times. Florence's sense of fun is displayed in the signs all around the place, some of them genuine antiques: "Out of Respect to Ladies, Gentlemen Are Requested Not to Smoke in This Room"; "Entrance Next Door"; "Grandmothers Are Just Antique Little Girls"; "Martha Stewart Doesn't Live Here"; and "Nice Lodging Rooms to Let Upstairs," my personal favorite…because there's no upstairs. The house is neat and airy and though filled with many interesting items has a spacious feeling abetted by the owner's own petite size. There's even a bunkhouse of sorts. She explained: "The children wanted to work here in the summer, and they had to have a place to live or they couldn't get a job, and then they couldn't get a place to live if they didn't have a job, so it was a catch-22. So we built a little room on the outside with its own entrance, and built-in bunks, and a little shower bathroom, and that's my guestroom. If they can't climb into a bunk, they don't stay!"

I asked Flo to tell me about her memories of growing up on a lonely little island 33 miles out to sea and she gave me great little vignettes of her childhood. "I do remember when the old Point Breeze caught fire [August 8, 1925]," she said. "We were living then at 120 Main Street, at the corner of Bloom; I was just six. My father had charge of the hose cart on Gardner Street; he went running off to the fire with another man, and they dragged the cart down to the fire themselves. Mother, knowing that the hotel guests might need places to stay, quickly made up all the beds just in case. My brother and I were so frightened by the glow the fire made in the sky."

Were you born at the Nantucket Hospital? I asked. "No—my mother had me at home. My brother had been born in the Nantucket Cottage Hospital, then on West Chester Street, and Mother described the nursery as 'a closet under the stairs with one window.' She didn't like the situation at the hospital—this was in the early days, when the nursery was probably just a small room. Of course later on, they had a real nursery on the first floor, and the maternity ward was on the second floor. So all the babies got carried up the stairs, and when people were coming in to visit they'd say 'Oh what a cute baby!' and cough and sneeze or whatever… It was quite different when I had mine. I had two children there, Drew and Debbie…and my third child, Dusty, was born at the new hospital. And at that time they were very conscious of diseases and viruses, so she came wrapped in an autoclaved piece of paper!"

Where was "home" when you arrived on the scene? I asked. "I was born at 120 Main Street. But they've taken the porch off—there was a porch on one side, and the boards used to warp in the off-season, so my mother used to walk up and down the porch with the carriage and you know, it sort of wobbled and lulled the baby to sleep. That was 1919. At that time my father was running the Island Service Company, where the Boat Basin is now."

Old-Fashioned Discipline in School

What about schooling? I asked. Florence's reply: "My mother taught us the kindergarten part of our education at home. Then for first grade we went to a Miss Cox, who lived at the corner of Gardner and Howard Streets. Oh, she was a taskmaster, scared me half to death—if you didn't do it right you got a crack over the knuckles, you know, the old-fashioned kind of discipline! Why did we go there instead of to school? I don't really know, but I just met Albert Brock in the Post Office, and he told me he went to Miss Cox too. She taught on a one-to-one basis. For the second grade I went to Academy Hill…when it was a wood building. I must have watched when they tore it down, because I vividly remember them taking the roof off, and then they swung a rope through a window and pulled the side of the building off… After that we did sort of half-day sessions down at the South School, on Orange Street. That no longer exists. I can remember walking home from school in the dark. In the winter, at the end of sessions, at 4 o'clock in the winter afternoon it got kind of dark. And there were no school buses.

"The South School was on the left-hand side of Orange Street; Ryder's Market was diagonally across the street. Right near there was a house we eventually bought from Mrs. Alice Fuller Davenport—I don't remember the number, isn't that awful? Then, eventually, Academy Hill School was finished, and I went there before we moved to California. I don't remember much about school; I was not a very good student. I'm sure that at one point I had Mary Mendonca as a teacher. Everyone had her; she was very loved and well known. She eventually bought the Victorian house on Main Street, up from the bank. In those days things weren't expensive. People would buy lots of property. My great-aunt Florence Lang bought properties all over the place, including a 100-acre piece out in Shawkemo that we lived in, summers…it had been the pasture for Louis Coffin's sheep. The barn on the property was moved up to the harbor part of the land, and that's where we spent our summers, in that converted barn. At first it was dormitory style, and we had no electricity or running water, but we did have a phone—my father insisted on that. I remember the old icebox with the drip pan underneath. When my father came home he'd bring the ice.

A very young Florence Ingall, wearing hightop sneakers and kneesocks, poses for the camera.

And we also had a kerosene stove and lamps; I was in charge of cleaning the wicks and keeping the chimneys clean and filling them. Oh, we also had a big demijohn—a huge water bottle on a stand—you had to tip it to get the water out. We used to go next door to the Harps—they had a gorgeous spring—and we'd fill our gallon jugs there and then fill the demijohn. We spent our summers there before we moved to California. My brother Bill and I had great fun out there—there was a lot of area to roam, and we went swimming and shelling.

The Cupola Was Heaven

"Then Dad decided to build another house up on North Liberty Street—what is now the State Police Barracks. While that was being built, we lived in the house on Orange Street, which now has been taken down. Oh, that was a beautiful Victorian house…the inner doors to the dining room were about five inches thick! And it had a cupola, which for the kids it was absolute heaven. It was like a big playhouse—we had a great time there."

I asked Florence how the move to California came about. "When we were living on North Liberty, my mother contracted breast cancer, and we went to Boston for her surgery, and then we went out to California. My great-aunt had a house in Pasadena, and there was a clinic out there that was supposed to have the latest in cancer treatments, so we took Mom there, and stayed for a winter…I turned thirteen that year…and then we brought her back, but it was too late. She died back here. I was the youngest; my brother Bill was two years older. And after that Dad couldn't quite face the music down here, so we went back to California and rented for a while, just for the winters. He thought the schools were very progressive there."

34

I asked Florence if she'd finished her schooling out west, and she replied that she had, high school and then college. Did she come back then? "No," she said, "by that time I'd lost my other parent, and my great-aunt helped me out—she sent me to Scripps College in Claremont. I majored in Art and the Humanities there…you had to major in the Humanities, so Art was my minor. The whole education process was great."

During our conversation, the phone rang several times, and there were consultations with the painter, outside on the porch/deck, so I had time to look around. The décor includes a figurehead of a beauteous maiden just over the fireplace, and I asked if it is a real one. "Yes," was the answer, "but I don't know what ship it came from. When we bought the house on Orange Street, it was all wrapped in a blanket on the couch in the main sitting room. My then-husband put it outside on the porch;

The Ingall family—Florence, her mother, Elizabeth Church Ingall, her brother William, and her father, Oswald D. Ingall—with their touring car at Top Gale, at Shawkemo Harbor. Top Gale was on land on which Louis Coffin kept his sheep barn; the Ingalls converted the barn, but Florence says that at first the whole family had to sleep up in the hayloft, dormitory-style. She said it was wonderfully rustic—kerosene stove and lamps—and that they used to get water next door at a natural spring on the Harps' property.

there was a roof over it, but it got a lot of weather. It looked dark maroon, paint was coming off, and it was cracked. Apparently her nose had broken and you could see a nailhead where they'd attached it. We took it to be fixed, and when the fellow started to clean it up, he found this beautiful light blue on the dress, and he reproduced that color, painted the brooch, and did a beautiful makeup job. It was really a remarkable restoration. And," she smiled, "because it came from Mrs. Alice Fuller Davenport's house, we call it Aunt Alice."

Near the front window was a quarterboard with the name "MELISSA TRASK," and Florence said, "That one is from a whole group…and there's another from the *Argo* over there. They were all in a collection that Wallace Long had; the children's father bought the whole bit, and we had them displayed outside the Island Service Company, but people were prying them off and taking them, so we moved them inside, and now half of them are out at the Life-Saving Museum and half are at the Historical Association. Some of them are from shipwrecks, some of them are reproductions that he carved himself. The *Melissa Trask* was a ship that was wrecked off the shoals here…I think the quarterboard is the original. In the 'old days' people kept busy doing that sort of collecting—they were packrats and collected those sorts of things, especially from the sea.

"My father ran Island Service, and my mother was a homemaker, and I guess she was pretty active in the town…I know she was on the School Committee at one point. She'd been a teacher before she married, and so she participated, and was also a member, of the Congregational Church. That's the church I was brought up in." And, Flo said, though she spends her winters in Weston, MA ("the winter dampness here is hard to live with"), in summers while she lives in her Easy Street home on the Faraway Isle, she takes part in many church activities, including being an usher, on a variety of committees, and one of the "Steeple People."

LITTLE FLORENCE, BIG LIMOUSINE

When did Florence come back to Nantucket to live? "Well," she said, "from college I went to stay with this great-aunt, Florence Lang. I was almost the only young relative she had, so she treated me almost like a granddaughter, and after I finished at Scripps she was not very well, though she did make the trip out to see me graduate. She lived in Montclair, NJ, her main house, but she also had a house in California and on Nantucket. Anyway, she asked me if I would stay with her, because she needed somebody to give her a hand. So I went right from college to Montclair." Florence paused for another chortle. "She had a man who drove for her, and of course it was just at the start of the war,

Elizabeth Ingall sits at the radio her husband made; she and the children, Florence and William, also wear headphones to listen to voices from afar. Flo says that her father and Harry Holden, in Siasconset, both built their own radios and had a bit of a competition to see who could reach the farthest on their sets.

and he decided that he should give himself to the war effort, so he resigned his position with her…and I became the driver as well. That was really a riot, because I'm very short, and he was a big man…now, this was not a limousine in the sense of today's limousines. It was a sedan with a window in between the driver and the passenger, and it had little jumpseats. He taught me how to drive it, and I'll never forget—I was scared to death of this car. It was so big…but he'd say, 'If you can get the front end around, the back will follow!' So here we are in the middle of the war, gasoline rationing, sugar rationing, butter, anything that was precious…and if you didn't have a coupon, if you weren't well known in the market, and I wasn't, you had trouble getting what you wanted. So here I go, driving to the supermarket in this great black limousine, and putting all the groceries in the back where the lady of the household usually sits, and it was quite an experience. We came down here to Nantucket to stay that summer; her house was on Hussey Street, the one with the sunken garden, a beautiful house. That was in 1942, the year I graduated. And then she decided I should have some business experience, so she put me to work at the Island Service Company office answering the telephone. That was really a riot, because they hadn't had a woman in the office and the men were so startled—they'd come up to the wicket and start to joke with the other men and then look over and see a woman, and go 'Wooops!'

"At Christmastime my aunt suffered a stroke—she was 82, so she had a long, good life. And she'd been a widow for quite a number of years. I called her my great-aunt because I didn't know what else to call her…she was not related in any way, but she was wonderful to me. It's kind of complicated: My father was born in Sault Ste. Marie, Canada; his true mother died when he was eighteen months old. Later, Grandfather, who was a mining engineer, married Florence Lang's sister, so that brought my father kind of into that family. The sister died soon afterward, so Florence and her mother took on her sister's stepson. They kind of gathered this young boy together and brought him to the States, put him through school, and so I was really her godchild. I was family to her…she married late in life and didn't have any children of her own; she'd lost her own parents and her sister and brother. She sent my father to Cornell University and then to Yale Forestry School, and then what was Amherst Aggie, an agricultural school. So he had quite a bit of education, but he couldn't seem to settle into something, so she brought him down here and put him in charge of this company that she and her by-then husband had bought. People came down here in a different way than they come now…they bought places and managed them, and bought lots of land. Island Service Company was on Swain's Wharf, and it was Swain's old company they took on."

The conversation returned to those early years on Nantucket. Florence recalled that it was a very pleasant life. "My mother was a Girl Scout leader, my father was a Boy Scout leader…and of course my brother was a Boy Scout and I was a Girl Scout. Our meetings were held at what was the Monahannet Club at that time. I participated in all the things that had to do with Girl Scouting, and then I got the idea I would like to play a musical instrument, so my father bought me a bugle! I took lessons, but I was so poor at it and so shy about making bloopers that I really didn't do much with it. I was the Scout bugler—for a very short time. I'm not musical in the least—only in my dreams! Oh gosh, it's been so long ago, I have a hard time recalling my childhood. When we moved down to North Liberty, we backed up to the fields that belonged to the Seacliff Inn at that point, so we spent a lot of playtime in those fields—and then the Seacliff Inn had their own farm—chickens and so forth, so we used to play around there.

THE ASHCAN THEATRE

"I remember too taking dancing lessons; Eleanor True was one of the teachers, and Elizabeth Sylvia. This I suppose was meant to promote agility and poise and whatever…We had performances at the old Seacliff in a big banquet room, and then we had a recital at the Yacht Club—I have some awful movies of it that my father took. He kept himself busy; when home movies first came out he started in with a big, heavy camera that you had to wind up. Island life was good…down here there were virtually no problems; I don't remember even being warned that I should be careful about anything except running in front of a car, maybe. We were given a lot of freedom to come and go, and we were kept busy. My father bought commercial cartoon films and educational films, and he had a projector, and we used to give little movie shows to the kids in the neighborhood or to the organizations like the Scouts, and we did this all in the basement. It was called the Ashcan Theatre."

What do you remember about the town? I asked. "Well, let me see. The A&P was on Main Street…and the dentist I went to was in the second floor where the Camera Shop is now. Where Spectrum is was the local bar, called The Spa. And we were supposed not to walk by there, because sometimes the men came out in not too good shape. The Dreamland Theatre came later." I wondered if Florence had ever felt marooned on the island, such as during the winter storms. Her answer was immediate: "I didn't consider it being marooned—I just thought heaps of snow were fantastic. But we also traveled off island. My mother's family were in Kingston, PA, and she tried to get there several times a year…so we knew about the outside world, absolutely. We reached a point where my father thought we should have a different kind of summer, and my brother was sent to a camp in the Pennsylvania mountains that was run by Dan Beard, the man

Little Florence Ingall, holding a toy bunny, and her brother William, mugging for the camera in the yard of their home at 120 Main Street on the corner of Bloom Street, where Florence was born. Florence says her mother always cut her hair in a Dutch-boy style, and she hated it, because she always feared Mother would snip off her earlobes, which were right where the hair ended.

Florence Ingall (Clifford) dressed as a sailor boy for Austin Strong's Follies, held for many years at the Nantucket Yacht Club. Flo had to do the Sailor's Hornpipe dance after she popped out of the breadbox behind her. She said that bread used to be brought to the island via Railway Express, and recalled that a man named Willie always delivered the bread to Roger's (now The Hub).

who introduced Boy Scouting into this country. And the next year I was sent to the nearby girls' camp…and the one summer I was there, I contracted the mumps! I put the whole camp staff into a panic, because they could've had a real outbreak. Actually, they were very lucky—only two of us got the mumps. That wasn't fun for me, and I really wasn't close to this other girl, but we were confined together, and a good part of our summer was spent isolated. We read…but you know, you're kind of dopey with the mumps. My mother sent a box, and it was full of little things, and every day I could put my hand in it and bring out one toy…and that was beautiful. Then, as we got better, we were allowed out of our confinement during naptime—maybe given a horseback ride or something. I may forget a lot of things, but not that!

"When my great-aunt died, I was kind of at loose ends. One of her relatives who lived in Montclair just one street down, a Mrs. Walter Kidde, took me in—they're the fire extinguisher people [another boat-horn beep]. And while I was staying with her, I went into New York and took photography classes…and then I came back to Nantucket and a while later bought this little place from her estate. I've had this house since 1943. I think one of the reasons my great-aunt loved Nantucket was that her father loved to hunt; they came down here to duck-shoot, and I've found one picture of her which must have been way out for her day—she was in knickers and a hunting jacket with a gun. He'd lost his son, and I guess she was his hunting buddy. That was a time when there was a lot of affluence—they'd go to Europe on a steamer with all these big trunks, and they brought beautiful things back. When her estate was being settled, there was beautiful china and glassware, and huge carved bears from Switzerland that were coat racks…"

"When I first came back I lived with my half-uncle, Ormond Ingall, and his wife…at that point this house was just an open day place—it had been built in the mid-20s, by a judge whose wife was a diabetic, and this was an open building, sort of like a gazebo, so she could get the air. The land belonged to my aunt, and after the judge no longer needed it, she used to have her friends in for tea, looking out into the harbor…the only thing in here when I took over was the tea set. Over the years it's grown like Topsy, a little here and a little there. It is comfortable, and of course I have heat in here now, so I could stay all winter if I wanted to. Anyway, I met my first husband and was married up in Long Island, and I had the three children here…they're all natives. Drew is the oldest, then Debbie and Dusty. Both the girls worked for Joe Lopes when he ran the Boat Basin…they were dock girls, and Dusty ended up being Assistant Dockmaster. She stuck with it, but Debbie went off and did other things. Debbie is in real estate, at Island Properties. Drew now lives in Vermont, but the others live here. Dusty, who's married to Michael Ramos, runs the office for Ramos Plumbing. She has a 5-1/2-year-old, Nicholas. I have four stepdaughters and seven step-grandchildren too, and as a result I have a big extended family." Here Florence showed me a great picture of the whole bunch, taken at her surprise birthday party on June 27th of this summer. "Quite a crowd," she said. "Isn't that a nice picture? In my second marriage I had seven children—his four girls and my three children…can you imagine—I had five teenagers at one time! That was I guess the hardest part."

The phone was ringing and the painter was needing a conference, and there was baking to do, so it was time to stop this pleasant gam. Florence Clifford's normal day is pretty active. "I keep busy," she said. "Sometimes I bake for my families—I bake it and get it out the door so I'm not tempted!" I commented that she looks to be in terrific shape, and she replied, "Well, I do all the things you do when you're active in a church. And the other activity is the Aquacize program at the High School, three times a week. I don't know what I'd do without it—it keeps me from being completely gelled. There's a group of us who've done it for years, and it's nice, because you get to know everybody."

I thanked Flo for a great interview, and before she left she showed me the piece below, which is a result of another of her activities: a memoir-writing workshop.

The Aroma of Summer
by Florence Clifford

To a great number of people, summer means a move to another place. Often this means a trip to escape the city heat or a change from the mountains to the sea. I grew up on an island that attracted many so-called tourists during the summer months. Our house was rented to some New York City people escaping the almost tropical heat of Manhattan. As a family, we moved "out of town" to a converted barn on a bluff overlooking the harbor. It was a life of freedom for my brother Bill and me, surrounded by a hundred acres of fields and hillocks and, of course, the beach and the water. There was no radio or television, and as a matter of fact, no electricity. My father enjoyed the tranquility of the country at the end of his work day and my mother met the challenge of cooking on a kerosene stove. They seemed pleased to have my brother and me in the great outdoors, using our imaginations for play. Much of our time was spent on the shore and in the water, exploring and swimming. Both of us learned to swim early. As I look back on those days, there seems to have been no real concern about exposure to the sun. Sunburn lotions and the SPF 15 factor were not yet a thing. My brother and I were instructed to watch each other for signs of our skins turning into wrinkled prunes from too much time in the water. Then we were to go back to the house to warm up. The inevitable was that we both got sunburned. The treatment was liberal amounts of Noxema, spread on like frosting on a cake. Its whiteness turned us from lobster-red to ghostly pale. In the process of soothing, the distinctly medicinal odor permeated the room where we sat or played. The aroma lasted and lasted. There was no question as to what had happened to both of us that day. The smell was a dead giveaway. It was an aroma that was a strong mixture of menthol and peppermint, and it was very STRONG. No delicate fragrance that! Dad wasn't exempt from this treatment either, if, after a Sunday in the yard, he succumbed to an uncomfortable sunburn. I've often wondered what our friends thought after an evening visit to our house. Were they offended by the aroma that permeated even our living room? Just perhaps they had also undergone such a treatment themselves.

Below—Florence in 2003.

Right—Florence at the beach, in a two-piece bathing suit that was considered fairly daring at the time.

40

A Woman of Gentle Vitality
Katherine Hatch Dunham

On a day of slashing rain and 40-mph December winds that were battering this little island, I visited Katherine Hatch Dunham in her warm and cozy home. We'd put off the interview for a couple of weeks because she said she'd overdone just a bit on her 87th birthday in November. Neat, slim, with bright brown eyes, Katherine now keeps an oxygen tank nearby, but that doesn't stop her from telling some great old island memories with a great deal of gentle vitality.

Yes, she's a native…and yes, that's her picture on the cover of this book. She's on the left, smartly saluting while Florence Ingall [Clifford] stands beside her, peering into the distance; they're getting ready to dance the "Sailor's Hornpipe." With a small cap, brass-buttoned jacket, and bangs, Katherine looks like a young sailor-boy, and told me she took her role very seriously indeed in the late '20s Nantucket Yacht Club Follies, dreamed up by Austin Strong. In fact, those shoes she is wearing are undoubtedly tap shoes. Looking at the picture, which had been provided by Flo Clifford, Katherine laughed and said, "Do you know, there's a dirty spot on those white trousers; my mother always used to say, 'No matter how often I clean you up, you always manage to get spotted!'"

Going to Dancing School

Katherine said that she was probably around 12 when this momentous event took place, and it was apparently the only venture into show biz that she experienced. "I was taking dancing lessons," she said. "My Grandmother Hatch, who came from Ireland and worked for one of the families in the Three Bricks, always said that I should do something—play the piano or go to dancing school or sing. And she said she'd pay for me to do it. So I went to dancing school. It was held in the home of Sam Sylvia's mother, right next to Academy Hill School, so you could go over after school. In the class, which included Florence Ingall, among others, we learned tap-dancing and ballet—and I could hit my head with my toes at the barre! And we got chosen to be in the Follies. Oh, it was fun. I wish I could remember the exact date. Jimmy Glidden's mother made those costumes; Mrs. Sylvia's mother made some, too. Then, when Mrs. Sylvia stopped teaching, I took dancing lessons from Mrs. Leroy True, at the church. I had those costumes up in the attic at 50 Orange Street for years, but I finally threw them out when we sold the house. Albert Johnsen drove his truck up beside the house and everything went out the window. Oh, I threw a lot of things away, but when you have a huge house and move, you can't keep everything! The house was on the corner of Flora Street.

"My family background on Nantucket? Well, let's see—my grandmother Hatch, as I say, was from Ireland, and she had an ice cream parlor in her house at 26 Orange Street. She rented that house for I think $10 a month from a man who spent winters in California. Later, she bought 50 Orange Street for an investment, but she never lived there, though my father did after she died, and of course I lived there for years. There was a big barn down on Flora Street in back of 50 Orange, and my father had a pony there, which I rode once…but it threw me on my head and I put my teeth through my tongue, and that was the end of my horseback-riding days. My brother George was a great horseman, though, used to race. Anyway, my grandmother made all her ice cream from scratch, and all by herself. She used to take ice, 100-pound blocks, in tongs and chop it in with salt in a big trough out in what she called the back kitchen, and she'd do two batches at a time, and then put burlap bags over them to keep them cold. She had as many as twelve different flavors: ginger (and I had some ginger ice cream this summer, hadn't had it since my grandmother made it), and strawberry, and frozen pudding—she'd put a little brandy in it and raisins—and chocolate and vanilla, banana, and more. She'd spiel all the flavors off for customers. She had one room there that she set up for customers, and I waited on tables after school…I was very young. There was no refrigeration—it was all ice and salt. The people in the neighborhood used to come with their bowls, and she'd fill them up and they'd take them home. One man used to come and he'd stand there in the front hall talking, and by the time he went home, his ice cream would be nothing but soup!" Katherine laughed.

"Grandmother Hatch was a widow by then—her husband had died of a stroke, fairly young. They had two boys, my father and my uncle. The house is still there—the Willards own it now—and there was a long shed, I guess you'd call it, where they used to keep big, empty wooden boxes from the cemetery. They weren't caskets, I know that. That was eventually torn down. My grandmother also took boarders; she had two rooms that she rented…" and here Katherine chuckled…"no bathroom facilities—commodes! There was a stove in each room and she'd take out all the ashes…she was a hard worker. I don't know how she ever did all she did. She died in her early forties…I think she worked herself to death. She was quite a woman.

"My father, Walter, was born in that house where my grandmother made ice cream…and when he was in the last year of school he and five other fellows had a runaround with a teacher, and they walked out. Grandmother Hatch wanted him to do something worthwhile, so she opened a shop, a grocery store, with him on Orange Street, right there on the corner of Martin's Lane. But she also made him have tutoring with Elma Folger, a schoolteacher who held private classes up on the Cliff. She didn't want him to lack an education. Later, she bought 50 Orange Street, where I lived for many years; I moved here to Hummock Pond Road in 1974.

Here, Katherine's maternal grandparents, Edward and Florence Thomas, top left, pose in front of the Wauwinet House with some friends on Arbor Day, 9/13/17.

Grandma Thomas with Katherine, at left, and a young cousin at right; they are in front of Grandma's house at the corner of Chester and Centre Streets.

"My father, Walter, lived to be 70-something—oh, I'm terrible about dates. His brother Irving used to have his own business delivering kerosene—for heating, you know—and sometimes he worked until 9 at night, keeping people warm…never collected half his money. My mother's father, Edward Thomas, owned the paint shop on Main Street on the corner, Paddack's Paint Shop." (Later, Katherine showed me a beautiful framed marriage certificate commemorating his marriage to Florence Chase in November of 1880.) "Grandfather Thomas," she went on, "died on Armistice Day, of pneumonia; he was very young. My great-grandparents must have had some money, because my mother's parents used to go to Boston every once in a while and everyone would stay in a hotel. My Thomas grandparents had three girls: first Alice, and then Ellen, my mother, and Louise was the other daughter. How did my parents meet? I really don't know…but they had two children, myself and my brother, George Edward, who was named for both grandfathers. He died before I moved out here to Hummock Pond Road."

ABSOLUTELY HATED SCHOOL

I asked Katherine about her school memories, and she quickly replied, "Hated school! *Hated it!* I never graduated. The principal told my mother, 'You could leave her there for a lifetime, and she'd never graduate.' One reason was that I'd missed too much school. I hurt my leg, and I was laid up for three months—old Dr. Roberts, who had an office on Pine Street, kept operating and operating, and then I got an infection…and finally I went back to school, but I should never have gone ahead…I got lost, just couldn't catch up. They moved me along and I went to freshman and sophomore grades, but then stopped…I just didn't pay attention. Two teachers I remember are Mary Mendonca and Julia Williams, who taught typing. I was very friendly with Julia. She lived on Farmer Street…she was a nice woman, who had a hard life.

"I got my driver's license when I was 16, and while I was still in school, in the summers, I worked down at the old Spouter Inn. Two sisters, old-maid sisters, had a tearoom there, with a few gifts.

Here Katherine poses with her father, Walter, in 1966, in front of Hatch's Package Store.

When I got the job, I thought I was going to help them in the gift shop, but all I saw was a dishpan! My mother and father were really upset. There was sort of a mound in back—I think it was where the old train tracks had been; it went right through where Hatch's is now. When somebody came in they'd put them out there on that mound so they could look at the water and take their orders…and then they'd start fixing the food from scratch. And these people would sit there…of course it was a beautiful view, but it would be an hour before the sisters got anything ready to serve. Once, they asked if I would drive them to 'Sconset to see the sunrise. I said yes, and set the alarm clock to ring very early—my father wasn't too happy about that—and when I came back, you know what they gave me? Fifty cents!" Katherine laughed and raised her eyebrows. "My father said, 'That didn't even pay for the gas!'"

Was this your parents' car? I asked. "No, I had my own. Grandmother Hatch insisted that when I became old enough I should have a car, and when my brother got old enough I was to share it with him. It was a second-hand car, a Chevrolet. Well, you want to talk about fights! Sometimes I'd go to the Monahannet Club, which was a girls' club that had dances and suppers and things, and I'd park the car and take the keys, but when I came out, the car would be gone! George wasn't old enough to drive then, but he'd take it anyway! He had a key made. I got into more messes, because I started to smoke along about then, and he'd say to me, 'If you tell on me, I'll tell Mom and Dad that you're a smoker!' So I had no alternative. Anyway, when he got old enough to drive, we had to share it, and that brought about *more* arguments! And finally, we needed tires, so my father said, 'OK, I'll buy two tires, and you each have to pay for a tire.' But my brother and I got into a heated argument, and George was so mad that he took all the wheels off! So my father said, 'This is it!' and he sold the car. He was tired of listening to us…every time we sat down to dinner we'd start arguing about who was going to have the car. So then we didn't have any car. Oh yes," Katherine sighed, "my brother and I had our differences. I guess my parents were a little strict. I was pretty well behaved growing up…though I have a few things I did that I know I shouldn't have…" She said this with a distinct twinkle in her eyes, but declined to tell stories about those experiences…except for one.

THAT FIRST SMOKE & QUITTING SCHOOL

"I started smoking," Katherine admitted, "with Lucille Ring Sanguinetti—in fact, she's a distant cousin of mine on the Hatch side. I used to go to her house on Saturdays in the summer, and stay for the day… Well, we snuck two cigarettes out of her father's desk and went behind his garage on Liberty Street to try them out. Lucille's mother came out in front and thought the garage was on fire! It was cement block, and why she thought it would be on fire, I don't know, but she did. When she saw us, oh, she was angry, and was going to send me home. I said, 'I can't go home!' because what was I going to say? I was scared to death my parents would find out, and how was I going to get out of that? So she let me stay…so that was my first cigarette. It didn't make me sick, no…and I became a heavy smoker. I stopped twenty years ago, but I'm paying for it now.

"Anyway," she went on, "I left school and got a job…I've always worked in a store. My father was going to open a lingerie shop, because there wasn't one here, but that never got started. Oh dear, I

Left to right—(1) Katherine stands saucily next to an airport fence in spite of a sign warning of JET BLASTS. (2) In 1936, Katherine holds her baby daughter Deborah Anne. (3) Here Katherine adjusts her daughter Deborah's wedding veil. 1956. (4) Katherine Hatch Dunham, a beautiful woman still at 87.

just can't remember what job I had then. I was married very young, at 19; my husband was a native, a Tuckernucker [pronounced "TuckerNUCKer"]. We were married in my grandmother Thomas's parlor at 8 Chester Street, in the house my grandfather had built for her when they were married. I had to come down eighteen stairs, and my hands were shaking so I could hardly hold my bouquet. But we got divorced after three years—he wanted a harem!" she laughed, "had girlfriends everywhere. He had three wives after me, so you can see what I mean. I took my daughter Deborah, who was very young, to Boston, and Fred Bennett, who I'd known when he was a minister on Nantucket, had a church up there, so he helped me find an apartment. I rented furniture, and then went to work at hotels. Yes, I was pretty independent—I had to be! I remember on December 7th, Reverend Bennett was driving me in to work and the car radio was on, and we heard the announcement of the attack on Pearl Harbor. He said, 'I guess I'm going to war.' So he did…he became a chaplain.

"I stayed in Boston four years. When I went up there, I didn't know anyone except Reverend Bennett. I did make a friend, though, and we are still touch—we've been friends for over sixty years. She's not too well now, and my daughter took me up to Wellesley to see her recently. Anyway, she lived in a nearby apartment, and we became friends. Her husband was in a hospital, he had tuberculosis, and this meant she was alone with two children. There was some money on her side of the family, so she didn't have to work, really. And her mother, who had a vacant wing on her house, said 'You girls ought to come here and live in this wing, and Katherine will save on rent money.' So we did, and my friend looked out for Deborah when I was at my job. That worked out well, but it wasn't an easy time; I was doing hat-checking at night and working during the day—well, I had to feed my daughter."

46

COMING HOME AGAIN

What brought Katherine and her little girl, by that time in second grade, back to Nantucket? "I was going to go to work in Buttner's store. The owner had a store in Plymouth and he'd opened one on Nantucket, and Juanita Killen was resigning from the Nantucket store, so my mother said why didn't I come home and work there…she didn't like the idea of me being in Boston alone. So I went down to Plymouth and talked with the owner and he said I could have the job. I got all set—my brother came up in an old rattley-trap, got all my stuff in, and we came back to Nantucket. That was April, and I went to work, but not too long afterward, the man came to the island and said, 'Katherine, I have somebody coming down to take your place…she's been working here during the summers and now she's graduated from school'…so he gave the job to her. After I'd moved and all!" A sigh. "Well, I ended up working for Eleanor Royal in her clothing shop on Federal Street—you know, where there are three shops now, across and down from the post office. Eleanor had lived in Plymouth and knew the owner…she was supposed to run his store, but he fired her and gave the job to his girlfriend. So that's how she came to open up her store, which was just a summer shop at first. Then she decided to keep it open off-season, and wanted to know if I would run it for her in the winter. So I did, and I loved it.

"At that time, Deborah and I lived with my mother in an apartment in the basement, at 50 Orange Street. It was nice, just big enough, and Deborah could walk to school. But I had a runaround with Eleanor, so I left and went to work at the Nantucket Drug Store; in the winters, when there wasn't so much business, I worked on the soda fountain. And then my uncle died, so I went down to help my father at Hatch's Package Store. The hours you had to put in there, though, to keep on top of things! I ran that store after my father passed away. But you had to work until 11 o'clock at night, and the responsibility…it wasn't easy. I finally sold it and went to work for Coffin's Gift Shop, where I stayed for twenty years. I hated to leave them, but I was having problems with this leg. I don't like to see that store closing…but the rents are so high!"

"So," said Katherine, "that's about the size of my life… After I moved back to the island, I didn't do much but work, though I used to do a lot up at the Congregational Church… And these days, where do I go? Well, from this chair to that one," she laughed. "I really can't exert myself, but I do read all the time. Right now I'm reading a book by Jude Deveraux called *Legend*—I don't know why I'm reading it, but it's a really funny book…I don't watch much TV…I have the news and things on in the morning.

"My daughter and one of my two granddaughters live here…and one great-grandchild, Julia. She was born in Colorado on December 31st, 2000—two hours from being the first New Year's baby. She's a beauty—she is right here on the island now, and I really enjoy that." Katherine paused and smiled: "I've had a good life—it could have been worse. I was always working. I didn't have any hobbies, but I liked working. It's been a pretty happy life."

A recent photo of Katherine Hatch Dunham (known to all as Gramma Dee). Great-grandson Randy is at top right, great-granddaughter Julia in center; over Julia is Katherine's daughter Deborah Taylor; at bottom, Katherine is flanked by granddaughters Marsali (at left), Randy's Mom, and Laurie, Julia's Mom.

48

Skipper of the Old
Skipper Restaurant
Bill Beers, 1997

When I called Bill Beers for an interview in September of 1997, I was told he'd celebrated his ninetieth birthday the night before and had played tennis all morning, so he was taking a little nap. Every year, in June and September, he was in the habit of staying with Milton and Shannon Kaye at their home at 24 India Street. But he was definitely not your ordinary vacationer. Just ask an islander about him, and the likely response will be, "Oh, Billy Beers—the Skipper Restaurant. What a nice fellow!"

When I asked if his party the night before had been a surprise, Bill responded, "Well, I had an inkling, because they wanted to be sure that I'd be available for that date. It was really engineered by Joan Murdoch Bernhard; she was our hostess and treated us all. She'd been a waitress at the Skipper from the very first year, so she knew all these people who'd been involved with the restaurant in those years I owned it and gathered them together—Dutch and Bing Swain, and Regina Keightley and her husband…and there was a fellow named Beesey Mellon, Dick Parker, Ben Larrabee (both he and Dick Parker worked for Miss Prentice one year before I came). And also Marcia Gardner Tooker, and Woody Woodworth—he worked for me, and his father was the accompanist for the Harvard Glee Club when I was a member. And Woody's first wife, Carol…she works at Tanglewood. There were sixteen at the party—I was surprised; I never dreamed that many could assemble. It was a wonderful event." Bill stopped a moment, then chuckled. "Regina Keightley is just now getting used to calling me Bill—they used to call me Mr. B."

Bill, who looked extraordinarily tan and trim, said he plays tennis regularly. "Oh yes. We play with Hugh Rainey, who came from Scotland and is a superb tennis player; and Larry Stentzel, who's also very good. And I play with Marcia Gardner Tooker, who worked for me in those first five years. And Thérèse Woodward, née Paradis, which is a Nantucket family, and she's a good player also. Good friends! You know, it is tough to leave the island after my visits with Milton and Shannon, but I always know I'll come back again.

ROUND TRIP TO NANTUCKET: $3.95

"The first time I came here was on the New York, New Haven & Hartford, which owned the boat system, and we went to New Bedford by train and then came over on the ferry. We spent a couple hours on the island and then went back, and it cost $3.95—round trip! I guess that was in the early '30s. Yes, I did get sand in my shoes; I only had to walk up Main Street and back and I was hooked. Loved it. I guess I came back for summer visits, but then I realized that Nantucket was an ideal spot for a summer theatre. I'd been in the theatre and had good friends in the theatre, so three of us put in a thousand dollars each and announced our plans for a summer theater at the 'Sconset Casino. And it was Katherine Cornell who posted our equity bond—you had to post a bond to cover two weeks' salary for your permanent cast. Then we imported New York stars, such as Violet Heming, Blanche Yurka, and…oh, who was the gal who was in movies with W.C. Fields? Can't remember her name. But they were interesting people, though perhaps not many remember them now. Our first theatrical production was *Candida,* because Morgan Farley, who was one of the three, had done it with Katherine Cornell. So she came over, and also on the island that year was a very famous actress—oh gosh, I can't remember her name right now—and I asked her to please be our guest. 'Oh no,' she said, 'the box office is one part of the theatre I thoroughly believe in.' She wouldn't accept free tickets to our production; she bought hers.

"Well, that was my first adventure on Nantucket. I withdrew and the other two carried on for several years. I had a restaurant in Boston, in Copley Square, called the Toby House, and I realized that I needed a summer business, because in the summer your businesspeople in Boston and your residents of Back Bay are away—summer homes and summer vacations—and I didn't have enough business, so I needed a summer place. And I decided Nantucket was the place. My aunt said, 'Bill, if you find a proper restaurant, I'll help you financially.' She was Mrs. Ledgard Sargent, of the Sargent School of Physical Education at Harvard. However, she died that winter, so I thought I couldn't go ahead with any plans; but in the fall, without my seeking it, two people who knew Miss Prentice of the Skipper Restaurant came to my Boston restaurant and suggested I talk with her, because she was thinking of withdrawing. So I did, and we hit it off right away. She and Gladys Wood owned the Skipper, then Gladys ran a real estate agency—there were only two or three on the island then. She owned a wonderful house on Main Street, very Medieval Englishy, with funny old diamond-shaped windowpanes. Anyway, Miss Prentice made me a proposition I couldn't refuse. That was in 1943.

"One outstanding thing about my first summer, 1944: we served on the deck of that old schooner, and a European, Rose Walder, a wonderful singer who had escaped from Germany just in time (she had a Jewish background), was visiting me. And when the bells began to toll the victory on D-Day, she stood up on that deck and sang the *National Anthem*. It was very moving; America meant so much to her. It made us all stop and think. The summer season, of course, was not as long then, but I continued with the Skipper for 25 years, till 1968. I bought a lovely historic house here, at 27 Liberty, but eventually sold it. I had the most wonderful crew of young people who worked for me through those years, before and during college. The surprise party was actually a reunion of quite a few of the young people who worked for me during the first five years I ran the Skipper. Dickie Parker, who grew up here on Nantucket and ran the Mad Hatter for a while, came all the way from Colorado. And others came from distant places, and we had cocktails at the Yacht Club and then dinner at Cioppino's, and it was beautiful. The president of Harvard, Neil Rudenstine, wasn't able to come, but he'd worked for me one summer, and was exemplary. And Rhoda Dorsey, who became the president of Goucher, worked for me several years; after the last summer she worked she went to London with three scholarships—she was a very smart girl. When she was doing her sidework before we began to serve, she'd be singing English folk songs," Bill laughed. "She couldn't make it to the party, but wrote a lovely letter. And they want to do this yearly—I don't know how long I'll last, but we'll see."

SERVING THE CELEBS

Tell me more about those days at the Skipper, I said. "Well, the Skipper had the honor of refusing to serve four very glamorous people—Elizabeth Taylor, Mike Todd, Joan Blondell, and Eddie Fisher came in as a party just as we were closing, and we didn't have a table for them. So we had to refuse them! We did serve Faye Emerson and Skitch Henderson, and they were fun, because they wanted to come back into the kitchen afterwards and see all the workings of it. And we served Jimmy Melton, the famous tenor. Oh, a lot of well-known people came into the Skipper. It had been a famous place for a long time—way before I ever saw it, my mother and I had seen a full-page advertisement on the back of the *Saturday Evening Post*—the most circulated magazine at the time—for Valspar Varnish, which was waterproof, and the scene was pouring boiling water onto newly varnished tabletops of the

Skipper. Think of the publicity that brought! My mother looked at it and said, 'Bill, do you think we'll ever see that place? And she did see it, for the full 25 years we were there! Just a little side story here: For many years Mother and I drove up here from Florida, and I finally said, 'Mother, I think it's time for us to fly,' and she had never flown. We boarded the plane at Miami and soon the Captain's voice came over the loudspeaker: 'This is Kevin Shaughnessy, your pilot…' and Mother said, 'We know him!' We'd met him in Boston…and that made her feel so good and so safe. She immediately let the hostess know she was on the plane, and he made us feel very welcome.

"Anyway, the Skipper. So many stories. We did get some extraordinary publicity one time when Garry Moore, who did the TV show *I've Got a Secret,* came in with a party from his yacht. Everyone was so excited, and the busboys kept pouring water at the table to be there as much as they could. A very good waiter named Bunky was serving the table, and after Garry Moore paid and left, Bunky came to me and said, 'Mr. Beers, I know I gave him good service, and he stiffed me!' But I said, 'I'm sure he'll come in tomorrow; he's planning to get some chowder to take out, and I'm sure he'll remember.' But he sent somebody else in and didn't come back. Bunky called his mother and said, 'Who do you think I waited on? And he stiffed me!' And she said, 'I'm going to call *I've Got a Secret* and tell them!' She did, and they called Bunky right away and told him they wanted him on their first program—he was so excited he was walking on air, but a couple of days later, he said, 'Mr. Beers, I think somebody's playing a practical joke on me.' I said, 'I'll tell you what you do. Send a telegram to the show and ask them to confirm your engagement.' He did, and they called right back and said that they had reservations for Bunky at the Hotel Taft, and were expecting him. Well, we were all in my living room watching the television when it went on, and sure enough…the questions were put to Garry Moore rather than to the panel, and took him right up to his summer vacation and his yacht in Nantucket Harbor, and dining at the Skipper, mentioning the name! And they said, 'And you were waited on by college students?' 'Yes.' 'And you didn't tip your waiter?' 'OH!' Moore said, 'didn't I tip him?' Bill Cullen said, 'He won't get through college that way!' So Garry Moore took out a lot of money and gave it to Bunky, and of course all his expenses were paid—what a thrill for him. Well, that gave the Skipper nationwide publicity, and the next summer people came in asking to be waited on by Bunky. Isn't that a grand story?

SKIPPER OF THE SKIPPER FOR 25 YEARS

"Really, the Skipper was in an ideal location. It was a much-loved restaurant. Once, after I'd withdrawn from it, a man approached me in the A&P market; he was hot under the collar. He said, 'Do you know you've taken away from me one of the things I most loved about Nantucket?' I didn't know what he was talking about at first, but then I understood, and said, 'Yes, but I gave it to you for 25 years.' And then he calmed down. I sold it to a gal who'd worked for me as a waitress—Alice Erickson, a lovely person, who'd come back to the island to raise her family. And then she rented it to a man who called it the Relaxed Lobster, which we all laughed about, because a relaxed lobster is on the way out…or dead! And after that Mr. Fee purchased it.

"A lot of my former workers stay in touch with me. When I decided to give up the Skipper, people said, 'Don't you miss it?' And I said, 'The thing I miss is the wonderful crew I had working with me—we worked together!' Johnny Brock, of Brock Insurance here, worked for me, and he was one of the best employees I ever had. And Harry Ostrander, who now owns a house here, worked for me for several years, and Bing and Dutch Swain, who grew up here and worked for me, come back and visit. I kept my Boston restaurant for a few years, and then I sold that and started a successful restaurant in Florida in the winters, and it grew, and I really didn't want another big restaurant. At the Skipper, you know, we fed 300 people on a small day, and 600 or so on a large day. And it took 36 people to run it! I didn't want another big one, but the place in Florida grew, darn it! I realized I'd either have to enlarge it and invest money that I didn't have, or sell it, and I sold it."

I wondered if Bill had intended to be a restaurateur from the very beginning. "No," he said, "I was in the theatre in New York City. Never a leading man…I was in fact the juvenile. I was in a good play with Mary Bolen, who was well known then; and I was in a couple plays with Basil Rathbone. It's interesting—in that play with Mary Bolen, one of the little parts was taken by Jimmy Cagney. Did I spot his talent right away? Well, he spent most of his time backstage turning handsprings and doing gymnastics!

"I wasn't a New York native," Bill continued. "I went from Cambridge to New York to a school of the theatre, and while I was there I had the opportunity to appear in *Abie's Irish Rose*. It was the longest-running play on Broadway. Here's how that happened: The sister of Ann Nichols, who wrote the play, was in the same school as me, and one day she came running in saying, 'Bill, the stage manager can't find one of the actors; he has a very small part. You run over—you could do it.' So I ran over. The stage manager primed me on the two lines I had to say. So for one performance I was in *Abie's Irish Rose!* Then, after that year of school I was in Provincetown in a summer theatre, and later I was at the Cape Cod Playhouse. I was serious about acting, but after a while I realized it was very hard to earn your living in the theatre, and I bowed out. Then I began to take up singing as an avocation along with running a restaurant. And I had a job, at Trinity Church, right across from my restaurant, for five years—baritone, first bass. Of course I had been trained in music earlier, and I got to sing with other musical groups, including the Boston Symphony, and was a featured singer on a radio program with an organist doing popular songs—don't remember his name. I also sang at the Isabella Gardner Museum…so I had a nice artistic avocation going on. I didn't give it up altogether, but was only involved in musicals here on Nantucket, with Mac Dixon; I was in *Brigadoon* and *Carnival*. Mac was a dear friend. I knew him from way back when his aunt Jane Wallach was alive." Bill stopped and chortled gently, remembering those days on the Nantucket boards. "Ruth Ann and Charles Flanagan were both in *Brigadoon*—I was the leading man, Ruth Ann the leading lady. I remember I was able to lift Ruth up and whirl her around in one scene! I don't think I could do it now," he laughed.

"After I sold the Skipper in 1968, I kept coming back to my house for the whole summer. And then I was pulled into the Nantucket Musical Arts, with Jane Wallach and others, and I took that over for several years as manager, not president. Then Eva-Maria Tausig got pulled in, and we would have big confabs, and then she took it over. At some point, in Florida, I was inveigled into involvement with the theatre there—it was a wonderful regional theatre—part professional, part amateur—and I directed that for a while. I never directed on Nantucket, mainly acted…Mac was in full charge."

STUCK ON NANTUCKET

Bill stays amazingly active. "In Florida I play tennis," he said, "and I have both speech and singing students…I've had students in every theatre there—the Burt Reynolds Theatre, the Caldwell Theatre, the many pro and semi-pro theatres. I teach in a very leisurely way, I don't push it; and just the keeping up of my little house takes a bit of effort; and I ride my bike over to the ocean every morning, often see the sun rise. I don't go swimming then, but do later on in the day. It's wonderful to swim on Christmas day!"

What keeps Bill Beers coming back to Nantucket? "Oh," he answered, "I love the island. The only thing that disturbs me is the tramping of the tourists and too many automobiles... One of the things about Nantucket that makes it unique is the assembly of early architecture, the beautiful historical houses, the cobblestones, the church bells, the church towers, and then of course the unsurpassed beaches...I love to go to the beaches, and to look out over the moors. I hope there will be careful management of expansion in the future. Yes, there is still room for houses to be built, but somehow the proliferation of automobiles has to be managed. What should be done? Limit cars one to a family? Not allow cars on the island? Well, I don't think you could achieve that—people wouldn't put up with it; it would infringe on their personal liberties. It's a real conflict, isn't it? Personal liberties and the good of all of us...and that's to be solved in many places. But I am an optimist. Nantucket is a truly unique spot, one of the most untouched early American scenes we have. And I'll keep coming back..."

✎

Bill Beers died in Del Ray, Florida, in 1998.

MORE ABOUT THE SKIPPER

The Skipper Restaurant, a popular island dining spot on Steamboat Wharf for residents and Nantucket visitors for nearly a half-century, was originally a two-masted schooner named the **Allen Gurney***. It had carried cargoes on some 57 voyages since being built on Rondout Creek on the Hudson River in 1867. Captain Allen Gurney, one-time master of the ship, was one of four brothers who had gained respect as ship-builders, maritime agents, and master mariners on the east coast in the early 1900s. Gradually, the schooner became reduced to delivering coal, and it was a familiar sight in Nantucket Harbor for many years.*

Miss Prentice & Miss Wood. *The Skipper dining establishment wasn't always a jauntily awninged shipboard eatery and drinkery, though. It was initially a tearoom/restaurant located at 14 Liberty Street run by two intrepid and hardworking women, Margaret Prentice and Gladys Wood. Miss Prentice was a dietitian who'd been a driver for the California motor corps and also ran a canteen for soldiers in Antwerp, Belgium during World War I. Gladys Wood, a Massachusetts gal, was also a "canteener" in Luxembourg and elsewhere with the 81st Division. In 1920, the two got together and started the tea-room on Nantucket, putting up a sign of a jolly skipper looking at the island world through a telescope. There was a dining room, veranda, and, according to an undated newspaper account (possibly from a New Bedford paper), "a gayly [sic] parasoled lawn where tea was served. Friday was selected as chowder day and people came specially for it." The women also served a good lobster salad and steaks and chops "for the most ravenous male." Miss P. made the salads and "presided over the pantry" and Miss Wood took care of the service, "assisted occasionally by Smith College and Y friends."*

The Black Hole of Calcutta. *The menu was orange, and at first announced, "If you don't see* what you want, ask for it. It may be in the Skipper's Chest.' Some of the elderly ladies," the article says, "thought the phrase indelicate, referring to a part of the Skipper's anatomy that might better not be mentioned." Later, the menu bore such notices as "The Skipper announces with great regret that in order to save the lives of his crew, his house will hereafter be closed on Sundays," or "Skipper's Cupboard bare. Come back tomorrow." The place was both too popular and too small, however, with "one sink, dreadful ice-boxes, and very cramped pantry space." So Miss P. and Miss W. looked for a new space. What they found was the Allen Gurney which was "unseaworthy, grimy, with a hold like the Black Hole of Calcutta." It had "come in during the winter with a cargo of coal for the Island Service Co." and stayed at the wharf "in a leaking condition." In other words, it died in service, right there in Nantucket Harbor. In spite of dire warnings of financial and possibly other kinds of disaster, the women thought it was the answer to their prayers. They eagerly pursued the possibility of mooring the ship next to the wharf owned by the New York, New Haven & Hartford Railroad, consulting with the harbormaster and making many trips to Boston seeking permission to moor the deceased ship at Steamboat Wharf. Successful in this mission, they bought a building on the wharf which had been built in 1890 to serve as the I&M print shop on land way up near Monument Square off Milk Street; after it was moved to the wharf, it became the shelter for a merry-go-round called "Flying Horses" on the wharf (which validates the claims of many old-timers); and last it served as a "sanitary laundry."

The women leased the land from the railroad early in 1921, had the ship floated right in front of the wharf during a very high tide, and moored the Allen Gurney by the building. Next, according to the early newspaper account, they had two large holes made in the ship's sides so that the water would rise and fall in the hold with the tide. Lots of cleaning needed to be done, and the two women rolled up their sleeves and did much of it themselves, scrubbing, caulking the decks, painting. The erstwhile laundry was made into a two-story affair, the top for bedrooms and bath for cook and waitresses and the bottom floor for work space and a really efficient kitchen with good refrigerators and a dishwashing rack much like the one Miss P. had worked with in the canteen at Antwerp. The Allen Gurney's small engine became the motor for the ice-cream freezer. The women painted the tables green and orange, erected a brightly striped awning, hung the Skipper sign from the Liberty Street tea-room, and made cretonne curtains adorned with tropical parrots. They also had two small bedrooms, a bath, and a living room made, portholes "gayly curtained, well-filled bookshelves, and a desk."

Miss Wood retired in 1924 to start her real estate business; Miss Prentice stayed with the Skipper until 1944, when William Beers bought it and ran it for almost three decades. The place was in business for almost fifty years in all. A reminder of the old Skipper remains as the long spar which became the tail of Nantucket's Old Mill. And the memory of the late Bill Beers lives on in the hearts of all those whose lives he touched.

This is what the old Skipper looked like at the dock. That's Easy Street in the foreground. Used with permission of the Nantucket Historical Association.

Living Happily Ever After
Walt & Eleanor Lucas, 1998

When Walt Lucas opened the door of his Vestal Street house to welcome me, I realized I'd known him, sort of, since I came to the island. This was the chipper-looking, neat-mustached, pleasantly smiling man I'd see all over town, always walking. I'd been told he was a professional photographer who'd had many pictures in the likes of *Life* magazine; I'd also been told: Sure you know Walt—everybody knows Walt!

And when I walked into the living room of his neat little late-1700s house, I didn't expect to see a roomful of oil paintings, some finished and some in various stages of completion—a boat resting on the shore, several renditions of the Statue of Liberty, Sankaty Lighthouse, and a young girl deliberately painted in American primitive style. Walt explained that he's trying to get 25 or so paintings together for a one-man show. But I thought you were a photographer, I said. "Oh, I am, but I've been painting for some time," he replied. "Nobody knows me—see, I don't use my name. I was brought up to believe that if you're good, people will find out about you…only people who are not that good use their name all the time. So I hardly ever do." He told me that he's been a member of the Artists' Association of Nantucket for years, was once on its board, and exhibits photographs and paintings regularly. ("Have you seen my photograph of the ghost at Hadwen House?" he asked me.) So it turns out that photography was where he began his career, and for some years he's also been concentrating on painting.

ART IS IN HIS BLOOD

How did this all come about, anyway? "When I was very young, I always had a camera," Walt said. "A little Brownie or something more fancy. When I was in my teens I studied photography with Ansel Adams and Margaret Bourke-White, who did all those *Life* covers when that magazine started. There's something interesting I didn't discover until I was about 50 and started putting two and two together," he said. "My dad was a professional lithographer, and he'd come home with big sheets off the press and after dinner we'd clear the table and he'd put these big sheets out, color proofs and so forth. He'd have his magnifying glass and would check everything…he was doing lithography for artists like Georgia O'Keeffe and Alfred Stieglitz and John Marin, the watercolorist, all these famous people! I didn't know them at all…I was just a kid. Also, my great-grandfather, who came from England and started the clan here, was an artist and a photographer. So I guess it's in my blood…" Walt laughed, adding, "I have a picture showing his whole family, and he's got his hand around a bulb to fire the camera while everyone, including him, was posing… So that's kind of my background."

What happened after your studies with Ansel Adams and Margaret Bourke-White? I asked "When I was 19 or so," he answered, "I was drafted, and so I was over in the Pacific for almost five years. The first island we hit was Guadalcanal, and I was there a year and a half." Having studied with such well-known photographers, he said, it wasn't hard to get assigned to the photography unit. "At first we did stupid things—pictures of documents and so on. Finally I switched over into Intelligence, and then we did more important things, like installations. We were always in a safe area—we had a few air raids, but nothing spectacular. We always came in right after the battle, so we were reasonably safe. We went all the way up into the Solomons, into New Guinea, Manila, and then Japan, where we were photographing the whole island, right from the caves at the southern tip, Kyushu, to the northern region, where they ski…and of course Hiroshima and Nagasaki. All the pictures were of course government property…"

Walt was sitting and gently rocking in a chair that had an interesting squeak; it let forth an occasional *quaaack* like a duck. Walt assured me with a grin that it was the chair, not his bad knee. I asked him what he did after the war. "Photography," he said, not surprisingly. "That was around 1946, I guess. I worked for American Optical Corporation, so a lot of my photography was in big magazines like *Life*. Eleanor and I got married as soon as I got back. I think that was in…1946." Obviously proud of his wife's accomplishments, Walt outlined just a few of the things Eleanor's been involved with on the island: she started the Center for Elder Affairs here; she also worked with Bernie Grossman to get Landmark House started, and was hired by the Council on Aging of Nantucket and Elder Services of the Cape to start some programs for Nantucket seniors. "Wherever we are," said Walt, "my wife and I always help, and that's why, even though she's retired, Eleanor is still involved. I have a four-wheel-drive truck—we contact older people and make sure everything is all right. If people need help in the winter, grocery shopping or whatever, we do things like that." Eleanor, it turns out, is a multitalented person. She got her degree in French and Romance Languages at Radcliffe and much later learned Russian at Indiana University and Dartmouth, as part of a government program that began in the Sputnik era, about 1957. I talked with her later to get more details about her civic activities and also about Walt, since he turns out to be pretty modest about his accomplishments, and Eleanor told me that when the government tapped her to learn Russian, it was a particularly fascinating time, "because I was no spring chicken then." Eventually, Walt had told me, she taught Russian and also spent some time in that country to enable the U.S. to learn more about our huge and interesting sometimes-ally. On one memorable trip, Walt went along, and he and Eleanor learned so much that they gave lectures on Russia to Chamber of Commerce and church groups when they returned.

SHE MET HIM IN THE DARK

Eleanor said, "When Walt and I married, I was an industrial editor at American Optical Corporation. We met because I was putting out the company newspaper, and since he was the advertising photographer, he had to do the paper's photographs." She paused for a moment, then laughed: "I met him in the dark, really. But he came out into the light after a while. We had a lot in common; he's also interested in absorbing all kinds of knowledge. After the war he studied at the Rhode Island School of Design. While he was still in the Army, he also attended the Rochester Institute of Technology to study chemistry and photography so he could develop his film properly in the heat of the tropics. "He's always been interested in art," Eleanor went on. "For about twenty years, he taught the photography courses for the town's adult education classes."

I asked Eleanor how she'd describe Walt. She laughed heartily: "I'd say he has a mustache…I think." Didn't she know, really? "Well, we've been married a long time. Let's see…he had knee surgery, and after that he started walking downtown two or three times a day. He carries dog biscuits around in his pockets because he loves dogs, although he's never had one himself—that's because he worries too much. He's a worrier, so that's why he likes other people's dogs." She laughed again. Walt had told me that they were "never quiet; we're doing something all the time," and Eleanor agreed, saying, "Oh yes. I volunteer at the Seconds Shop, am on the board of the Homestead…and I worked at the Maria Mitchell for years, giving nature courses and walks…but now I'm engaged in following up my own interests—nature, and wild plants."

A Thing for Islands

Walt told me that he and Eleanor were married in Belmont, MA. "That's where she was from—and then we lived for a while in Charlton, MA." Then the Lucases built a house in Connecticut and finally moved to Nantucket. What got them to the island? (Quack *quaaaack* went the chair as Walt thought over his answer.) "First of all," he finally said, "I like islands. When I was a small child my family spent every summer way out at the end of Long Island. It was a spit of land, very narrow, like Coatue…and then the big tidal wave came in the late '30s and wiped everything out. But I like islands; I like the ruggedness and the spirit of island people. And of course during the war years I spent most of my time on all those islands in the Pacific. *Anyway,* Eleanor and I used to go to the Cape, Wellfleet and Truro, out that way. Then one day we said, 'Let's take the boat and go over to Nantucket,' so we came over and fell in love with the place. That was, I guess, in the early '50s. And then we had friends we'd visit in 'Sconset…it's a long story…and finally we got our first place, the cottage in Quaise, which we still have. Another thing that brought us here," Walt continued, "was that my wife's aunt through marriage was Jared Coffin's great-granddaughter, and when she was a little girl (this is the 1800s) she lived at Moor's End on Pleasant Street, the house Jared Coffin had built. You can see a picture of her if you go to the dining room of the JC House; in the big dining room upstairs there's a huge oil painting, two little boys and a little girl, and that was Aunt Marian Coffin as a child. She lived to be almost 100, and died, I think, in the 1960s. So Eleanor had Nantucket roots through marriage…not me, though. My family all came from England."

Getting Involved

So, you moved to Nantucket and lived happily ever after? I ventured in the silence that followed. "Oh, yes!" was the resounding response. "As I say, we started some things, got involved—I did work for the Chamber of Commerce years ago, and also the Civic League, and I also started to do special work for the Historical Association. They have a large collection of glass plates, negatives from the early 1800s, but many are in terrible shape because they weren't processed properly—they've flaked out, silvered out…and every so often somebody wants a print from one of those and I do a lot of delicate retouching. I'm working on a big NHA project now. They're getting ready for a big show at the Fair Street Museum on the shipwrecks all around Nantucket."

Walter Lucas is a man who obviously enjoys life, including doing some things that others might consider work. But what does he do to relax? Turns out he has a large collection of CDs and records. "I love classical music," he said. "That's all I ever play. My mother wanted me to be a classical pianist, and I studied all the time, but then I couldn't take it any more, so I gave it up. I never go to the movies. Most of the stuff is trash…anyway, if you wait two years you'll see it on TV. I watch television and enjoy the Lehrer Report, and the Philharmonic, whatever it's playing. I also like the science shows on Channel 21."

Have Walt and Eleanor ever had any regrets about their decision to live on Nantucket Island? I asked. "Oh, no," Walt said. "This is a terrific place…as long as you've seen the rest of the world. I don't get off much at all. But Eleanor spends the winter in our place in Florida—she can't stand the cold weather, and I can't stand hot, sweaty weather. So I wake up early in the morning—I don't eat much—and I start painting right away. I paint all day, or three-quarters of it. And I take walks," he continued; "they clear the air—and I do my own cooking. I make all the bread we eat; I have for years. And that's fun. It's relaxing, you know, pounding away at the dough. And it's good exercise, too. I make three loaves at a time and put a couple in the freezer. Let's see—what else? Basically, making bread is my hobby. Oh, and I love to pick berries—blueberries, cranberries, beach plums, anything that's around—because that gives me a chance to think. Beach plums haven't been too good lately. I make my own jam, because I figure it's got more nutrition, with the skins on." That must, I suggested, taste wonderful on your home-made toast. "Oh yes." Do you also make pies? I asked. "I don't, but my wife does," said Walt. "She's got some great recipes. We had people over last night for dinner, and Eleanor made strawberries soaked in orange brandy, with some orange zest—you let it stand for a whole day and serve it over a touch of frozen yogurt—and was that delicious!" Do you have secret berry-picking places? I wondered. "Sure—of course! We go out to 'Sconset for the cranberries. There's a swamp that Maria Mitchell sold, I guess to the town, with a beautiful cranberry bog, and nobody used to know it was there. You need boots to pick, or you hop from one hummock to the next." And the bogs are great for bird-watching, too, I observed. "Oh yes—we're both bird-lovers. I feed wild birds both here and in Quaise…we even have ducks, and I have tame rabbits that come right up to me to let me feed them. I like things like that."

CHECKING OUT THE *ILIAD*

And then there's reading. One whole wall in this room of the many paintings is covered with a bookcase he built himself (oh yes, he also has a workshop: "If you own two places," he said, "you're always doing repairs"). "We both read a great deal," he said. "In fact, just a couple months ago we ordered a new translation of the *Iliad*. We compared that with the old one, to see the difference. That's the kind of stuff we do. I don't read novels, except cheap little mysteries which I can read in one night because it clears my brain. And I like a good biography."

Walt is rocking, the chair is quacking, and I'm thinking, Do these two people ever sit still? Then, reflecting back on my question about the decision to stay on the island, Walt said, "We have a good support group here. We belong to the Angler's Club, and have all kinds of younger friends. This is one of my philosophies—I keep in touch with the young crowd; that's very important to me. Too many people retire, sit in a chair, and they're dead in three or four years."

Time to leave, after taking a walkaround to see all the paintings more closely. Oh, I almost forgot, I said. Do you have a picture of the two of you in the early days, and one of you today? Guess what? Like the cobbler who doesn't tend to his own shoes, here's a professional photographer who claims he doesn't have any pictures of himself! So you can bet I asked Eleanor if there were any pictures lurking about that I could use for the article—a wedding picture, for example. She laughed, and said, "Oh God, no! Our wedding picture is a joke. You wouldn't want it!" (I asked Walt about that later, and he told me they'd carefully posed, with the camera on a tripod which the minister's wife was supposed to trip. "Well, she didn't and she didn't, and finally I made a face…and that's when the picture was taken, so we don't show that.")

Oh dear, what'll I do about pictures, then? I asked Eleanor. Her response: "Call him and threaten him—he'll find one."

So I did. But I had to get pictures from someone else! Walt and Eleanor Lucas are what Nantucket is all about. And the lesson from their lives is that if you really want to live happily ever after, you stay busy, help others when you can, and laugh a lot.

Eleanor's Beachplum Sweetmeats

I coaxed one recipe out of Eleanor Lucas, and just for fun, here it is. The sweetmeats, she said, may be used in baking muffins, sweetbreads, cakes, etc.

1. *6 cups fresh-picked beachplums (at least 80% ripe)*
2. *Freeze (may be frozen up to 2 years)*
3. *Defrost*
4. *With thumb and forefinger, squeeze out pips*
5. *Measure pulp and any liquid which has accumulated. Put in saucepan with equal amount of sugar. Bring to boil. Simmer 15 minutes. Drain through sieve or cheesecloth for 1 hour. Put any liquid in glass jars, leaving——inch space from top. Cool. This may turn out to be sauce for ice cream or desserts, or jelly (depending on ripeness of plums).*
6. *Spread strained beachplums on wax paper on cookie sheets. Leave for 24 hours. Freeze for future use. In use do not defrost.*

❧

62   *As of 2003, Walt was in a nursing home off-island.*

Above—Walter Lucas, a familiar figure on Nantucket with his fur cap and cameras. Photo by Terry Pommett. Far left—Walt Lucas on a photo shoot, c. 1960s. Used with permission of the Artists' Association of Nantucket; photographer unknown. Far right—Walt took a series of photos of Main Street mansions; this one, entitled "Long Ago and Far Away," is of a hauntingly beautiful woman in one of these homes, taken in 1950. The photograph hung in an Artists' Association of Nantucket show in February, 2004, and the picture of it was taken with permission of the AAN.

Interviewing an Interviewer
Martha Walters, 1997

*M*artha Walters was as enjoyable as an interviewee as she is an interviewer, which she's been for years. She was very forthcoming and there was plenty of twinkle in her remarkably sky-blue eyes. Since she wasn't born on the island, she fit into the "Life Before Nantucket" category, about which she commented: "Well, a lot of people don't think life even begins until they get to Nantucket!"

Martha and her family came to the island every summer when she was a child. "I was born and raised in Boston in the Back Bay," she said, "and also went to school there, on Marlborough Street. Then I went to Radcliffe, where I majored in Government, and went on to law school. After graduation I worked in my father's real estate law practice for a while, but I didn't find that too exciting. I finally left and went into something very far afield…and that was radio. I was offered a job at the Yankee Network, which at that time was comprised of six New England stations; they'd been looking for someone to take over women's programs. And I was there until I married one of the executives, and it seemed a wise thing to retire, so there'd be no conflict of interests. Which," she added with a raised eyebrow, "I have always regretted."

MOTHERHOOD, THEN HARVARD

When her son Charley was born, Martha decided to stay home while he was small, even though she had all the instincts, training, and experience of a bona fide career woman. (Charley Walters is familiar to most islanders as the long-time proprietor of Musicall and an ex-Nantucket TV interviewer himself.) "I feel sorry for the girls today who have a baby and then go off to work and miss the most exciting time," she said. However, when her son went off to boarding school, Martha, now divorced, went off to Harvard, where she "kind of supervised" the fifty teaching fellows in the required course in written English. "I also had a lot of contact with the students," she said, "which was very enjoyable. Many of those students and teaching fellows have remained good friends to this day."

Martha stayed at Harvard for six or seven years, and "then I decided it would be nice to move to Nantucket, because we'd always come in the summer when I was a child and when Charley was a child. Nantucket was really home," she added. "I would pick him up at school on closing day in May and we'd dash for the boat, and then in September we'd dash for the boat to go home, and he would finish his summer reading on the top deck. We also came for Christmas and holidays. And we always rented. My father never wanted to own a summer house…and I'll never forgive him for that! When I moved year-round to the island in 1970, Nantucket was a quiet little village…and the next year the developers were coming in like crazy, and they've been coming ever since. By that time Charley had finished college, so he came down too and bought the record store from Gene Mahon [when it was on Centre Street, where Paul LaPaglia's Antique Print Gallery is now]. For a while I didn't do much here, except working part-time for a couple of stores. And then I got the idea that there was really not much coverage of social events in Boston…

"I grew up when Boston had five or six newspapers, and they made a big thing of social events. Then, back in the '70s, it was down to two papers, the *Globe* and the *Herald*, and they weren't doing much. So I went up to Boston and talked to the manager of the Ritz Carlton and the manager of the Four Seasons, both of whom are still close friends, and I told them about my idea for a social-news paper called *Round and About Boston,* and they thought it was a great idea. So I started to publish that, and I would go up to Boston for any events I wanted to cover, and one year I lived up there during the winter, but I really did miss Nantucket. Wintertime to me is the best time on the island."

In the meantime, Martha was writing an arts column and a social column for the *Inquirer and Mirror.* "But," she said, "I left the Inky Mirror to do my own thing. I started to publish a Nantucket social-events paper, *Around and About Nantucket.*" And as if that wasn't enough, at some point Martha consented to be the news reporter for a new island radio station. "Looking back," she laughed, "I wonder how I really did it…We had a tiny room out at the airport which had all the equipment, and I'd go out three times a day and do the news, and push all the right buttons myself. I don't think I could do it now. It was great fun. And you know, in this very small town of Nantucket in the wintertime, I could get enough news to do three different five-minute segments." One of her criticisms of big-time news programs was that you get almost the same news at 11 p.m. that has been broadcast at 6 p.m.—but Martha never had any trouble finding something fresh for each broadcast, and she raced over to the airport with it for her three daily trips. "I was practically on the police force," she laughed. "I spent more time there than the policemen did. And also the fire department, and oh yes, all the Selectmen's meetings."

When Channel 3 came to Nantucket, Martha was a natural. "In those days," she said, "they had no newscaster, so they used to ask people in town to do it. Quite a few of us—Johnnie McLaughlin and most of the Selectmen and other people around town—would read the news. Finally," she went on, "I started my TV program *Round About Nantucket.* I've interviewed many old Nantucketers who've since died…there's quite a hodge-podge of taped interviews, some of which are still in cardboard boxes hidden away somewhere, which we'll have to find."

Martha Walters has hobnobbed with and interviewed well-known island, national, and even international figures, and only one of them, she said, has ever refused to be interviewed. "It's an interesting story. Somewhere around 1980, I was standing in front of Tonkin's with a woman from Town & Country Real Estate, and she said, 'Good heavens! Here comes Frank Sinatra—and he's feuding with Town & Country, so I'm leaving—I don't want him to see me.' Well, I looked down the street, and coming toward me was this rather small man who looked as though he just got off the pickle boat. I thought, 'That cannot be my great idol, Frank Sinatra!' He and his wife went into Tonkin's. I told myself I had nothing to lose and followed them in and asked him if he'd be on my program. He didn't say anything, and then his wife said, 'We are on vacation, and we're saying no to everybody, because if we say yes once, we're really hooked.' I said, 'Well, I can understand that, but Bill Harbach told me you were coming.' Sinatra looked at me and said, 'You know him?' And I said, 'Yes, I've known him for quite a few years. Actually, I interviewed him last week.' So we chatted for a few more minutes, and then I thanked them and started to leave, saying, 'By the way, if you see Paul Keyes, say hello.' (He and Harbach produced Sinatra's big shows.) And he looked at me and said, 'You know *him,* too?' And I said, 'Yes, actually we were in radio at the same time. I got there first, and everything Paul knew about radio he learned from me.' And then," she smiled, "I left."

COAST TO COAST WITH NBC

Who were some of the other notables who obviously didn't refuse to be interviewed? I asked, knowing there were many. "Oh," she answered, "of course the ones who were here, like Russell Baker and David Halberstam…and oh yes, the late John Chancellor, that charming man. I interviewed him at the Jared Coffin House, and I started off by saying, 'You know, you're on NBC from coast to coast…' He looked a little taken aback, I guess thinking of all his contracts and so forth, and I said, 'That is, the Nantucket Broadcasting Company, from Madaket to 'Sconset.' He liked that," she remembered with a laugh.

Asked about some of her most memorable interviews, Martha chuckled and said, "I had one interview some years ago that was funny or it was a disaster, depending on how you looked at it. I knew a lovely young man—he was the best man at my son's wedding. He is a good talker—if you say 'Good morning' to him you might find yourself engaged in conversation for a half-hour. He's never at a loss for words, and an interesting fellow, so I asked him if he'd let me interview him for my show. He came in all dressed up, and brought his dog with him. And the camera started rolling. I said, 'Hello—it's nice to have you here' and gave him the leading question, and he answered, 'Yup.' And I tried again, and for the whole fifteen minutes I got monosyllabic answers…so I did most of my talking to the dog. I told him later, 'Tom McGlinn, this is going to go down in history, because nobody will ever believe you didn't talk!' I don't think he was embarrassed or shy—it was just that he'd never been on that side of the camera before. And as a matter of fact, after that he became my cameraman."

Martha Walters has a delicious sense of humor and laughs easily. Quizzed about all the other activities she's involved herself in on the island, she mentioned benefit events and fashion shows, and also the Tree Fund, in which she's been an important participant for many years. How did that come about? "Walter Beinecke owned the White Elephant back then, and he spoke to the manager about doing a party there to build a fund to take care of the elm trees, because of the influx of Dutch Elm disease that year. The manager asked me what I could do, and I suggested having a cocktail fashion show, so that we could get the men to come for cocktails, and that worked out beautifully, because once a man gets dragged to a fashion show, he'll come back time and again, and enjoy it. It's been going on for years, and it's worked." And after a bit, I observed, you even put some of the men on the runway. "That's right," she replied; "a couple of years ago I got Pierre Salinger to model a fur jacket…and he had a great time."

Like most good conversations, this one wandered to and fro, from past to present and in between. Martha talked about her earliest memories of summers on the island. "It was a very, very simple life in those days. You went to the beach and you went to the Yacht Club and you went to bed early at night, both children and adults. A big event would be a cookout. At that time the summer people were mostly from Boston and the suburbs, and they were quite content to be left alone. But unfortunately, those days have gone. The worst things about Nantucket today are certainly the traffic problems, and the hordes of tourists who arrive every day and wander around… Why do tourists stand right in the middle of the sidewalk and chat?" She laughed good-naturedly and added, "I've been doing a lot of writing for the Tourist Department of the Province of Quebec, and I always say to myself when I go there, 'I'm going to play tourist and I'm going to get in everybody else's way!' But I never quite have the nerve."

"Of course," she added, "there are awfully good things about Nantucket. For me, the best thing is that you can be just as busy as possible or you can just enjoy your own company, and no one is going to disturb you. And if somebody calls you at 5 o'clock and says, 'Can you come over and have a bite to eat tonight?' you'll say yes…but if you lived on the mainland, you'd never admit you were free!" Martha admits she's a pretty urban person, traveling often to Boston. "My whole life was in the city until I came here." She added thoughtfully, "Nantucket is beginning to see itself as a small Manhattan, getting a little too chi-chi…It bothers me that there are an awful lot of empty trophy houses. The people who are building them are not permanent-type people, and when *W* finds a new resort area to publicize, they're all going to go there. And then," she laughed, "those houses will probably all become bed and breakfasts—because they all have as many bathrooms as they have bedrooms, so there's a big expense saved. I think that's a good solution."

Although Martha maintains a schedule that would leave most people breathless, checking out and writing about the Boston and Nantucket social scenes, she still finds the time, not to mention energy, to get most places by walking. She had a knee problem a few years ago that threatened this habit, and a surgeon wanted to operate, but ever-cool Martha decided to let it cure itself. She did, she admits, ask the doctor how, when this was usually a young athlete's problem, he could account for her sore knee. "He looked at me with a very sober face and twinkling eyes, and said, 'I really didn't want to mention that age has a deteriorating effect.' Well, I just burst out laughing; I loved him for saying that!" Anyhow, she's still walking. Walking…and also observing that very lively and fascinating social scene that is Nantucket.

&

Martha Johnson Walters, social maven and interviewer extraordinaire, died on January 15th, 2004 at 86. A gracious and community-involved woman, Martha walked everywhere, and almost always wore a wonderful hat. Nantucket will miss her.

Far right—Still the picture of style, Martha Walters at a party in September, 2003.

Above—Boston Back Bay's Mr. and Mrs. John William Johnson with their three-year-old daughter Martha.

Above—On January 1, 1936, Martha had her coming-out party at a tea dance followed by dinner at the Ritz-Carlton in Boston.

Above—Martha's wedding to Alvin C. Walters, at King's Chapel, Boston, August 1949.

70

A Conversation with Cary
Cary Hazlegrove, 1998

7 1

CARY HAZLEGROVE

The interview with Cary Hazlegrove, Nantucket-based photographer extraordinaire, was great fun, but not quite the kind of information-gathering mission I was used to. I don't know if it was the day, the mood, the stars, or just a sudden case of interviewer's block. Wednesday, August 19, was not a beach day; it was cloudy, chilly, and blowy after a night of soaking rain following a muggy week. The island mood wasn't the best; because of the coolness and the clouds, there seemed to be a half-million island visitors in the core area aggressively intent upon having fun. Meaning that to get to the interview at Cary's office in the Pacific Club building, I had to ford my way through a turbulent sea of shoppers—rough waters complete with rocky shoals (cobblestones) and sharks (stressed-looking people in large new RVs).

Ms. Virginia Page Boxley Bullington Is In

But probably what did me in was Cary's enchanting, beautiful baby—just over six months old and a winner. No doubt about it—everyone needs a baby fix now and then. The appointment was on the third floor of the Pacific Club…and it became apparent almost immediately this wee human being was in charge. Questions would be asked and answered, then the talk would shift to what color her eyes might eventually be, or when that second tooth might pop out, or to just plain infant-oriented gibberish. Yes, this was a conversation of sorts, and not even all in English. Hence this article is set down in the form of comments, responses, and descriptions of what this bright girl-child was doing to entertain her rapt audience and vice versa. Despite the total absence of repertorial perspicacity on my part, I did manage to get some "life-before-Nantucket" facts, and Cary Hazlegrove showed that she is a thoroughly gracious, funny, and very positive person. And a great mother.

MM: What's her name? [The smiling baby is swinging happily in a duck-decorated swing suspended from the doorway between Cary's office and a small reception room.]

CH: It's a big name: Virginia Page Boxley Bullington. Bullington is my husband's last name and Boxley is his big family last name. [Silly noises from both Cary and Mary as they try to make VPBB smile. Ahhhh*CHOO!* says Cary. Baby grins.]

MM: [to baby] Oho—you're giving me two big eyes, aren't you? [to Cary] There's nothing quite so disconcerting as a baby's stare, is there? Not a blink.

CH: It's wild, isn't it? Here's what makes her laugh: Achew!! a*CHOO!* Ah-Waaaa-*CHOOO!*

MM: [recovering from laughter] You were born off-island, weren't you?

CH: Right, I was born in Virginia. But I did not name my child after my home state! I lived in Virginia all my life until I moved here in 1978. When I graduated from Hollins College in Virginia ["the charm farm," she adds in a slight but clear southern accent in an aside accompanied by a mock-significant look], I came to Nantucket on a whim; an old boyfriend had told me I'd really love it. So I came up here, and never left! I've lived here almost half my life now.

MM: You've been here for twenty years—shouldn't you say "chahm fahm" by now? What was your major at college?

CH: I had a double major—studio art and art history.

MM: What did you hope to do when you came here—did you have something special in mind?

CH: No, I didn't. I was a child of the '70s [rolling her eyes and sweeping her arm outward] and I came up here just to get a job. I didn't really have a plan, like all the young kids do now…I thought I would live every day the way I wanted to. The first person I worked for was Gene Mahon. That was when he had the Camera Shop and the Roadhouse, where the Faregrounds is now, on Fairgrounds Road. Remember that? And now he and I end up sharing office space.

MM: Is that how you got into Bluegrass music? I know you sang for ten years with the Fishhandlers—that was a terrific group.

CH: No, I've always sung…I just started doing it, because I really love singing. [She picks up the baby and walks about with her as she talks. Virginia looks around at me as if to say "Do I get attention when I want it or what?] I just kind of fell into it, started singing every time I could and then they asked me to join them. We had such a good time doing that. We all—Richard Cary, Michael Kopko, Fritz Warren, Chip Plank, and me—just sort of converged.

MM: Are you singing at all now?

CH: Yeah, I sing on the Milestone Road a lot in the car. I love to sing and I sing all the time, but I don't get up and sing any more. My husband Andy is a professional jazz guitar player, and he's here for the whole summer, working up old jazz standards—Cole Porter, Johnny Mercer, things like that. He's having a great time doing that and playing private gigs.

MM: Tell me a bit about your growing-up days. [Boo! say I, making faces at baby.]

CH: Well, I'm the oldest of four children. Every child in my family has been an artist…it's great. My mother is a painter; and my mother, my brother, and my sister Page were all at Rhode Island School of Design together…my mother was getting her second BA in painting; Bill was in graphic design and Page was in glass. Page died very suddenly and tragically last September. [A quiet moment, in which Virginia gets an extra-warm hug.] It was a great upbringing, a very artistic but very traditional upbringing. I have an incredible mother who is one of my closest friends. None of my family lives here. Mom and Dad came up for almost a month in June to help me with the baby. I'm very very close to my family. My sister Sarah is a photographer and my brother Billy is a graphic designer and a photographer.

MM: [after making a few strange sounds for the baby] When did you become interested in photography?

CH: I was drawn to cameras at a very early age…even in kindergarten, I remember being totally astounded when somebody's father was taking pictures with a Brownie camera…And I was editor of my yearbook—my parents gave me a camera when I was 16 and I just really have been drawn to photography ever since. I think that deep down in my heart I'm a frustrated painter, and one of the things that's really great about photography is that it's instant gratification. I don't have to spend a tremendous amount of time working on canvases and things like that. My mother is a brilliant painter.

MM: For me, taking pictures is hardly instant gratification. I have a film that's been in my camera for a year. I keep trying to finish it, and now I'm beginning to suspect there may not be film in it! How would you suggest parents get their kids interested in photography?

CH: First of all, find out if they're interested. I really think people are pushing kids too much these days. [She deposits Virginia back into her little swinging throne.] If children show an interest, I always let them photograph. If kids are having a shy attack or being unwieldy, I'll pick them up, let them look through my viewfinder, and show them how to take a picture. Some kids are so turned on by my equipment, and other kids could care less. I mean, if a child is interested, then pursue it, but…camera equipment is expensive, and it breaks, and it's finicky, and it requires patience, so I wouldn't just throw camera equipment at kids unless it's something they have an interest in…and you can tell. Be careful—don't push kids too hard. I'm really hoping not to push my child at all. I just think everybody has his or her own rhythm.

MM: Virginia [who is trying to eat her fuzzy rabbit at the moment] seems very relaxed and unpushed. Were you thrilled to find out you were going to have a baby after all those years of relative independence?

CH: Yeah! I woke up at forty and thought, "Oh my God, I forgot to have babies!" Have you seen that T-shirt that says, "I can't believe I forgot to have children"?

MM: No, but I've seen *"Oh my God,* I think I left the baby on the bus!" [Even baby enjoys this, smiling and showing her tiny tooth.]

CH: I had a very easy time getting pregnant, and I had a very easy pregnancy and a very easy delivery…*Lllllllook* at her…[Her voice has gone up an octave and Virginia's eyes widen as she no doubt thinks, "Crazy grownups!"] I don't really know if hers are going to be brown or blue. She's like a chameleon—if you have her outside, she has blue eyes; if you have her inside, they're brown. She has very smoky eyes; I don't know what they're going to be.

[After a minute or two of baby talk, the discussion swings back to the Fishhandlers while the baby dreamily sings "Ah-bla-bla-bla." The phone rings yet again, the baby eavesdrops, and I try to get back on track.]

MM: So, talk about what you're doing now…besides your wedding and family portraits, your baby, and your annual multimedia slide show. I imagine you have lots and lots of spare time. [We both laugh; baby exclaims something that may be the equivalent of "Heh heh."]

CH: The slide show is in the Performance Center of the Methodist Church; I've been doing those since 1988. This year it's "Nantucket: Messages from a Small Island." And I've done a series of books called *Weekends for Two: Fifty Romantic Getaways.* I just finished my third in the series, on the Mid-

74

The Fishhandlers, a great bluegrass group that entertained on the island from 1980 to 1988. From left to right, the late Fritz Warren, Richard Cary (holding his harmonica), the late Chip Plank, Michael Kopko, and Cary Hazlegrove. Cary, by the way, took the picture! (Photo compliments of Richard Cary.)

Atlantic. The other two were on the Southwest and New England. Bill Gleason, who's from California, is the author, and I do all the photography for him. [Virginia, on the couch now, is babbling pleasantly, as if taking part in the conversation.]

MM: Are you going to continue on that project?

CH: [Sighing and bouncing Virginia.] I don't know…the baby…the only way I would do it is if we did the Caribbean…[She breaks off to have an important conversation with baby.]

MM: How long does it take you to do one of those books? [I actually pay little attention to Cary's answer because the baby is smiling at me, and I can't focus!]

CH: About forty days—[putting her face close to Virginia] *WOW…BIG GRIN!* She's a good girl. I love her so much!

MM: You were so lucky to have an easy pregnancy and delivery…

CH: It was very easy. But she was a colicky baby…[Virginia looks profoundly amused—for sure, she's thinking, "Well, did you expect me to be easy *all* the time?] She has one tooth…it just broke out a week ago. I thought she had sand in her mouth.

MM: [I ask to hold Virginia, take her into my lap…and once again valiantly try to reestablish the focus.] Tell me more about what you did to pay the rent when you first came to Nantucket in 1978. [*"Bouncy bouncy whee!"* say I then, completely losing my dignity.]

CH: I did housecleaning, I worked at the Camera Shop and the Roadhouse, I worked at Company of the Cauldron, I worked at the Brotherhood…

MM: The Roadhouse had jazz then, didn't it? Did you sit on the piano and sing torch songs? [I can't help it, I'm kissing the back of this kid's neck and considering renting her for a day. Virginia looks sidelong at me, plotting to grab my spectacles.]

CH: She really is interested in glasses—can't figure them out. Country music is really what I'm most interested in singing…I sing more country/rock stuff. When Andy's playing all those great standards I'll start singing those and he'll just stop and look at me over his bifocals—I mean it's like "You're singing this in a different key than I'm playing it…" [laughter] I know all those songs by heart, because they've been played at my family's summer place in northern Michigan for years—songs like "In the Still of the Night" and "Bewitched, Bothered, and Bewildered."

MM: Do you ever go off-island for any significant amount of time?

CH: No, except when I go to Austin, Texas, in the winter, which I started doing about four years ago.

MM: [To baby: *Ahhhboo!]* Is that where you met your husband?

CH: No. We grew up together in Virginia. Our families have been best friends for three generations, and we re-met at his father's funeral in about 1987, and got married in '90. Um…no…we saw each other again in '89 and got married in '91. I'm awful with dates. [Virginia becomes super-wiggly and I hand her back. Cary takes her, making a beautiful Brooklyn Razzberry sound.] Andy absolutely loves this baby.

MM: What's held you here on Nantucket? I'm sure you've seen a lot of changes take place here.

CH: I have, Mary, but you know what? I'm much more of a 'glass is half-full' than a 'glass is half-empty' person about Nantucket. I mean, there are changes everywhere, everywhere, and you know, the traffic is really the only thing that I abhor. That and going to the grocery store. And my husband has taken over that duty this summer and Naomi, my wonderful assistant in the other room, has done all my posting and banking—I haven't been to the bank once! What a luxury! I've been having the most unstressful summer, even though I'm working at a full clip.

MM: Yes, but you're working right in the center of town. Bet that's not easy.

CH: Right, it's a pain in the butt! [laughter] I think Nantucket has changed, a lot. And I have to say that in photographing children I've seen a real shift in the kind of people I'm shooting. Kind of unleashed. And spoiled. But I'm very optimistic about Nantucket. It's weathered some serious stuff, and I think it'll be fine. I don't know what's going to happen. I think that everything is happening at a very slow rate. It's like being pregnant—it doesn't happen all at once. It happens very slowly. You know, there are so many people who are negative about Nantucket; but it really is just an amazing place. I'm at Sankaty Beach Club all the time, and you know the Hoicks Hollow Road public access to the beach—there's never really anybody there! I mean there are tons of places where you can be alone. It's just such a beautiful spot in the world. This is the epicenter of Hell, right here! [We can hear the noises of the cars and people in the street below.]

MM: You sound pretty happy about your life. If you won a million dollars in the Lottery, would you be doing the same thing?

CH: Yes. I might buy a nicer car. [laughter] I don't even know if I'd travel...I'm so darn tired of traveling; I've done so much traveling with this book. There were 164 inns to photograph in almost every state in the country. I like just being at home. I'm a homebody. If I won the Lottery I would do the same thing. I love to work. It's my center. It's a great way to make a living.

MM: And is Virginia always with you?

CH: Yes, except when I do family portraits and weddings—then my husband takes her. I just carry her everywhere and let her be herself. I will take her home for her afternoon nap; I usually don't come in to work until 11:30 or 12. She sleeps pretty well; this morning she got up at 10 of 8. Sometimes she's like a fish on a frying pan, but she does sleep.

MM: She is a wiggler, isn't she?

CH: Oh honey, she wants to walk and roll!

MM: [Still trying to get a handle on the interview...] Is there anything besides the traffic on the island that peeves you?

CH: Just the traffic. And I really hate the mopeds. I can't stand 'em. Especially if you live in 'Sconset and have to deal with the Milestone Road. It's a mess. The traffic issue is the only thing I think that really needs to be dealt with. The building...you can't stop building; the only thing you can do is pray that the people next to you have as good taste and give their last dime to Conservation—that's really all you can do. You know, one thing about these trophy house that's so great is that they have a lot of property with them, and they can't be subdivided...What I think is, bring on the big houses, because you know what? They're not eighteen little ones.

MM: Do you see a change in the type of people who come to Nantucket?

CH: Yes, I do, but you see people's best and worst behavior, when you get all crammed in one place. [Now Virginia is quiet, and Cary makes rhythmic high "tooty-wooty-wooooty" noises.] She looks like a Gerber baby, doesn't she? She will never be a child model.

MM: You never had any jobs out in the mainland world?

CH: Nope. Never had one, never will. If I had that million, maybe I wouldn't work as hard. I work very hard. I'm shooting between twelve and fifteen family portraits a week, including weddings and [big sigh] the whole thing.

MM: What an adjustment it must be for someone who was quite independent for years to have a baby…

CH: Well, life really hasn't changed that much. It's only one baby! And I've been working as hard as I did last year—maybe even harder. But I could not live my life without Naomi!

MM: Since my interviewing cap plainly isn't on very straight today, let me wind up by asking what questions I should have asked you? What would you like to say?

CH: [Thoughtful pause.] You know what? Be kind, tell the truth, eat good food. [More laughter.] You know, everybody treat each other nicely. Enjoy Nantucket for what it gives you, because the place gives back everything you put into it…and it's just an amazing place to live. There's a lot of old stuff floating around in the air here…

MM: Do you believe in ghosts and spirits of old Nantucket?

CH: I don't know if I believe in ghosts or spirits per se; I do believe there's a certain energy that is very there if you're attuned to it. And I don't think a lot of people are. I think they're kind of missing the boat on that. I love Nantucket…always have and always will, and I'll probably be here forever.

MM: You've never been even tempted to move?

CH: Sure—when I was pregnant last summer and I had hormones from hell. I felt great, but I had never experienced PMS in my entire life, until I was pregnant. And that was a really scary thing for me. [I swear, Virginia growled a baby *grrrr* at this point.]

MM: I guess it's time to end this whatever-it-is. I think Virginia Page Boxley Bullington is terrific; I love your photography; and I do think that in your spare time you ought to consider starting another Bluegrass group. Nantucket needs it.

It had been a fun and interesting session. Certainly different. But the next time there's a baby attending an interview, I think I'll just turn off the tape recorder, get down and do a rousing game of Pattycake.

This image of Cary Hazlegrove and small daughter with big name, Virginia Page Boxley Bullington, is one of few, and it was taken by Cary Hazlegrove's sister, also a professional photographer.

78

A Very Magic Life
Richard Cary, 1998

This man wears so many hats you're almost out of breath when you listen to him talk about his life. At this writing, he's artistic director, business manager, technical director, resident set and lighting designer, public relations department, head custodian, furniture mover…and heaven knows what else. All this for the professional theatre company he started in 1985, Actors Theatre of Nantucket. And in the past he's done all this and more—during the '70s he was also a custom house designer, contractor, and builder—all while he was doing "the theatre thing." His name is Richard Cary, and on the day I interviewed him at his Hinckley Lane home he was also being head lawn-maintenance man. You get the feeling that he literally never sits still. But he did stop mowing to talk about his life before…and on…Nantucket.

"I was born in 1942 in Medford, Massachusetts," he began, after setting a bunch of pictures and yearbooks and lists of plays on the table and making himself a big cup of coffee. "My great-great uncle or grandfather or something, Lorin Dame, was the principal of Nantucket High School for about four years back in the 1860s. My grandfather ended up buying land on Hinckley Lane in the early 1920s or so, and my mother always came here in the summer, so I came with my parents for vacations. The old Hinckley farmhouse was the family place—I guess originally there were about six acres. It was once a working farm; actually, there's an old journal with the cost of chicken feed and all that stuff in it. So I feel very connected to the island. What did I do as a kid here? Jumped in puddles, went to the beach, went to Robinson's 5&10 and the A&P and the bowling alley, all on Main Street…to me, Nantucket was always home in my life, because we moved around so much. I always knew I'd come home to Nantucket eventually.

"Ooold Rrrags & Bottles"

"I went to college at Carnegie-Mellon, and between my freshman and sophomore years I saw a posted notice that said 'Intern wanted, apprentice jobs available, Straight Wharf Theatre, Nantucket.' So I grabbed the opportunity and spent my first whole summer here, working in the theatre. That was in 1961. It was an amazing experience! This was a professional company out of New York; they did ten classic plays, even a Japanese Kabuki. And out of ten plays I had five character parts. One of the most memorable was in *Juno and the Paycock*—I was the panhandler's voice. I had to call down over the stage from way up in the attic—[in a shouted Irish accent] *'OOOLD RRRAGS AND BOTTLES!'*"

Wonderful story, but we're getting ahead of ourselves, I said. Tell me something about your life before Nantucket, off Nantucket. Cary responded: "Well, my father was called up to serve during World War II. He'd been raised in Japan—his father was a missionary in Tokyo—so he spoke Japanese fluently and ended up being an interpreter/interrogator for the Navy. Evidently he saved thousands of lives by convincing die-hard Japanese generals to reveal information that would stop battles. His name was *Harry Cary!* I was born during the war, and while my father was away we moved to the Washington, DC area and I ended up being raised in Annandale, VA, 19 miles from the heart of DC. And then in 1953, the whole family packed up and went to Japan. My father worked for the CIA." Richard made a scary face and commented, "Can I say that?" He laughed and went on: "We spent from '53 to '55 there, and then returned to Annandale. I spoke Japanese, but it's all gone now…" It turns out that

Richard lived in Japan during the fifth, sixth, and seventh grades, and from the eighth grade to the end of high school he was back in Annandale where, he said, "I was the first boy cheerleader in the state of Virginia!

"I had a great time in high school," Richard said. "You know, the Honor Society and the Spanish Club and the Drama Club and the A Capella Choir... And the school provided many opportunities to do theatre: I was a natural for the stage." He showed me yearbook pictures of those days: playing the ham on the stairs, acting in a play, crooning à la Elvis onstage, and many other photos, in all of which he seemed to be having that great time. Did he know at that point that he wanted his life to be in the theatre? "Oh, yeah. But I was also a good mathematician, so I was led toward architecture. At the age of fourteen, I added a whole wing to our house, and that was going to be my career." But the theatre was in his blood. "I went to Carnegie-Mellon as an architecture major and of course it's the best drama school in the country. Early on, my roommate and I went to see *Twelfth Night* and he turned to me during the performance and said, 'Isn't that where you're supposed to be?' And so I switched majors as fast as I could, but I couldn't switch to acting because it was midyear, so I became a playwright major, based on my writing, my poetry. I think in many ways that was a key event, that I didn't go into acting specifically, because then I'd have been an actor only. By going into play-writing, I became exposed in depth to writing and reading plays, obviously, and also to theatre history, directing, lighting, design, voice, speech—the whole nine yards." At this point Richard heaved a dramatic sigh and continued: "So...being a carpenter, being an actor, and graduating as a playwright, qualified me for...absolutely nothing at all!

The Cary family in Medford, MA, in about 1943. From left to right, Richard, age 1; his mother, June; his father, Harry; and his brother, Lorin, age 3.

Summer of 1956, and Richard is ready to go for a bike ride.

But I'd worked in the Straight Wharf Theatre, and in my sophomore year I did summer stock at the Antioch Area Theatre out in Ohio, known for its Shakespeare summer program."

FORTY BUCKS A WEEK

Did Richard go right into acting after that? "Well," he replied, "you can't just say, 'OK, now I'll go out and earn a living as an actor'—it just doesn't seem to work, unless you're extraordinary. After I graduated in 1964, it was Vietnam time and I was waiting for my draft call, so I sort of blew that summer. I went back out to Yellow Springs, Ohio in the winter…it was a nice little community in which to grow up a little bit. And I sort of gravitated into set design at the Antioch theatre. In the summer of '65, Jacques Cartier, the founder and artistic director of the Hartford Stage Company, came to direct a Shaw play, *Captain Brassbound's Conversion,* and I played the Scottish minister. One of my projects as an apprentice was to build 26 rifles for the African and British Army, and I made all 26 overnight. That impressed Cartier. In the fall, when I received my 4-F because of a curvature of the spine, I was a free man, so I called Cartier up and got the job of carpenter and apprentice actor in Hartford. I got 40 bucks a week and had a job in the theatre at a time when the regional theatre movement was booming. The following year I became the technical director, which gave me a real salary, and was also assistant resident designer."

The next theatre jump was to the Arena Stage in Washington, where Richard became master carpenter. "I met people like Robert Prosky, Ned Beatty, James Earl Jones, and Jane Alexander, and she and I still cross paths," he said. I recalled seeing Jones and Alexander in New York in *The Great White Hope,* and Richard said that had been his last show in Washington, for which he "built the whole damn set." He was doing so many

In 1959, Richard won a high school talent show, impersonating none other than Elvis Presley.

Above left—Richard Cary as a dapper high school sophomore. Above right—The Carys posed for another family photo in Annandale, VA; Richard was a high school student, his brother Lorin was in the service.

things at once at that point that the stress was terrific. "They wanted to do rolling rep the following summer and didn't increase the staff, so I ended up having to build eight sets all at once…it was a crazy summer. I decided to resign from the theatre, retire, and become the writer and poet that I was. Then I got a call from my old classmate, actor Jamie Cromwell. He was starting a theatre in Springfield, MA, Stage West, so I helped him open up and stayed for three years. Then I was going to retire to Nantucket and be a carpenter and the hell with other things. As I said, I'd always known I'd come home to Nantucket eventually. And I needed a break from the theatre, because I'd been in it, wall to wall, for twelve or thirteen years, and very intensely all the way…in wonderful theatre. Being the technician, you have much more access to everything than if you're just an actor. You get to see the shows, and meet the actors in a different way, as kind of their boss." Here Richard assumed a pose and barked melodramatically, *"DON'T TOUCH* that furniture!" Having learned the craft simultaneously with playing just enough character roles to be eligible for Equity, he decided that wasn't what he wanted at that juncture, so it really was, at last, back to Nantucket.

CHIPS OFF THE OLD BLOCK

In March of 1970, Richard moved out to the old Hinckley farmhouse, where "the wind was blowing the rug off the floor at night…had to sleep by the fireplace." He and his then-wife had a child, Donick, who went to Nantucket schools and is now a writer for *The Simpsons*. And, by a later marriage, there is a talented daughter, Martha, who has appeared in a number of Nantucket productions and, he says, "This is not just somebody who *wants* to act; she's someone who *can."*

The first thing Cary did when he arrived on the island in 1970 was to sign up at the Theatre Workshop as a set designer and technical director…"and I never heard from them," he said, "and praise the stars they didn't make use of me in that capacity, because I suddenly realized I didn't want to do that; I wanted to act again! I really consider acting my true profession…I love directing, too, but that's the practical side. I design and build shows to help make my living, and also to bring professional theatre to the island. Anyway, I did nothing but acting for ten years for Theatre Workshop—it was great! I played, among other roles, Alfred Doolittle in *My Fair Lady,* the father in *The Fantasticks,* Old Skipps in *The Lady Is Not for Burning*…I directed that, too…and lots more. I got to do *The Rhinoceros* and some Irish plays. Then I began building houses in 1971. [That old thing about earning a living again.] I was one of the designer/contractor/carpenters who were in demand during the '70s. We were like the 'hippy carpenters'…Mitch Blake and the late Carl Borchert and Bruce Killen and…my God, it's hard to recover from losing those two guys.

"Then, right at the very peak of my building career, in the winter of '79, Theatre Workshop asked if I'd like to direct a play, and I said yes. We were using Bennett Hall at this point—Straight Wharf had burned down in about 1975. I directed Mary Roberts Rinehart's *The Bat.* After that they asked me to take over for Mac Dixon; at the same time I was a contractor and designer, and the first thing I wanted to do was build us a theatre, so, along with Elizabeth Gilbert, president of TWN at that point, and George Fleming, I helped negotiate a contract with the Congregational Church. Those were some of the happiest years of my life, designing and rebuilding Bennett Hall—which had been a gymnasium, really, with bleachers on one side and a raised stage on the other—and directing plays, starting with *Harvey.*" This is a painful memory, Richard admitted, because for some reason, he says, his name is rarely mentioned as Bennett Hall designer/builder or artistic director in any accounts of TWN history. But he shrugged, saying, "It's extremely difficult to take over from a living legend [Mac Dixon].

"Mac was very tired, and moving in and out of Bennett Hall each time we had a play for four years had been very difficult," Richard continued. "We'd lost two of our set and lighting people, and I was pretty much without help. In the meantime, Fritz Warren, along with David McCandless, David Larrabee, and Mitch Blake, worked as carpenters on the new Bennett Hall. And at about that time Fritz and I started as members of the Fishhandlers, a Bluegrass band." Richard picked up a picture of this wonderful group and read off all the members' names: "That's Fritz (his death was such a blow—it drove me back to cigarettes), then me, Chip Plank (we lost him last year, too), and Michael Kopko (who's directed a few plays for Actors Theatre), and the wonderful Cary Hazlegrove. Well, we had such a ball! We played out at the Wauwinet House for about three summers, and they could only get about 200 people in a room and there'd be 200 outside...and then we started at the Box when the Wauwinet was sold. Their sound system then was awful, and we flopped. But we had a couple great reunion concerts at the Unitarian church and one whole night at the new Bennett Hall—we did all the songs we knew." Richard plays harmonica and sings tenor.

"In the fall of 1980," he continued, "we got Bennett Hall up and running, and in the summer of '81 I got them back into summer theatre. Some of the people in those shows were Warren Krebs, Libby Oldham, Bob Lehman, A.T. Wilce, Del Wyn, and Randy Lee. When I took over there were like five people at the first audition, and by the end of the first year I had brought 120 new faces onto that stage. And I formed the dance company under Linda Gallagher and ended up doing *Nutcracker Suite* every winter. And the Christmas Pageant at the Congregational Church...I was the technical director, the lighting designer, you know, the whole thing, and doing six plays a winter...which is what community theatre is all about." But then came what Richard referred to as "the darkest piece of history": "I resigned in the fall of 1984 and made a very unfortunate move to Reston, VA. I knew quite soon that I was in the wrong place, so I called up the Bowmans, who owned the Folger Hotel, now the Point Breeze, and said, 'Can I come back and start a theatre in your ballroom?' They said 'Let's try it!' and back we went to Nantucket and at this point the house I'd built was rented, so we ended up living in the basement here in my parents' house. But I started a theatre. On May 11th I met with several people who'd been supportive of a professional theater company, including Bob and Barbara Bowman. Bob stood upstairs in the hallway to see if the noise from a play would make too much racket and we applauded and cheered, and we heard a monologue from Ionesco's *The Bald Soprano,* which was one of the wonderful TWN productions I did, on a double bill with Edward Albee's *The Zoo Story,* a dynamite production, so good that it paralyzed the audiences...Anyway, I'd burned the TWN bridge, and the Terrapin Company started out in 'Sconset, and Theatre Workshop was committed to do summer theatre, so there were three theatres on the island, and all flourishing—it was great!"

"We were at the Folger Hotel through 1991, and that last year we had to move lock, stock, and barrel out of the way for the Prom, the Garden Club Show, two weddings, and something else...it was just too much. We'd already been renting the Methodist Church space for rehearsals, and in 1992 I decided to move permanently to the church in the hope of establishing a permanent home." You don't want a bigger theatre? I asked. "Oh no—it's perfect. It seats 100, and it's intimate. I love that space."

At that point Richard mentioned the very present concern of theatre-involved people on the island: lack of permanent space. "It's getting pretty scary for the theatre groups here," he said. "I know some people think that a theatre is not viable on the island, but it is!" The problem is not only the space, it seems—it's also the rent. "Maybe we just can't beat this game; maybe Nantucket is pricing itself out of our capacity to do what we want to do," he said. But clearly, he isn't willing to give up on his dreams. "Nantucket is a wonderful place for a permanent theatre, maybe on the edge of town, with parking, maybe with the buses going to and from; I think this is quite viable." His agenda, he said, is "a permanent building and a permanent professional theatre company. I loved community theatre, don't get me wrong, but I can't ask community theatre to pay my way...I mean, I can't pay the bills with a community theatre budget. And ATN is a professional theatre company, where everyone gets paid—that's not what makes it professional, but the idea is that in such a group you commit yourself to a full run, five or six nights a week, a professional presentation so that you go beyond learning lines and doing a good show, you go into the profession of it. I think Nantucket should have a community theatre that is productive all winter, because most of us on the island have to work too hard in the summer to be able to give ourselves to a production through the summer months."

So you're talking about a professional theater company in the summer and community theater group in the winters? I asked. "I don't know," he answered. "Something tells me that Actors Theatre should have its own roof, and its own space, so it can do what it does without clogging up the politics of what community theatre ought to be...I would use such a space fulltime from Memorial Day to Columbus Day, and there's so much talent available—with my own theatre space we could have Williamstown right here, without a blink. And then there'd be a permanent building on the island for guess what? Community theatre all winter! To me, that's a perfect dream." He stopped and a smile appeared under the Mark Twainish mustache. "Wouldn't it be great if someone said, 'Let's start a million-dollar campaign with my $500,000 check'? There are people who come to Nantucket who could underwrite a building...I just don't know how I could take a year to not be doing anything else but saying, 'Hey, can I talk to you about getting some money from your trust?' If everyone who gave last year gave twice that and said, 'Put half into the building fund,' we'd be well on the way. And there's a whole population that's new to the island, people who don't even know there's a theatre here, and some of them might say, 'You need $2000? Well for heaven's sake, why didn't you ask?' It's a perfect way to pull them into being a thriving part of this community...".

It's obvious that Richard Cary loves the island; before that short, fateful move to Reston, he says, he'd lived here fulltime for almost two decades, only going off twice, once to teach at Antioch and once to get his teeth fixed. There's certainly stress and frustration involved in keeping Actors Theatre thriving. And it is thriving: "It was very nip-and-tuck in '92; we almost folded," he said. "And now we're utterly healthy. But it was hard work to achieve this."

Nantucket is home for Richard. He admits that the island has some problems that concern him: "I'm appalled," he says, "when I see houses built in Trott's Hills or in the Wannacomet land that should've been forever wild. And if employers can't house their employees, if people can't live here year-round for less than $1500 a month, it gets to be like you're stepping on your own feet. And I honestly don't know what the outcome will be. But Nantucket has a soul that can't be beaten…it really does. There is a magic here."

That he plays a vital part in the creative and artistic life of Nantucket is undeniable. Whatever develops, you can be sure the engaging, positive, lively, and energetic Richard Cary will be right in there pitching for better and better. And always with a smile and a flourish.

Update: Richard now winters in Asheville, NC, with his wife, Cheryl; in 2004 his Actors Theatre of Nantucket celebrates its twentieth anniversary.

Left—Young Martha Cary poses with her dad in 1986. Photo by Jack Weinhold. Right—What? A monk? Richard Cary? Here he is, dressed for his role as the chaplain in the Antioch Area Theatre production of Christopher Fry's *The Lady's Not for Burning.*

86

Looking very Mark Twainish, here is Richard Cary. Photo by Jack Weinhold.

Che Sera Sarah:
"Whatever Will Be Me"
Sarah Leah Chase, 1998

*T*he day was rainy and gray, but not unpleasantly so; not many cars were on the road, the birds were singing lustily (it was, after all, mating season), and the winter-solemn landscape was turning gently, deliciously pastel, in virginal early-May pinks and faint greens, made the more impressionistic by the lingering fog. Spring was here! and I welcomed the excuse to ride far out of town for an interview with Sarah Leah Chase.

Is there anybody on Nantucket who doesn't know who Sarah is? She's been a familiar presence on the island since she was a young teen (which she still looks like), and her cookbooks are known all around the world. We settled ourselves comfortably on a sofa, Sarah facing a huge window looking out over the misty Tom Nevers moorscape.

I asked Sarah to tell me about her life before Nantucket. "I grew up in central Connecticut," she began, "one of four children. I have an older sister and brother and a younger sister. When I was 13, I came to Nantucket for the first time to be a mother's helper for an aunt who had moved here and was kind of like an older sister to all of us. She was my father's youngest sister; both of their parents had died when she was 14, and my father was made her legal guardian. So she grew up in our household, until she got married. Shortly after that, she and her husband moved out here and started an antiques business, Paul Madden Antiques. (Paul and De moved off the island in 1987.) I came here in about 1970 to work as mother's helper with their three-year-old son, and just instantly fell in love with the island, and knew that I wanted it to be part of my life forever after. Coincidentally, my interest in cooking was cultivated because my aunt is a wonderful cook, so in addition to the child-rearing duties I would frequently be sent out on culinary errands and asked to do little culinary chores (chopping, dicing, peeling), and I just loved it. Every day I would go to the Nantucket Bake Shop and get a loaf of Portuguese bread, and go to the farm wagon and pick out the best tomatoes you could buy, and this or that type of lettuce…so I learned. And, as often happens on Nantucket, the husbands come home for lunch and I was responsible for putting together a lunch plate for my uncle."

Sarah continued: "De is a wonderful cook and she inspired me, really. I never actually studied cooking at all. I went to Miss Porter's boarding school in Connecticut, and there I regularly had jobs helping in the kitchen. But I always say that my culinary education has come from keeping my eyes, ears, and mouth open wherever I go.

"After boarding school I went to a series of different colleges—I used to joke that I could write the underground guide to colleges from personal experience. I started at Middlebury College in Vermont my freshman year, and I was kind of isolated up there so I applied to both Harvard and Wellesley, and got accepted at Wellesley, where I went for my sophomore year. It's a beautiful place and I wasn't at all unhappy there, but I still had Harvard on my mind, so I applied one more time for transfer and did my last two years at Harvard and got my degree in European History there.

"When I'd graduated from Miss Porter's, I was just fixated on this idea that I had to go bicycling in Europe. I had studied a lot of European art history, and it piqued my curiosity. Then I read in the back of a magazine about this Canadian company, Butterfield & Robinson, that did European bicycle tours. I called them to get a brochure and decided this was what I wanted to do. But my parents had four kids in private school and were not about to send me off to Europe for the summer. Up until that point in my life I had saved every single penny that ever came my way, and so I took my life savings to pay for the trip. But I was $300 short," she laughed, "and a bachelor uncle who was over one night drinking my mother's cooking sherry was so impressed that I had saved all this money that on his third glass he said, 'Oh, I'll give you the other $300.' So that summer changed my life."

Sarah continued to go on the bicycle tours throughout college as a guide, she said. But she didn't stop coming to Nantucket. She said, "I'd usually be in Europe for a month or so, and then I'd go back to Nantucket and pick up another summer job and do it until I went back to school. I continued working for my aunt and uncle some, and then I had waitressing jobs too. I cooked for Frances Carpenter on and off one summer; and another summer I lived out in 'Sconset—in that house just beyond the rotary, the one with the big awnings—for a lady from Palo Alto, Mrs. Finell. She gave me one of her little cottages and I sliced the cantaloupe and put the bread in the toaster oven and made her bed and vacuumed [all this was said very fast, punctuated by a good deal of laughter], and then I had ten other jobs, working here and there.

"I did some sewing, too, for Our Store, where Vis-à-Vis is now. I wasn't very fast, but everything else I did was so frenetic, and I found that the sewing and the rhythm of the machine and all that very soothing. My mother taught me to sew, and I used to make some of my own clothes growing up. And actually some of the money that sent me to Europe was money that I earned sewing. I used to make pillows, and I remember selling all I had to a store in Farmington, Connecticut, one day, and I was sad, because my whole room had been filled with pillows. And then," Sarah laughed, "I thought, 'Would I rather have the pillows or the money?'"

THE ELF WHO CAME TO DINNER

"When I was at Wellesley someone gave a lecture on the concept of choosing a major. He said that you should feel like a violinist feels when he loves and knows a piece very well—his fingers just float over the strings, and that's how your major or what you do in life should come to you. When I was a senior at Harvard, all my classmates were sort of blindly applying to business school, law school, med school—because that's the program they were on—and that was going to determine the course of their lives. I just didn't want to do that, and I remembered the analogy and I knew there were two things I loved: cooking and Nantucket; and so I decided that I would open a shop on Nantucket. Although the prepared-food idea is very common now, in the early '80s, it didn't exist. In summers when I was on bicycle trips in Europe, we'd go into these little stores in small villages in France, and I'd marvel at the great food they had, already made, and I thought that there would be an audience that was sophisticated enough on Nantucket to appreciate that sort of thing. At that time on Nantucket, most people still liked to cook some, though that's not necessarily the case now, and I thought I'd be like the little elf who would complete the meal—if they didn't want to do the side dishes, the concept was that I would do something that was good enough for them to pass off as their own and I'd put it in a real dish, too…at that time Nantucket was small enough that you could be sure you'd get your dishes back the next day. So that's how the idea to be this little culinary elf that would complete meals for people came about.

"The summer after I graduated from Harvard I tried out the business concept at what is now the Bagel Shop but at the time was the Upper Crust. Kathy Grady owned it, and she gave me a little refrigerator case, and I did stuffed grape leaves and potato salad and chicken salad, just to see if the concept would fly and be popular. That was in 1981. My original store was at 21 Federal, which up until that point had been Emmons Corner Guest House. At that time Federal Street was kind of a dark, sleepy street, believe it or not. There wasn't much going on. The thing I loved about that time

A family Thanksgiving 1975 at 17 Union Street; Aunt Diane (Madden) is at top left with her arm around son Parke, who Sarah came to Nantucket to babysit; Richard, a college friend of Sarah's is at top, and then, far right, a young Sarah with Lolly the dog.

Here's Sarah Leah Chase on one of her culinary events—this one aboard ship.

on Nantucket, and it was very short-lived, was that there was a chance for a creative, energetic soul to open a business and not lose her shirt doing it. "My investment for all the equipment to open Che Sera Sarah back then was only about $10,000, but today it would probably be $150,000. Or more. My rent was $750 for the entire first floor, and there were three bedrooms in it that I wasn't using that I rented out at a fair rate of $300 a month, so I had my rent covered. And people could come in and select their foods...the shop was in that front little room, that first dining room at 21 Federal, and the kitchen was where the back room is. It was called Che Sera Sarah from the beginning. [In the introduction to her *Nantucket Open-House Cookbook,* Sarah says that the meaning of this name was roughly "whatever will be me."] I was there for two years, and then the building went on the market for half-million dollars, and was turned into a restaurant. And I moved down to Washington Street and that at the time was Siberia! Way out of town. I was there for a couple of years, and then Bob Kuratek asked me to go into partnership with him at the Boardinghouse Restaurant. I did some of my specialties from Che Sera Sarah, and directed a lot of the menu choices. A year and a half later, I left the partnership and reestablished Che Sera Sarah where the Chanticleer to Go had been; that was formerly a men's clothing shop. It was a great location for me, and my first book, *Nantucket Open-House Cookbook,* came out at the same time I got established down there in 1987. That was the first cookbook I'd done on my own. In 1985 I had co-authored the *Silver Palate Good Times Cookbook* with Sheila Lukins and Julee Rosso; that was my introduction into the cookbook-writing field."

Her books and her regular columns in the *I&M* prove Sarah is a solid writer with a very engaging style. "I was originally hired to test recipes for the *Silver Palate* book," she said, "but they needed some help in the writing, and that's how I came to be a co-author. I found that I really liked putting the writing and the cooking together. I took a lot of creative writing courses in college, but I'd sit in literature classes and observe the professor criticizing writers, and I decided I was too thin-skinned to go right into writing; I would imagine this professor down the road saying, 'This was the early Sarah Chase,' or whatever, and then I thought, Well, if I cook, it's a way of keeping the creative juices flowing— and nobody can pick up a chicken salad I made ten years ago and say, 'This was the early Sarah.' So I was then able to begin writing, kind of cocooned in the guise of discussing food."

After writing *Nantucket Open-House,* Sarah wrote another Nantucket book, *Cold Weather Cooking.* She also wrote a cookbook with her brother called *Saltwater Seasonings,* which features Maine cuisine. Her brother, Jonathan, is a culinary whiz, too; he has a restaurant in Blue Hill, Maine. "He also went to Harvard, where he majored in Economics," Sarah said, and then laughed: "so the two children to whom my father gave a Harvard education have both ended up behind stoves.

Suddenly Famous

"When I wrote the *Open-House Cookbook,*" Sarah continued, "I didn't expect success like the *Silver Palate* book—that had huge success, and was immediately on the *New York Times* best-seller list. Quite simply, that made it easier for me then to get my own book deal. I thought maybe a handful of people would want to know what was in my brownies, or how I made my chicken salad, and I was totally unprepared for the reception it got. It came out on the 4th of July in 1987, and I had ordered 75 copies to last me the whole summer. They all sold that weekend, and unbeknownst to me, people were taking the book to the beach and reading it like a novel…and I'd be stopped on the street for autographs. People felt all of a sudden that they knew so much about me, and that made me feel very exposed, because basically I'm shy…" Here Sarah paused and laughed, turning the same pink as her sweater. "I'd rather cater a cocktail party than actually be at it. Ironically, I've found that motherhood is a great way to somewhat overcome shyness…you know, people come up and talk, just out of the blue, in a way that would've made me leery in the past, but now I know it's just a friendly motherhood bond, and there are infinite things to talk about.

"Oliver [born July 25th, 1997] has changed my life, and delightfully so. It's funny, everyone in the family thought I'd be the first one married, with lots of kids, and instead I went on my career path, but the second I had Oliver, as much work and as much surprise I felt at how demanding motherhood is, I wouldn't change it for anything. I just love the understanding it has given me of what goes into making a human being. When you're little, you never realize all that's done for you. And this has given me a tremendous insight into what a marvel being a human being is."

What, I wondered, was Sarah working on now? "My latest books, *Pedaling Through Burgundy* and *Pedaling Through Provence,* are part of a series based on my bicycle tours, which I continue to do for Butterfield & Robinson, on the adult level. I'm working on a third, *Pedaling Through Tuscany*…but somehow marriage and motherhood have made my concentration a bit less than what it used to be. On those trips, we always stayed in top-notch places and sampled the cuisine of the different regions. When I decided to do the cookbooks I went back and researched, to capture the essence of the cuisine for each region, working out recipes. I've tried to walk a fine line between being loyal to the cuisine I'm representing and at the same time keeping in mind that my market is the North American market…you have to know the type of recipes your audience likes and the kind of things they can get, and sometimes you have to change flavors to make them as intense as what you remember having over there. A perfect example is the ratatouille in my Provence book. It's roasted rather than simmered because I feel that method gives you the strength of flavor that you get in the vegetables in Provence that we don't get here. I have to work somewhat like an impressionist painter who makes a rough sketch and then goes back to a different environment and creates a scene from recollection, and the recollection is often intensified and personalized."

THE ESSENCE OF SARAH

What makes your recipes uniquely "Sarah"? I asked. "Well," she answered, "I like vivid, distinctive flavors. And, as for anything that's creative, you develop a style, much like a writer or painter—something that becomes unmistakably…an essence of you…but trying to put words to that essence is very difficult. So yes, I would say there's something that maybe makes a signature Sarah Chase recipe, but trying to say exactly what it is, is hard. I think on the one hand it's a juxtaposition of flavors that people may not have thought of combining, and oftentimes my recipes deliver a sophisticated product without having to go through a lot of sophisticated techniques." Is there one thing you prefer creating above all others? I asked. "I love making salads," she said, "and actually that was the original core of my shop, many different salads. Main-course salads are sort of my signature thing, and have been for a long time. For example, cold Chinese noodles, or a Moroccan carrot dish, which is a cold carrot salad; or my chicken salad, or cous-cous. A lot of those ideas came from spending summers at my aunt and uncle's house on Union Street. When my aunt cooked, she never cooked just enough for the meal—there were always leftovers, but the food was so wonderful you looked forward to having it the next day, and often we ate it cold. I talk about this a little bit in *Cold Weather Cooking*. A lot of the recipes in that book were tasted the next day, cold, to see if I really wanted to include them."

As in many interviews, the discussion eventually focused on Nantucket Island, the joys and

Sarah and Nigel show off their new baby Oliver in July, 1997.

Sarah Leah Chase and young Oliver, 1999.

Clowning a bit, Sarah imitates a poster.

Sarah and husband, Nigel Dyche, celebrating his 40th birthday in New York City.

pains of living here. "I do worry about the ever-increasing influx of wealth on this island, and the values that a child will pick up, living here," said Sarah. "But as for the pluses, there's a tremendous safety factor—people don't lock doors; they leave keys in their car. You just can't do that anywhere else. And I like the social structure here a lot, in the sense that oftentimes in Suburbia, you'll just have a certain type of friend, but here our friends are from all different age groups and walks of life, and I like that. I like the cosmopolitan aura; some of that has come with all the wealth of exposure to different, fascinating people who happen to be on Nantucket...and sharing Nantucket is a common thread that makes for friendships that might not otherwise exist.

"I have to say," Sarah concluded, "that through the years Nantucket has been very good to me. I've tried to be good to it and carry on my business and my dealings with integrity and honor, and I think that all the other opportunities that I've gotten as a result have somehow been anchored by my being on Nantucket."

96

Growing Up In a Different Nantucket

Richard Ray, 1999

Perhaps the most-often-asked question on this island, next to "What do you do in the winter here?", is "Are you a native?" Naturally, Richard Ray's answer was yes. "My father was born here," he went on, "and his family can trace its heritage back to Peter Folger, who was one of the half-share holders. We are part of the Hamblin/Ray family tree that's related to Ben Franklin. When Nantucket was first settled, people were needed to make barrels and casks for storage, and that's where the Ray and the Hamblin families came in—we were the coopersmiths, the ones who made the barrels." And obviously, I said, you don't do barrels any more. "No," Richard laughed, "I do baskets but not barrels. Everybody here does baskets! Anyway, my mother is from Prince Edward Island in Canada. She has some island roots because some aunts and uncles settled here, and she visited them. She and my father met in a Nantucket/Cape Cod/Worcester connection; they found each other in various places throughout their early years, and they were eventually married and I showed up in 1947." And you were born in the Cottage Hospital? I asked. "Yup. I held the record for the largest baby…I think I was 13 pounds and something. I had an older sister, but she passed away before I was born. She had an open valve in the heart, which can be fixed by twenty minutes' worth of surgery today. But fifty years ago it was incurable. And she lived till she was about four years old. My parents were prepared for it, knew it was one of those things that were going to happen."

Have you spent your whole life here? I wanted to know. Richard answered: "I've paid my dues—I spent ten years in America. I went to kindergarten and elementary school here, and what we called junior high, which is now the middle school, and I started high school here. I was not the model high school student. I didn't do well for a number of reasons, and following my sophomore year my parents sent me away to a private school in Maine, hoping that I would at least learn the fundamentals of a decent education." It looks as if you turned out OK, I said. "Yeah," he said, "and interestingly enough I absolutely loved it up there—it was an opportunity to get a fresh start, and it worked. I went to school there for three years. From there I went to Northeastern University and got involved in an accelerated program, and I did a four-year stint in a little over two-and-a-half years; we went to school straight through, no vacations, summer, holidays were shortened. I majored in Radiation Physics. Physics was something I had picked up in high school and delighted in. Along the way, because I knew I wanted to work with people, I decided I wanted to get into the medical profession, so along with my Bachelor's degree I also picked up a certification as an X-ray technician. I could have taught or worked in a nuclear power plant or been an X-ray technician, and I chose X-ray technology, because I wanted to get that person contact." Richard paused and grinned. "Back then I was a person kind of guy…I don't know, any more. In 1969, I started working in Cape Cod Hospital and worked there till 1978. And I met a lovely lady, a nurse, and we got married in 1970; sadly enough we were divorced in 1978. Following the divorce I moved back here for a sense of security—I had been promised a job here as an X-ray technician at the hospital. When I arrived, that job fell through…and at that point I was also raising a three-year-old daughter. My parents were still living here and so I moved in with them, and it was all very comfortable and worked very nicely.

DOING THE BREAD-TRUCK THING

"While I was looking for something a little bit more permanent, I put time in as a maintenance person out at the airport, and I drove a bread truck. That was a marvelous job that came along at the right time—I needed something that would provide me an income yet was a little more relaxed, and because of some wonderful friends on this island and some fabulous interactions, I had a great year doing the bread-truck thing." All Nantucket working people seem to have had a myriad of jobs, I commented. "Oh sure," he answered immediately. "It's fun! It rounds out an individual's character. Anyway, one day the telephone rang, and a member of the then Board of Selectman said, 'Hey, Richard, the job of Health Inspector is about to open up. Why don't you put your name in?' Well, I'd had some Public Health courses at Northeastern, so I applied. I didn't know what a resume was, and was told to submit one! I bought a small book at Mitchell's Book Corner on how to prepare a résumé, put one together overnight, submitted it the following morning, and about five days later received a phone call telling me that I had been selected as the island's Health Inspector. Well, I felt pretty proud about that—and then I looked at the list to see who had applied. I was the only one on the list with any medical credentials at all!" What, I wondered, does the Health Inspector *do?* Richard's answer: "The Health Inspector addresses food-service establishments, does licensure inspections, gets involved in lodging houses, human habitation issues...and here we spend a lot of time with septic systems and groundwater protection; it's an environmentally evolving position. It is also a catchall, because it's a small town...or it certainly used to be. So as well as being the Health Inspector, technically I am the town's Hazardous Waste Control Officer, the Rodent Control Officer, the Director of the Division of Weights and Measures for Nantucket...I seal all the scales...Yeah, it's a catchall, and those are just some of the things that we do." I observed that Richard didn't look at all stressed, with all those responsibilities, and he smiled and said, "I just hide it well!"

THE OTHER MOTHERS

What were Richard Ray's school years here like? "I remember all or most of my teachers, because it was a very comfortable experience. First of all, the classes were small. At that point there were three schools on Nantucket...when I was going through the elementary school there was the old North School, which is Academy Hill, and there was the South School, which was the old Cyrus Peirce School, which was where the high school stands now—that's where the kids from the south part of town went. And then there was an elementary school in 'Sconset. None of us were ever together as a complete unit until junior high, which was seventh and eighth grade. And that was on the top floor of the Academy Hill School building. It was a great education—you knew all the teachers, saw them in the community on a daily basis, and it was a very friendly atmosphere and a delightful childhood. You're going to hear me use the word 'was' a lot, because Nantucket was then a very family-oriented atmosphere. It had to be...it was so small. At point there were 3,500 or 3,600 residents of the island... It would be hard for me to understand somebody not having had an excellent childhood here back then."

And you were all sort of "enclosed" in one place, I said. "Sure," he agreed. "You'll find that if you ask most Nantucket kids my age now who their mother was, obviously they'll say their own mother, but if you ask them 'Who is your other mother?' there's going to be a list of one or two, because every one of us had somebody we considered our other mom. And that was usually our best friend's mom because you never knew who was going to be staying over at what house, you spent a lot of time with your friends—there were not places to go—you couldn't get in the car for a weekend and travel somewhere. So you had to make your own fun; kids did that in groups of two and three and four, and usually you ended up with a best friend. I certainly had mine—he is still on the island here." And you've maintained that friendship? I asked. "Oh, absolutely. It's funny when you think about it—I went away to prep school, and that was frowned upon by a lot of the students here, because a lot of them had the misconception that (a) if you're going away to prep school your parents have a lot of money, and (b) you're kind of snobby and that's the way you want to be. That wasn't it, in my case. I was doing so poorly in school here...I flunked everything my freshman year, everything. Well, I think I passed math. And I didn't care—I was going to parties and enjoying the social life. My father had had to drop out of school to help his family through the Depression, so he really didn't have a lot to offer me as far as helping me to study was concerned. And Mom was a practical nurse at the hospital...they were both working hard to stay here, so I was kind of on my own with homework and stuff, and I wasn't doing well at it. So my parents sent me away to school because they knew there was something better for me. But when I came back here, after my first winter away, I was absolutely flabbergasted at how many of my local friends really weren't talking to me that much any more, because I was branded a prep-school kid, and that was the stigma that prep-school kids carried with them. We had a lot of them in the summertime, and they kept in their own little groups—the summer kids and the local kids did not mix at all. That was back in the early '60s and Nantucket had been discovered as a summer place to go.

"But I had six or seven very good friends who are still friends. And I value that probably more than anything. One particular character, Bill Barrett, who works for the post office, is without question my best friend—if I've got a brother it's Bill Barrett. We don't see each other all that often, but the friendship will be with me forever. He has stuck with me through thick and thin and that's what I appreciate most about an individual. Frank Powers is another one who's been there for me, and I've been there for him, hopefully. But it was such a shock for me that first summer, coming back and finding I'd been branded, and I thought, 'What did I do wrong? I thought I was bettering myself, I get back here and now I'm an outcast.' I got over that, though."

What, I wondered, did kids do for entertainment when Richard was growing up? "Well, regarding the dating scene, there weren't a lot of formal events. In the summertime, there were the movies—the Dreamland Theatre was the only one we had then, and it closed down in the winter except for a Wednesday- and a Saturday-night movie when I was younger...but most of those were thirty years old and we'd seen them twelve times...The dating scene consisted of house parties, for the most part, and during the summer—and this goes to show you how much things don't change—it was the 40th Pole. That's off the Eel Point Road...and kids still go there. There were a lot of dances—music was certainly a big part of the kids' lives because it brought us together at dances and sock hops and things like that. Back then music was a catalyst for a social gathering for us; now it's a catalyst for a political statement.

"Sports? I was on the football team here...I didn't put in as much playing time as many of the other players, and that may have been my downfall in high school—that's where I decided I would rather go to parties and have fun and not study, because the parties and the social aspect of being a football player and things like that were much more rewarding at the time. That was the only sport I played here, but when I went away to school I discovered soccer, found I had a natural ability for the sport, and loved it."

ROMANCE ON THE BACK OF A FIRETRUCK

Did island kids work during the summers? "Absolutely! I was 13 years old when I got my first job, working for Sid Killen as deck boy down at the old Jetties Beach. I have a son whose first job is as a deck boy down at Jetties Beach!" I asked Richard about his children, and he answered, "I have a daughter, Heather, by my first marriage, and Edie and I have three kids—Travis, Hillary, and Adam. I met her after I'd moved back here and became the Health Officer. She was a University of Miami graduate, and her parents had been coming up here for years—she was a summer kid. I'm sure she and I had crossed paths many times and never knew it. After graduating, Edie decided she wanted to spend the winter on Nantucket and see what it was like, and she joined the Nantucket Fire Department as a firefighter and EMT. Our first date was on the back of a firetruck! We decided to go out to dinner on Stroll weekend, and we ended up going to a fire. We were married in…" (Here he raised his eyes to the ceiling, laughed, and thought for a moment.) "It was 1979, I guess."

Are you happy about your children growing up on Nantucket? I asked. His answer: "Ab-so-lutely! I wouldn't have it any other way. It's a different world—as I said, back when I was growing up here it was very family-oriented. There are issues that exist now that we didn't deal with back then. Back then, it was smoking and beer-drinking that were terrible. You certainly did things with your friends and off on your own, but you spent a lot of time with your family, because there were things that everybody could do. I went hunting a lot with my dad—rabbit hunting, pheasant hunting, duck hunting—just the two of us, with a couple of shotguns…we'd go walking out on the dirt roads, and just talk. The rapport was fabulous; I hope my kids have as many stories about me as I have about my dad.

"I love dearly what Nantucket was, and I do love what Nantucket still is," Richard said. "I want my kids to have those same feelings about Nantucket that I have about my childhood years. And they do, because we've made extensive efforts to be a family. My kids, whether they want to or not, are going to remember the wonderful Sundays where every one of us and the dog went out at noontime on Sunday and hiked the moors; we picnic everywhere. In the summertime we have moved as a huge group, with all of our friends, and we'd have a beach party every Sunday, with all the family. There has been a standing rule in my house that being a health inspector, a firefighter, an EMT, or the naturalist that my wife is…they all stop on Saturday night. Nobody does anything on Sunday that isn't family-oriented. The kids know that Sundays are family days, and they don't object; they love it, because they know other families and their friends will be there, and that we'll all we'd have a great time. Sometimes we've been on the beach for twelve hours, cooking two meals there. And in the wintertime we do goofy stuff—we're probably one of the few families that have had a barbecue up at Great Point in February. And it was wonderful! We laughed for three hours—we froze to death, and couldn't get the burner working, but we had just had a wonderful time. I'm blessed with a very great wife, who comes up with all of this stuff; it's been a lot of fun."

"When I was a kid, in the summertime my mother and dad and I went to the 19th Hole, and we thought it was way out of town! And other families were there, all my friends...so it was just a big beach party every Sunday. And in the winter we would all go to church, and then we always had a big traditional dinner. And then at one o'clock the three of us would pile into the car and go for a ride. I'd sit in the back seat and listen to the car radio, and listen to the two of them, and I have wonderful memories of that. The island is 14 miles long and 3-1/2 miles wide, so nothing is new! It's the same old stuff, but we had a ball with it! And nobody said, 'Aw, how come you can't come over on Sunday?' because everybody knew that Sunday was family day, because you never saw Mom and Dad because they were working so hard, and you wanted that."

MISCHIEF IN HIS HEART

I asked Richard if he'd always been extroverted. Friends of his had told me that he definitely has mischief in his heart. "Oh, yeah," he answered. "It's what keeps me going. I've been described as having this other individual inside here [he tapped his chest and smiled]; he's called Little Richard...and sometimes it's very difficult to suppress Little Richard. He gets out once in a while, but there are times in my life when he's spent *WAAAAY* too much time out. However, if anything has gotten me through life, it's been a sense of humor and the ability to sit back and look at something and realize that it may not be such a big impact way down the road as you think at the moment. You've got to put things into perspective. With my work, there are times when you need to take things seriously and times where if you take them too seriously, you're going to be totally and completely ineffective."

A friend of his told me to ask Richard about motorcycles, obnoxious cars, summer drivers... A slightly wicked grin told me I was going to hear the answer from Little Richard himself. "I guess the drivers on this island are probably the people who can irritate me more than anything

102

else. Because of what I do, I'm a rules and regulations kind of guy; there's very little gray area—it's either right or wrong. That doesn't mean I'm an authoritarian, I just have my values, and when I'm out there driving, they seem to manifest themselves. I object to individuals who stop in the middle of streets to have conversations...it is not something I would do. A long time ago we could get away with that here, but in the middle of summer when you've got 75 or 80 cars on Main Street and Bozo up at the front is talking to somebody leaning against the car, it becomes very irritating."

"I also have some problem with people's abilities to handle signage on Nantucket, particularly in places like parking lots. Look at

Richard Ray on his favorite mode of transportation.

the sign right out there! It says, 'ENTRANCE ONLY—DO NOT ENTER,' and it's facing the driver who's already *there!* Now, some bonehead thought that up—it's at the wrong end! It's the dumbest thing I've ever seen. We don't help the situation by putting signs like that up! A majority of folks here in summer seem to be driving Connecticut cars, and I have a problem with them [another roguish grin]—it seems to me that for them, the signs that say 'DO NOT BLOCK— FIRE LANE' seem to spell 'PARK HERE.' I don't understand that…so I've been known to take those big cement signs and roll them up against the driver's door so that it's facing the guy. Another thing: I am convinced that if you banned vanity plates, thousands of phonetically challenged Connecticut people couldn't come here any more…what in hell does a license plate that says 'Quaise' mean to somebody in Darien, Connecticut? Get a little Nantucket bumper sticker, but don't drive around South Carolina with a plate that says 'Great Point'…who cares?"

TRASHING THE DIGNIFIED IMAGE

OK, now tell me about the Harley, I said. This elicited more laughter. "I had a midlife crisis when I hit 45. I've had a lot of motorcycles in my life, but I gave that up the day that my first daughter was born…because I realized I need to stick around for a while. Well, I don't know whether I've thrown caution to the wind or what, but because of a longstanding island friend who owns a Harley, I started to get the lust again. So at 45 I bought myself a Harley. Now, as the Health Inspector for the town of Nantucket, during my working hours I realize I have to maintain a certain sort of decorum…but it's very nice to throw on a pair of old blue jeans, a holey old Black Harley T-shirt, my leather vest with all the Harley patches, my turtle-shell helmet, and take the image of the Health Inspector and absolutely trash it!"

What do your sons think of all this? I asked. Another laugh. "About a year ago my oldest son said, 'Dad, I'd like to ride the Harley.' I said, 'Well that's…probably OK. Why?' 'Senior Prom's coming up, Dad—I want to take my date to the Prom on a Harley.' And he did." Richard is obviously very proud of his kids. "They're the greatest kids on the face of the earth," he said. "That's Richard speaking. Little Richard would also tell you that there have been times when Hillary's been up at the end of the driveway with a 'For Sale' sign around her neck. And people have taken her…and brought her back…they didn't want her either! And I love that too, because of all my kids, Hillary is the Little Richard."

What are the best and the worst things Little Richard has ever done? "Well, the worst thing he does is to become very irresponsible. And he doesn't listen to people. I had problems with that, many years ago, but a lot of that Little Richard's gone. The best? In his own mischievous way he is able to convey a message, and do it with a sense of humor. Very few people will ever walk away from a conversation with me and not know where I'm coming from. I can have a feeling and make it known while couching it in a sense of humor. I'm trying to be honest, trying not to offend anybody—but there are individuals and situations that need amending. I have spent most of my life on this island, and I have seen what it was, what it is, and I think I can see what it will and can be. And I think it's time that things have to be said and things have to be done before we totally lose it.

"If you don't like something, you've got to say something about it or it's going to perpetuate, it's going to become a bigger problem than you ever anticipated. In my first ten years here as Health Officer, I watched the effect the change in the housing situation had on people here. A silent majority is alive and well here; most of these people don't like the situation, but they're tolerant, and I don't think that's appropriate. That wonderful two-word phrase, 'Act up,' associated with the devastating disease called AIDS, is appropriate here. The AIDS advocates, several years ago, had to do something that would garner attention—yes, a negative attention, to an extent—but it focused people on the point, so that later on that point could be appropriately addressed. Perhaps that's the stage I'm at in my life right now. I feel like the guy shoveling coal in the bottom of the *Titanic* when it gets hit by the iceberg. And the Captain sticks his head down and says, 'Hey, we've got an iceberg…we're sinking. But don't mention it to anybody—we don't want anyone to panic.' My statement here is, 'I won't, until the water reaches my lower lip.' When that happens, then I'm going to mention it to somebody. Now the water has reached my lower lip and I'm fed up with what is happening around here and somebody's gotta say something about it. I'm not a saint; I'm not a guiding light; I want people to look at something and make their own decision, but if they're going to make that decision, I've got to do something that sometimes may be construed as slightly controversial. And I don't care any more what people will think.

MAKING CHANGES

"I have to rehearse some of the things I have to say, and think about them…I've tried not be off the cuff too frequently because that can be troublesome. But it's kind of productive to open up a situation and get somebody's attention with a sense of humor…something humorous or something controversial, they'll turn their head and they'll look. Once you've got their attention, then you start on the serious side of what you were discussing, and you pull them in, and you make them believers, and if you can do that, you can make changes. I don't know where that's going to take me…" Do you have political aspirations? I asked. "Sure. I would like to put myself in a position where I can make perhaps more changes on an islandwide basis than I can make as a health officer." Would you run for Selectman? I queried. "I'd think about taking a shot at it. You can quote me on that, but please also say that it could perhaps be the biggest wakeup call of my life. I could do quite well and gain that seat, or I could get three votes. But I think the preparation is there for the job, in that over the last twenty years I've come to understand that every time I make a decision I irritate somebody. It doesn't matter what the decision is— somebody's going to be pleased with it and somebody won't. And if I can accept that, I think I can deal well with controversial issues. I hope the sense of humor lasts…it's running pretty thin."

I told Richard that I had hopes of interviewing his wife Edie, and he smiled and waxed a bit eloquent about their relationship. "I sincerely believe that opposites attract. Edie is a very different individual than I am, and I think the two of us, in our totally separate personalities, have so balanced it that our kids have perhaps been getting the best traits of both of us. But we are very different people. It's fun…and that is to the benefit of the kids. I wasn't an environmentally oriented kind of person, as far as animals were concerned—I'm becoming that way now, but it's only because of my association with Edie, and the kids have seen that, and they've appreciated it. I deal with human beings; Edie deals a lot with the natural world, and the kids have seen how to deal with both. She's given so much to this family thing, and I'm very proud of what she's done. Edie is an extremely talented and a fascinating person."

Well, so are you, I said, and meant it wholeheartedly. My thanks to Richard, Big and Little.

Richard Ray in his office, 2004.

Nantucket: It Still Feels Right

Jim & Margareta Nettles, 1999

They're both creative artists: he's an actor and she's a weaver. In some ways their callings are related, because they both start with an idea, expressed in a script or in a pattern, that must be carefully thought through and properly developed—in his case a character in a play, a personage necessary to the validity of the piece, to whom his actions and spoken lines must give life; in her case a design conceived in her own mind or predetermined, either of which requires particular materials of specific textures, hues, and strengths and for whose completion an exacting procedure must be followed for a successful and beautiful final product.

Jim Nettles is certainly familiar to Nantucket residents and visitors for his many and varied roles in plays produced here. And Margareta Nettles has been perhaps the island's most prominent weaver, maintaining a studio for many years to teach the art to others and to create exquisite pieces that have gone to fortunate buyers all over the world. When I asked them to tell me about their lives before Nantucket, Jim said, "I was born and raised in New York City, and I stayed there until Maggie and I left in 1975." Maggie said, "I moved to the United States from Sweden in about 1966; I had a scholarship to study weaving, and I started out in Washington, DC, then moved to New York." Were you a weaver in Sweden as well? I asked. "Oh yes. I was trained in art school and have always been a very serious weaver. I have stayed in the weaving and not deviated at all."

FAST-TALKING, DANCING AROUND, & WHATNOT

How did the two meet? Jim: "We met at a Swedish celebration for Lucia…" That's the one with the crown of candles? I asked. "Yes," he answered, "the Lady of the Lights. I love telling this story." He grinned. "I traveled with a pack of friends on weekends to play a lot of daytime basketball and then party all the rest of the weekend. We knew this schoolteacher, Fred Hershkowitz, and he was our bulletin board. We'd call him up and say, 'Hey Fred, what's going on this weekend?' On this particular weekend he gave us *three* parties to go to! One was on the Upper West Side, one was someplace in Midtown, and the other one was in the Village. We decided to go in that order—start in town and work down. So here we are, eleven of us…" Margareta quipped, laughing, "None under 9 feet…" and Jim said, "I was the smallest one in the group.

"So," he went on, "we crashed this holiday party, and it was wonderful, so I stayed. I'd been partying with my friends for years, the same thing every weekend—we'd do a lot of fast-talking, dance around, sleep around, drink around and whatnot. And it was really becoming boring, the same old kind of thing. I was about 33. I hadn't met 'that person' yet, you know. And I was looking. This party represented something different, because people were sitting around talking to each other…" Margareta added, "We were talking about Swedish traditions…and we were dancing Swedish traditional folk dances." Jim said, "Yeah, and so I stayed, and eventually I talked with Maggie and we talked into the morning hours, and that was it." Margareta added, "We had no idea that we were going to end up together, but it was a nice conversation and it felt very comfortable, and the next day Jimmie called me…" Jim: "…early in the morning, about 6:45…" Maggie: "…and said, 'Can we get together?' And I said, 'Well, let's wait a couple of hours.' But we did go out for a walk the next day and then we talked to each other for a week on the telephone, and then Jim called and said, 'I'd like to cook dinner for you…'" Jim: "It was one of those things—you find somebody you can talk with and whatnot, and it seems right, feels right, you know, why not take a chance?" Maggie: "Thirty years later it still feels right. It's more right now than ever."

Did you get married before you landed on Nantucket? I asked. Jim answered: "We got married on Nantucket in August of 1970." And how did Nantucket enter their lives? Margareta: "I had been invited to Nantucket through Maryann Beinecke; I'd met her through a mutual friend in the city and she was very interested in what I was doing with weaving. She brought me to Nantucket to work with her through Nantucket Looms in the summers, and…" Jim interrupted: "…it was a weaver's guild then, the Nantucket School of Needlery. It used to be where Obadiah's has been, on India Street. Maggie was brought to the island to teach the faculty there. She maintained her studio in New York, but in the summer she would come up here, because she had the school, so from 1970 on I came to Nantucket."

THE REWARDS OF "CLEANING UP"

Jim explained that they'd met just before New Year's Eve, 1969. Shortly afterward, Margareta's father died and she had to return briefly to Sweden, but when she came back the romance was still very much on. Jim said, "We spent New Year's Eve together—I was living up in the Bronx and she was living on 98th and Broadway. The following May I moved my gear to her house; in June we conceived our daughter; and in August of 1970 we got married. OK?" Jim settled into a much more responsible life. "We stayed in New York till 1975," he said, "and I worked there and commuted to the island in the summers. In New York I was the manager for a drug rehab center, and then I worked for the police academy in the 77th Precinct in Brooklyn, to help train policemen how to develop ways of dealing with crises in the community, and how to service people more effectively, using the agencies that were already set up in the community as resources—in a sense, the idea was to get the police out of the cars and start doing like they did in the old days…It was interesting how I got that job, because I had applied with all these [candidates with] Ph.D. and M.A. degrees and shucks, I didn't get a degree; I was out there in the streets. I went to the interview at the police academy and the Deputy Police Commissioner and all these big-brass people and whatnot were there, and they started interviewing me. I'd worked for the court system, in crisis intervention kinds of things…so even though I didn't have the credentials in terms of a sheepskin, I had a whole lot of experience, and I was good." Margareta interrupted: "Remember that a close friend of ours asked you to apply because he knew your skills and experience." Jim agreed: "He said 'Give it a shot, see what happens.' I had been a criminal in my younger days…" Jim was grinning, so I asked him if he was pulling my leg—he's a great kidder. "Oh no!" he replied. "From 16 on I was…and then when I came out of the service, I just went down the wrong track; I was out on the streets hanging out, and using drugs." Can I quote you? I asked. "I don't care. It's true," he answered. Was this when you were playing weekend basketball and crashing parties? I asked. "No, that was after I cleaned up. I met Maggie after I cleaned up."

What made you clean up? I asked. Jim's shocking response: "Suicide, thinking about suicide. I had a gun; I used to sit around and click the gun and think 'What the hell am I doing here? I have nothing, is it always going to be like this?' And I woke up one morning and said, 'What the hell is wrong with you? You don't want this s---; you don't want to kill yourself!' My mother was a dreamer and she'd instilled all these wonderful dreams in my head; some may think of them as fantasies, but shucks, most of them have come true. Things do change, turn around." How did you turn your life around? I asked. "There was this program at the Phoenix House, and you couldn't get in there unless you were clean. At that time I had myself like a $150-a-day habit, but I also knew they had a bed open right then. So I got all spruced up and went down there and pretended I was clean as the pure driven snow, and I kicked into their program…and I don't think they ever found out." And you stopped just like that? "I stopped. I had reason to stop. I've always been a good eater, always taken care of myself…so that got me through and when I came out of there, I met Maggie!" Smiles all around.

Jim continued: "At the end of that police academy interview I said, 'You know, I probably have committed some crimes that are not on the books, and I have committed some crimes that are on the books, and I've been sent away, too. Those are crimes that I have done in the past, and I'm through with that, and I'm on a new track now, you can see how my job record has been.' So when I walked out of there the guy who was heading up the project came running out and said, 'Where'd all that come from?' I said, 'You told me to be truthful.' I got the job. And later I had to interview a couple of the policemen who'd arrested me. I said to myself, 'Ain't this something?'"

Didn't you have any fears about telling them all this during the interview? I asked. "No," he said. "You are what you are, you can't turn back the hands of time." While he liked what he was doing, working within the community, Jim said, "I hated the bureaucracy, hated the idea that people kept insisting I wear a suit and a tie, when that wasn't my makeup and that wasn't where I was coming from. I think just being who I was and telling it like it was, was enough…those were my credentials. I wanted to help people."

When and where did Jim and Margareta tie the knot? Margareta said, "We were going to get married in Vermont, but our friends here, Bill Euler and Andy Oates and some others, said we should get married in Nantucket. So there was a wedding put together—this was in 1970—and we were about ten people in all. And it was wonderful, because we got married in the State Forest, and the night before, we went to put some little ties on the trees so that we would know where to go the next day, and we couldn't find them [laughter], so we just went to another tree and everybody just kicked off their shoes. That was August 19th…" Jim: "August 28th." Maggie: "…and you know the flowers of the Indian Pipes? They were all around. And the pine needles were just like a rug…" Jim: "…and the sunbeams were coming through…" Maggie: "…and it was at 5:30 because then the clock hands were going up…." Jim: "Yes, you get married when they're going up, because then your cup fills up." Maggie: "So that was this beautiful wedding, and we could hear the waves…" Jim: "…and our minister was David Coles—he was also an artist here on Nantucket. And the same person who produced *Dracula* on Nantucket…" Maggie: "…John Wulp…" Jim: "…was responsible for our reception." Maggie: "And it was a very important time for them, because they did this Dracula that then went straight to Broadway…" Maggie continued: "And you know, we saw that every night for a while, because John did it on Nantucket."

MOVING TOWARD NANTUCKET

What Jim called "another epic" in their life together occurred when the couple took advantage of an offer from Maryann Beinecke to move to North Adams, MA so that Margareta could teach weaving in a defunct mill complex in which the Beineckes were developing a group of artisans from all over the U.S. "Maggie and the Beineckes were sharing the same kinds of dreams," Jim said, "and we were ready to leave the city. I knew that if I stayed any longer I was going to slip back to meeting my friends, going out to basketball, and so forth, and I'd grown tired of all that. In fact," he laughed, "my friends used to call me henpecked, which was great, I loved it, because it meant that I had arrived and they could see that. They were jealous—I had a good thing!"

In 1979 the couple finally moved to Nantucket full-time. They sold their house in the Berkshires but there wasn't quite enough to buy a house on the island. However, in Jim's words, "through the grace of some friends we bought this place." Margareta said, "We were so lucky." "But," said Jim, "I now had no job (I'd been running the CETA program for North Adams), so I went to work selling and buying scallops for the Nantucket Seafood Company, and later I worked in the Marine Home Center." Like many, if not most working Nantucketers, Jim has had a variety of jobs. At one point, he said, Margareta taught him how to weave, and together they worked on a big commission: rugs Margareta had designed for Jackie Onassis.

What holds you on Nantucket? I asked. Jim responded: "We made an investment in '79, and we bought at the right time and it's paid off, so we have a home that we couldn't have anyplace else. And it's a safe place to be…" Margareta said, "From the moment I stepped on the ground on the island I knew that this is what I loved. It's been the greatest gift ever to be able to live here." You knew it was your home of the heart, I said, and she answered, "It is my heart, and I could not have wished for anything better. And it has served my profession, for me to be able to work in a place that was conducive to exercising what I knew how to do…[she sighed and shook her head]. I see that God put me here. I love the island."

Jim and Margareta have a beautiful daughter, Anita. Margareta said, "She is wonderful; more than being beautiful, she has a wonderful…" Jim: "…soul, a wonderful soul." Anita, Jim and Maggie told me, spent her earliest years in New York City, but went to Nantucket schools when the family finally moved here, later attending a challenging private school in Charlemont, MA. She attended Wheaton College but switched to the Culinary Institute of America to pursue her still-serious interest in cooking. Presently she runs an island landscaping business, and we assume she finds her way to the

Far left—Jim and Maggie Nettles, celebrating his 49th birthday. Top right—Jim Nettles with daughter Anita in 1980. Photo by Beverly Hall. Bottom right—Maggie and Anita. Directly below—Margareta and Jim Nettles on their wedding day on Nantucket, 1970.

kitchen now and then. Has she ever been in a play? I asked Jim. He answered, "She was in *I'm Not Rappaport* with me." Margareta said, "Oh! What a thrill that was!" and Jim allowed as how she was "very good."

Jim started acting in 1982. He said, "Richard Cary, who was director of the Theatre Workshop then, coerced me, with Maggie's help over a period of a couple years, to go down and audition, and I did for *Death of a Salesman*. I played the waiter. And I forgot my first line." What, I asked, was that line? Jim's reply was somewhat confusing, since he'd almost forgotten what he'd forgotten, but his answer, amidst some hilarity, was: "It was 'We ain't got no mice. We don't serve no mice. Or meese. We don't serve no meese in this restaurant.' And I was hooked. From then on." Margareta said she'd never even been tempted to get into the theatre except as a devoted audience member and "Jimmie fan," but she did say that it was no surprise to her that Jim would be good at acting. "I sort of knew, not really consciously, but I felt that he had something in him, you know, and then he did this first play, and then I knew, I know what he has."

Margareta and Jim travel to Sweden occasionally to see her people, but Jim admits to not being fond of his old stomping grounds: "I don't love New York any more," he said. And he sees what remains of his family only infrequently. "My brother died from drugs at an early age," he said, "and I lost my mother and father when they were fairly young by today's standards. I grew up in a dysfunctional family; my father would not tolerate fear in his sons, and as a result I didn't trust my emotions and couldn't share with my parents how I felt, so I grew up with emotions I wasn't able to let out, and I didn't trust anybody. All my emotions were locked in, all my dreams, all my intellect, were shut off. Until…" Thoughtful silence. Well, I suggested, cleaning up and meeting this beautiful weaver from Sweden and ending up with a good strong marriage and a life on Nantucket must have been helpful. Jim answered, "Yeah, and being in the theatre has helped, because it had me search down in myself for the different emotional levels one has to use in acting." Margareta added, "I've seen Jimmie go into himself and get things for when he is doing a play, and he just keeps finding these things, and pulling them out, and it has so much strength!" Then she commented that "you have a chance to feel better when you live on this island because you live in a very healthy way here…you know, your attitude toward the rest of your life is stronger because you have been able to live in a very positive way."

She went on: "Everything may not have been totally easy all the time but, because of the chances that we've had to make our life here, we can form ourselves around what the life of the body is. Nantucket has been extremely helpful for me artistically and in every other way." Jim added, "Me too…I may be a good actor, I may be a bad actor, but the point is that I was given a chance to find out if I had anything—that is what my solace is on Nantucket, that I can do that."

This couple shares a very positive attitude about the future, despite Margareta's bout with cancer. "Our goal," Jim said, "is to get out and see more, and we want to travel—go to the Midwest, go to the Grand Canyon, go to the desert in Southern California…" Margareta nodded and Jim went on: "We want to get on a train and let it take us to where we want to go." But this doesn't mean for a minute that they won't always return to the home of their hearts. Jim feels that one of the best things about the island is the very fact that "you live in a fishbowl here. What I mean is, you're not watched, but your life is lived out in the open. That's nice, because people get to know you and see you; it's the kind of community that…" Margareta: "…is very open." Jim: "Yeah, and forgiving, when it's time to forgive, and understanding, and supportive."

So for Jim and Margareta Nettles, who have made their lives and based their careers here on the Faraway Isle, the passage of time has brought about both a drama and a weaving, neither of which is finished, with some interesting nubs in the fabric, perhaps a forgotten line here or there, a lot of hard work, courage, many rewards, and the knowledge that they are experiencing a rich and worthwhile existence. As is true for so many people living here, life before Nantucket very providentially led these two home.

Margareta Nettles died on March 3, 2003, after a long battle with cancer.

Jim, Anita, and Maggie Nettles.

Destination: Music
Mollie Glazer, 1998

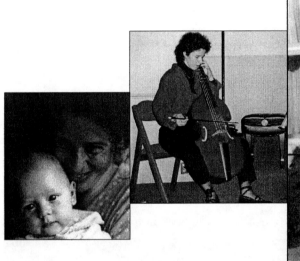

*M*ollie Glazer, one of the finest cellists you can hope to hear, is a familiar figure on Nantucket's music scene. Despite some apparent stumbling blocks, such as a seeming ineptness in her own first string experience and an uninspired (and uninspiring) music teacher or two, something kept gently pushing Mollie forward into a life in which music is the linchpin.

What was her life before Nantucket like? "I was born and brought up in Springfield, Delaware County, outside Philadelphia," she said. "My mother was a music teacher, and when I was very small, I used to sit on the stairs and listen to the piano students who came to the house…it's kind of a cool memory. She was never a performer; she taught elementary education, in the days when they didn't have a music room in the school, and she would push a piano from classroom to classroom. Can you imagine? She didn't enjoy it—it was a very hard job, and she had to prepare big programs a couple times a year. When I was in third grade she went back to school and got a second Master's degree, this time in Library Science. She said that she'd always been envious of the school librarian because her life was so quiet! So she became a school librarian…and gave up music." Did she give you piano lessons? I asked. Mollie answered, "No, she sent me down the road to a piano teacher. I thought that was very smart of her. I was five or six; I think she saw that the interest was there. Even before that I would try to pick stuff out on the piano. I have a very strong memory of my nursery-school teacher talking about how to tell the difference between your right and left hand. I knew that the right hand played the high notes, and that's how I always figured that out."

When did you start on other instruments? I asked. "I was fortunate to be in a school district that had a very strong in-school music program. That doesn't exist in most places any more, as you know. And during the four years I was there, the high school produced at least two dozen professional musicians. The elementary school offered string and band instruments to fourth-graders, and I took violin. I don't think I had a really good teacher, because my parents have a home movie of me playing, and the positions were awful, the sound was awful, and the bow-hold was awful…things that as a teacher I zero in on right away with students. Also, when I would practice, which was not very often [with a smile], my father would torture me by putting on a Jack Benny record. That was mean, don't you think?" Laughing, Mollie sang the familiar sour old triad scale the comedian used to play on his violin.

Mollie said that her late father would have loved to be a musician: "He grew up during the Depression, so you know, just forget about it ever being an option. He had a great passion for music, and I must say I have a lot of that from him, because he played music night and day. I grew up listening to musical theatre, to big-band music, to opera, to organ music. He loved big theatre organs—and actually was president for a while of the American Theatre Organ Society and the Theatre Historical Society. So he traveled the country looking at old theatres, and wrote four or five books about the history and architecture of the old theatres in Philadelphia. He did this when he retired; before that," she added, making a face, "he was an accountant." But he encouraged your music even though he teased you, I ventured. Mollie grimaced and replied, "Mmmm…I suppose he did. I used to play this piece on the piano that I liked a lot, and I would play it really fast to see if I could, and I would hear my father say to my mother: 'Please tell her to stop that!' But I've heard the horror stories of people who really put down their musical kids, and that didn't happen to me…of course they supported me. But I was an extremely sensitive child, and so it was not fun to hear that…"

A Little Violin Improvisation

Did you love taking violin lessons? I asked. "I was bad at the violin," Mollie said, "and I didn't compete well with my friends who were also playing violins. I was in the second violin section in the sixth-grade orchestra, and we had twenty violins, which was amazing by today's standards. But I was way in the back. And I figured out that if I put the violin between my knees, it was easier to play…and all my friends were learning vibrato on the violin, and I couldn't do it that way. But I could do it like it was a cello. The director let me do it, and then he let me switch to cello after that year. And I loved the cello from the very beginning. But again, I didn't have a good teacher in high school—he played in the Philadelphia Orchestra, which impressed all my relatives, but he was not a teacher. I mean, people are teachers or they're not. It's a real gift.

"What made me continue? I don't know, frankly. I was driven by some unknown force…Anyway, I switched to the cello in seventh grade, so I had a good five or six years in it…and then I didn't go to college right away; I didn't know what the heck I was doing. I mean, it was beyond me that I had to decide something; I was just confused and overwhelmed. So I took a year off, and…I changed cello teachers! I studied with Elsa Hillger, who I believe is still alive and still playing—she's in her nineties now. And she was the first woman, other than a harpist, to be in the Philadelphia Orchestra. Now, *she* was a teacher!

Finding Her Way a Little Bit

"That was a very pivotal time. I was very depressed that year, and my mother was afraid I was going to live at home forever! I got various jobs, like waitressing…I was finding my way a little bit. And on Saturdays I played in the Youth Orchestra of Greater Philadelphia; that was really a great experience. Afterward, I would go for my lessons at Elsa Hillger's house. It was very exciting…I was 18, I would go into the city by myself and have this whole musical day in the city, and it kind of gave me feelings of independence and power. Elsa wanted me to stay in Philadelphia and go to the Conservatory there, but I wanted to get away from home and go to a university. So I picked the University of Connecticut, and got a music scholarship there, which totally amazes me because I felt I couldn't play anything. I had to go play an audition, and I don't even know what I played. But I saw later that this teacher on the audition committee had written 'Very very musical.' So she saw a potential. Talk about karma, how you meet people in your life who really change you and shape you…I mean, if it wasn't for her I wouldn't play the cello now. Her name is Mary Lou Ryland, and she's still a professor there. She's been coming to

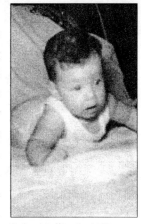

Baby Mollie, in 1958.

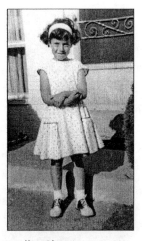

Mollie Glazer, at age six.

Despite the pigtails, the young Mollie Glazer looks very much like the today Mollie.

Nantucket and doing cello quartet concerts with me."

Mollie went on: "And I picked the University—I had very clear criteria. I didn't want 50,000 students; I wanted a rural area; and it had to have a music department. Gee, if you think about it, when you pick a music school you should pick a teacher first. But I didn't know about that...But look what happened! So it was really totally amazing." And you began to know that the cello was your career, your life? I asked. "Yeah! I was there for two years, and then found that limiting and transferred to New England Conservatory. There weren't the players at UConn to play with...you know, it was a state school. But I grew so much in those two years; Mary Lou took apart my hands, basically, and taught me how to play the cello." So you were sort of learning the instrument all over again, I said. Mollie laughed. "Yeah, well I never learned in the first place.

"Anyway, I actually ended up getting my degree in the viola da gamba, not the cello. Because when I arrived there, the teacher was not a teacher...I changed my major, basically, so that I could have a good teacher, and I knew the gamba teacher, Laura Jeppesen, was very good." Mollie showed me her viola da gamba, which is incredibly beautiful. She explained that while it is the same size as a cello, it's a seven-stringed fretted instrument, as opposed to the cello, which has four strings and is not fretted. "Gamba," she said, "actually means legs...so it's a 'viola of the legs,' because it doesn't have an endpin like the cello, and you have to balance it in your legs. I had a student cello when I went to UConn, and after a year Mary Lou told me I needed to get a fine instrument to be competitive in the music world. So after one year at UConn, I gathered together all my waitressing money and $3,000 from my grandmother, and bought a really fine cello...which has tripled in value since then. And I also bought a middle-ground gamba.

118

"Laura was a really great teacher. She recommended that I go to Europe after graduation and study with her teacher, Wieland Kuijken. I applied directly to the Royal Conservatory of the Netherlands, in the Hague, sent a tape, and got in! And before I went to Holland I bought a really

fine viola da gamba from Laura. That's the one I still have. That has also tripled in value. You know, that's the thing about buying instruments; they're better than mutual funds...but of course you'll never sell them. I'll never sell them. And in Europe, I bought a baroque cello, and then I moved back to the States, and I had these three instruments with which to go out and parade my skills.

SCHLEPPING AROUND WITH HUGE INSTRUMENTS

"I lived with my parents for a few months, and I would take these trips in my mother's car, first to New York, then Boston, Washington, and Philadelphia, and I'd play for everybody, trying

Mollie in her early twenties, holding her beautiful viola da gamba.

to get work." I got a mental picture of Mollie toting these huge instruments around on subways and busy streets and observed that it must be a bit scary traveling with big instruments. And how on earth do you transport them on an international flight? She laughed, and replied, "It's not so much scary as a lot of schlepping! Actually, the cello that I bought in Holland was from 1770, and you know, you have to buy a ticket for each instrument, and I couldn't buy tickets for all of them. I was young and a little naïve, and I put that one in baggage, and the neck got broken on it! And did I weep when I opened that case up. But insurance paid for it, and it got fixed, and there you go. So it was OK."

Returning to her search for work in the States, Mollie continued: "I got my first work in Philadelphia, and the first group that hired me in New York was the Waverly Consort. I had to do temp secretarial work for a while to make ends meet, but after about a year and a half I had a ton of music work. I chose to live in New York, because that's where I got the most work. And I lived there until 1992. I had such a diverse life in New York. Any time you go out, you call your answering machine, and it feels like it could be the Lottery…you know, it's like, 'Ooh, today maybe somebody will call me with a tour to China! Or maybe somebody'll call with a concert in Carnegie Hall. Or maybe…'" That was definitely the positive Mollie.

She did get to go on some fabulous tours, and also played at Carnegie Hall. "That," she said, "was in a new group called the Classical Band. It was formed so New York could have a period instrument orchestra of its own…because people were grumbling—'Why doesn't New York have a great baroque orchestra, like cities in Europe? We have great players here—let's start one!' We played Beethoven, Mozart, Haydn, Schubert…and we did four concerts that year in Carnegie Hall. It was great! I loved that experience for everything it was worth. We had a three-week tour in Germany, and made a couple of CDs…but it didn't work out, because the artistic director of the group absconded with the money and…bla bla bla…and there goes that orchestra, see you later. But that was the best year I had anywhere; that was the '89/'90 season. I also played in pits of Broadway shows; and once I had the experience of getting on stage, as a sub in something called *The Three Musketeers,* at the Ed Sullivan Theatre. I was in period costume playing the gamba; I had to do that without a rehearsal because I was a sub. I was terrified! But you know what it's like to be a freelancer; it's feast or famine, so in the feast periods you'd have it all in one week…and most of the time you have to throw it together in two rehearsals, or three, if you're lucky. But I loved it; I loved all those experiences. The downside was sometimes having to carry two instruments on the subway; that was intense, but it was all worth it…"

Why did Mollie leave New York? She laughed: "Well, frankly, I had always wanted to live in New York, and as soon as I got there I was looking forward to getting out. I mean it was so exciting, and so full of opportunity—but at the same time it's not a lifestyle I like. It's draining, and there was all that heavy schlepping around on public transportation. I did get a car, but that didn't help me very much. You can't park anywhere, and the stress and the bla bla bla…I was always applying for college jobs in other states; I even considered joining a band of musicians in Utah one year, and another in Seattle. And then in the spring of '92 I found that the White Elephant Hotel on Nantucket was advertising for a piano player. I had never played the piano professionally, but I had always played the piano, and I took lessons as a kid, and always enjoyed that. And I convinced the guy I could do the job; he hired me on the phone without ever really hearing me! I had three months—I went to the Lincoln Center

Public Library; I Xeroxed; I bought a ton of music. And I practiced and practiced and practiced…I went to a jazz teacher who helped me learn how to read those lead sheets…I learned about 3rds and 7ths and all kinds of things. I did a crash course and I took that job at the White Elephant and played there for two months." Mollie later said that she'd come to the island briefly in 1979 to visit a friend attending Leonard Shure's chamber music camp in Wauwinet. "I got a terrible sunburn, but I thought this place was so incredibly beautiful.

"The White Elephant job was for two months. I got room and board and played 24 hours a week. First they offered me $100 a week, and I got 'em up to $200, but frankly, I wasn't experienced and I didn't feel like I could ask for more. It was mostly fun, though sometimes it was a drag, when nobody was there and I was playing for the bartender. I had one day off. I'd brought my bike, and I biked this whole island. I loved it! About halfway through, I realized, This is so great! I'm so relaxed! I was meeting a lot of musicians on the island…Why did I decide to stay? Well, I met Barbara Elder, and she told me that the string teacher who'd been commuting had decided not to come back, and there was a job at the Nantucket Chamber Music Center. I was making probably three times more in New York, but I decided to stay, and I did that for quality-of-life reasons. It was a very interesting time and a very scary time…but what the heck?"

I asked Mollie how she made enough money to stay on the island. "Well, actually, to make ends meet, I went back to New York that first fall three or four times to do gigs. In December I'd go for two weeks and make a whole bunch of money—Messiahs and Brandenburgs, and all the stuff you do at Christmastime. And then that petered out, and I stopped hustling for it. I stopped having the desire…as much as I loved all that freelance work, one of the main reasons I left was that I felt like a hamster on one of those wheels—you know, you're going nowhere fast…And musically it wasn't very gratifying any more."

Marrying a Native

How did you meet Skip, your native Nantucketer? I asked. "I met him doing country line dancing at The Pines. Deborah and Mark Beale had taken me out to dinner and we went there afterward—Gary Mehalik's bluegrass band was playing then; it was winter of 1994. And I watched him when he was alone on the dance floor with his three kids. He had his six-year-old up in his arms. It's kind of embarrassing…but I saw a 'look' in his eyes, love for this kid, and he was twirling him around, and I was spinning around myself, watching. He was teaching people line dancing, and then there was a couples' dance and he came over and asked me to dance. And this was the thing that was really weird…I felt as though somebody pushed me out of the chair. Something was saying Pay attention! This is important!" Ah, I said, love at first sight. Well, yes, she admitted, smiling widely.

So, I said, you've settled down into this house in the woods, and you have lots of students and a successful business supplying music for weddings, and you perform a lot…and as if all that isn't enough, you're in the thick of doing a big show, *Faraway Land,* for which you've written the music. Do you really enjoy being so busy? "Oh yeah!" was her prompt reply. "This has probably been the busiest summer of my life. *Faraway Land* [written by islander Donald Noyes] is my first musical— I'm not a trained composer, though I've written full evening-length dance scores. I'm wearing a lot of hats for this production. But I'm not complaining. I have a very low tolerance for boredom. I really love my life; I have a very rich, full life, very diverse. I like it that way." What does Nantucket have for you that no other place in the world offers? I asked. Mollie grinned and answered quickly: "My husband. And my stepchildren—they're fantastic. And a home; there's a stability, a center here. For me as an artist, the best things about the island are that I have felt very welcomed here. And as a creative person, I have felt that I have this territory in which I can do stuff. All I have to do is come up with the ideas, and I can put them into motion, too, but I get a lot of support for them."

There was so much more to talk about: the occasional frustration of not always having enough musicians on-island to play with, or the challenge of building a string program at NCMC, or that sometimes it's difficult to set up a concert program because increasingly, something else is going on that would interfere with attendance. It's true that community groups such as the NCMC or theatre groups, for example, are having to schedule around ever-larger off-island-dependent events; there is the danger that truly community things may be stifled. "I don't get involved with judging this," said Mollie. "It's happening whether we like it or not, and I think the best thing to do is to go with the flow…there will be casualties, but I think ultimately Nantucket will be more of a cultural place. Can you imagine a performance center here? Or an arts festival with major players, with a teaching kind of facility for kids? I get a little overwhelmed when I think about it. I mean, I kind of came here to get out of the ratrace a little bit, and create my own world here, but…" She stopped with that "but," and it was plain that some of the changes that may come to the island hold promise that excites her.

Far left—Future musician Isaiah Williams, very young, and his mom, Mollie Glazer. Isaiah's middle name is Sebastian, because, Mollie says, his birthdate missed Johann Sebastian Bach's by 8 minutes! To right—Totally wrapped up in her music: Mollie in 1996. Below—A pensive Isaiah between Mom and Dad, Mollie Glazer and Skip Williams.

A Best Friend Named Principessa

Ethan Philbrick, 2003

We began the interview by carefully parking the cello in a safe spot, then watched as a pair of cardinals came to the window feeder to dine and eavesdrop. Ethan Philbrick was just going on 18 when I interviewed him in the summer of 2003, and a week away from embarking on a big adventure: living in his own apartment in Boston while he attends the New England Conservatory of Music.

How do you ask someone so young to describe his beginnings? Ethan plunged right in. "We moved here when I was a year old," he said, "and it's been wonderful growing up here—I can't think of a better place a person could grow up. I liked the schools here, and stayed through my sophomore year. But I was going up to Boston every Saturday to study, and it was like I was in two places; I didn't really feel as if I was anywhere, and it wasn't necessarily the greatest situation. So I applied to a lot of different boarding schools around Boston so I could keep on studying at New England Conservatory. I ended up going to Walnut Hill School, an art school in Natick. That was a really big move for me and my parents. My sister Jennifer had just gone to Harvard, and I was supposed to have two more years at home, and here I was, going away to school—my mom didn't want me to leave home at all. But we sort of compromised and my parents got an apartment in Boston, so I'd spend the weekends with them there." Neat trick—he didn't have to commute any more, but he made his parents commute! "Yeah," he laughed, "but it worked, and we enjoyed it.

"Walnut Hill was really interesting," he continued, "because everybody there had something they were passionate about; they were very directed and focused—they knew what they wanted. The school has music, drama, visual arts, creative writing, and dance…and you also have your academic education. The music department is actually the biggest department, and there were some incredible players…it was a really cool environment, and it completely changed my course. The Conservatory has a program at Walnut Hill School, so we'd go to Boston every Saturday just like I'd been doing from Nantucket, and we played in the Youth Philharmonic Orchestra, as well as taking our lessons there. I started cello with Mollie Glazer here on Nantucket, of course, when I was in third grade. At Conservatory, I studied first with Emmanuel Feldman, and then Mark Churchill during my senior year."

Anyone who's heard Ethan play in the last few years knows that he and Nantucket's superb musician Mollie Glazer are well-known for their improvisatory "matches," making really good music at the drop of a hat. I wondered what more traditional teachers thought of this. "Well," he said, "it's definitely not very common, especially at a place like Walnut Hill, where everyone's so directed and work in their practice rooms four hours a day. But I've grown up hanging out a lot, going on walks, doing other stuff, and have not stayed in my room practicing a lot…I'd practice, because I love playing the cello, but it wasn't something I felt I had to do. So it's completely natural for me to use music as a totally free expression…and that's something a lot of classical musicians aren't used to. But look at Yo-Yo Ma—he's starting now to do that. My teacher Mark Churchill is really intrigued by it, and thinks it's a great asset."

NOT AN IOTA OF STAGE FRIGHT

I first knew Ethan when we were both in the 1997 production of Donald Noyes' musical drama *Faraway Land.* He was then in middle school, and was already being noticed for his exceptional musical ability, yet was a completely agreeable kid who threw his whole self into whatever he was involved in. Asked to perform a small vocal solo, Ethan jumped right in with no qualms, which was a bit unusual. He seems to be one of those fortunate people who don't suffer either stage fright or self-consciousness in performing. "It's really interesting," he said. "Performing seems to be something that comes naturally to me, and I realize that's not so for a lot of people. I don't really get stage fright, and that has a lot to do with my parents' attitude, I think, because they're completely open. Sometimes a competition will get me stressed out, because the whole point of it is that you're getting judged, and that's not necessarily the best feeling. But when I'm just sharing something, like in performing, I don't get nervous." That easy enjoyment of what he's doing comes through in his playing, puts the audience at ease, and makes for a very positive atmosphere—very important for a performer.

In the spring of 2003, Ethan brought some friends from school to Nantucket to play for Mollie Glazer's premiere of her *Beyond Measure,* "and it was an absolutely incredible weekend." But soon after, he was slated to solo in the Elgar *Cello Concerto* with the Youth Philharmonic, and he admits that he was "sort of worked up about that, because it's easy to think of that kind of performance as some sort of competition or something you have to do...but I finally said to myself, 'Wait—I'm just doing something that's beautiful, and I'm going to be sharing it with other people. It's not something I should get stressed out about.' I realized I'd have to spend time practicing so I wouldn't embarrass myself...but my attitude was that this was just going to be a fun thing, and who cares what everyone's going to say about it? And once I took that attitude, it ended up being a really incredible experience."

FALLING IN LOVE WITH MUSIC

Are Ethan's parents, Nat (writer) and Melissa (attorney), especially musical? "Well, my dad played classical guitar in middle school, and when he got to high school he got an electric guitar and played in a garage band. And my mom used to play percussion in her school band—bells, the glockenspiel... But when I was growing up, it wasn't like, 'Now that you're a certain age, you must start learning a certain instrument,' which happens in a lot of musical families. We always had a live-in babysitter in the summers because my parents had to work, and one summer, when I was four or five, our sitter was Trina, from Kentucky; she played flute, and she practiced an hour every day. I'd sit outside her door while she was playing, and I can still remember that feeling when I listened—I'd be dancing outside there, and thinking, '*WOW,* she's playing music!' When she left I asked my parents if I could play the flute. They thought that was OK. I wasn't in school yet, so we talked to Miss Moores, the elementary school music teacher; she gave us Dorothy Thompson's name, and she recommended I start on the recorder, because my arms weren't very long...and the flute would've been a stretch.

"My mom was really great—she started playing with me, so we were learning at the same time." Ethan laughed, "I had a little green plastic recorder that we bought at the pharmacy—I still have it. Eventually my mom stopped, but I kept going. I don't know why, but it was always something that seemed very important to me. As soon as I began, it really defined me...everyone at school knew me as the kid who played music. So the fact that I play music has always been a big part of me and my life. That Christmas, my parents gave me a flute, and I kept that up until about the seventh grade. But in third grade, Mollie Glazer, who'd just gotten a grant to start a music program, came into our general music class and demonstrated cello and violin for us. She actually started a ton of third-graders that year, and I started the cello then. It was pretty easy for me, because I already read music, so I was sort of ahead of other people who were struggling to read music. So I just took to it and kept it going. But it wasn't till seventh grade that I thought, 'Hey, this cello thing might be what I want to do more,' and stopped playing the flute to concentrate on cello.

"My parents had such an incredible attitude…I know so many people whose parents would lock them in their practice room and make them practice four hours before they'd let them out. To my parents, music was just a wonderful thing I did, so they didn't do that sort of thing. So music sort of stuck with me, in a big way…it was just automatically very serious and real, and something I was really there for. My parents weren't making it important, I was."

Ethan says he still gets the flute out of the closet now and then and plays it. He added, "When I was playing with the Pep Band for the NHA football games, I became so interested in the piccolo that when we played 'Stars and Stripes' I got to stand up and do the piccolo solo." He took enough piano lessons from Deborah Beale and at music camp to enable him to accompany cello students during their lessons. He's been teaching during the summer, allowing busy Mollie Glazer a bit of a break; he said that not only are all his students very promising, but the teaching process is yet another way of learning more about music. "And it's been great to watch these kids just absorb music and love it and have fun…and also to play with their peers."

PRINCIPESSA, ETHAN'S BEST FRIEND

Now it was time to talk about that cello leaning on a chair on the other side of the room. Is this the cello on which he learned as a child? "No," he explained. "This one was made in Venice in 1821; I got it in November of 2001. Before that I had a cello that was made in Chicago in around 1997. So this is really my first cello that I can really connect to. She is great." She? "Yes, my cello is definitely feminine." He laughed, a bit embarrassed. "I don't really think of my cello as a human being…but it's

126

Left—Ethan Philbrick, the very young cellist, playing at the Cape & Islands String Jamboree in the mid-90s. Photo courtesy of Mollie Glazer. Right—Ethan Philbrick with his one-time cello teacher Mollie Glazer, after a concert.

definitely a woman cello. She's very slim, actually quite a small full-sized cello, which makes her very easy to play. She's a really light color, so you can think of her as a blonde. And she's from Italy, and is somewhat stuck-up—she doesn't like humidity, and she sort of freaked out when the Youth Philharmonic went to Guatemala on tour, started opening up, and didn't like it very much. But anyway, I call her Principessa, because that's 'Princess' in Italian." That concert tour, so casually mentioned, took place in June of 2002; the group played in Panama and Guatemala, and it was, according to Ethan, "an absolutely amazing experience," one not without its little dramas. Guatemala, he said, is still completely stricken by decades of civil war: "Everyone has guns, it's just so sad. And music is so needed, and they know that, and they really yearn for it. I've never heard and seen people just grasp music so readily and so beautifully." But, he said, "I performed under a lot of not necessarily desirable conditions…we actually played some chamber music concerts at the ambassadors' mansions in each of the countries, in beautiful, huge rooms. One had a marble floor, and the cello has a metal endpin, which slid around on the floor, so I actually had to hold it with my legs the whole time I was playing. But it worked out fine. The other mansion had beautiful hardwood floors, and I didn't want to mark them up with the endpin, so I had to hold the cello that way again." He chuckled. "At my house, you can see a 2-by-2-foot-square place in the room I grew up practicing in, where there's just hole after hole, and there's one big one right in the middle where you can actually see through the floor to the basement!"

Watching Ethan during his recent concerts on Nantucket made it clear he'd not only grown very tall, but that his fingers are beautifully long. Do you find that one arm and hand is more developed than the other from cello-playing? I asked. "Yes," he said. "The fingers on my left hand are a good inch longer than on my right. That's common with cellists." Is Ethan cautious about what he does (sports, lawn-mowing, whatever) in order to keep from hurting his hands? He laughed and shrugged. "I don't let caution impair my life…I mean, I'd rather do what I want than worry about my fingers. I live a pretty well-rounded life. Cello-playing isn't the whole world…you know, there's so much more out there, and it really saddens me when I see all these musicians who are only doing their music. You can't live in fear of hurting your hands, or practice all day…how much fun is that?" In other words, life is to live, and not just in the music mode."

Speaking of recent concerts, Ethan admitted he'd become a bit bored with all the necessary practicing. So one day, he simply took Principessa and rowed out to his family's boat, where he simply stunned everyone within earshot by playing around with a beautiful song called "Ashokan Farewell" that had stuck in his mind after seeing Ken Burns' Civil War series. Imagine that lovely melody sung by that lovely instrument wafting its way over the water.

YO-YO MA BECOMES A FRIEND

Ethan has had a remarkable honor in his young life: the opportunity to play cello for and with Yo-Yo Ma. He explained how that had come about: "There's a public radio program called 'From the Top' that showcases classical musicians under eighteen; so they came to Walnut Hill and auditioned students. During my two years at the school, I played in a chamber music group, a piano trio, with two really great friends: Yung Jin Choi, a violinist from China, and Alex Rabin, a pianist (he did my Noonday Concert last year with me on Nantucket). There was a violin and cello duet that Yung Jin and I had read a few times and had fun with, and we thought, well, why don't we just go and play this for them and see what happens? We did, and the next day they called to ask us to play for the January show, and said, 'Our special guest that day is Yo-Yo Ma, and Ethan, you're going to get to play a piece with him!'" Ethan said that he was on a cellphone on a sidewalk in Natick when that call came in, and he reproduced the amazed yelp he'd made upon receiving that good news. "Yo-Yo Ma is just the most lovable and human person ever…there were three other cellists from Chicago, all under twelve, and they were really scared. He sensed that and laughed and joked with them to get them to relax. It was beautiful…he is just such a nice person. Playing with him was one of the most exciting musical experiences of my life. And then I played last December [2002] in the Youth Philharmonic at a concert, which began with the 'William Tell Overture.' Everybody knows that overture [he hummed the "Lone Ranger" theme], but it actually starts with a cello solo…it's like the sun rising. It's beautiful…a cello solo then a cello quintet. I asked if I could play the solo because I love it so much. But I began to worry—what if I messed up? I finally concluded, 'How can I do this music and be nervous? Go for it!' That was exactly what I needed to do. The concert was in Jordan Hall, and the first thing in the concert was my solo. You just play this low E and then an arpeggio up, and then everybody else comes in. So I was the first 'noise' of the entire concert. Yo-Yo Ma was there, because his daughter is in the orchestra, and afterwards he came up and told me I'd done a great job, and we talked a lot, about what I was doing the next year and stuff… It was incredible! I mean, he is world-known, but he's a human being, a friend. He gave me his number and we scheduled some conversations about what I was going to do in the next year. We just talked—it wasn't like me getting advice, it was just a conversation about what I'm thinking about, what I want to do."

The decision about what to do when he graduated from Walnut Hill required a lot of serious thinking on Ethan's part. "I didn't really know if I wanted to go to a conservatory or a regular school. I had two horrible months, February and March, trying to decide. It was a tough point in my development…I wasn't sure if music was where I was going to be most happy. And at the same time, I was having all these auditions for college. I knew I loved music, but it was a very confused and not very happy time. I was forcing myself to practice, and traveling around for interviews, so it was really hard. But I finally decided to go to the New England Conservatory; I thought it was a pretty cool concept to go to a school specifically for music—maybe I wouldn't want to do it for four years, and who knows what will happen? I'd love to try so many other things. But I think I made a good decision. And the big change is that I'm going to be living in my own apartment, completely on my own…I've been living in dorms for two years. It's a huge step, but very exciting. And I'll be studying with Paul Katz, an incredible cellist.

Ethan's interview took place just days before he embarked on his new life as a college student. During the summer he'd taught cello and also played at Eat Fire Spring Café on Old South Wharf on Friday and Saturday nights and at Cambridge Street Restaurant. He said, "I played with Mollie Glazer sometimes, and also a lot with Bob Walder, a gifted guitarist. We do a lot of Latin jazz—he's mainly a Flamenco guitarist. I've been doing a lot of jazz and improvisation, which has been very interesting. Jazz is really cool, because you have this tune and you play it and then the element of improvisation comes in; I thought it would be easier, and that I could do that sort of free improvisation I do, but you have to follow certain rules for jazz. I've really enjoyed it—it's been a very interesting journey."

CHANGING THE WORLD THROUGH MUSIC

I asked if Ethan's aim was to be a member of a major symphony orchestra, and he responded, "I don't think symphonies are where I'm going. They just don't excite me right now…all these people who have been in there for twenty years and they're bored but they're making money so they can't venture out. I just think I'd like to go out there and find out! Yo-Yo Ma has sort of cleared the way for us young cellists now to go out there and just completely change the world of music. That is what I want to do. I was talking to someone in the Youth Philharmonic who was going to go back down to Guatemala to play and I thought, 'God, I should go too, and just set up in the streets and play and people will drop their guns!' That's the kind of thing that excites me, and that's where I think I'll be going…but who knows how that will happen? At the same time, there's nothing more exciting than playing music with other people…maybe that'll happen, maybe I'll find some way to do that too.

"I have so many dreams. I could be anything; I love music and it does things to me that nothing else can do, and so I know music will always be part of me, because it has been for my whole life. I would never leave music…but I think I would love to do other things, just see what else is out there in the world. Who knows what I'm going to be in ten years?"

As for today, Ethan says he's having fun. "I know you have to make sacrifices if you really want something, be willing to give some things up. But I never feel like I'm sacrificing anything. I haven't been able to go to the beach every day this summer, because of the teaching and sometimes I've had to stay home and practice, but it's always been with an incredible reward. So I don't really look at doing music as involving sacrifices."

After the interview, Ethan took his Principessa out of the case, and played a Bach piece. It was absolutely beautiful, brilliantly played, and to make it even more delightful, behind him on the windowsill a chickadee actually sat listening attentively. It's obvious that Ethan is going places, and I admit to hoping that it will be as a cellist. But whatever he does in life, with his enthusiasm and positive outlook, as well as a genuine desire to make music matter to the world, he'll go far.

Left—June, 2003 photograph of Ethan Philbrick and his sister Jennifer, a student at Harvard. Right—Ethan Philbrick in June, 2003, as a brand-new graduate of the Walnut Hill School.

Through the Magic Door
Clara Urbahn, 1999

*D*riving to 'Sconset on that late-January morning was only the beginning of the magic experienced in the next couple of hours. It had been lightly snowing for a while, and the trees along the Milestone Road looked as if they'd been sprinkled with confectioner's sugar. "Shadows" of rust-colored pine needles formed scallops along the road where the overhanging branches prevented the snow from landing, and the only other colors in the world seemed to be the muted greens and browns of the trees and the soft blue-gray of the low clouds that were sending down large, lazy flakes. I'd considered canceling the interview, thinking the drive might be too slippery, but going slowly on the deserted road gave me the opportunity to be awed by the silent, snowy world. It truly was a winter wonderland, and I half-expected red-capped elves to pop out from behind trees, leading small deer on ivy halters.

When I drove into Clara Urbahn's drive and got out of the car I made the first tracks in the fresh snow. An icy ocean roared nearby. Clara, a dark-haired, strikingly attractive woman, opened the door and while we said our hellos grabbed the collar of a gallivanting dog, which was welcoming me with perhaps an overabundance of enthusiasm. After banishing the sociable Dudley, Clara led me through the house, and as we approached the living room I saw the most amazing sight: chairs in a friendly circle, chairs that were animals…and a life-sized yak presiding over the assembly. I must have gasped, and I certainly felt like a child who'd gone through a magic door and right into a storybook. Patting the yak's hairy hide, Clara said, "Isn't he fun? This a long hair is made of witches' wigs!" It seems she'd happened upon a goodly supply of the wigs while doing her shopping for materials for the huge creatures she creates—whether she'd already made the yak and it awaited its fur or the idea for making it hit her when she discovered the wigs I didn't ask; I was simply overcome by the enchanting room.

A MOUSE IN A TIARA

Moving through a hallway whose walls were embellished with dozens of photos of friends and family, we ended up in another room more fabulous than the last. Seven-foot-high animal figures awaited…a rabbit dressed to the teeth and carrying a basket, a white mouse adorned with dazzling "diamond" tiara and huge sparkling earrings, wearing lots of pearls draped over a green satin gown festooned with many short, fluffy white feathers which swayed in the breeze created by our entrance. I had an immediate feeling that I was underwater, and these feathers on the creatures and costumes on stands around the room were slowly undulating in the current. In one corner was a green frog costume and in the opposite corner a giraffe chair; beyond the wide doorway was a room whose facing side looked like a stage, because along its length maroon velvet curtains were pulled shut. I almost sat on the floor to await the show that was sure to begin when those curtains opened. Instead, I perched myself in the lap of a delightfully goofy-faced polar bear and prepared to begin the interview. What a place! And Clara was chuckling as she introduced me to her creatures, knowing full well the spell they produced. She's clearly as enthusiastic about what she's doing as are those who view her beautiful beasties.

This room and what she's producing in it represent Clara Urbahn's latest creative effort—all the creatures and costumes will ultimately be inhabited by human beings in a staged musical production of the book *Emily's Tale,* written by Buzz Williams and beautifully illustrated by Clara. "We collaborated on that book for about two years," she said. "It was a lot of fun." She went to the mouse and said, "This is Emily and [pointing] that's the fairy, and over there is the frog—they're all characters in the book."

Clara finally sat opposite me and, because of her visual problem and her generous nature, she pays close attention when you talk. Her eyes are dark and bright, and it's difficult to believe that she isn't seeing you clearly. Where did life begin for you? I asked. "I grew up in Guatemala," she said, "and lived there till I was 10. My parents met there in 1941, and my father, an American, was looking for land to start growing cardamom. That's a spice—you put it in your coffee and your hamburger, among other things; it's also used medicinally, and Arabs say it's an aphrodisiac. My mother and father met at a coffee plantation down there when she was 17; she was studying under the portrait painter Rosamund Tudor…anyone who likes children's books might recognize the name of her daughter, Tasha Tudor. My parents married about five months after they'd met, and had five children; I was the middle child, nice and safe—I loved it. Nothing to prove!"

WILD, WOOLLY, & BEAUTIFUL

Clara continued: "My mother trained us to look through a window and see everything as a painting. That was a wonderful exercise. I think it makes life a little more exciting if you practice this every day. It was a wonderful way to start life off, as if you're living in a painting, in a way. My mother was an enormous influence on my artistic education. We went to school in shack huts with cobblestone floors—it was a very romantic time. There were parrots in the trees, and monkeys. One of my sisters had beautiful blond white-wheat hair—she must have been three or four years old—and there was an orangutan in a tree, and it jumped down, grabbed her, and tried to drag her up the tree. We didn't know what to do, because every time we got close enough to try to get her away from this orangutan, it would show its enormous fangs. And then, thank God, out of the blue a huge Great Dane walked by, and the orangutan freaked and went running back up the tree and we got Lynn back. But I'll never forget it! That was a wild and woolly place and it was very beautiful. It also had a restlessness about it politically. Whenever there was an election for a new president you had to sleep in the hallways for protection from any flying bullets. My mother used to read Beatrix Potter to us a lot during this time, and we'd 'fall into the illustrations.' And if we heard a gun go off, she would tell us they were celebrating the president's birthday. She had such a terrific imagination, you know, just everything so colorful…"

I like your expression "fall into the illustrations," I commented, and Clara replied, "Oh, it's exactly what you do, but also she led us there. We left Guatemala in 1958 and went to live in Orlando, Florida. But my father kept going back because of the land, and he helped the president and the country a lot. After we moved, I went away to school in Massachusetts and I was having trouble reading, and really didn't know why, and glasses didn't work. We found out later on, when I was about 19, that I had an eye condition called Stargardts [Stargardts Maculopathy]. I had always dreamed of being an illustrator for children's books, and I thought 'Oh rats! Maybe now I won't be able to.'" At this point Clara laughed and then triumphantly related the next line in her conversation with herself about this genuinely disturbing development: "I said, 'No! I will be able to—I'm just going to *do* it!' So I did. I studied my favorite children's-book illustrators—Maurice Sendak, Arthur Wrackham, Andrew Wyeth, of course…and Beatrix Potter, top of the list—and I put them all in a big stew…and came out with my own style.

"To me, ink drawings and soft watercolors are dreamy. I've learned to put a little whitewash over the watercolor to try to soften it up, give it more of a thickness, a richness or whatever. It's a style I've kind of dabbled with." I told Clara that I love her animal illustrations precisely because they look tactile, as if they're coming "roundly" out of the page at you. That's exactly what this artist intends, and she seemed delighted that it came across that way. But clearly, she's not one to rest on her laurels. "I think you can never be quite satisfied with your art…you want to be happy doing it, but you also want to be not quite satisfied with it, so that you'll keep moving forward and make it grow and move through another door. I love illustrating, but I knew I needed to move, and I wanted to make it three-dimensional—that's why I started making yaks and full-size horses and big creatures. I think it was about ten years after beginning illustrating that I moved into that."

PART OF LIFE'S DEAL

It seems to me pretty challenging to paint illustrations with a major vision problem, and significantly more so in the case of designing and putting together and costuming huge animals, so I wanted to know more about that formidable venture. Do you mind talking about this? I asked, and her answer was immediate: "Oh, no." She's quite candid about her lack of vision and there's not a scintilla of self-pity in her attitude—quite the opposite. She said, "When I was 19 I was told that within a year, people wouldn't have faces any more, and I wouldn't be able to drive, or read. And I accepted all of this as part of life's process; it's part of life's deal—if you're handed something, you just work with it." But what a terrible blow that must have been, I said. "Well, but it was OK. The only thing I questioned was the illustrating—that was the thing I really wanted to be able to continue doing. And it's actually been a blessing in disguise. I use a magnifying lens on one eye and that has enabled me to do very close detail, where if I had good eyes, I might illustrate like a runaway train, and forget detail. You know the saying 'God is in the details'? I love that. So now the magnifying lens makes me slow down and I have to zone in really closely. If I'm illustrating a book, I do 19-by 21-inch illustrations, and then they shrink them down. But the blessing—because I think it all works for you, whether it's a handicap or a crisis or whatever—the blessing is that the poor vision has made my art. I've become more aggressive with it, sort of, and hungrier to make it move into another dimension. I think that's why I moved it from the illustrating into making three-dimensional things, where you can walk around them and look at them.

"For the time being," Clara said, "I've put illustrating on hold, because I'm moving into something else." And this movement hasn't simply halted at the creation of big critters—eventually that wasn't enough for Clara, who explained, "When I did big bears or horses or yaks, they were fun, but they weren't moving. So I thought, 'Well maybe if I try to make these things

Left—Miriam Osterhout Rosengarten, Clara's beautiful mother, an artist herself, taught her children to look through a window and see everything as a painting. Right—Clara's father, Frederic Rosengarten, was an avid music-lover; when he wasn't busy on his cardamom plantations, he played the piano every day and also wrote music.

constructive, what will that be? Well, furniture! So that's when they moved from standing form to sitting form…you can sit on them, and they can be part of your furniture." She laughed, exhilarated by even the telling of the permutations of her work. "So that was great for a while," she said, "and now I'm onto a whole new venture which I'm so happy about…now I'm doing costumes, animal costumes; people will get inside them."

At this point, Clara (who moves through her house with absolute assurance, making it difficult to realize how little she actually sees) got up and went to Emily, the splendidly dressed mouse, and showed me how a person will don the whole figure. "And this is something new I'm discovering with costumes—when you put this head on, it's heavy. The actor has to move with the head, and so the costume is almost telling the actor how to move more gracefully. The actors will have to move like this [she moved slowly, as if she were dancing], and it's almost like a dream state, the way you would dream it. So it's a curious thing regarding where all this is going. Who knows? That's what's fun about it!"

GETTING PEOPLE'S FEATHERS DOWN

It sounds to me as if you've never spent much time weeping and wailing about what happened to your vision, I said. Clara replied, "No—I've found it an interesting and very curious thing. You remember I told you my mother trained us to look at everything as a painting…for me it became almost became surreal, because when someone doesn't have a face that you can see, you listen more. You're sitting there in front of me, and you have no face, but I absolutely feel your energy, because I've become much more sensitive to my environment, more audio-centered. I listen more; if I hear in someone's voice that he or she might be sort of fragile that day, I'm careful to be more sensitive. Yet if I saw the way I did growing up, I might be more numb, not as sensitive to a person's voice. You see what I'm saying?" The phone rang, and Clara calmly walked to it, turned it off, and continued: "If someone's voice is tight, they may be anxious, and you want to try to bring them out more, let them feel they can put their feathers down and feel as though they're safe here. The voice is the door to the heart—it tells you exactly what's happening. So the vision problem has actually been a terrific present."

What a great image, being so sensitive you can induce a person to unruffle his or her feathers! And Clara confesses she loves feathers—they are present in almost every costume she makes, and they definitely add to that dreamlike movement of her large creatures. (Before I left, she presented me with a dramatic long red ostrich-feather boa, saying that she often does that for the kids who come to visit!)

Thanks to her mother's training, Clara was prepared not only to be an artist but to accept challenges and keep moving ahead. After discovering her eye condition, unable to attend RISD as she'd wanted because reading was impossible and her vision was deteriorating rapidly, she moved to Philadelphia, and "shortly afterward," she said, "I moved to Nantucket. That was in 1972." How did that happen? I asked. "I

La belle Clara, in an ostrich-feather hat of her own creation that looks alive.

Clara, with son Jason, in 1972.

Among her many other amazing accomplishments, Clara has helped build several churches, and here in Cabrera, in the Dominical Republic, she started a school; now she is the godmother of 1000 children there. 1998.

met and married a physician who was going to practice on the island, and we had a wonderful son, Jason. I'm very proud of him."

Although the marriage ended, Clara, who'd taken to the island instantly, knew she'd keep coming back. "I found that everything about this place held me…I was under a spell, no question. It was like a warm glove to me, and I could absolutely find my bearings everywhere. I found so many new friends; I was just crazy about living here. And I felt like I belonged, really. You know, every bird has its tree. I felt every day as if I were walking through a painting. The world here makes a lot of sense to me…it's always felt right. I've stayed here off and on for years."

Eventually, Clara said, she met Eric Urbahn. "On our first date he told me about his dream to sail around the world. Little did I know I'd be on that boat from 1990 to 1993!" Did you paint while you were sailing? I asked. "Yes. Eric designed me a wonderful studio below; there was enough space for a drafting board and I would hook myself up to a bungee cord because if there was a rogue wave or if the weather was rough, I'd be bouncing back a lot in my chair and I didn't want to end up in the head! I could work under way for days at a time, and I loved it! Eric is an architect, and taught me many things that helped me in my illustrating world."

But mostly, I said, you seem to have taught yourself—learned by doing. "I did," she said. "There is an absolute blessing in disguise in this, and if anyone is in my situation, I think that if you just follow your heart it'll teach you. I really love what I'm doing, and I'm very excited about these costumes…I can't wait to put the people in them! They're brand-new, a week old. No one's been in them. This one [pointing to a large red velvet cape with lots of feathers] is going to be a frog who's overweight, kind of vain and puffy, so I wanted to have a costume with a massive look. You want to see the conduct in the way the costume looks, because costumes can talk. Toulouse-L'Autrec, who is one of my favorites, loved feathers, and used them in most of his paintings. I think they 'talk.'" She moved to Emily the mouse. "These feathers, for instance, talk differently than the frog's, which are a bit aggressive—Emily's are shorter and softer, you see." Clara tilted her head and considered the tall mouse. "Emily definitely has some growing to do, as I guess all of us do."

KEEPING ART ALIVE

Poor Dudley was pining to come in out of the snow and join us, so Clara let him in and dried him in her lap with a towel while she continued to talk about her art. "The fun that keeps the magic of art going is that you never know what you're going to meet…you can have this idea and start off if it's on paper or doing a sculpture, but it's never going to look like what you originally started off with in your mind. That's what keeps it alive, that you never know what you're going to meet." I can in no way understand what you are seeing in the world, I said, except that I'm so very nearsighted that without my glasses I just see big blurry colors and shapes, and it's beautiful, like a painting that's been dissolved and softly diffused…but I'd like to know how else your vision affects the way you do your art. "When I illustrate," Clara said, "I do it in pieces like a puzzle. I don't see the illustration as a whole, I see it in pieces. And this is what's great in what the magnifying lens allows me to do. It draws me in, one inch from the paper, and I fall into the piece of the puzzle, into the graphic

Left—On their boat, the *Finback*, Clara and Eric Urbahn made a fabulous journey, circumnavigating the globe. They started in Nantucket; after rounding the Cape of Good Hope, they returned to the Faraway Isle two-and-a-half-years later. Right—For a number of years, children and adults alike have delighted in sitting in the laps of some of the creatures Clara has created. This one is an entirely nonfrightening bison.

detail…probably if I didn't have the magnifying lens or this vision, I wouldn't bother with the detail. So it's made me focus in on these little pieces. And also I try to practice that every day when I focus in on who I'm talking to, what I'm doing. That trains you spiritually, I think, just to focus in. The world can be chaotic, and there is a lot of stuff going on, and there are a lot of distractions, but if you just relax with whatever you're doing, everything you have to do will get done. In the old days I would manically put myself in 7th gear to get everything done; maybe I'd have gotten it all done by the end of the day, but I'd be exhausted, I wouldn't have enjoyed the moments that I had to go through for each little thing. When I focus now on what I'm doing, I realize that I'm enjoying that moment, and when I'm finished with it, then I'll go to the next thing, focus in on that and not worry about the hundred other things…"

I asked Clara how her life had changed since she first came to the island in the early '70s. She'd already spoken about the continuing and exciting evolution of her art, and I knew that the long marriage to Eric had ended. Again, her answer was quite reflective of her philosophy regarding her challenging life. "I think once again I have to go back to my eyes. They have been like a teacher to me, because they've made me focus in on really finding peace in myself. If I don't have that, I'll have a restlessness, and I won't feel a contentment with the world. My eyes have made me sit still, and be comfortable, and be peaceful. I've had to work with everything that they've offered me, and that's made me appreciate and be grateful for what I am able to do, and what I do in Nantucket. My vision made me slow down for obvious reasons, and it's made me just feel a oneness with everything, you know? And I don't feel aggressively hungry to go searching for beauty, because I have it all in my back yard."

I commented, "You're a tall, slender, and beautiful woman and the way you move and respond in no way suggests you're having any difficulty seeing—how do you let people know that you can't really see a lot?" Clara answered promptly. "Well, I don't use the word 'blindness,' which I did at first, because it can make people uncomfortable, so I just say 'I'm very nearsighted—I'm like Magoo.' [She laughed heartily.] When you do that, you don't even think about it yourself any more. If you focus too much on it, then you're distracted. And I forget most of the time that I even have this condition any more, so I guess I've finally sort of become one with it, and I'm glad for that, because through the years it's taught me so much, and…I'm glad I've caught up with it."

GOING AT FULL GALLOP

Don't think for a minute that Clara Urbahn stays in her beautiful, magical house all the time, inventing bewitching creatures to make. She very much lives on the island, enjoying walks on the beach, small social events, and even horseback riding. "I used to ride on the beach with Jillian Fleming, and she'd say, 'OK, Clara, there's nothing in front of us, *let's go!*' So we'd go at a full gallop down the beach. I couldn't see what was ahead of me, but I trusted Jillian…our horses would gallop along neck and neck, and the sand would be kicking up, and it was magnificent!" She paused, then said, "Another thing that interests me is my spiritual life; it is very important to me." Do you meditate? I asked. Her answer: "Yes I do; I pray, which is a form of meditation, and I think even in your art you're meditating. I believe in prayer; it gives you a sense of peace. I believe in the divine, and I think that everyone is here to become friends with it. And then you're always coming from love, not fear, I find. There's something about having reverence for something outside yourself. It brings you into God-centeredness instead of self-centeredness. And if you practice that, you're more apt to be thinking of the other person, or thinking of how you can help a situation, or what you can do to make this a positive situation, or if you have a problem how you can fix it. In meditational prayer you always end up with the answer—it comes to you."

In Clara Urbahn's philosophy of life a vital element is to keep moving forward without fear; this means trying new things, growing, and always being ready to go through another door. That's her outlook—a good word, I suggested, for her in particular. "Yes," she said. "My outlook has come from looking in and bringing it back out again with art. The art really became my medium in relating to many things. It is very comforting, and it is also terrific to be able to create. I think art is love in whatever we do, whether it's writing or music or something else, and if you're able to share that, you're sharing love. And the icing on the cake is when you can make that love or that art serve others. That's really wonderful, if you can move it to that, I think. So it works all the way around."

I'm so glad I didn't stay at home on that snowy Nantucket day. It was hard to leave all those beautiful and fascinating creatures, which included their most magical creator. Clara Urbahn had led me right into the painting that is her life, and it was a very worthwhile journey.

Don't think that a serious visual impairment is going to stop this adventurous woman; she often took the wheel of the *Finback* during the trip she and Eric Urbahn took in 1990–1993. Here she is, sailing toward Africa.

Always Moving Forward
Donald Noyes & Yoshi Mabuchi, 2000

They came around Brant Point in 1992, but it didn't take them long to get involved in island life and acquire a "family of friends" here. And, given their successful ventures on the island, it's not surprising that they quickly decided Nantucket was home. Donald Noyes (author and playwright) and Yoshi Mabuchi (restaurateur) soon translated a beginning oriented toward mere economic survival into a permanence marked by their purchase of a house, the opening of a popular downtown restaurant, and production of an exuberant musical drama centering on the Great Fire of 1846.

Don and Yoshi seem to be opposites: one somewhat shy, quiet, and slight; the other gregarious, forthcoming, and, well, altogether different in physique. But they are a committed couple and have been for almost a quarter of a century.

THE WORLD WAS ON FIRE

Ever reticent in talking about his beginnings, all Yoshi would say at first was, "I was born in Tokyo more than fifty years ago, during the war—1943. But this is not important." Don asserted that it was of legitimate interest to readers and filled in the details: "Yoshi was born during a firebombing in Tokyo. His mother actually had to take up the floorboards of the house and crawl underneath into the sewer for protection, and she gave birth to Yoshi there, with no one to help her. Alone." Yoshi added, "The house was on fire...she cannot run away. We survived; but our house caught on fire three times"; that was during the constant firebombings that took place during those terrible years. When Yoshi was born, his mother's other children had already been evacuated from the city. Don explained: "In Tokyo and all the big cities in Japan, all the men were conscripted into the service or factory work. And all the children over five were evacuated to the mountains by the schools and the Red Cross. So Tokyo was left to women and babies. That's why Yoshi's older brothers and sisters were not with their mother. And by the time the war was over and the children were brought back by the Red Cross, his siblings were teenagers, and Yoshi was a baby, so he never really knew them. As a result, Yoshi didn't grow up like most people do with sisters and brothers, because they came back home and were going on adults, and he was a small child. And then they married when Yoshi was still very young."

Your mother must have been quite a woman, I said to Yoshi. He nodded, and there was a silence. Don said, "She was a very brave woman; she was actually honored when she died, in about 1990, for staying in Tokyo during the firebombing, which ruined more of Tokyo than the atom bomb ruined Hiroshima. Here's a story for you: Yoshi's father died of burns from the war years—he had been in the Army. When he died, Yoshi's mother had nothing. She was told she could collect her insurance money from his death, but to do this she had to go to another part of the city. Now, Tokyo is a very spread-out city, not like New York. When the buses were finally running again, she went by bus across town, which took all day—the city was in ruins—and got to where they were giving out the disbursements. And because of how much the money had devalued because of the war, she got exactly the amount that it had cost her to take the bus. She told me—in translation, of course—that it was the only time she cried. She didn't get enough to even buy food—she got enough just to get back home again. Those were bad years in Tokyo—cold winters, and hardly any food. She would beg chocolate bars and trade them for rice. She was an amazing woman. She had gone through the Tokyo earthquake in 1923; I think her first husband was killed in that...the older brother and sisters were children of that marriage. And then she had to suffer the war years...she told me, "Governments make wars, Mr. Noyes—we people only suffer. But we go on, don't we? We have to go on." She was, like all Japanese women, petite and feminine, but a survivor. All her daughters had proper dowries when they got married, and she got Yoshi to college. I don't know how she did it." Yoshi nodded in agreement, and said, "I was first one in family to go to university." And Don said, "She loved Kabuki Theatre…much as my mother loved Shakespeare."

It must have been a very difficult life, growing up in a city that had been burnt practically to the ground, and under occupation…but Yoshi plainly didn't want to talk about the privations. I asked if he'd ever dreamed he would end up living in the United States, and he said, "Yes, dreamed, because at that time the school was under the American system…they were changing the educational system over. I went to high school in Tokyo, and then I went to Tokyo Science University and received a degree in mathematics. After college, I worked in a big company, using my math background…" Don added, "He worked for Miura Publishing Company, which did expensive coffee-table books, and Yoshi was the lead salesman for them."

Don mused: "Yoshi's mother survived a war; my mother, Harriet MacCormack Noyes, survived something perhaps not as horrible but nevertheless devastating to a seven-year-old child: physical and emotional abandonment. But, like Yoshi's mother, she never became bitter. And although she has been gone for several years, I still reach for the phone to tell her when something important has happened to me. A Buddhist priest once told me that before we are born, we choose who will be our parents. If that is the case, both Yoshi and I chose well."

SHOES ON THE MENU

At what point did Yoshi become interested in the restaurant business? It turns out that happened as a direct result of his passion for traveling. Yoshi explained that ultimately he quit his job: "I wanted to see all the world; I went to eighty countries." Don added, "He would get a job in Norway as cook or dishwasher and support himself, or go to Turkey or Africa or South America, finding jobs, usually in restaurants. He was actually caught in a blizzard in South America once, where they ended up eating their shoes! In Russia he was followed by the Secret Police. He'd get a job, support himself, everywhere he was, and that's where he learned about the world and restaurants." Finally, "the money was out…no money," Yoshi laughed, "so I came to United States to work, in 1976. And ended up here, in Nantucket. I was first in New York City, working mostly in restaurants. Because of my language, my experience, you know."

Don chimed in: "Another of the reasons Yoshi left Japan was that it is a very regimented society, and it's a married society. Family is first. So there's no 'single culture' in Japan like we have. Yosh wanted to escape some of that regimentation and see the world. Anyway, when he landed in New York he wanted to stay in this country, and I wanted to have my own business, so we were both leaning toward the restaurant life. For a while I worked in New York, in the offices of the Graduate School at Columbia University. One of my jobs was to do the entertaining for the Dean's wife—I'd have to contact a caterer for a wine and cheese party, or a party for the British Ambassador, or whatever, and so I got familiar with table settings, caterers, foods, menus…and I did Meals on Wheels in New Haven, so I really had a hand in the food business. And Yoshi learned how to do sushi in New York."

Don said that he was born and raised in New Haven, Connecticut, along with three brothers and one sister. "I went to Teacher's College in southern Connecticut," he said. How did you two meet? I asked. "He picked me up—literally," said Don, deadpan. "I was doing social work at that time, and involved in the theatre a bit, off and on. A friend of mine who lived on West 76th Street had a party and invited me…she was getting engaged. When I left the party it was snowing, and I tripped going down the slippery stairs. Yoshi had arrived the day before in New York and was walking by, and when I stumbled in the snow, he held me up and helped me get my balance. He spoke a little English, so then we went to have coffee and got talking. My father was sick at that time, so I had to go back to New Haven, and then I came to New York again and later Yoshi visited Connecticut. And then he moved to New Haven and we opened a restaurant, which we ran for twelve years there. There was no Japanese restaurant in that whole eastern section of Connecticut then, and Hatsune really took off. Hatsune actually was Yoshi's mother's name."

LOSING & FINDING

I knew that Hatsune had been an award-winning restaurant, and asked why they hadn't stayed in New Haven, where the theatre, which is decidedly Don's cup of tea, is active. He explained: "When New Haven became a drug and crime city overnight during the recession, we lost everything—our restaurant and our house. No one would come to downtown New Haven any more. Thirty restaurants, including ours, closed in downtown…that was in the early '80s." What made you decide to come to Nantucket? I asked. "Well," Don said, "someone we knew on the island told us there was no sushi here, which was strange, because people who come to Nantucket are educated, have money, and travel—and those are the people who eat sushi. So we moved here in 1992, and in the first year we cleaned houses and saved our money, and then we were fortunate and got the lease for our location on East Chestnut for Sushi by Yoshi. We opened the restaurant in 1993, and it was an immediate hit."

144   When you came to the island, I asked Yoshi, did you have any idea that you'd stay? He answered with a smile: "No, we just came here for survival." And they survived very well indeed. Yoshi opened up another Japanese restaurant in Hyannis and, in 1997, started Tokyo Tapas on the island; both restaurants were eventually sold. Don said, "We sold the Hyannis restaurant to get the down payment for our house here. We consider Nantucket our home…and when we came here, we were just looking to make a living. We're staunch communicants of St. Paul's Church…active in our church and the theatre and the business community. Yoshi does a lot of charities for the business community—we contribute to AIDS, the church, and Food Pantry. We took advantage of them the first year and in the second year when we opened the restaurant, we gave them $500. We had said we'd pay back, and the guy said, 'No, that's not how it works,' but we did and we do every year."

Do you plan to travel back to Japan? I asked. Yoshi answered, "Yes—for a long time I couldn't afford it, but now I'm thinking about going sometime." Don agreed that there was a possibility they'd A there for a vacation someday, adding that Yoshi hasn't seen his family for a very long time. There's never been much opportunity to establish a closeness with his siblings because of their difference in ages and the way the war separated the family, but it would, Yoshi said, be nice to see them again. Everyone needs family. So it must have been wonderful for Yoshi, robbed of a conventional childhood and family by a war, to have been able to adopt and be adopted by a large, extended group of relatives. Yoshi agreed with a wide smile. "We're very family-oriented, actually," said Don, "and Yoshi's been Uncle Yoshi in my family for almost a quarter of a century. He's known the nieces and nephews since they were five and six years old. He's godfather to half of them …and we have great-nieces and -nephews now. Yoshi's just part of the family, and has been from day one."

Don's idea of relaxing is to write, and he always has some project cooking—literally, since the desk where he does a lot of writing (all in longhand, mind you) is in the kitchen, where both Don and Yoshi are very much at home. A social get-together of any kind at their house involves great food, and it's not all sushi, either. Both, by the way, were involved in the production of *Faraway Land*, Yoshi as one of the producers, Don writing the book and the lyrics. "It was his idea," Don says, also giving his partner credit for being a candid and helpful "in-house reviewer" of everything he writes.

Yoshi is a superb gardener and a professional-calibre carpenter, as evidenced by carpeting, floors, decorations, and floors in their house as well as a beautifully decorated sushi bar. Both read voraciously, Yoshi ordering books in Japanese regularly via Boston and New York. Sometimes they read the same book in both languages, but Donald says it was too late for him to learn Japanese by the time he and Yoshi became partners.

As with most islanders, adoptees and long-timers and natives alike, Nantucket represents the best of all worlds to these two. It's a community, they say, that has become both home and family. They appreciate the changes that have occurred over the years, seasoned by perhaps a little more than your ordinary trials and tribulations, and they subscribe wholeheartedly to Yoshi's life philosophy. Don puts it this way: "I tend to sit and ponder past events…what did we do right or wrong, what can we do about it? Yosh has the right idea though; he says, 'Forget it—go forward.'" Yoshi added, "Yes, live now…do what I can do; the past I can't change." And I thought that a phrase I'd read recently fit this couple very well: "Every wind brings change, chance renewed." Sort of the spirit of the faraway land which they have made their home.

Left—Yoshi Mabuchi and Donald Noyes. Photo by Mara Lavitt. Right—Yoshi Mabuchi at age 17.

146

An Extraordinary Man

Donold King Lourie, 2000

Although the interview started out ordinarily enough, it soon became apparent that there is nothing commonplace about Donold Lourie. A good sample of his humor is the explanation he gave me for the unusual spelling of his first name (Donold, not Donald). "Two reasons for two O's," he said. "Dad said 'oh-oh' when he first saw me. Mother couldn't spell."

Don was born in Evanston, Illinois, went to public school in Winnetka, spent two years at New Trier High School, and then graduated with honors from Phillips Exeter in New Hampshire. But he didn't pass Go and proceed directly to college. "In late 1943, I was in the Army Air Corps," he said, "where I learned, and then taught, electronics. After that, I was a buck sergeant, had six or seven B-29s to look after, and was on the way to Japan when the war ended with two Big Bombs—dropped from B-29s, I believe. Not mine. It wasn't until 1946 that I started at Princeton, graduating in 1950. I was in the Woodrow Wilson School of Public and International Affairs, but they allowed a lot of flexibility with other courses, so I took a lot of things like philosophy, and had a minor in English, which was what I was really interested in. Then I went to the University of Michigan Law School, graduating with a JD in '52. I looked around and got a job as an Associate at Debevoise & Plimpton, a law firm with about 32 lawyers then…today there are over 400. But I didn't stay there long—in about 1956, I went with the St. Joseph Lead Company, which later became St. Joe Minerals. It had mines in Canada, Argentina, Peru, and Missouri, this country's Lead Belt. I was Secretary and Vice President of that company for eight or nine years, and did mostly legal and administrative work."

MYSTERY & LOVE STORY

148

Donold called upon his first-hand perceptions of the mining industry and the big, bad corporate world to write a novel called *Dark Rainbow*, centering on that industry. He describes it as "both mystery and love story," in which "a conglomerate's purchase of the Rainbow reserve, believed to contain rich silver deposits, raises questions of fraud and murder." The story, he explained, shifts from Missouri mines to Cro-Magnon caves to Manhattan skyscrapers in an exploration of the impact of money and power on integrity and love.

Eventually, Donold Lourie left St. Joe, having been "head-hunted" by Citibank, one of the largest commercial banks in the world. "That was a completely different kind of job: operations," he said. "As Senior Vice President, I had responsibility for all the back-office functions of the bank—record-keeping, check-processing, and the like. It was a bit like being in the hold of a ship, where everything that makes it work is underneath. I stayed at Citibank until 1967, when I left to start a computer software company—Bradford Computer & Systems, which later became Bradford National Corporation. Four of us started that, and it grew quite large, from four to over 4,000 employees and revenues of $200 million. I think in all we raised over $50 million in sales of stock and it wasn't quite as easy as it is now.

"During its development, I went up to Columbia University to get a Masters of Fine Arts degree. I'd been writing all along—poems and short stories—and was also taking courses in French and Italian literature. I tried to balance off my writing with that seed-venture capital company. Eventually I just had had enough of business, and was making enough money so that I thought I could leave the computer company and really do nothing but write. The only things I had published then were some translations of Italian poetry into English.

"Getting the MFA degree took quite a while, because I had to work at the computer firm and by then my eyesight was declining. But finally I left the computer business behind. Before graduation, however, I was asked to get involved with a man who had a cartilage product that appeared to stimulate the immune system in such a way as to make it possible to hold back some very serious diseases, among them cancer. I didn't want to go back into business but needed money, and I thought it was a worthwhile endeavor. That was the second seed venture company I got into. We raised over $15 million for the pharmaceutical research company. And I was taking courses in painting, English literature, and sculpture, but my real interest all along was writing. I wrote a novel called *The Chocolate Rabbit* for my MFA at Columbia. It takes place during wartime, and the protagonists are two men who later go into law and business—in a way it's somewhat like *Dark Rainbow,* involving corporate conspiracies, greed, and so on. I've never tried very hard to publish it. After that period, I wrote *Dark Rainbow*—I seem to take about ten years for each one I write. Meanwhile, I was writing lots of short stories and poems."

The Terrific Selma

So…Don works on yet another degree and decides he wants to do nothing but write. What happens then? "Well," he replied, "in some recent writing I refer to the '70s as a time of anguish and decision. My vision was getting worse; my marriage was failing; I had left my business and my associates there, and life was full of difficulties." Those difficulties led to an exploration of what he described as his "rather stoic, almost cavalier reaction" to his failing eyesight. "I can remember weeping only once," he said. Meanwhile, in the process of working on *The Chocolate Rabbit,* it had become clear that he needed someone to take dictation and type the manuscript. "For a while," he said, "I'd used stronger and stronger glasses, then hand-held magnifiers, then large electronic magnification screens…but my eyesight continued to decline. I couldn't even see what I'd typed on big TV-like screens. So I looked around for someone to help me." This is when bright and beautiful Selma Rayfiel came into the picture. Don said, "Selma had been working for Farrar Straus as an assistant editor but had left to do her own writing. She needed to earn some money, though, and was doing proofreading, but it wasn't enough. The editor she'd worked with got us together, and she was terrific!" He laughed. "She was so terrific I married her…but not right away. We met in 1980, and were married in '88. Now she's working on a mystery—she doesn't tell me very much about it, though she has read parts of it to me. But she did a tremendous amount of work on *The Chocolate Rabbit* and also on *Dark Rainbow* and things I've written since."

Before describing what you're working on now, I said, would you mind very much talking more about your loss of vision, which is now total, and what you've done about it? I knew that for some time Donald had given talks to partially sighted people, under the aegis of his Vision and Company. "In about 1970," he answered, "thirty years ago, I had begun to notice some funny things. At that time I was still with the venture capital company, and my partners and I were making calls like mad on people to try to drum up business. One day I went to the elevator after one of these calls and started pressing the button…but it wasn't there. I'd missed it by about 5 inches. That was really the first indication that my eyes were getting worse. The doctor examined me and said that my macular degeneration had worsened. There are two kinds: the dry kind, in which you get older and the corpuscles just don't feed enough blood into the retina; and the wet kind, which I have, in which too much blood is fed in. Today there are laser treatments that can seal off the leaking vessels before blood gets into the retina, but the technology wasn't nearly as good in the 1970s. So not much was done about my condition and it got slowly worse. I went from magnification with big lenses and lights to electronic magnification, to voice, which I do all the time now. It's rather ironic—I hope not symbolic," he laughed, "that I've never 'read' either of my two novels. Now my eyesight is completely gone, and I don't lecture as often as I did. I travel to life-care centers and try to explain, mostly to older people, how to get through the day as a practical matter. Most people didn't really know about talking watches, talking typewriters, how to use certain kinds of magnification lamps and computers, how to label their clothes, comb their hair, put toothpaste on a brush, cook, find the food on their plates, and so forth. They were amazed. The trouble is, as you grow older, you have less energy and willpower to get over the loss of vision…and it's very hard to get people going again. They lose their self-esteem, their independence when they can't see. My lectures focus on practical things and as much humor as I can muster, and I think I do some good."

A Different Kind of Vision

When I first met Selma and Donold, he could still see a bit "around the edges," and was always so skilled and graceful about his vision problems that people could scarcely believe he wasn't really seeing much. He used to say things like, "Oh, your earrings are so pretty—I can see them sparkling and swinging," and "Your dress is wonderful…you look so well in those swirling colors." And he got around mostly by himself: took taxis or was driven to town, where he stepped surely and quickly, getting where he needed to go without fuss or fall, and most often alone. He swam and walked regularly—still does—and in a dinner or party conversation, he looked right at you—still does—and the fact that he had a serious vision shortcoming was hard to believe. Donold "saw" and still "sees" whomever he's talking with, in perhaps a fuller, more engaged way, than most sighted people. This man connects beautifully.

Years ago, I received a call asking if I'd be willing to type up a manuscript, a memoir by Donold's mother of her growing-up years on a farm in Illinois. Don eventually published the journal for members of his family, and it contained so many well-articulated and educational references to a country life of the past that it now resides in the Illinois State Historical Society annals. Selma and Donold brought me the manuscript (she was so busy with her own writing that Don elected to get outside help for the keyboarding), and it was a charmer. So was he. Twirling his white hair up into twists as he talked passionately about whatever, an open smile well-creased into a face that knows how to welcome response and ideas, he made it almost impossible to believe he could hardly see. An exciting conversationalist and a superb listener, too. Selma, never in the least patronizing or oversolicitous of her independent and fast-moving husband, is one of the brightest people you'll ever meet, even though usually somewhat reserved "out in the world."

Donold's father, who died in 1990 (his mother died in 1994), was an active man himself. "He was Undersecretary of State during the first two years of the Eisenhower administration," Donold said.

Left—When he spent summers at his grandmother's home in Illinois, Donold had to feed the chickens—a task he claims he hated. Right—Donold Lourie in his first days in the U.S. Army Air Corps in 1943.

"The Secretary of State was John Foster Dulles. Dulles wanted to get the State Department down to a smaller size and Dad helped with that reorganization. He did lots of traveling, but the hardest part for him was that he had to take temporary leave as President of the Quaker Oats Company. He was also the Senior Warden of his church in Winnetka. And he was an All-American football player at Princeton, and later won the National Football Hall of Fame gold medal. He was an interesting man—not at all literary, just a wonderful person to get people working together. While not a high-powered, strong-minded leader like Sherman in *Dark Rainbow* [a man you love to hate as the book goes on], he was awfully good at what he did and people liked him. He started as a salesman at Quaker Oats, and went up rapidly. Mother grew up in Lincoln, Illinois, on a farm, and fell in love with my father when he was the football hero at Princeton…that was in 1921, and they married in 1922."

THE NEW BOOK

There were two Lourie daughters—Nancy, who lives in Steamboat Springs, Colorado, and Anne, who died at the age of 42. Anne is the subject of a book Donold has almost completed. "It's a very sad story," he said. "Annie died, whether accidentally or on purpose, of an overdose of pharmaceuticals, in 1972. She had a terrible disease, eczema, and was sent away from home to Tucson for its climate when she was quite young. I was about nine then, and remember how tragic this was. The condition was a terrible torture for her; she used to claw at herself, and had awful scars. Our parents had tried everything available then: salves, baths, gloves, hands tied to her bed, quack remedies. It's a terrible, sad story. And there is still little that works for that disease. In her twenties, she took massive amounts of cortisone and was, of course, not happy; ultimately she became an alcoholic. She did become a good member of AA, and helped many others, but then got hooked on prescription drugs. Selma is working on the last draft of this book now, copy-editing and proof-reading. It's very close to being done." [Published in 2003, the book is entitled *Postponements: Memories of My Sister.*]

In the book, Donold tells of the impact Annie had on his life, "from my ability to feel more intensely to my petty dislike of salves and lotions…." One beneficial effect he mentions is a sense of gratification, of completion as he searched in the difficult 1970s for a fulfilled writing and personal life. "Annie," he recalls, "would often hold up her arm so that a patch of burning skin could cool down. Sometimes she would blow on the tormenting patch. Air is what the pangs of guilt and anger need, not festering containment." Was his stoicism about the "thickening fog" that his vision experienced, he wonders, "because the fog seemed, still seems, so much less terrible than the growing effects of Annie's disease?"

NEXT…

What's in the works next for this man who doesn't let anything stop him? "I have a choice of going back to work on *The Chocolate Rabbit*…or I could look at the short stories and get them published—they're pretty good—and maybe some more poetry." With the help of Selma and his "talking computer," Don will continue writing, as he's always wanted to do. He says, "Now I use a computer whose operating system is Windows, but I don't use the mouse or turn the screen on. The method is based on a screen reader built by a company in Florida…it tells me everything that's written, and with it I can search the web, scan letters or books, which are read to me by the voice. The voice can be modified, be male or female, be made faster or slower, as you want. The voice was terrible at the beginning, but sounds much more human now than in the old days…it'll spell words out for you, tell you what the punctuation is, where you are on the page. It's quite wonderful."

Never one to rest on his scholarly laurels, Donold hasn't let his vision problems stop him from accumulating more knowledge. He's learning Braille, and since 1990 he has gone regularly—alone—off-island and into Cambridge to take courses in European and French history, and full-time courses at the Harvard Extension School in such subjects as Victorian and Romantic poetry and literary criticism. "I'm just addicted to learning and to trying to get more information into my peanut brain," he said, laughing. At the time of this interview, Don had just completed a year as Chair of the Atheneum's Strategic Planning Committee, developing a five-year plan for that great institution, so for a while his Cambridge classes and his writing have slowed down. But you can't stop this man!

LIVING IN THE ATLANTIC HOUSE

Before I let him escape back to his talking computer, I asked Donold how he had discovered Nantucket. "A friend of mine at the law firm told me about the island, and subsequently I rented a house on the 'Sconset bluff in 1967, and in '68 I bought the house we're in now. It was built in 1848 as a hotel, the Atlantic House, and people would come out from town on the little train and get off down by the water, and then come up here in horse-carts. In the '20s they picked the whole structure up and turned it around a quarter-turn, so that it faced south rather than east. Sometime around the turn of the century it became a dancing school in the summers...can't you just picture the little girls dancing out on the lawn, much to the amusement of neighbors?" Anyone who's been fortunate enough to have attended one of Donold and Selma's traditional early-May tea dances knows about that beautiful yard and the generous ballroom. "That event started out as just a 'Sconset affair," Donold said, "as a way to celebrate spring, get people out of their houses, something a bit different from a cocktail party. We started with loudspeakers and records, then asked a few people from town, added an orchestra...it's sort of a way to pay people back, because we don't do too much socializing."

Don still walks and swims a lot, and often alone. "I tell my kids [Peter, a writer and teacher, and twin James, a teacher; and Anne, a remedial reading teacher, Samantha, a chef, and Catherine, an advertising executive] that Selma ties a rope to a tree and to me, and then I can't possibly go out too far...but the truth is that now she usually hovers around me. If not, I come out of the water and can't find my

Left—Don Lourie in his corporate days. Right—Donold Lourie enjoying the Dolomites in Italy.

own things, and I go straight to someone else's towel." He chuckled: "Sometimes there's a beautiful woman lying on it. Some surprises are good." Good heavens, you are the eternal optimist, I said. "Well, I do have my moments, but I like life too much to get down too far," he countered.

The island, particularly 'Sconset, does something for Donold, he says, that no place else on the earth can do…and he's traveled extensively. "There's just a wonderful atmosphere—it's so peaceful out here, and even in summer the hectic pace hasn't come to 'Sconset. I particularly like the island in the fall, winter, and spring…there's a special solitude here…you can hear the rip tides, the waves. Selma and I walk every day, and I walk alone, too. I know the roads very well, and of course that's another reason for me to live here. I can even navigate at night. I'd like to stay here, and die here; it's home to me. I've been here for 32 years now, in this house, and just can't imagine going anyplace else."

Nantucket is fortunate to have the talented Louries as residents. As the old Nantucketers used to say, they're the "finest kind."

154

A Prima Ballerina in Our Midst

Michele Poupon, 1997

Anyone who has lived on Nantucket for more than a few months is aware that many of the people one sees in the coffee shop, at the grocery store, in the line at the post office, or atop a ladder leaning on a building may have led an entirely different life before their arrival on the Faraway Isle. For a lot of people, Nantucket is the "home of the heart" and represents a significant life choice. Michèle Poupon is a good example of someone who pulled up her roots and replanted them here. Her parents, Paulette and Charly Allemand, had done the same, long before Michèle concluded her career as a prima ballerina in Europe.

I visited Michèle in early April at her home in a wonderfully secluded area in which the birds were loudly heralding springtime. She walked me around the property, in which one garden after another appeared at the end of a path cut through the vegetation. An enthusiastic gardener, Michèle has protected all her cultivated patches of land from rabbits and deer with wire and screening. There were rosebushes just breathing the warm air and beginning to expand, leaves ready to burst into welcome green; two types of raspberries, currants, and even a large area with infant and adolescent apple trees, under which Michèle was planting vegetables, making use of every inch of protected space. Daffodils stood here and there, their yellow blooms just about ready to explode, and unprotected by mesh or wire since for some reason they don't attract the rabbits and deer. One cleared circle at the culmination of a path revealed the small observatory Michèle's father Charly had recently built.

The outside graciously flowed inside, where sunlight and growing things also abounded. There was a huge vase of forsythia, forced into bloom to honor the recent birthday of Michèle's mother, Paulette, in the dining room. Everything, from the artwork on the walls to the collection of objects in a large print tray, to the many tiny lights suspended from wire "bridges" overhead, to the classical music that was playing on the stereo—everything said, "An artistic soul lives here."

WE WERE OH, SO HAPPY

We sat and talked about Michèle's life before Nantucket, and a fascinating story it was, told in a charming French accent and punctuated by gestures of the hands and arms that made it clear that although she is retired, Michèle is still very much a dancer. Ballet began for her when she was seven years old. "I was a sickly child," she said, "but with a lot of energy, and the doctor didn't know quite what to do. So he suggested to my parents that I try some classical ballet, and see what happens. My grandmother, who had a friend involved in the theater, arranged everything. She and the friend took me to a matinée to see a ballet performed by a group whose ballet master and choreographer was Boris Pilato, who was to become an important person in my life. After that I met the prima ballerina, who was Pilato's wife, and she invited me into her dressing room. She spoke only German and I spoke only French, but somehow she showed me how to do some ballet movements. She thought I had ability, and I soon became her pupil—and the very first student for Pilato's ballet company.

"We were oh, so happy," Michèle continued. "After I had been studying for about six months, Boris Pilato wanted to do the ballet *Coppelia,* which has all those puppets in the second act. He asked his wife, 'How is your little French girl doing?' and she said, 'Michèle is very talented; why not come and see her for yourself?' I remember that moment as if it were yesterday. I was on the barre, exercising, and it was like somebody put ice-cold water over me. I just couldn't do anything right; I seemed to have two left feet, and nothing worked. But I worked after that with my teacher and everything became OK and I began to perform with his group. More and more students came, and a few months later, three of us danced the three little swans in *Swan Lake.*"

By then, said Michèle, she couldn't imagine doing anything else than ballet. But it was difficult to handle odd-hours rehearsals and go to public school, which rather frowned upon absences, even of a promising ballet student. So the decision was made to send her to private school that could accommodate both rehearsals and regular classes. All this took place in Bienne, homeland of her parents and a French-speaking area of Switzerland. However, Pilato eventually decided to take most of his troupe to Bonn, Germany. "He was very sad to leave me in Bienne," said Michèle. "Oh, such a big story there, but to make it short, he finally found a way for me to live there with a family with four daughters. It was great for me because I was an only child, and suddenly I had four friends to live with. My mother and father stayed in Switzerland. This was a big sacrifice, but my mother let me do it because she understood that I loved the ballet and that was the only thing to do. She really is a wonderful lady. Our relationship has always been so beautiful, and she has always seen me as a friend. And this friendship is still there."

So at age 13 it was off to Bonn, birthplace of Ludwig von Beethoven. There, Michèle made friends with a young girl from Cologne who shared her enthusiasm and talent for ballet. "We were the two youngest girls," said Michèle, "and we grow up and we get better, always in the first row, you know, and they called us 'water drops,' because we worked to be like one in the movements. We heard the music the same way, which is important, so you don't have to look at each other, you just follow the music...and you work like water drops." Soon the girls were joining the troupe in its travels to distant cities, such as Barcelona, to perform in operas and ballet. "It was there we met Placido Domingo, who is my favorite singer, performing the opera *Tannhäuser.* It was a very demanding life, but I loved it," said Michèle.

Michèle Poupon with her partner, dancing Stravinsky's *Firebird Suite* in Essen, Germany

Michèle Poupon in the role of Cinderella when she was prima ballerina in the Boris Pilato Company in Europe.

In time Pilato's ballet troupe moved permanently to Essen, Germany, where it gained critical acclaim, and in 1964 the beautiful dancer was named prima ballerina, in spite of being from another country. "This is a title of honor," Michèle explained. "It is like 'Sir'—when you have been named prima ballerina, no one can ever take that away from you. That was a really big day, but…you won't believe it. Instead to be happy I start to cry, because I think now the joy and the freedom to dance is all over. Now everyone will look at me with a magnifier." Fortunately, she said, that didn't occur and dancing did not become a job instead of a thing of joy. She remained with Pilato for the remainder of her career. "We were such a good team, and we were like a family," she said. "And it was wonderful—he has so much knowledge and imagination and is such a musician, he could do everything with nothing."

In her career, Michèle Poupon performed in many operas and ballets, including several, she said with a laugh, in which she dies. "I danced the part of Ophelia in *Hamlet,* and I died in that, of course. Also, in *Romeo and Juliet* I died." Other performances in which she survived included Françaix's *Les Demoiselles de la Nuit,* Adolphe Adam's *Giselle,* Bartók's *Music for Strings, Percussion, and Celeste,* Stravinsky's *Firebird Suite* and *Rites of Spring,* and many, many more, all choreographed by Boris Pilato.

Michèle Poupon seems to be one of those rare and fortunate people who adore what they do, yet are able to let go of that career when the time is right, to proceed to the next stage of living. "I danced 34 years of my life," she said, "and stopped dancing in 1981. That was a hard decision, but Boris Pilato retired, and I saw that it was the time for me to stop also. I couldn't imagine dancing with anyone else. Working together in the ballet is very *intime,* and you don't have to make much talk. You understand each other and it goes just so, you know? After I stopped dancing I first thought to teach—I had moved to Zurich—but then I decided I wouldn't. So I started to do needlework, a lot of embroideries, you know, and enjoy nature and do gardening—all the things I never had the time for before. Oh, the time goes by fast, fast, fast."

Meanwhile, Michèle's parents, Paulette and Charly Allemand, had moved in the early '60s to America—first to Newtonville and then to the quiet little island of Nantucket. And in 1989, Michèle followed, moving into a house she had never seen but that her parents said she'd love. And that has proved to be a very happy move for the whole family. With her parents close by, the relationship has remained remarkably close. "My mother and I, in some ways, are very different," she commented, "but in many ways we are so alike, especially in the arts." Since she has been on the island, her well-known mother, Paulette, has been teaching theory, coaching instrumentalists, giving vocal and piano lessons and recitals, and casting her positive influence on all aspects of the activities of the Nantucket Chamber Music Society, in which she has figured importantly.

A few years ago Paulette, with Peggy Krewson (another prominent teacher, choral director, and performer on the island), decided to do a performance of Grand Opera choruses—an ambitious and successful undertaking for all those involved. They enlisted the help of Michèle for the necessary choreography for the Polyvetsian dances, and she proved to be very much up to the challenge. She had only two professional dancers, for the lead dance roles, and had to help select and work with a group of about sixteen volunteer ballet dancers, none of whom had had much or any experience—but who definitely had enthusiasm. That took a bit of bravery, I suggested. "Oh, but they were very brave too," Michèle replied. "And they were very nice, because at that time my English was not so good. I saw that they were really happy to do this, and with such good will." However, at first blush it seemed impossible that anyone could make almost immediate dancers out of amateurs. Said Michèle, "I looked at my mother, and I saw Peggy, and we were all thinking, 'Oh my God!' They were thinking, 'What will she do with them?', but I got started. In Europe when you are a dancer, you know, there is very much respect and you are quiet and observing, and you take it very seriously, are very committed." And, she went on, here on the island of Nantucket a few short weeks from a public performance is this group of people, laughing and talking and not taking things too seriously. They were, after all, doing it for fun. "So," Michèle continued, "I was tough with them sometimes, but they were not at all resentful. They realized what they had to do. And they were happy, too, with the costumes, which my mother and I had made. So it got better and better."

Prima Ballerina But Never Prima Donna

The next time she was enlisted by her mother and Peggy Krewson was for a performance of parts of Verdi's *Aïda.* (These women are famous for attempting what others think is impossible and doing it, enriching the musical lives of performers and audiences alike.) In this instance there was bona fide trauma involved. In Michèle's words, "Before the second performance, Peggy came in and said, 'Guess what? We have no Aïda.' Greta Feeney, who had the lead role, had been taken ill. We had to do something! Well, Peggy sang the part and I mimed the words and did the actions." Michèle, luckily, had had experience with saving the day. "Even when you are prima ballerina it's OK—I will not lose something from my crown, how do you say it, if I dance one scene in the group when there is a need. I did that often, and I did like it. But I must tell you, it's more difficult to get back in the chorus than to get out. Because once you are prima ballerina, you have all the freedom to dance by yourself, and you have the whole room [here she stretched out her arms in a wide ballet pose], but in the chorus you have to look now for the arms, so you don't bump people, and you must be precise with all the others. You work hard for it, but it's fun too."

Michèle Poupon has moved forward in her life, and seems to be the "compleat" retired professional artist. She recalls and treasures her past as prima ballerina in a major European ballet company, one that, like her own dancing, was consistently critiqued positively, but in no way does she pine for and live in the days that used to be. Her light-up-the-room smile and attitude, as well as her every movement, bespeak a fulfilled person. I'd always thought of ballerinas as being somewhat removed from the real world—above it all, literally and figuratively, distant, ever so slightly haughty in the company of mere mortals. After all, ballerinas can fly.

But Michèle is a great example of a well-balanced human being despite her extraordinary talent and illustrious past life. Perhaps, Nantucket being a magical place, she has come to exactly the right spot in the world.

Three young swans in *Swan Lake*. Michèle is in the center.

Voila! A Life of
Passionate Serenity
Paulette Allemand, 2000

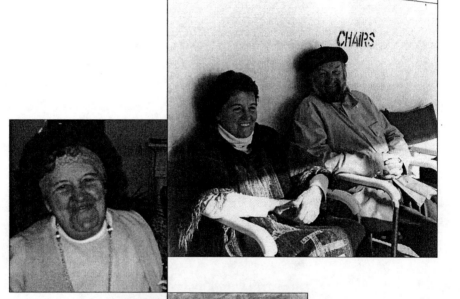

*I*t's entirely possible that no one on the island of Nantucket has ever seen Paulette Allemand scowl. There's an open and welcoming smile on her face *toujours*. Everyone who knows this generous, talented woman is her friend. And if you know her, she will greet you by giving you a wonderfully warm European kiss on each cheek.

Paulette speaks with an extraordinarily charming French flavor, accompanying her conversation with enthusiastic hand motions and facial expressions. This is a person whose countenance bespeaks serenity; yet there is an amazing energy and passionate intensity about her that is entirely positive.

THE FAMILY THAT SINGS TOGETHER…

"I am born in Switzerland," Paulette began, "in Bienne, which is a bilingual city. My parents were watchmakers, but also musicians. They were doing this other career because with music, you know, you are not always making enough money. They took us all the time to concerts, and my father was a director of the town's orchestra; he played the organ—the harmonium, really, because at that time some churches didn't have organs. And you know you have to puuuuump this instrument…and I was doing that for my father—like Bach—he had also students to pump for him. I am the daughter of the performer and *voila!* I am doing the same thing. It was really a nice life. And we were doing little concerts almost every Sunday for the mother of my mother—she was in one sense our publique. I was playing the piano, because I was fast to sight-read music, you know? My sister and my mother were sopranos, my brother was a tenor, and my father the bass, and I did the alto and the piano. That is the way I got my training…and we did enjoy that. My father taught me also painting—he was so talented—and my mother the same thing. They were playing guitar, mandolin, piano, trumpet, harmonium, organ…you understand?"

So, I said, you didn't feel forced into music. "Oh, no!" Paulette exclaimed. "And you know, in church or with the society my father was directing, they did have always concerts, and my family performed all the time." Wasn't it Hindemith, I asked, who wrote a lot of music intended for families to perform together? "Yes!" Paulette answered, "and Honegger, too. I knew the aunt of Honegger. I did have a friend who was a conductor, and she knew Madame Honegger and took me to meet her. Her house had a big terrace overlooking the mountains, and it was always full of people from all around the world. She was looking like an Indian—we said her face was cut with *une hâche*, a hatchet, because it was really strong. When I went to meet her, it was something like fifty people there, and Madame did love the blackberry pie, so my friend brought that for her. She was sitting at the end of a long table; I was on the other end, and she suddenly got up and came to me and asked, 'What is the date of your birth?' And I am wondering what she wants…and she said, 'Come to see me tonight at 8 o'clock!' And then she went back and eat the pie like nothing happened. We talked that evening during three hours, and it was incredible. She said, 'I never saw so much talent. Now you have to work! You have to work with children…' And I was already doing a lot with children. I was teaching the mothers, with the piano or voice, and their children I taught rhythm too. It was the Dalcroze Méthode [a method of teaching children to appreciate and enjoy music]. Jacques Dalcroze saw that children often have a lot of problems to read and study music. And you have to teach them the notes, the solfège, the rhythm, and things like that, but they don't want to do that…they want to play! So he said, 'Why not put all those children together in the rhythmique classes?'" With this method, she went on, the children are prepared in the basics of music in an enjoyable way, so that they take to music naturally.

Were you performing as well as teaching then? I asked Paulette. "Yes," she replied. "I was 28 or so at that time, and I was teaching and performing in many cities; all the mothers with the children—I went to them, usually in one house, for the rhythm classes. I was renting a room for teaching rhythmique and yoga. You know, for singing, the yoga is so perfect, and you really learn the diaphragm breathing. In that time, you understand, it was not like now—now you find everywhere classes in yoga, but in that time, no. How I came to yoga, it was a very strange thing. We did have a concert, and I had in it a long aria, très dramatique…and you know with very long phrases like in Handel and Bach…you never can breathe. The rehearsal with the orchestra and the chorus was at four in the afternoon, and the concert was to be that night. So when it came my turn, I tried to make the conductor understand [my tempo]…but he was conducting slower and slower! And I was almost dying there, trying to get those long phrases. During the intermission I went to him and I said, 'What are you doing to me?' And he laughed: 'Well, I was just trying to see how long a phrase you can sing!' I said, 'Oh, it was not fair, don't do that to me tonight!' And he asked me, 'How are you doing these long phrases?' And I said, 'Oh, I do yoga.' You see, I had found a book on yoga by Gesu Dian, and I found that it worked really well for my singing. Then the conductor said, 'Do you want to meet Gesu Dian?' He took me to the class of Gesu Dian—that was maybe six months before we came here to America. I took lessons with him, and I remember before the class he had us sit for 20 minutes in silence…you don't say a word…it's no noise…it's like the golden silence going on. It's an incredible atmosphere and experience to do that. You really start to hear the silence. After the class, Gesu Dian told me, 'You have to breathe'—and that is where I get my breathing technique." Wasn't it fortunate, I commented, that you seemed to meet him at exactly the right time? "You know," said Paulette, raising a finger, "there is a saying: 'When the students are ready, they find the master,' and that is true!"

Where did Paulette study music, besides with her family? "When I was 11 years old, the Directeur of the Conservatorium in Bienne had an audition. There were 120 children auditioning. For that you have to play something…then he makes you hear intervals—you have to sing a third, a fifth, whatever he asks—and he plays something and now you have to sing what he did play. A lot of things like that, and finally you had to play. And I was playing the little sonata of Mozart [she hums it] and I win the prize! And the prize was all your study until the end of your schooling. That was a great blessing for my parents, you can imagine, because we were talented, but we were not rich people, and I don't think they could have done all that. So that was great for me." And that was your grammar school, high school, and college education, at the Conservatory? I asked. "Yes. And it was wonderful," Paulette replied. Following that, her remarkable career as a teacher, parent, concert singer, and pianist kept her extremely busy on the European music scene. "Many choral conductors," she said, "also did like me to prepare the accompaniments before they had the orchestra, which was very expensive, to come in. There, you know, you have to pass examination to be in the chorus, the orchestra, so there were very excellent-quality musicians."

LOVE AT FIRST SIGHT? OH, YES!

How did Paulette meet Charly, her husband? I asked. Paulette smiled and answered, "Charly is born in Indonesia…there are three brothers in the family. The father was a mining engineer…that is why his parents were there, so Charly and his brothers went to school there, and they even spoke the language. In 1928 or '29, there was a government monetary crisis, and that happened while they were back in Switzerland for their long vacation, and they were told they should not go back. Charly and I met in my town, Bienne…because you know you have concerts, things like that, so that is how we met." Was it love at first sight? I asked. "Oh, yes! Oh, very very nice. And he was always really very supporting…What year were we married? Oh, my goodness…I can't remember." Paulette and Charly have one child, Michèle Poupon, and she too inherited the love of and involvement with the arts—in her case it was classical ballet. After her retirement as prima ballerina of a major European company, Michèle moved to Nantucket, where she and her mother collaborate frequently on the Grand Opera productions that have become a fixture on the island music scene. "We were extremely fortunate to have even one child," said Paulette; "it was very difficult. But you know, I have the feeling life is really…how you say…it has all been planned, voila…everything is already done long time…" Do you mean, your life was meant to be exactly as it is? I asked. "Voila, voila!"

When and how was it that Paulette and Charly come to the States? "Oh," she said, beaming, "that was the story of Charly [pronounced "Sharlee"]. Charly was a physicist, and he was working for a steel company from Stockholm, Sweden. Now, that company was working for America, and Charly was the technical director, and always sending the research results, so in the 1960s they said Charly must come to America…and we did have three months to make up our minds. That was in the '60s. But we were ready…Michèle was in the theater…it was a great life. When she could come from her performances in Germany, we would spend time together, and we were always going on vacation together. You know, we are more friends together than parent and child, and that is something which should be much more understood. We stayed friends, and we share everything together. Parents should say to their [grown] children, 'You have your life, we have our life…but we support you. Don't do things for us, do things for you…take the responsibility, do what you can.' And it's so good. Look, we don't educate or have children for us! You understand? So that was a beautiful teaching, and

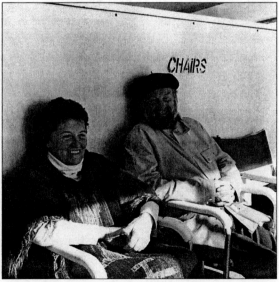

Left—Charly and Paulette in Guadaloupe at a Club Med at which their nephew worked, c. 1967.
Right—Here are Paulette and Charly Allemand on the boat en route to Nantucket, sometime in the 1960s.

when it was the time for Michèle to go on her own, I cannot cry about it—you don't grieve, you support. Many parents are too *possessif!* You are born teachers, but in one sense as parents you receive more…when you have the child you are older by age, but they are teaching you! And that is what I learned with Michèle—it is incredible what she taught me.

INDIA VS. NANTUCKET?

"Charly came here to America in 1961, but not completely…he was coming for one month, two months, three or four times a year, so they finally find it will be much more easy to have Charly here. We went to Newton, Massachusetts in 1966, with the Jarrell Ash Company—yes, that was Susan Jarrell's family. [Susie Jarrell is another vibrant force in Nantucket's music scene.] It was a spectography company. I asked Charly what that is—spectography is the study of the decomposition of the light, something like that…the *optique*…it is very vast…and that is the best I can describe it to you. Charly did the Ph.D. in Switzerland about…I can't get the right word…about something small…you know…" Atoms? *"Voila! Les atomes!* And he was at that time working with India also, with a research institute…so we almost went to India instead of to here!

"Now, Dick Jarrell was the director of Jarrell Ash, and Kiffy, his wife, called me one day in Newton and you know, I didn't have any English at all, so she told me, 'I go in June and July to Nantucket; you have to come there—you will learn the language.' And you know, here the women are the leaders, it's not like in Switzerland, where it is the man, not the woman, so she said, 'Dick, you bring Charly every weekend!', so that's what we did. I was living here during the summer, and the men were coming Friday night until Sunday night. We stayed in a big house in Surfside, near the beach. It was incredible—I was spoiled right away! In that time between Fairgrounds Road and Surfside there were no houses…and when it was fog it was no plane—it was so quiet there. After that we came every year to Nantucket, because Kiffy was giving to people who worked for the company a vacation in the house, which was very nice."

Left—The Allemands travel back to Europe annually; here they pose with the modest background of the Swiss Alps. Right—Posing in hats someone has presented them at the La Comballaz Chalet in Switzerland, 1995. Michèle Poupon, their daughter, says they look like "Swiss hillbillys."

When did the Allemands finally decide to move to Nantucket year-round? "We came one weekend for Labor Day, maybe four or five years after we first came. And we go right away to the beach! Now, Mary, we didn't put anything on our skin, and we were on the beach from 11:30 or so until 5 o'clock. And there were so many people, and they said, 'Paulette, you have to give us a yoga class.' And I remember when I start to stretch, I was so…" Paulette stopped, searching for the right words. You felt as if your skin was too tight? I volunteered. *"Voila!"* she said, laughing. "I didn't know! Then that night, when we went to sleep, I said, 'Charly! You are red like a lobsTER.' And he said, 'Oh, you didn't see yourself?' That was Friday night, and we were there until Monday afternoon, because it was the last weekend of the summer, OK? Then we decided the next day we don't go to beach; we put on long sleeves and went to promenade in Nantucket. We had thought about the New Hampshire and the Maine to retire, but you have to shovel snow, so we were thinking that in Nantucket even during the winter it's not too much; and it's not big—you can really do, you know, things in town, it's adaptable. It's ideal! So this day we met Madame Doucette and said 'We want to come here to live,' and she showed us first one big house, and that was too expensive, because we were still living in the house in Newton. So she closed the book, and we thought, 'Oh, no.' And she told us she was remarrying and was building herself a house that would now be too small, so she showed us this house!"

Charly decided to retire in 1981, which is when Paulette came "completely" to Nantucket and became totally involved with music here, as well as yoga. "But Charly just kept right on working, and commuted," she smiled, "and he only really retired this year." Paulette teaches singing almost every day, and although she no longer teaches yoga classes per se, she includes yoga principles in her vocal teaching. "And I still practice yoga daily," she said. I'd heard rumors that this animated woman still does the standing-on-your-head pose once a day, so I asked if it were true. "Oh yes," she said. "Usually at night, and sometimes the morning." And do you also meditate? I asked. "Oh yes," she replied, "but you know, in one sense it's 24 hours a day of meditation…you understand? Everything can be a meditation. And yoga—you can do yoga even if you can no more walk," she went on…sit up straight, feel your spine stretch…you can do a lot. And it helps so much in singing. You know the Cobra position [in which one raises up from a flat, face-down position on the floor, arching the back]? Usually people push themselves to do this…but no, a cobra has the energy in the tail, so you have to breathe that energy, and that is what makes the cobra big, puffed out." So that it's not your body

changing, it's the energy changing your body? I asked. *"Voila!* It's incredible, the feeling—and the same with the Bow position. When you stretch the bow, the master said, you do not focus as if you were aiming a bullet. You can not see the target, because the target is yourself. You understand? You have to in one sense match your

166

Left—Paulette has been an active participant in Nantucket's music scene; here she is after a concert, with Barbara Elder. Right—Enjoying her surprise 80th birthday party, Paulette poses laughingly with husband Charly.

center with that center, and then everything will happen. Now, this is true for everything you do, even picking up a book…everything must be prepared…but it cannot be intellectual—you cannot think too much."

THE SECRETS OF LIVING WELL

What does Nantucket Island and this country have for Paulette and Charly (and daughter Michèle as well) that no other place can offer? "Oh, that I can answer right away," Paulette said. "It's the way Americans are open and free, and we like that so very much." At that moment a handsome bright red cardinal lit on the wet deck railing outside the large music room Charly built onto the house—a room familiar to most musicians on the island. We admired him, and then Paulette smiled. "You know, when we came here we did have a lot of shocks—not negatif shocks, but good ones, through that kind of freedom. We especially liked that because in one sense in our marriage we were living a lot like American people, because we supported each other's careers; we were open. People could feel free to come to our house. And it's so good when you feel that way!"

We chatted a bit about Paulette's paintings (she no longer paints—too busy with music) and also about Charly's sculpture. She showed me a beautiful life-sized carved hand on a windowsill, its thumb meeting in a circle with its forefinger, the other fingers curved gracefully. "Unfortunately, he doesn't do that much any more, but he did it because someone told him the hand was the hardest thing to do." Paulette and Charly, with their upbeat attitude, seem to know the secret of living well…with a willingness to try new things and do the old things well.

Paulette is an extremely passionate person, very energetic and intense, full of vitality and motion and excitement about everything she does and says. Serenity and passion and the gift of pure enjoyment in making things better. To know Paulette Allemand is surely to love her.

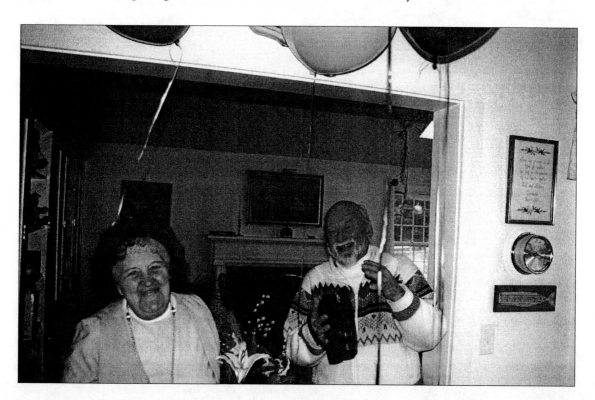

168

Life Before Nantucket:
All Six Months of It
Charlotte Matteson, 2000

*C*harlotte Matteson's family connections with Nantucket began in 1918; she has been coming here every summer since she was an infant in the 1950s, and for thirteen years has lived here full-time. When she told me she'd been born in Providence, I couldn't help but ask if, given her family's long history here, her parents were guilty of shortsightedness...they could, after all, have had a native. Charlotte replied, "Well, my mother was trying to have one child and she ended up with two at that point. When my sisters, Bliss and Lydia, were eight and six, Mother was literally in the labor room having what she thought was her third child, and she gave birth to twins. Elizabeth is about seven minutes older than I am.

"Mother was given the house at 86 Main Street as a wedding present in 1940 by her father," Charlotte continued. "In 1918 my grandparents, Albert and Ruth Read, were invited to Nantucket for a weekend, and they liked it so much that they decided to rent a house up on the cliff for a month in 1919; by the end of the month they'd bought this house. My father had a chance to buy the East Brick—but there were two kids at that point and a cook and a nanny, and he decided on this house because it had two bathrooms and the East Brick had only one! That's fine, actually, because this house is sort of anonymous—people don't know about it when they come up Main Street. It's called a Greek Revival half-house because the staircase is on the outside wall rather than in the middle. It was built by Zenas Coffin in 1834.

"Mother summered down here from the age of four, every year except 1970, when my father was sick. And I've been coming here since 1953—we have a picture of Mother and Daddy in the back yard here with Bliss and Lydia on either side, and they're holding us, the twins, when we're six months old. We usually came down about the third or fourth week of June and stayed all summer; Daddy came on weekends and for the month of August.

"My father was a Trustee of Estates for the John Nicholas Brown family, the Brown University people—his grandfather and father had done that also. He loved Nantucket, and did a lot of surfcasting, and we had family picnics out on the beach. He'd designed a very wide grill with mesh underneath so that the coals would be up off the sand. My Aunt Charlotte had a place up on Gosnold Road, so we used to go to the beach there, and Eel Point, the South Shore, Cisco...When we were really little—before 1963, when the hurricane blew through and ruptured the beach—we'd go out to Smith's Point, and it seemed to take forever; it was much farther out then. I remember our parents used to have to put us on leashes and little harnesses, otherwise we'd just go."

Charlotte kept coming back every summer, even during college and grad school. And her first job ever was on the island. "When I was about ten, Erica Wilson, who had just moved here, was offering needlework classes. At that point Lizzie and I were being taught the 'finer graces' of regular, straight, ordinary, run-of-the-mill sewing back in Providence, so the next thing I know I'm over at Erica Wilson's around the corner learning how to make a little fish eyeglass case. When I was fifteen, I started helping Erica with the children's classes. She was designing for Columbia—Minerva at that point, the company that was distributing her kits, and she'd scratch out a design on a piece of paper, hand it to me, and I'd do it. I mostly knit now," Charlotte said, adding, "I have an image of my mother sitting in a chair and we'd have the radio on—didn't have a TV then—and she'd knit and read, and listen to the radio, and sort of keep an eye on us...all at the same time. Unbelievable woman."

What was your typical summer like as a child? I asked. Charlotte said, "We badgered our parents forever about getting a horse. My father grew up in Providence and literally in back of his house was a stable, so he grew up riding, and as eight-or nine-year-olds Lizzie and I had the typical passion for horses. On the island, Clara McGrady—she was also involved with the Miacomet Raceway—had the Hilltop Stables, and she used to rent horses. You could go trail riding and there were classes for kids. So instead of taking sailing or tennis lessons like our

sisters did, Lizzie and I went riding at least twice a week. It was great. I stopped riding when I was a teenager, in large part because I had to make a choice back in Providence whether to sing on Saturday morning or go on with horseback riding. Lizzie kept riding, and I decided to sing—but for a long while, riding was the thing, and I used to read an incredible amount, too, so the Atheneum was one of the sources for my existence here."

STAY OUT—THIS MEANS YOU

In the cupola of 86 Main, over the third floor, which looks out on the rooftops and back yards in the area, can be found some very familiar signs of active kids in the house: scrawled on a bedroom door were the words "P.U., Bliss" and "The 5 Good Workers Club. Private. Period. Stay Out. This Means You." "Oh yeah, it was a club," said Charlotte. "There was a big age gap between my older two sisters and Lizzie and me. Bliss and Lydia had their own life…they were in the Yacht Club and we were riding horses. When I was about five, I got up to cupola once and was scared to death I wouldn't be able to get down the ladder. But my sisters went up there all the time; they had sort of a clique of kids that they knew down here, and of course I wanted to be part of that. We occasionally used to see the fireworks from up there, too. When we were growing up they used to have Baptist sings on Wednesday nights…this is in the '50s when many people had black servants, and the women would go there and sing these wonderful hymns—we used to go up Pine

In 1919, Albert Read and his wife Ruth, Charlotte Matteson's grandparents, bought a house built by Zenas Coffin in 1834—86 Main Street. Here are the five Read boys: from right, Albert, Charles, Frederick, Malcolm, and little Robert.

Here are the Read boys grown up: from left in back, Charles, Frederick, and Malcolm; in front Charlotte's grandfather, Albert, and Robert.

Street and sit on the back steps and listen to them.

"Another thing we did in the summer was to go around the corner to Liberty Street, where my Grandmother Read lived, to watch TV. She was Ruth Bucklin, who I'm partially named after, and Granddaddy Albert was one of five Read boys…he died before I was born." She got up and showed me a wonderful old photograph on the wall of her Great-Grandfather Read, his wife, Mary-Elizabeth Bliss Read, and their five sons, Albert, Frederick, Malcolm, Charles, and Robert. There were lots more photos and paintings of relatives displayed, each with its own interesting story. A striking portrait of her mother as a young woman shows Charlotte's strong resemblance, and nearby is a delightful painting of Charlotte's great-grandfather at about age five: "Everybody loves those striped socks he's wearing," said Charlotte. In the living room is a large old photo of Great-Aunt Ella Matteson wearing a superb, colossally large hat. "She built the house that we lived in on George Street in Providence…and my Matteson grandparents lived across the way. She willed the house to my father, and we all grew up there."

SETTING HER BRAIN ON FIRE

Tell me about the school years, I requested. Charlotte answered, "We all went to a private girls' school, Lincoln School—it still exists. Bliss and I both graduated from there; Lydia graduated from Hinckley School in Maine in 1967…and there was a whole slew of Nantucket kids who went up there—Bryan King, Karol Lindquist, Richard Ray, Bruce Killen, Tobey Leske, Gray and Susan Worth, to name some—so it was perfect for her. And Lizzie went to Rocky Hill Day School in East Greenwich, Rhode Island. After Lincoln, I went on to Mount Holyoke, and later to Yale Divinity School; I received a Master of Divinity degree from Yale and Berkeley Divinity School—Berkeley is the Episcopal part of Yale Divinity School." Why, I wondered, hadn't Charlotte become a priest? She groaned; apparently this is a question she has to answer with fair frequency, especially because she is so active at St. Paul's Church, in the choir and as a vestry member, among other things. She explained: "My parents were always involved in Grace Episcopal Church in Providence—Daddy was head of the ushers, Mother was head of the Altar Guild. Ironically, we never did very much here at St. Paul's, but we had been raised as

Left—Twins Elizabeth and Charlotte Matteson, enjoying a summer's day on Nantucket. Right—Charlotte at about four.

Episcopalians and I went through the sort of teenage trauma of not wanting to go to church. Then, when I went to college, I thought, Well, maybe I should know what I'm walking away from—maybe I should take some religion courses. So I did during my sophomore year, and just loved it—the department, the courses, everything. I was a biology major; I was going to be an oceanographer. By the time I was a senior I was a double major. Religion departments can really be awful, but if they're good, they just set your brain on fire. And I was really lucky at Holyoke. I did my senior thesis on Quakerism and whaling in Nantucket and spent my senior-year January term doing research here. It was fun.

"And then when I graduated," she went on, "I realized I didn't want to get a Ph.D. in oceanography; I was tired of science. I wasn't sure what I wanted to do, so I lived in Providence for a couple of years and was really involved in the church, and then I decided to get my Master's so I could teach. That was in 1976, when the Episcopalian Church decided to ordain women. I talked to my priest and he suggested I go to divinity school. And I thought 'I don't want to be a priest!' But I looked at divinity schools, and went down to Yale and loved it. It offered what I wanted; I could get my teacher's certification as well as my Master's degree, and they were more than supportive. I made it pretty clear I wasn't interested in becoming a priest— I really didn't see myself that way. I wanted to get my certification, I wanted to work at a private school, I knew I wanted to work as a chaplain. I talked a lot to the bishops and agonized over this...and I finally said, 'If it's this much of a struggle to decide, then I'm clearly not meant to do it.' And that was a good decision. I love the church; I love being part of it, but I really don't like the authoritarian sort of ecclesiastical hierarchy you have to go through as a priest. I understand it, but I don't like it. It's partly the way I've been raised...all women's schools...and I didn't want to be in a situation where the bishops could say, You can't marry this person, or You have to live here...It's not quite that bad, but you have to have your bishop's approval for what you do. And I think I've found my calling in terms of working in the church, especially with singing."

BEEN THERE, DONE THAT

After receiving her degrees, Charlotte spent a full year on Nantucket. "Winter was very different, and very little was open then, but I loved it. And then the Taft School, where I'd done my senior internship, offered me a job. I loved teaching, and loved the school. I taught freshman biology, several senior electives, such as physiology and invertebrate zoology, and worked in junior/senior courses in the religion department—mostly death and dying and biomedical ethics. I was at Taft for seven years, and then I woke up one morning and I didn't want to do it any more. Literally, that's the way it happened. I love kids, but it was exhausting, and I had no life of my own; it was really frustrating for me. I realized I was spending a lot of time thinking, What's it like to be on Nantucket today? So I basically took a sabbatical down here; that was thirteen years ago, and I haven't left."

Did you have any interest teaching on the island? I asked. "No!" she said emphatically. "Everybody asked me that, and I kept saying I'm leaving teaching because I'm tired...why would I want another job in teaching? I worked for Elizabeth Gilbert for a while, at her needlework store. Then I worked part-time at the Camera Shop...it was a good job, because I got to meet everybody who lives down here in the wintertime. And then I worked as rentals manager in real estate for three or four years. OK, been there, done that, so I left and did housecleaning for a while…I've done just about everything. Now I'm working at Geronimo's." And, I added, you're very active in St. Paul's, plus doing a good bit of soloing in various concerts and presentations. And teaching voice. You chose singing at an early age, didn't you? I asked. "Yes, and I've kept that up; at Holyoke I was in the choral group and I sang in the Yale Divinity School Choir, and when I came here I was in a sense locked in as a singer. I've had a different sort of training; I'm not a Broadway singer, I'm not a pop singer…I have sort of an English choirboy's voice…" Charlotte described the Reid Method, a vocal technique she she's been teaching to a varying number of students for about five years.

A HEALING PLACE IN SPITE OF IT ALL

Sounds as if your life has changed a lot in the last thirteen years, I said. Are you glad you came back here to live? Charlotte responded, "Yes, I love being here; it's enriched my life. I've gotten a lot of focus here, learned a lot about myself from other people. I've discovered I like living in small towns; it's harder because you don't have the privacy thing, but you can walk into the Stop & Shop and know twelve people. I've always been really interested in the maritime history of the island, the emotional history…and I would like to get more into that kind of thing—go and read diaries at the Foulger, for example. My family's always been a New England family—we're descended from Roger Williams, and we've been in New England for thirteen generations. I really love that sort of history. And living on Nantucket has given me a real sense of the environment and my connection with it, which I really like. But there are problems…I used to take the dogs out to Altar Rock and walk around; now, in summer, it's hard not to run into trucks and Jeeps speeding down the road. But I do treasure the environment, and I'm grateful for all the people who've donated their property to the Conservation Foundation or taken charge over their property to protect it, because it makes all the difference in the world."

Here Charlotte heaved a heavy sigh. "I remember Main Street when it had the 5&10, and a little grocery, and you could do all your shopping and stuff downtown…now you go down to Main Street to buy property or expensive artwork or really expensive clothes. It isn't Main Street as I remember it—I understand why, I just don't like it. And back in the 1950s and '60s people who came to Nantucket had a sense about what it was about—the history, the whaling stuff— and now people use it for their elegant summer places, and I resent that a lot. A lot of people come here, and it's like How much money can I throw at it to get what I want to get out of it? That's distressing." She laughed: "I was getting a sandwich a couple days ago and there were two guys standing there in their tennis whites and rackets and I realized that they were wearing clothes that were probably more expensive than what I earned last week! It's my choice, to work where I choose…but it's very difficult to be in that situation. Another thing I'm distressed about is that the working people here who want to have homes can't raise their families down here…not everybody can afford $150,000 for property, and then build a house on top of it."

Charlotte has a thoughtful premise that's worth thinking about in today's world of instant millionaires: "I think there's just too much money out there, and people don't know how to spend it. They haven't been trained to spend it for others, they've been trained to spend it for

174

themselves. There's a lot less charity work going on, a lot less giving of self to help others…There used to be a different attitude about money. My parents gave us a real sense about its value—it carried a responsibility, you respected what it could do for others. It's the lack of that attitude that's prevalent today. One of the reasons I stay involved in the church, I think, is because there are a lot of like-minded people there, caring about one another."

But all in all, Charlotte obviously cherishes her island and does her part to keep it healthy. "When I moved here to stay year-round," she concluded, "I thought it'd just be for a year or two. I'm grateful I've been here this long, and I've been lucky to be able to find work and have the support system I have here." So in spite of all the problems with escalating growth, Charlotte Matteson considers Nantucket "a very healing place." It's home.

Charlotte Matteson with the late, great Abby, and Cori.

The World's Busiest
Potato Grower

Lucy Apthorp Leske, 2000

Although I'd known Lucy Leske for about a decade, I wasn't aware that we'd both been born in the same small central Massachusetts town, Holden. When she was eight, her family moved to Texas, and another move in 1972 took them to central Florida, where she attended high school. "That was where I took my first biology classes," she said. "I had a fabulous teacher who took us on lots of field trips, and I just fell in love with biology." But that wasn't where her love of growing things came from. You can read her well-written and edifying weekly column, "Gardening by the Sea," in the *Inquirer and Mirror* and it's almost a given that such lore has to come from lifelong experience in the art of gardening. In her first years of life Lucy was intimately involved with her father's vegetable plot. "I loved that garden. I used to go down and hang out and pick peas and eat them right out there in the sun," she remembered. "Dad used to start his seedlings in the house on a tiny sun porch that was connected to the closet that ran between the bedrooms. It wasn't heated, but in the spring it was sunny and warm there. My bedroom used to smell like…well, green, with all those little seedlings growing. I think that all your life you are drawn to those nostalgic sorts of things through your sense of smell—it's the most fundamental sensory perception function in a human being. I think that is why I grow plants…because I like the way they smell. Anyway, that's what I attribute my love of science and gardens to.

OUTDOORS WITH FINGERNAIL CLAMS

"When I finished high school I was tired of the hot weather, and really missed the changing of the seasons, even though I'd left Massachusetts when I was only eight. So I went back to New England for college and have been here ever since. I went to Mount Holyoke, and I chose my major earlier than most classmates. I took a biology class and knew instantly that's what I was going to major in, so there was no struggle—it was pretty clear. I took a lot of biochemistry classes, and also things like English and music. But in my major I focused on environmental classes, things that took me outside. By the time I was a senior I taught one of the environmental labs. My senior thesis was about freshwater fingernail clams…they're in freshwater ponds and swamps in the woods all around the South Hadley area. I measured their birth rate and compared that with the level of acid in the ponds and how that was related to acid rain pollution. So it was a really outdoorsy, naturalist major. I really consider myself not a botanist or a horticulturalist, but more of a naturalist. I'm interested in nature and communities of living things and how they relate to the landscape, and also how humans relate to and impact those communities in that landscape. How people, plants, and animals connect to the landscape in which they live."

What did Lucy do after college? "Well, of course, all of this is related to Nantucket one way or another," she said. "Ever since I was little I'd been coming to Nantucket to visit my grandmother— Mary Lou Apthorp. She's now 92 [Mrs. Apthorp died in January, 2002], and living in Our Island Home. She had bought the house right next to the Youth Hostel in Surfside during the war; I remember her telling me stories about how her two sons would go and hang out with the Coast Guard guys while they were manning the radio, looking for submarines. When my dad grew up and married, he'd bring Mom and my brother and sister and me out here. And during college, between my junior and senior years, I decided to come out here and work for the summer. I lived with my grandmother out in Surfside—this was 1979—and I worked at Cap'n Tobey's Chowder House as a waitress, on Straight Wharf. And darned if I didn't fall in love with my boss, Tobey Leske.

POTATOES & POTATOES & POTATOES

"At that point," she said, "I needed money more than I needed my B.A., so I took a semester off and stayed on the island for the fall…. Well," she admitted, laughing, "part of the rationale for staying was the man, part the money. My parents were shocked. They wanted me to graduate from college, and they were worried that I was going to move out here and grow potatoes for the rest of my life. I remember arguing with my mother and saying, 'If I want to live out here and grow potatoes for the rest of my life, that's what I'm going to do!' And darn it, that's what I'm doing now…I'm growing very fine potatoes, thank you very much!" Was she growing fancy types, with all her gardening knowhow? "Plain old potatoes, purple, Peruvian, Ruby Crescent, Yukon Gold, Early Ohio, and others." And what does she do with all these potatoes? I asked. "Eat them!" she said.

"So I spent that fall in Nantucket, earned some money, and then went back in January and finished my college career…commuting occasionally between South Hadley and Nantucket. When I graduated, I moved out here fulltime. And then in 1982 Tobey and I were married at the Sankaty Head Golf Club. I only worked at the restaurant for one summer—I was not the best waitress in the world, let me put it that way. I started working at the Marine Lumber at the Garden Center, for Alice Erickson…she lives on the Cape now. She was remarkable…I'd had other jobs in between—at one point at that little dress shop on Center Street, sewing buttons on dresses…but in 1982 I went to Marine Lumber and worked there for six years. That's where I met most of the people in the landscaping industry, which was really taking off then. I continue to network a lot with those people. That's where I really learned a lot about landscaping and large nursery plants…and Alice taught me so much about plants and roses. I joined the Nantucket Garden Club, where I was exposed to some wonderful, talented women who were very knowledgeable about gardening and flowers.

THE GARDENER BRANCHES OUT

"When we were first married, we lived in a little apartment in Monomoy, and I had my own vegetable garden…and I haven't been without one since. Then we bought our first house on Fairgrounds Road in

Left—This picture was taken at Surfside in 1978, the year Lucy came to Nantucket. She stayed with her grandmother, the late Mary Lou Apthorp. Right—Lucy at the beach in Florida at age 20.

All ready for her Junior Prom, Lucy Apthorp (Leske),
with her date, Rusty McClelland.

Dressed up for a party during college, Lucy looks
very serious.

1983, and did all the landscaping ourselves. During that time Bob Kaldenbach was publishing a newsletter called *The New England Farm Bulletin,* a very basic, sort of anti-establishment, nontechnological approach to farming. Then he started *The New England Gardener* on the island, and that was distributed all over New England for home gardeners. About a year later, he and his wife decided to leave the island, and advertised these two bulletins for sale. I needed something beyond the challenge of managing a retail garden center, so Tobey and I talked it over—we wanted to start a family, and we thought this would be a way for me to make money while I was working at home. That was pretty naïve, obviously…but we bought the *Gardener,* and over to the house came all this antiquated Radio Shack computer equipment with the mailing list on it, and I wrote the whole thing. It was an eight-page newsletter with subscribers all over New England. At one point we had up to 12,000; there was no advertising, so the whole thing had to pay for itself through subscriptions. I got into direct mail with a vengeance, and learned the hard way that writing is no way to make a living." That brought a big shared laugh.

"We published the *New England Gardener* here on Nantucket for five years," Lucy continued. "And that's how I became immersed in writing about gardening. I love writing. That's my father's avocation—he likes to write poetry and is working on a novel. He counseled me that there's nothing better than having a monthly or weekly deadline, and to never give that up—that it was a wonderful discipline and an incredible experience to have to write something every day. So, while I had the newsletter, I approached Marianne Giffin at the *I&M,* and asked her if she was interested in a gardening column. I started writing for the *I&M* in 1988, just after our first son, Colin, was born. Wyatt was born in 1990. I was publishing this newsletter and writing a column for the paper, and was still working at Marine Lumber, and I had a baby. Something had to go, so I finally quit my job at Marine Lumber and focused on writing and raising the kids. And it soon became clear that the newsletter wasn't going to be able to support itself, so I sold it in '89."

Growing into a New Career

In spite of giving up her job at the Home Center, Lucy became ever more busy. She got involved in doing some landscape design projects, but that became too physically demanding. "We needed to have two incomes in our family," she explained. "Tobey was in the construction business then, which in the early '90s was going through a slump. So we decided that I needed to find a better way of making a living besides writing. And that's when I approached Nancy Martin at Educational Management Network [a consultancy/search firm for higher education], to ask her advice about what I could do with my skills. She said, 'Come to work for me; I need a writer.' In 1992 I went to work for her fulltime. On day one I walked into the office; everyone was traveling, and on my desk was a list of instructions which told me to reference three candidates, and the first person on the list was the Dean of Harvard Medical School! So it was a pretty heady first experience. Nancy had told me I was going to take to the job like a duck to water, and from the very first day I absolutely loved it.

"Back then at EMN, everyone just kind of did everything…I wrote position descriptions, did referencing, lots of sourcing and recruiting, stuffed envelopes, answered phones, did the mail, everything. I'm now a consultant, and that was a very gradual evolution…it wasn't like one day I was crowned or anything, it just sort of gradually happened. Nancy Martin is a marvelous mentor, and it's a privilege to work for someone so well regarded nationally, who understands this business inside and out. She recruited all the staff from Nantucket, and built this business till it became a national competitor. [EMN merged with a larger search firm, Witt/Kieffer, in 1988.] We do high-quality work, serving a field that I passionately support. I love and am proud of the work; in this tiny, island-based business, we have an impact on the leadership of institutions that I fundamentally believe in. And through the leaders we help place, we affect the lives of thousands of people around the country. I think it's the best job on the island. Furthermore, we collect all our fees from off-island, so the staff income positively impacts the island, particularly in the wintertime. We don't have to add another 100 visitors to the island for us to grow our business off-island."

The Secret: A Perfect Partnership

What does Lucy do for relaxation? She continues with her own gardens and her regular column, is active in the Garden Club, and slips in some sailing with Tobey whenever possible. "Tobey and I have always sailed," she said, "and when we were first married we used to race in the Yacht Club races on Sundays. In about 1989 we'd bought a sailboat, and right about when I started working for Educational Management Network we made the decision to rent our house in the summertime, so we lived on our boat in the harbor for three summers. At this point my kids were little, and there was also a dog and a cat on board. We lived on a mooring, not even at the dock, and had to go back and forth in a boat. It was quite a challenge." At about that time I remember seeing Lucy often on her way to work, whizzing along hellbent for leather on her bicycle. "I still ride the bike for exercise," she said.

It must be difficult to handle all the traveling that is required in your EMN job, with a family, I said. "Well," she responded, "recently Tobey made a change in his life. He'd gone back to the restaurant, but the hours were more than he could handle…and we both believed that one of us should be home with kids when they came home in the afternoons, so he decided he'd change the pace of his life. Now he does a lot of volunteer work, as well as consulting—he's helping St. Paul's with the rectory renovation project—and he also does real estate home inspections for buyers, and delivers boats as well. This makes for a very flexible schedule and we needed that. It's a wonderful setup; he's a marvelous cook. He even does all the grocery shopping and enjoys it—I hate it! All this time I've kept writing the *I&M* column every week and for a time also had a column in a national magazine, *The Kitchen Gardener.* I've also written for several local publications, such as *Nantucket Magazine.* I really enjoy all this a lot."

I knew Lucy had been working on a gardening book for a while, and asked her about it. "Ohhhh," she groaned, "how do you write a book in 15-minute sound bites a month? I have about three-quarters of the material, but it needs finishing touches, like taking the pictures…I work on this during the weekends. I like to write, and have been writing essays, études, my father calls them, on small-town life. Nobody's seen them but Tobey and Tom Congdon and my father, so I have an audience of three. When I write on weekends, it relieves the stress of what I do during the week. My job is very demanding, physically and mentally, but I love it. When you write about gardening, you're not thinking about work, you're not consumed by it, and that's healthy. And I ride my bike, love the outdoors, and we sail when we can. In the winter I work on the landscaping; I've worked hard at putting plants in that do more than just bloom for the summer. Really, from the moment you order or start seedlings, you're thinking about gardening for at least ten months of the year—making compost, ordering, seeding, and weeding. She laughed, adding, "And I now have four chickens. I don't use chemicals at all in my gardens or the landscaping, and I have to manage the insects, because they read my column, know where I live and what I'm growing…I have every insect on the planet visits my garden…people have never heard of the bugs I have. I grow very strong and healthy plants, but you have to fight the bugs, and chickens not only eat all the bugs, they manure the garden and give us eggs in the winter. Their names? We just call them the Biddies."

NOTHING GREENER ON THE OTHER SIDE

What does the future hold for the Leskes? I asked. "Well," Lucy said, "I knew when I married a man who was born here that we'd never leave, and that's fine with me. It's very important for our kids to grow up in a great, supportive place. I love the winters here. We'd really like to stay…what keeps us patient with the summer melee is the closeness and richness of the community in the wintertime, and as long as that fabric remains unbroken, there's nothing greener on the other side. The beauty, the connectedness—you just don't get that in other places. That said, there are a couple of things that are even more important to us than the community and the beauty of the place, and that's the education of the children. While right now the public schools are doing a very good job, we keep a close eye to see that they get what they need.

"In the late '80s I served on the Nantucket Conservation Commission that helped write the regulations in place today governing the construction of building projects close to the water. The only thing that disturbs me, and there's nothing that can be done about it, is that as the population grows, there is an impact on the undisturbed areas, so the things that make life beautiful here are being encroached upon. Tobey does all kinds of volunteer stuff for the harbor, future planning for the island…The other day we were talking about a metaphor for what's going on here, and it's this: When you want to go to the opera you buy tickets, and some of them are very expensive…you pay more for the front rows, less for the back…but you're not excluded from the opera until the place is full…being there's not based on social status or anything. When it's full, the people who come to the door have to go somewhere else…they missed it, and that's just the way it is. I don't feel that certain people should be allowed to live here and some not, but at some point it's going to be full, and I guess we have to decide sooner rather than later what the seating capacity is."

Lucy Leske, this woman born with a strong energy gene, chuckled at this point. I'd asked her about the future. She said, "In my next career, which is presumably going to start some twenty years from now, I've decided I'm going to lead nature walks…helping people inspect and examine things like caterpillar cocoons and the vein patterns in an oak leaf. That's what I'd love to do." Sounds like a great plan.

Left—Lucy and Tobey Leske with their boys: Colin, at left and Wyatt at right. Right—Summer 2002. Lucy at her desk at Educational Management Network/Witt/Kieffer, a Nantucket-based consultancy.

Withchety, Chewink
& Psssh Psssh Psssh
Edith Andrews, 2002

This interview is a bit different, because it's about what Edith Andrews does, rather than the story of her life. Born and raised in New Jersey, Edith graduated from Penn State, received her M.S. from Cornell, and came here summers until she moved here fulltime when she married Clint Andrews. She was shy about discussing her life or providing photos, but her long-time importance here as a bird expert is undeniable. She did comment upon her Nantucket Folger ancestry: "They used to say that if you had island forebears and lived on the island for 25 years, you might be accepted by the islanders. But my daughter Ginger is a real native."

Birds are Edith Andrews' life. And after all, aren't our birdsongs Nantucket voices?

It all started in May, when the birds were frolicking and courting and singing their feathery little heads off starting at 4:30 a.m. in the branches of the big trees outside my second-story window. Suddenly, and thereafter frequently, I heard a birdcall I didn't recall having heard before. It was clear and close, but I just couldn't spot the bird. Its call couldn't be put into words, as many birdsongs can, so I went around for days asking people if they knew which one of our feathered friends sang this: whereupon I proceeded to sing: D-C-G...the D and C being eighth notes and slurred, the G a staccato quarter note. If that sounds dumb and unclear to you now, it certainly did to most of the people I asked. But then one day, on the phone to my daughter in Plymouth, I heard the same sound! She was outside, and said she thought it was a Baltimore oriole, because she had two pairs in her big yard. Of course: *oriole, oriole, oriole*—a neat three-note call.

That started me thinking about all the birds whose songs and messages are much more easily described because they are words or phrases...i.e., their calls have been "Anglicized" for the convenience of interested birders. Yes, I'm an interested birdwatcher but can't seem to remember which is which. Oh, I know the "regular" ones, and I even have cardinal, bluejay, mourning-dove, and chickadee couples regularly visiting my window feeder. And I can I.D. them all by their sounds. But what of other birds?

I did what any sensible bird-challenged person on Nantucket would do and phoned Edith Andrews, who many call the Bird Lady of the island. Could I interview her and work up a little collection of Anglicized birdcalls? She was, as always, most gracious, and when she arrived, the first thing she said was, "Well, I have a mystery...I just can't remember at the moment which bird says whoops! three beers! and it's driving me crazy—I've heard it in the field, but I can't remember who said it."

WHO WAS THAT MASKED BIRD?

What, I asked, are the sounds of some of Nantucket's birds? Edith answered, "One of them is the common yellowthroat; it says witchety-witchety-*WITCH!* Even beginning birders can really hear that. He perches up on a bush and sings, with his head thrown up in the air." I admitted to being partial to this bird—it's tiny, and the black band across its eyes looks for all the world like a mask. If you feel like a mini-adventure, go sit on the steps of Steps Beach early in the morning, and you'll see yellowthroats darting back and forth and singing. Another good place is in the area near where the swings used to be at Low Beach.

"The yellow warbler also sings on Nantucket," said Edith. "It says sweet-sweet-sweet-I-am-so-SWEET! Says it real fast. The eastern towhee says drink-your-tea...and sometimes it'll just say drink-your...or just drink. It also says its name, as many birds do: toWEE or cheWINK. In fact, in a lot of places they call it a chewink." Is that the same as the rufous-sided towhee, which I see in abundance over near Macy Lane and Skyline Drive? I asked. "It is," Edith answered. "They've changed its name to the eastern towhee now. When I first started birding it was a red-eyed towhee, and then they changed it to rufous-sided, and now it's the eastern towhee." Oh, the ubiquitous "they" ...who are "they" who change birds' names, and why? "Well," Edith said, "'they,' the ornithologists in the universities and museums, are the ones who change the names. There's a towhee out west that is known as the spotted towhee, and for a while they split the western and the eastern towhee, because they were separate...then they put them together because they thought they'd hybridized and made one species...then they split them again. And there's also the white-eyed towhee in the south, but that's the eastern towhee too."

I mentioned one of my favorite birds, the scrappy, fierce little sparrow hawk, whose name has also been changed. "Oh yes," Edith said. "They changed it from sparrow hawk to kestrel. American kestrel. Yes—I don't know what gets into them...sometimes they can mess things up when they change the names. This bird says *keek-keek-keek-keek*...that's the best way I can say it." I recalled seeing plenty of these little falcons, sitting on rails and telephone lines, watching intently for prey. If I thought they were cute, I changed my mind when I saw one swoop down, grab a mouse, and take it to the top of the tree to tear it apart, all the while glaring around as if to say, "Just try to get this away from me!" I seem to remember these saying *killy-killy-killy* when I visited California, so apparently this bird too sings a different tune now and then.

It's fairly easy to whistle some birds' songs, like the cardinal's sharp "upside-down whistle," as someone once described it; it's like a whistle for a dog, only it goes from up to down in tune. And of course cardinals have quite a variety of songs. Their *burgee-burgee-burgee* seems somehow appropriate on this island, where burgee flags stream brightly from visiting sailboats. Some birdcalls simply can't be "translated" into words because they sing more of a melody. Edith agreed: "That's true, yes. I'm not musical, so I can usually do better with the ones that say things, that I can put words to. Let's see—the red-winged blackbird says [and she really sang this call, in spite of claiming she wasn't musical] *okalee, okalee*. He makes a lot of different sounds, but that's one you hear in the spring." When I lived in upstate New York, the redwinged blackbirds seemed to say poop-uh-*CHEE!* Maybe, I joked, it had a New York accent. Edith laughed and said, "Well, they do have different dialects. Song sparrows sound different further west than they do here in the east. It's like people—geographic distribution, I guess.

THE LOVE CALL OF THE CHICKADEE

"And of course you know the chickadee's call—you can't mistake that. It says its name: chick-a-dee-dee-dee." And doesn't the phoebe say its name too? A high, plaintive PHEEbee? Nope, said our sage: "The eastern phoebe says pheeBEE pheeBEE...but when you hear PHEEbee, PHEEbee, higher on the first note, or PEEtoe, that's a chickadee—that's the love call of the chickadee in the spring."

Ducks have their quack and oystercatchers say *wheee!* and hummingbirds say *hummm, I* mused. Well, they don't say it, Edith reminded me: "Their wings make the humming noise, not their throats. But they certainly do make a sound. I caught one in a mist net once and it cried like a baby! It *screeched!* It was loud. I was amazed; I had no idea!" In California, I recalled, the Anna's hummingbirds are extremely aggressive and not frightened by anything. I've seen them fly out at people from their flowers at the very busy edge of a San Francisco hill, in a perfect rage because someone dared to walk too close. I've also heard them make a very fast, twitter-chipping, the tiniest scolding you've ever heard. "In this part of the country," Edith said, "we have the ruby-throated hummingbird...we get others by accident; the rufous hummingbird might get here by accident, but the eastern one is the ruby-throated. They are lovely birds."

Then we went from the sublime to the ridiculous-crows. They caw-caw-caw, sometimes in code, it seems. They sit in the big trees at Academy Hill, often at the crack of dawn, and send messages to their cousins and sisters and aunts over in the Lily Pond area, getting answers only slightly less raucous and noisy. Cawwww...caw-caw. "That's a language, of sorts," said Edith. She proceeded with her bird translations: "The yellow-shafted flicker, a relative of the bluejay, says wicka-wicka-WICK!" And does a catbird sometimes sound like a kitten being tortured? "Oh, the catbird does meow like a cat...but you could be hearing a starling, too. Starlings imitate a lot of other birds. They have picked up the wolf whistle! I never have been able to whistle—I wish I could." Another copycat, of course, is the mockingbird, which seems to imitate all the other birds, and which will sometimes copy a whistle executed by a human bird. These guys are also quite bold, and will come close and peer directly and inquiringly at you while you're pretending you're a bird expert making attractive avian noises.

188

Pssssh Psssssh Pssssh

A hint to people learning about birds: Edith said they are attracted when people make pshhh-pshhh-pshhh sounds. Many people have had the awesome experience of doing that sound, or the alternative wishy-wishy-wishy (not spoken, just sounded) at exactly the right moment in time and at just the propitious place, and watching as dozens of small birds flocked to nearby trees or bushes to investigate the creature that was making this enticing sound. I've found that it works sometimes after a rain...and it does seem as if the colors you're wearing have something to do with whether birds will get close to you or not.

"The barred owl," Edith observed, says "Who cooks for YOU? Who cooks for YOU? Furthermore, she said, "The ones in the south say Who cooks for YOU-ALL?" No, really? Yes, really! Talk about dialects! We decided to give the loon a try and Edith thought my rendition of that shy bird's haunting laugh-cry, ending in a sort of tremolo and tailing off with a sad downturn, was pretty good. That's a waterbird, but how about shorebirds? According to Edith, their calls, for the most part, are hard to translate, but the godwits, with their long upturned bills, whistle (surprise) *godwit.* Incidentally, willets, which say *wee-willet, wee-willet,* also have a long, sharp bill, but large sandpipers, such as the long-billed curlew or the whimbrel, have the same bills turned downward. (Did you know that there's a sandpiper called the wandering tattler? I don't think he wanders to Nantucket, though.) The killdeer, a beautiful bird with two striking bands around its throat, said Edith, also says its name: killDEE, killDEE. Looking up shorebird behavior, I found that the killdeer will, like the inland pheasant, pretend to have a damaged wing if someone or something gets too near its nest, and will walk just far enough ahead of intruders to get them away from its nest, but not near enough to allow them to catch up with it. The killdeer is a type of plover, and of course Nantucket knows about the piping plover. One of these started a new nest recently after some fool destroyed the first one, and the section was then closed off because of its status as an endangered species. Edith said, "Well, it was a surprise that it re-nested with two eggs—as someone said, if they'd just left it alone the first time it nested, instead of destroying the nest, it would've been hatched and done and gone by now." Plovers aren't particularly shy unless they're nesting, Edith noted. Referring to the expired whale that beached on the island earlier this season, Edith said, "We watched them pull the whale off, and there was a piping plover right on the beach with all the people around; it was running back and forth, and didn't seem to mind at all. But it's when you get near the nest that it gets alarmed."

A bird that tends to live in inland marshy areas on the island is the American woodcock, whose call, Edith noted, "starts out with a *been been been* on the ground, and then it does all these wonderful twittery noises when it's way overhead…just beautiful." This bird is a type of sandpiper, actually. A sanderling, she added, likes the sandy shoreline, and when in flight says *plick.* Other shorebirds? Edith said, "We have the little blue herons here on the island; they seem to be in migration. But the great egret and the snowy egret both nest here." It's a snowy, she said, that you often see in the harbor—and if you go out on Straight Wharf and look over toward Children's Beach, you'll probably see this handsome wading bird; it's as bold as you please, prancing around amid all the harbor hubbub, looking for meals in the tidal detritus. You can also see snowy egrets easily in the Folger Marsh, out near the Lifesaving Museum on Polpis Road; they walk so deliberately, placing one foot carefully down, picking the other up high, and I've observed them actually stepping slowly up to people's fishing pails and stealing bait, quite audaciously. The way to tell a snowy from a great egret? Said Edith: "If it has yellow feet, it's a snowy; it's wearing yellow slippers. If it has a yellow bill, it's a great egret." And if that's not enough yellow or greaters and lessers for you, there's a greater yellowlegs and lesser yellowlegs…which both look very much like the willet.

The conversation came around to inland Nantucket birds again. Edith said, "The song sparrow says *hip-hip-hooray-boys! Spring-is-here!* It goes together, but if you listen carefully, you can hear that. It starts out with two notes hip-hip. Someone said it's like Beethoven's Fifth— *hip-hip-hooray.* And the black-throated green warbler says *tree-trees-murmuring-trees,* real fast." We stopped a moment to look at the jays gobbling up sunflower seeds on my windowsill. "You know," said Edith, "bluejays imitate other calls, too. I've heard them sound like red-tailed hawks. But I can't imitate that.

"A chestnut-sided warbler says I-wish-I wish-I wish-to-see-Miss-BEEcher," Edith went on. "And the ovenbird says teacher-teacher-TEACH! And that one is loud! We only get those on migration—they don't nest here, so we don't hear them very often. If they happen to sing while they're migrating through, we're lucky to hear them. And they sing most when they're courting. Now, a rose-breasted grosbeak sounds something like a robin; they just pass through in the spring—they nest in Massachusetts, but not on Nantucket." The robin, I said, seems to have a number of sort of bubbling sounds. "That's a good way to describe it," Edith said. "Both cardinals and robins stay year-round. There is some exchange with robins; some of the northern ones come here for the winter and ours go farther north for the summer. And that's true of the starlings—they are year-round, too, but they migrate."

When I asked if any birds on the island have migrated here in the past and then decided to stay on, because the robins seem to be here year-round now, Edith said, "Well, some of the young ones that go through will linger...they stay, but they don't nest here—they're too young, like the black-bellied plovers that've been hanging around Eel Point; they must be young birds, so they haven't gone north. They have to go north to breed and nest...all the way up to the tundra, so they have a long way to go."

Whoo-Whooo Are Nantucket's Ground-Nesters?

We talked a bit about Nantucket's ground-nesting birds, which are very fortunate because, except for feral cats and human beings, there are no animals that seek them, such as skunks, possums, and weasels. "Feral cats," Edith said, "are a problem for Nantucket birds; they do a lot of hunting...but of course they get mice, too. Among the ground-nesters, there is the short-eared owl, and pheasants nest on the ground, and some towhees will nest on the ground; or sometimes they'll build a nest a few feet up. The barn owl will take a wooden box...it would nest in a cavity if we had big enough trees—that's the way they did in the old days. We have several kinds of owl on the island, including the barn owl and the saw-whet owl—that is a little tiny one, and it nests in cavities also; they used to nest in the State Forest, but we haven't found them there lately. We don't have great horned owls, but we used to have long-eared owls; they nested in the Forest too, but not regularly—I don't know whether it's too much human disturbance or what. The snowy owl comes in the winter, and we had one at Eel Point that came and stayed until April this year! And it will go to the tundra to nest." I'd thought that the owl I'd seen very late one night on Ram Pasture Road was a snowy, because he'd looked very white, sitting in the middle of the road. I thought he—or she—looked like a big roll of newspaper, so I stopped to pick it up. With my radio playing classical music and a starry sky above, I got out of the car, saw to my amazement it was an owl, thought it might be hurt, and of all silly things, said, *"OH, are you OK?"* It looked at me long and hard, not 8 feet away, then took silent flight, its big wings extending all the way up over its head, almost meeting, then all the way below its body. Edith agreed that that was a *Wow!* experience: "That sounds like a barn owl—they can look quite white at night. And they're strictly nocturnal, too. Sometimes we go out at night, mostly to listen to birds—for instance, we went to try and hear whippoorwills this spring, without any luck. But they nest on the island too."

What is Edith Andrews' favorite bird? She laughed and said, "People always ask that! My favorite bird is the one I'm looking at! Well, I like the Carolina wren, which incidentally has a nice loud call I can hear without a hearing aid, and it says *video-video-video. Or weetier-weetier-weet.* That's a favorite, and that's one that never used to nest here, but it's moved northward, just like the cardinal...we never used to have cardinals this far north, but they've extended their range north and so have the Carolina wrens, and once they get to Nantucket, they stay year-round. So they nest here, too."

What are the birds you fear for most on Nantucket? I asked. "You mean because of loss of habitat, and feral cats? Well, the ground-nesting birds like the short-eared owl—it may be nesting back on Nantucket, and I think someone did find a nest last year. The harrier seems to be holding its own, and we have quite a few pairs. The ospreys are doing well; in fact, yesterday I went with Bob Kennedy—he's doing a study of the ospreys; he had a lot of experience down in Virginia with ospreys, banding and such, and he has a snoop stick. That's a mirror on an extendable pole that can be extended to 40 or 48 feet. Granger Frost has an osprey pole with a platform on his property and we went to see yesterday afternoon [this interview took place in June] if the eggs had hatched—there were eggs the last time they had looked—and there were three babies in the nest, and you could see them in this mirror very well. So that's pretty exciting. The mirror is only about 6 to 8 inches, but holding it just right over the nest, you can see the contents very well. I always wanted a snoop stick...but you know, it's awfully hard to find nests. However, when you put up osprey platforms, you can see them. I did some banding of ospreys when they first started nesting here, and the first one that I ever banded ended up in Colombia, South America, three years later; it was found...dead. It may have been shot for the band...a lot of people do that sort of thing. They think it's worth something, that they'll get money for it. Anyway, a lot of ospreys spend the winter in South America, and there have been lots of recoveries in Colombia, particularly."

How about the mist nets Edith had mentioned earlier? "We use those to track birds' movements, to see what's here; usually I do it in migration, particularly fall migration, and we get some idea of how many of each thing is going through. And that's when I get a lot of the warblers, in their fall plumage. You put the mist net between trees or bushes, and it's 30 or 40 feet long and has four panels—it's a very fine net, like a hairnet. And a bird is easy enough to extract from the net; you take it out, put it in a bag, and take it back to the banding table, and then put the little silver bracelet on its leg; each one has its own number, and you can keep track. I do some banding in the summer, too, with my breeding birds, and that way I keep track of how many catbirds are breeding on my property, for example, and how many yellow warblers, and common yellowthroats. Those are the ones I get mostly. But some years they do better than others; keeping track of their longevity is important." When I've seen Edith on television banding birds, I've noticed that she talks gently to them all the time she's handling them. "Oh yes, I do," she said, smiling. "They're sweethearts—they're all little sweethearts."

I asked how Edith had gotten started birding, and she replied, laughing, "I don't know. Well, I did see a black-throated green warbler outside the bedroom window when I was in my youth, and I found it in our bird book...I think that turned me on...although I was interested always. I just was born that way, I guess. I was lucky."

...& I'll Squeeze It Till It Squirts!

Edith told me about a simply unbelievable birdcall performed by the warbling vireo: *If I see it I will seize it and I'll squeeze it till it squirts!* "It all goes together, faster than I can say it," she laughed, "but if you're careful you can hear it. I still wish I knew who says Whoops! three beers! That'll come to me. Let's see—other birds that say things: the white-throated sparrow says Sam-Peabody-Peabody-Peabody-that's an easy one. The eastern meadowlark says spring-is-here. The goldfinch is pretty easy when it's in its spring plumage; now that's one that's here year-

191

EDITH ANDREWS

round. And it changes plumage—in the spring it gets that lovely gold color. And as they fly overhead, goldfinches say potato-CHIPS, potato-CHIPS. They're very sweet."

There are, as Edith had said, variations in bird families, often according to where they're from; for instance, in the east we have the raucous bluejay and its cousin in the west is the darker Steller's jay; island oystercatchers, which bow toward each other during courtship, are black and white on the chest, while they are all black on the west coast; both have strong, long, pointed red bills for prying shells open. And of course many different variations of hummingbirds, and even bluebirds: "There is the mountain bluebird and the eastern bluebird," Edith said, "and they're separate species in the same families."

What's Edith's advice regarding birdhouses? "Well," she said, "you have to know what bird you want to attract, because different birds take a different-size opening into the house...tree swallow houses would be the most logical around here. And put it in an open area, where the bird can fly into it. There are plenty of books on how to build birdhouses for different birds. If you build the right kind of house, the right birds will come...if they're there. You ought to know what birds are in your vicinity, in your yard, first."

HINTS FOR BEGINNING BIRDERS

When you see a bird you don't know and want to be able to go to your bird guide and identify it, what's the best thing to "fix" on—size of beak? color? tail shape? size? pattern of flight? Edith had some advice for people learning how to enjoy and know birds. First of all, obviously, it's easier when the bird has landed somewhere. She said: "It's better to start when they're not fluttering by so fast! If they're on the ground, you use a kind of yardstick: take the robin and the house sparrow (most everybody knows these birds) and ask yourself, 'Is it smaller than a house sparrow? Or is it larger? Is it smaller than a robin or is it larger?' You want to get some idea of size." Then, she said, look for specific characteristics (beak shape, color, tail length, for example)..."and it helps if you can have a binocular, to bring the birds closer." I complained that by the time I get the binocular up to my eyes, I'm looking at everything but the bird— branches, leaves, etc. Edith said, "The way to use a binocular is to start with something like a road sign and just bring the binocular up to the eyes...look at the sign and bring your bino up without moving your head or anything, and see where it is, and then practice focusing. Find the bird first with your eye, and then without moving, bring the binocular up to your eyes—see if that works."

Well, we'd talked about a lot more things than Anglicized names for birdcalls, but already I'm sighting and identifying birds better. However, I still need work: at this very moment, I'm hearing a *pick-a-whir* outside, and don't know what it is. Before I let Edith Andrews escape, I asked her what were the best birds she'd seen this year. She answered promptly: "The forktailed flycatcher, a black and white bird, kingbird-like, with an enormous tail, 10 to 12 inches long. These come occasionally in the fall, not spring, and are very rare—and they do not stay. Then there was the lazuli bunting—Nonie Slavitz, who's an excellent birder, found that. It was seen in Somerset Lane, in Bartletts' field. It's a first for the east; Massachusetts has never had one. It stayed for two or three weeks. Then there was a sandhill crane that stayed two or three weeks."

Finally, Edith remembered what bird says *whoops! three beers.* It was the olive-sided flycatcher. I looked this one up in my bird guide and found that it's found in northern coniferous woods, looks a bit like the eastern phoebe except for a larger head and bill and a shorter tail. Its song, says my book is *whip-three-beers* (but plainly, on Nantucket, it's *whoops! three beers),* and its call is *pip-pip-pip.* So after all this, I find that the song can be different from the call. I'll have to ask Edith about that.

Edith Folger Andrews, on the day she was honored for lifetime achievement by the Maria Mitchell Association, 2003. Photo by Barbara Vigneau.

The Art of Building a Woodshed

Ginger Andrews, 2000

*G*inger Andrews, who's often smiling when she speaks, seems to be given to waving an arm and either quoting a famous dramatic line or making one up. Even her phone messages tend to be wry and erudite quotes. "All the world's a stage," she declared from our interview spot just outside her kitchen door, "except for my house, which is the prop room."

It was one of those bright and sparkling deep-blue September days that refuses to let you stay inside, so we moved outdoors, where we heard the occasional aggressive shrieks of a power saw and the racket made by some sort of hydraulic lift just next door. "They're always doing work on the houses around here," she declared. Do you mind it? I asked. "Oh no," she said with a philosophical shrug, "that's Nantucket, after all."

Explaining the reference to a prop room entailed getting up and going back into the house. Ginger stepped inside the kitchen door and pointed upward. Over the door was a sign: STAGE DOOR ENTRANCE. "That's from the old Straight Wharf Theatre and was actually thrown away one summer. I don't know why they decided to throw it away, but I grabbed it. I hung it over the kitchen door on the inside, because there's little in the house that hasn't appeared on a Nantucket set at one time or another." We went outside again and talked just a bit about Ginger's parents, bird expert Edith and the late Clint Andrews, both of whose well-known interest in the natural sciences influenced Ginger's growing-up years.

Tell me about being a bona fide Nantucket native, I said. "I was born in the Cottage Hospital, which had just been moved from West Chester Street, so I think I was one of the early arrivals. I went for the first ten years of school here, and at the end of tenth grade I went away to a place called Simon's Rock, which is in the Berkshires—it's part of Bard now. It was called the Early College—we used to call it the Late Prep School," she added with a smile. What was the reason you went off-island for that part of your education? I asked. "Well, I did very well in some of the standardized tests…which don't really say how intelligent you are, they just prove that you're good at taking standardized tests. And I guess there was a general feeling that I ought to go to college. My memory of going to school here after first grade I would say is of hours and hours of soul-killing boredom, so yeah, I didn't like school much. Simon's Rock was pretty exciting. They actually had a film course, and of course when I was growing up there were no movies here in the winter at all. I always say that I ended up in theatre because I couldn't choose between art and English—I couldn't give up one or the other. The theatre is very satisfying because there's some relic of wholeness there that has become fragmented in other forms of entertainment.

THE QUAISE MARSH ENVIRONMENT

"I was brought up in this house, right here, until I was ten, and then my father went to work for the UMass Field Station, and we went to live out on the Quaise Marsh. It was an incredible spot. I used to love to follow the deer paths through the underbrush and I think the first summer we were there, I spent practically the whole summer in the water. In those years, Beverly Hall had the children's gallery down on the South Wharf, which was a really exciting place to be. She used to take me to art museums in the city, and so on. I remember being really impressed with what [sculptor] Louise Nevelson did with the stuff she picked up on the beach, because of course, Nantucket natives are great scavengers." Ginger stopped to laugh. "That comes in very handy when people need props for things, as you've experienced yourself." (I had just borrowed two 1940s phones from Ginger for a performance of Menotti's *The Telephone*—that was my first experience with the "prop-room" qualities of Ginger's house. It's literally filled with furniture, artwork, costumes, sculptures, objects of every imaginable kind that can be and have been used for many, if not most, staged performances on the island.)

Ginger Andrews' father was a native, but her mother grew up in Maywood, New Jersey. "She went to Bogota High, then to Penn State, and she came here summers…I'm a native, for what it's worth." She said that a bit sardonically, and we recalled a recent letter to the editor in the *I&M* in which a woman had written, "I'm an almost native," and the reaction of some of our native-born friends. We agreed that there's probably no such thing as an almost-native, and I had to ask if there were some things to which a bona fide native is entitled. "Well," Ginger answered, her expression denoting some consternation, "in some ways I think it's an overrated thing. I mean, so what? [Another heavy sigh.] One of the problems we have on the island is that some of the natives have said, 'I'll get mine, and the hell with the rest of them.' Basically, I do sometimes feel like an indigenous person, having grown up here. I've seen forty years of changes on the island, and I would say that as a community it's been pretty much destroyed; you know, it's turning into one big gated community, and the only thing missing is the armed-response sticker over the ferry dock that tells people they're not welcome here unless they have megabucks.

"Before I went off to school, being an only child, I spent a lot of time hanging around with my parents, and got very involved with their interest in the natural sciences …if there was a beached whale, we went to look at it. Once there was a thresher shark or a hammerhead—I remember that it was incredibly ugly—that washed up at Madaket. I went with my father, hauling lobster pots, fishing, clamming, all those great things. Now I hardly ever do them," she added with what sounded like regret.

Some moments of reflective silence ensued, and then Ginger said, "You know, it's kind of an accident that I landed up back here…I graduated from Simon's Rock after four years with an Associate of Arts degree, so then I had two more years to finish college and I went to Denison, but in between I took three years off, and Nantucket in the 1970s was a really exciting place. There were a lot of artists and it was possible just to get a caretaking job, stay for the winter, and write your novel. Some people wrote them, some people drank, you know, and some people got siphoned off into the theatre…

"For those three years I was back here, I went scalloping with my dad, wrote a lot of letters, worked in the theatre. I had a summer job at the Theatre Workshop, and I sort of bounced back and forth in the arts a little bit. One reason I landed back on the island was because if I'd gone to New York I'd still be coiling cables, and being here gave me a chance to do more. Originally I wanted to be a set designer, but I ended up in lights because I'm not the kind of personality that makes carpenters want to work overtime on a set after they've done a full day of carpentry.

"This summer," Ginger said, "when we did *On the Isle* in 'Sconset, they had a song to the tune of 'Get Me to the Church on Time,' but the words were 'To Live in 'Sconset's Very Hard,' and every time they got to the chorus they drowned it out with the sound effects for a moped and a motorcycle and a lawnmower and a leaf-blower, and finally an airplane. The point was that to live in 'Sconset is very hard—you can't hear a darn thing. One noise stops, another starts up." At the very moment she said this, a power saw uttered a long, chilling scream. "I used to call this The Island of Perpetual Construction," she yelled. "I get up early, but *ERRRR-RAAAANH-KITCHUNK-KITCHUNK-KITCHUNK!* starts at 7 a.m. They seem compelled to start at 7, make noise for an hour to assert that they've done something, take a three-hour coffee break, and then they work slowly through the afternoon." Her laughter said that she'd gotten used to it, however, despite the fact that this was hardly the ideal atmosphere for a taped interview.

THE MAGIC DOOR & THE WONDERFUL MAC DIXON

I was curious to know if Ginger had been interested in the theatre before she went away to school. "I went to the plays with my parents and some of my classmates, at the old Straight Wharf Theatre…they were terrific, and sometimes they were in them, so we'd go to the theatre and come home and discuss the plays, and it was great fun. There was a door that went backstage; it was down on house right, and it looked intriguing, and people kept going through it looking important. I always wanted the right to go through that door. Well I managed to get back to Nantucket before the 'causes-unknown' fire that burned down the Straight Wharf Theatre in 1975, so I actually managed to go through the door a few times."

Who were some of the theatre people with whom Ginger worked in those three years? "Oh, well, Mac Dixon. I stage-managed mostly then, because I wanted to learn all I could about theatre, and I thought stage-managing was the way to do it, because it encompasses all the aspects of production. And I learned so much from Mac; I mean, if America had any respect for artists at all, Mac Dixon would have been declared a living national treasure. He studied with Boleslavsky and Madame Ouspenskaya; he had had a Broadway career; his aunt was Jane Wallach, who worked with Antoinette Perry, for whom the Tony awards were named…Jane and Mac were tremendous resources to Nantucket. They really unified the theatre community here, drew people in and kept it going.

"I learned a tremendous amount about the craft of theatre from Mac, and to watch him work was amazing. Just the sheer preparation he did before a show, and the time he would take…he could turn a gawky, shy American teenager who'd never been onstage before into a snappy Cockney British callboy—that's like an assistant stage manager—in about twenty minutes. Some of the people I worked with at Straight Wharf are still here—Eric Schultz, Charles Folger, Maggie Lee, Ursula Austin, and Margaret Hitchcock, for example—and some went on and had full-time careers in the theatre…While I was still in school I did summer stock off-island, and in my first year I worked at the Lenox Arts Center, where I just kind of hung around and watched Richard Foreman direct…that was a completely different experience from watching Mac Dixon direct, but equally interesting. Mac was very traditional, from the old Broadway sort of established school of thought, and Foreman was and still is completely wacko, avant-

Left—Ginger Andrews. Right—Looking pensive, Ginger in the 1970s.

garde—you know, *Rhoda in Potato Land*—that was one of his plays, and *Dr. Selavy's Magic Theatre,"* a musical based on the artwork of Marcel Duchamp.

"After the Nantucket hiatus, I went back to school, and once again I got sucked in by the theatre. I was an assistant in the sculpture shop, and worked for the prop department. After I graduated from college with a degree in Theatre, I bounced back and forth between Nantucket and New York a bit. I made various semi-successful at living in New York, and did some freelance stuff there. I worked with Joe Papps' Public Theatre briefly. Somehow the time went all too quickly, what with one thing and another, as it will…"

"After Mac sort of retired, in the early '80s, I was doing lights here on the island and enjoying it, and scalloping, and writing, and trying to be an artist—I used to do quite a lot of silk screening and I would make prints for other artists—Andrew Shunney, Clara Urbahn, George Murphy, etcetera—and I printed my own work also. Here's a funny story: At one point in my periodic frantic despair at being an artist I decided I was going to clean out my portfolio [she made a wide sweeping motion with her arm]. So I spent about two days weeding things…and I finally got this giant portfolio full of stuff I was going to throw out. It was a nasty, rainy, drizzly, cold, raw, soggy winter afternoon. I took it out to the Landfill; I heaved it into the dumpster and thought, 'All right, that's the end of that!' Well, four days later, sure enough, I ran into a friend, and she said, 'Did you throw away a portfolio?' I went, 'Ohhhhhh, *no!*' So my work is now gracing the Artists' Association, Kidder-Peabody, and the DPW office at the dump."

Tell me about the writing, I said. Are you still doing that? Rolling her eyes as if in pain, Ginger said, "Ohhhhh yes, off and on. It's agony. It's hard for me to finish things, and if I let anyone read them before I'm absolutely totally done, they just die on me, so I mostly write short pieces…I've written a few for the local papers [her term was actually "fish-wrappers"!] on ecological subjects. I also wrote occasionally for a little gardening quarterly which I really liked—after my dad died I got into gardening."

"EKING BY," À LA NANTUCKET

Ginger contemplated why she has always kept coming back to the island: "You know, it's nice…I think Nantucket has a bunch of different niches…you have your music niche, and your ecological niche, and your beach niche…and theatre…I've really been fortunate in that I grew up in the ecological niche and I also had a space of my own in the artists/theatre niche, and now I guess now I'm part of the alternative healing niche as well."

Most islanders, I commented, seem to have been employed in a number of different and sometimes quite divergent jobs. Ginger agreed: "One year I worked for the Artists' Association. And let's see, I did silk screening, house cleaning, dredging for scallops, opening scallops…I don't think I ever got paid for gardening. And of course I've worked in various aspects of the theatre…lighting has been part of my income, but I've had some very bad experiences with that. I'm just not enough of an entrepreneur, and you know, getting paid $15 an hour and then finding out that your services are being charged out at a higher rate, so the person you're working with can make $55 an hour…that's a typical Nantucket employer story. But working many jobs is definitely part of the Nantucket scene…I mean, I'm self-employed, and if I'm overwhelmed I usually can get a friend to help me, you know…and I've helped people in my time too." Is the lighting work pretty steady throughout the year? I asked. "Well, yeah…it doesn't quite add up to a part-time job, but it's close enough that I eke by. I rent out part of this house. As far as the lighting goes, during last summer I got to light Hillary Clinton, the ultimate celebrity. I don't have TV, so it was a little difficult; I couldn't check my work, but I gather from some people who saw her speech at the Methodist Church Performance Center on one of the news channels that I made the right choices." Did you get to meet her? I asked. "Oh no, of course not," Ginger responded. "I was back behind the TV cameras and the lighting stuff…that's usually where I am."

More machine noise, then blessed quiet. Ginger said, "Let's see…what was I pontificating about? Oh, interesting people I've lit, which is kind of like asking the rock about the wildlife that crosses around in front of it. But…ummm…I would say that I kind of put Hillary Clinton in the middle. I've been providing interior lighting for Atheneum lectures for two or three years, and I love that. And there've been some wonderful concerts that the Arts Council has put on. Of course the bad thing is that I hardly ever get to things that I don't work on…Probably the weirdest thing I've ever worked on, barring the summer stock at the Lenox Arts Center, which was by definition avant-garde and intentionally weird, would probably be a Christian rock group the Congregational church had one winter. I think it was in the early '80s, and the leader was one of those real Fundamentalist 'Don't tell me you believe in evolution' types. Now, I don't get paid for everything I do; I did this for the church. So this rock group didn't pay me, which would have been OK, but they also failed to thank me or acknowledge me, which is not OK…I mean, payment and thanks are the best, both of which I received from the 'Sconset folks for *On the Isle*. You know, thanks are good and payment is great, but to have neither payment nor thanks is really kind of churlish."

COULD THE WORLD FORGET ABOUT US?

Do you like where you are in your life, your career? I asked. Ginger was silent again for a moment, then gave an answer that more than hinted that she isn't entirely satisfied with the way things are, particularly after a very difficult summer owing to a repeat of her Lyme disease problems. She ended by shrugging her shoulders and saying, "Well, you know, it's like Thoreau said: You start out in your youth assembling lumber for a stairway to the moon and then in middle age you're content to build a woodshed. So I'm building my woodshed. I'd love to do more lighting. I'd love to work for other companies. I have a long history with the theatre here, and I've tried to maintain my own integrity, but as I've often said, where there are theatre people there will be drama…and so, you know, the skeletons and the arguments and the bloodbaths have continued and many really talented people who have been here have moved on."

What does Ginger see herself doing in the future—more writing? More painting? More theatre work? She laughed and replied, "You mean will I be cleaning houses when I'm eighty? Probably. I'll have to work several jobs to make a go of it, yeah, like everyone else." And what does Ginger think of what's happening on—or to—the island? "Well," she answered, "we had a big crash before, when Nantucket was a thriving oil-company town, and they behaved with the same standards and practices of companies today. When that changed and the island crashed economically, it was left very quaint and beautiful. It was starting to get built up again in the '20s when the stock market crashed. Soooo…a crash would maybe calm things down. Oh well," she concluded fatalistically, "the island isn't going to be here more than another 300 or 400 years anyway." What would you wish for the island? I asked. "Oh, that's easy enough. I wish that people would just kind of forget about us for a little bit, and that they would find some 'next new thing.' The best thing for Nantucket would be for people to lose interest a little bit and let us catch our breath. I don't know that a big crash would even help at this point. When people have multi-billions, who cares if they become mere millionaires, you know? The thing that constantly astounds me is the sheer waste of money and materials…when they have these houses done over and over and over again. Why is this happening? I think it's because it's the only way they have to assert control over their environment. They have too much money and they're too busy to actually do anything themselves, so they have it done for them, but it means that they don't have any feeling of personal, emotional, spiritual connection to Nantucket…God knows they're never gonna live here, you know? They might spend two weeks a year, or they might send someone in business they want to impress here, but they have these big, beautiful houses…and all they can do is say no to the carpenter. So they say no to the carpenter and the painter and the decorator, and they throw out the perfectly good old microwave and buy a perfectly good new microwave and throw that away…

"Maybe a good thing to talk about regarding what's next for me is my interest in alternative healing techniques. I've been studying Five Element Acupuncture with Eliot Cowan; it's really fascinating, and it actually goes very well with theatre in many ways. It's something I've always been interested in, because it follows the natural flow of energy in the seasons, the body, and the culture, as well as the individual. I've also been studying a sort of movement training called Continuum with a woman in California, Emily Conrad. Continuum is more about sensation and experience than talking, and I find that very interesting just from my perspective in the arts. One of the things I most enjoy about lighting theatre is that here, I'm able to do lighting without a computer board…it's small, I can do it manually, so the craft is really in the attention. Learning to look at and understand movement is really what Continuum is about, and it's what theatre is about. So yeah, I'm interested in the movement of energy, and this takes various forms…I think that the difficulties the theatre has had here reflect the difficulties of the community, because theatre is essentially a communal art, and if you don't have an audience, you can't have a theatre. I think we sometimes lose track of that as production people and performers because we're so intent upon getting the sets up and painted and the lights focused and the lines learned…and then…you're ready, and who's interested? Maybe nobody." Well, I commented, I think people are interested, but working people find it hard to go to the theatre after working a ten-hour day. Ginger agreed: "If you have three jobs, you hardly ever have time. You know, in the '70s people had *time* to be in plays, and it was kind of fun."

We had to stop; things to do, places to go. But Ginger left me hanging with a comment as I was leaving. "Sometime," she said, "ask me about my membership in the 'Virginia Woolf Walking, Writing, and Sipping Society.'"

Ginger says that "as the kid of two naturalists and the niece and great-niece of two Atheneum librarians (Barbara Andrews and Clara Parker), her sense of history comes with the territory she grew up in, and as of 2003, she's calling upon this knowledge in her capacity as Conservation Commission's appointee to the Community Preservation Committee. The CPC's mission is to promote affordable housing, historic preservation, and open space.

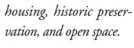

Left—A 1997 photo of Ginger looking as if she's enjoying a good joke with Martha Allen. Right— Ginger Andrews in 1982.

Wind in Her Sails

Adrienne McCalley, 2001

$\mathcal{A}$drienne McCalley has a long, long history on Nantucket—76 years at this writing. "When we first came here," she noted, "the *Nobska* was brand-new." She began life in the Hudson Valley, Poughkeepsie, in Dutchess County, NY. And how had she "happened upon" Nantucket? "Well, I have a long family connection with the island. My grandparents knew some summer people from here and came down in the late part of the nineteenth century. My mother was a very small child then," she went on. "She was born in 1881, so it's a piece back. Mother and her brother, as teenagers, used to come here and visit the Mitchell family; they owned West Brick, and also built the cottage down on Beachside as their summer home. Mother and my uncle had such a good time that after she got married, she wanted to come back here, bringing the children, but it was pretty far for my father to commute, so they didn't come back until 1925, when they bought a house. And so we came down to be summer Nantucketers on the *Nobska* starting that year."

EXPLORING ALL THE ROADS

What did you and your brother Ted Anderson (also an islander) do as children on Nantucket? I asked. "We practically lived at Sandy Craig's house a good part of the time—his family, as friends of my grandparents, had started this whole Nantucket thing. Sandy's and Suggie's mother, Maggie, was very welcoming of all little children. So I grew up on that beach. They had a pier—quite a few people had piers that stuck out into the harbor at that time...and some of them had summer houses on the end. Those piers were taken down every winter—can you imagine it?—because otherwise the ice would carry them away. My brother and I used to go swimming daily, rain or shine, on the west side of Hummock Pond. We had rowboats, and later on beat-up old outboard motors, and we had a pleasant, healthy youth. We belonged to the yacht club, but didn't have much to do with it, except to play tennis. I was made to go to various dances as a child. I won my first yacht club trophy in a Lucky Number dance down there when I was about six. As we got older, our father bought us a beat-up old car, because we would ruin the family car driving around on the moors, and we explored every single road on the island. We knew this island the way a lot of the islanders do not."

The island must have been wonderful in those years, I said. "Yes," she answered. "In the old days you had sweeping moor views. And even as recently as the early 1950s, I remember driving out the road between Shimmo and Shawkemo, and stopping with a friend of mine to pose on a hillock of mealie-plum [bearberries] to take a picture of her sitting there with a huge view of the harbor. Everything's up to here nowadays! I don't know if it was sheep that kept the scrub oak down—I do remember sheep, but they were always out in that area where they have them now, off 'Sconset Road. I don't remember them elsewhere, although I do remember some cows out Bartlett's Farm way, and at Hummock Pond."

A COUPLE YEARS OF "FIDDLING AROUND"

How about early life off-island? "I went to school in Poughkeepsie until I was boarding-school age, and then I was sent to the Masters School at Dobbs Ferry, which was called Dobbs. While I was there I got interested in music. I'd never been a very good piano student, because I couldn't read music, but there was a young teacher who was a very gifted pianist—I mean a real pianist, not somebody who just played Sunday-School hymns. She made her debut at Town Hall at the time I was in school, and we all went en masse to hear her. She awoke my interest in the piano, lit the fire—I learned a lot of the music literature just from listening to her. After I graduated, I fiddled around for a while doing the wrong things…and then…Well, my parents insisted on sending me to Finch, a junior college in New York, and I disliked it intensely, wasted my time, and resented not being able to do what I wanted to do…I didn't like the girls and the piano teacher…It just wasn't my thing.

"So the next year, my old piano teacher at Dobbs—not the one who inspired me so much—asked me to move in and be her babysitter. I did, and I studied privately with several people—a bad idea because you really should be in a school and hearing what others are doing. I tried very hard to catch up…I played by ear but I couldn't sight-read music…and still can't. Bad teaching when I was young. Finally, after two years of fiddling around, I went to the Mannes College of Music, and began to really work hard at it, with some very good teachers. You know, there are very few good teachers…a lot of people teach piano but don't do it well. When the war broke out, the man who was my teacher was sent off to war, and I was 'willed' over to a man named Frank Sheridan. He and Rosalyn Turek, the famous Bach specialist, were Mannes' artist/teachers. Frank was a very well-known pianist in the '30s and '40s. He had a big career, played with most of the major symphonies except the Boston, and also was well known in chamber music and solo performances.

"So I was Frank's pupil…and…" She hesitated, then laughed. "I don't know if I want to get into this story…" But she did. "It was the end of the school year and I came down then for some makeup lessons—he'd been away concertizing—and afterward, he invited me for a drink. The drink turned into dinner, and the dinner turned into a walk in the park…I was staying at the Barbizon, a women's hotel, and we said goodnight there and I went up the stairs. Then the phone rang: Would I come down and go for another walk in the park? Well, it was the beginning of a romance. We had to be extremely careful, because Mrs. Mannes, who started the school, was against this sort of thing. So I resigned from being his student and started studying with another marvelous musician at the school.

"Finally, Frank and I got married. And of course I was 23 years his junior—he died way back in the '60s. I was still coming to Nantucket every summer—I'd done that all my life. I brought him down here and he disliked it intensely—and things got difficult. He was a very temperamental man, and then he had a heart attack plus a pulmonary embolism, and was sick for months—the doctors

Left to Right—(1) At 11 months, Adrienne Anderson looks for all the world as if she's singing. (2) Already a beauty at age 7. (3) Adrienne Anderson at 12. (4) Adrienne McCalley near her family's Brant Point home—she kept her beautiful long blonde hair until she was almost 30.

down here told him he'd never work again…He was quite mean at this period…I was sorry for him, but he was abusive, and I just couldn't handle it. Well, he defied the physicians' predictions. I left him, and he turned right around, married another student, and lived ten more years…and did not die of a heart attack." Had you kept on with your own music after you'd married Sheridan? I asked. "Yes," she said, "and we actually performed together…we used to play the Mozart *Two Piano Concerto,* a lovely piece that Mozart had written for his sister Nannerl and himself. We played at Mannes, and with the Dutchess County Philharmonic Orchestra, and other places…and I kept on with my own studying. But then after I left him I drifted away from it.

A LIFELONG ROMANCE WITH SAILING

"I had stopped everything with music and was really very upset about my life, and sort of floated around for a few years. Frank had had his heart attack in July of '51; by 1955 I was kind of pulling myself together again, and I went back to teaching piano in New York, which I'd been doing at the Mannes School before my divorce. I taught at Turtle Bay Music School in New York, and one night I was coming home on the subway… You know those signs in the subway cars? There was an ad for the New York Boat Show, which was in the Bronx Armory. And I kind of had a yen toward boats. As things were souring in my marriage, I was wanting to pull away and do something different…maybe that was the Nantucket influence. Nobody in my family sailed, none of my friends." But you became an avid sailor, I commented. Adrienne smiled and said, "Well, I'm sort of an avid person. But I didn't actually start sailing until my late thirties. I was feeling very trapped, and had just broken up with a man who had started me sailing on Nantucket in the summer. He was not the right person for me, but I wanted to go on with the sailing. So after I saw the sign, I collected all kinds of literature on small boats and went to the show. My father's family had lived in Larchmont, right near the water, and there was the little Horseshoe Harbor Yacht Club there, so I joined that.

"And then a nice man, very well known in sailing, helped me choose the right boat, a Bluejay, which is a small Lightning, and I bought a book on sailing and went out in Long Island Sound and taught myself. The Bluejay's name was the Popsquatchet—that's a Nantucket name, you know. And

Left—Here is 6-year-old Adrienne Anderson, at left, all dressed up for the 1927 Nantucket Fête. The girls are in the garden of the West Brick, on Main Street. At the far right is Amy Ann ("Suggie") Craig, Sandy Craig's sister. Right—At 24, Adrienne Anderson was already thoroughly immersed in music.

this elderly man would sit on the porch of the yacht club—he had designed the Star, an Olympic-class racing sailboat, very prestigious (all the best America's Cup sailors come out of Stars)—and when I'd come in he'd say, 'Well, you did that very well—I saw you jibe…' And so I learned how to maneuver the boat, and in the course of doing this I met John McCalley." McCalley, it turns out, was not just a well-known sailor and photographer. (He published his *Nantucket Then and Now* in 1981, and it remains a favorite of island-book collectors.) "He was an economist," said Adrienne. "He had a Ph.D. in Economics and worked in the Research Department of the New York Federal Reserve Bank. And at the same time he taught courses at City College in Economics, and I met him at the Larchmont Yacht Club…and that was that.

"How did we actually meet? Well, some days when I went to the club it would be too windy to take Popsquatchet out—but I'd sit in it, just because I liked to be there. And John would come by in the club launch and say, 'Hey, kid, what are you doing?' I'd tell him I couldn't go out because it was too blowy, and he'd ask me to come with him in his Tern, a beautiful big boat like the old Vineyards they use to sail here, but more modern. As soon as I realized things were serious between us, I brought him to Nantucket. We sailed the Tern up here to Nantucket together—it's an open boat—all the way from New York, which was kind of a nice adventure. We arrived on a gorgeous blue June day, and he immediately fell in love with the island. The next year, 1958, we married and brought the boat up, and raced it out in the Sound in the Sunday Handicap Class here at the yacht club, but decided handicap racing wasn't much fun, so we traded in the Tern for a Rhodes 19. John and I and a third person would race in it. But husband and wife in racing sailboats either get along beautifully or it is murder! So that didn't last long…" She laughed: "Somebody said, 'You can hear the McCalleys all over the harbor!'

"After it became apparent that we couldn't sail together, John bought an 18-foot Marshall catboat, and we both became champions in our two classes. And that wasn't very popular at the Yacht Club, which was very much an Old Boys' club in the '60s and '70s…they liked to have their important members and officers win the races, not upstarts like us…and I a woman! Well, I could tell you lots of stories about that, but…well, it's changed now. The younger generation of men are more tolerant. In days of yore there were male chauvinists, with a vengeance, but women in sailing are much more accepted now. They may still have a little trouble with me, because I'm older than any of them…I turn more and more over to the crew now," she admitted. "I still sail in the Rhodes 19, though I haven't done much in the last couple of years, because the boat was smashed by another boat during a race and it hasn't been fixed yet…but I am dying to get back into racing."

MUSIC & THE THEATRE

In the fall of 1959 the McCalleys moved into 13 Vestal Street, and found island life fulfilling and happy. "John was pretty good at photography," Adrienne said, "and he'd gotten tired of life in New York and the Federal Reserve Bank and all the rest of it. During the war he'd worked in photographic research for the U.S. Navy, and helped to develop what became the Land Camera, the Polaroid. So he knew a lot about the chemistry of photography and how to take good pictures…he wasn't an amateur who moved to Nantucket and just decided to take pictures. He knew exactly what he was doing." John died in 1983 while he was working on another Nantucket photograph book; by that time he'd also photographically recorded separate albums for many of the Theatre Workshop of Nantucket productions.

I asked Adrienne to tell me more about life on Nantucket in the 1960s and '70s. In those years, she said, she experienced some of the happiest times of her life. That was when both she and John got involved in TWN. Under the learned wing of the legendary Mac Dixon, that group did a lot of sophisticated and difficult productions. Adrienne had roles in *The Pleasure of His Company* and *Man for All Seasons,* among others; was in the chorus for what she remembers as a "wonderful production of *John Brown's Body;* and played the piano for *The Fantasticks,* as well as for a brave and bold run of *Boeuf Sur le Toite,* written as a pantomime by Jean Cocteau with music by Darius Milhaud. "This was a very interesting piece," she said, "very Brazilian-sounding; it called for two pianos, and Flora Brennan, who was the school psychologist then, played the other piano. And a lot of islanders were horrified; they thought the theatre itself was the height of decadence." Nantucket Island of the 1960s, she said, was just a half-step removed from being a small, simple fishing village. "Of course what we did went over a lot of people's heads, but we went on. Mac didn't compromise—not only did he have a talent for picking exactly the right people for the right parts, but he did not stoop to bend his standards to suit a somewhat unsophisticated audience."

There was also a good little orchestra, Adrienne said, conducted by Estelle O'Grady. "Her husband was with the FAA here. And you know, people just came out of the woodwork to play in this group—I played the flute, Estelle played clarinet and her husband played trombone; Milton Zlotin [whose father-in-law started the Green Coffee Pot, which he later took over] played the violin—it turned out he'd been trained in Chicago, which surprised everyone; and Mrs. Miltimore, who, with her husband, ran a clothing store across from where Mitchell's Book Corner is now, was a violinist; and Mimi Haskell also played the violin. It was an awfully interesting group of people, and we gave concerts, good concerts—everything from Beethoven to Leroy Anderson...and this was in the 1960s!"

208

Left—Adrienne Anderson Sheridan in 1957, just before she married John McCalley. Right—Here, Adrienne poses on a dock at Mystic Seaport—she'd just become engaged to John McCalley, fellow sailor and a well-known photographer.

Sailing, music, and the theatre have all been important in Adrienne's life; she was quite a Sunfish champ for years, receiving three Senior Citizen Olympic gold medals in that class—in Bermuda, the Bahamas, and Miami. Other at the moment? "I just finished *The Life of Queen Elizabeth I,* a beautifully written book. I've gotten interested in English and Scottish history; I read about William Wallace, the liberator of Scotland in the thirteenth century, and now I'm into Queen Victoria." Thankfully, she still keeps up her piano studies and playing, though not publicly, in spite of a condition that has made it difficult and painful for her to spread and stretch the fingers of one hand…and also despite a 6-inch pin in her left arm as a result of an ice-skating accident.

It's difficult to believe that Adrienne McCalley is in her eighties when you look at her, and know how active she is, how straight and tall she stands, how young and energetic her stride. To what does Adrienne attribute her youthfulness and good health? She smiled and said, "I've stayed physically active…and it just never occurred to me to get any older than I had to! I see no reason to stop doing anything I've ever done." This is, surely, one important secret of a long, productive life.

Adrienne and John McCalley congratulate each other on winning the Nantucket Yacht Club races in their separate classes: hers the Rhodes 19 and his the Marshall catboat. c. 1968.

Never Bored, Always Busy

Jetti & Lou Ames, 2001

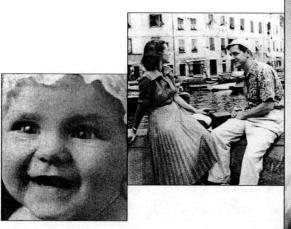

Jetti and Lou Ames, who spend most of the year on Nantucket and the winter in Tucson, have a long history on the island. Jetti's family started coming here in 1935, staying in 'Sconset at first. But, she said, "My stepmother thought 'Sconset was lovely but the beach wasn't very nice for swimming. Well, somebody drove her over to Wauwinet and she took one look—here was the harbor, here was the ocean, and there was the charming old Wauwinet House, and she made a reservation right then to come back the next year and stay there. So that's how it all started, and then Lou and I started coming in 1945." Lou chimed in: "We sort of had a second honeymoon here because I got out of the Navy in the fall of '45. We were married in '42, but the Navy got in the way, and finally the war was over and we decided to come here. I'd never been to Nantucket." But he liked it right away, and that's when their regular summers on the island started.

$15 A WEEK & LIFE UPON THE WICKED STAGE

Lou grew up in St. Louis; Jetti was born in Evansville, Indiana. She said, "I didn't come east to stay until after college, and that was to go into the theatre. And that's how I met Lou, in New York. He'd graduated from Washington University in St. Louis in 1940 and I graduated from the University of Iowa in the same year." Lou said, "I took a two-year hiatus in New York during college to 'find myself,' and then returned to get a Bachelor of Arts degree and went right back to New York. I got a job for $15 a week as a pageboy at NBC; I wore a gold-braided uniform and took tourists on tours of the radio station." Jetti said, "He was ahead of his time, really, because who was leaving college then and going off to do something for a couple of years and then coming back again? Not very many." Lou went on: "I had a little music education, so about six months later I was elevated to working in the music copyright division. The networks had decided to drop ASCAP and not pay their fees, so my job was to make sure that no copyrighted music got on the air."

Meanwhile, Jetti was steadily pursuing her lifelong dream—going into the theatre. "I'd gone to a woman's college the first two years, but left because with my voice being so low, I was playing only male roles, and I didn't think Broadway was ready for that. So I transferred to the University of Iowa, which had a wonderful theatre department and still does. And then I went immediately to a summer theatre, Chautauqua, in Lincoln, Illinois. I was going to come directly to New York after that. At the time that didn't seem unusual to me, because my family had always been very broadminded and supportive, only saying, 'You do go to college,' and I responding 'Yes, but I must major in Theatre.' But there weren't many girls' families that were letting them go to New York after graduating from college. Anyway, I had an ogre uncle. He and my aunt had no children and they felt they should protect me, and insisted I visit them in Waterbury, Connecticut, before I moved to New York. My uncle sat me down said: 'What do you think you're going to do, wait tables? How do you know you can act?' and so forth. Well, to shorten the story, I made a deal with him. He would pay for me to learn shorthand and typing and I'd stay there that year. They had a good little theatre and, if I could work there that year, I'd stay until May 1; then I'd leave for New York. That year I made many contacts in the theatre who prepared the way for me, and on May 1st I said goodbye to my uncle, who glared at me: 'Well, let me know when you have a place to stay and a job.' And so I got off the train in my little black linen dress with white collar and white gloves and my little hat, and took my test for shorthand and typing and got a job. I'd been sent specifically to a particular agent, because my contacts said she understood actors and knew what auditions to go to. She asked where I was staying, and I said, 'I don't know yet.' 'Well,' she said, 'I have an extra bedroom and bath and I'd love to have you use that.' It was on 57th Street, a very nice location. So I called my uncle and aunt at 5 o'clock and said, 'My address is such and such; my telephone number is such and such; and I have a job.' And then I met Lou."

Lou explained: "Jetti had a friend, Ann, from the University of Iowa who was working at NBC, and we had a few dates…and then Ann said she had a good friend she thought I would like. I don't know whether she was trying to dump me or not, but anyway, we arranged to have lunch with this strange lady and we met by the skating rink at Rockefeller Center…now, isn't that romantic?" Jetti said, "Can't you hear the violins?" Lou continued: "I guess we had an instant feeling for each other. We started dating and then Ann had to do without me." Jetti explained that before their meeting, she had fallen into a good living arrangement with Ann and two other theatre hopefuls. "We got a lovely apartment on Lexington Avenue for $100 a month—two bedrooms, two baths, and we each paid $25, less than what I was paying for my room…and Ann kept coming home and saying, 'There's this wonderful fellow in the music department—won't you come to lunch?' I would say I had an audition, or this that and the other, and I really couldn't care less. Finally, to shut her up, I agreed to have lunch and meet this fellow, Lou…"

SECRET AGENT MAN, SEVENTH HEAVEN, & PIERRE

Lou said, "It was 1941, and the war was coming on; I didn't want to be drafted into the Army, so I volunteered for the Navy and wound up in U.S. Navy Intelligence. For two years I was on anti-spy duty in New York, and then I went into communications school because I wanted to be on a ship. I went in as a third-class Yeoman, but

This photo of Jetaline Preminger is labeled "Miss America, 1919."

Jetti Preminger had a lead role in *Burlesque* at the Westchester Playhouse, Mt. Kisco, in 1951.

then I went to what they called the 90-Day Wonder School—in 90 days they made an officer out of me." Meanwhile, the apartment foursome had broken up—Ann got married and another girl returned to the west coast. "That left two of us," said Jetti, "so Laura and I moved into what could have been the original *My Sister Eileen* apartment. It was a tiny basement apartment on West 4th Street, in the Village; you could see people's legs walking by in the windows. It had a fireplace and a pet cockroach that came out and walked across the mantelpiece every night." Lou: "That was Pierre." Jetti: "We had a tiny kitchen and an even tinier bathroom with the old-fashioned toilet with a tank pull-chain…And we just thought this was seventh heaven."

Lou went to sea as communications officer on a small aircraft carrier in the Atlantic, where he spent two years chasing German submarines on the Atlantic. "We almost got torpedoed a couple of times," he said. "Our job was to escort troop ships from New York to England, and we spent weeks and weeks at sea looking for the enemy, and finding one or two occasionally. I was in the Navy for four years, and Jetti and I were married halfway through that period."

Jetti's theatre career was moving right along. "In December of 1942," she said, *"Angel Street* opened, and it was a sleeper…the play opened just barely, on the night of Pearl Harbor! And it was a tremendous success. (That play became the film *Gaslight.)* And immediately they decided to send a road company out. Well, there were five people in the cast: the lead, Judith Evelyn, and Vincent Price played her husband…and the English housekeeper and the detective and the Cockney maid, who was a real wench. And of course every female in New York wanted to get into the road company…" Lou said, "I knew Vincent Price and his family, because he was from St. Louis, so he was able to help Jetti get an interview." Then she was on her own, but her talent came through, and she became understudy for all three of the female roles. "That was wonderful," Jetti said, "because it meant that I

214

Left—Miss Jettaline Preminger and Mr. Louis B. Ames on their wedding day in 1940. Right— Jetti and Lou in younger days.

had constant rehearsals for all three parts all the time I was on the road, and then I started playing the maid on the road and later came back into New York and played for two years there."

IN A NUTSHELL, THE MARRIAGE WORKS

Wasn't it hard to be apart so soon after you'd married? I asked. Jetti said of their very long and successful marriage: "Well, you see, that's what's been so good about Lou's and my relationship—that we had an understanding about these things. It's more than an understanding, really—you have to be geared a certain way. I know too many people who've been separated like that and then something happened and they never really were together again…" Lou: "But in a nutshell, it works." The couple has two grown sons: Jonathan and Tabor. Jetti chuckled. "You know, they once told us, 'You and Dad spoiled us rotten,' and I said, 'What do you mean? We fell over backwards not to do that.' And they both said, 'Because we went to Nantucket every summer.' And it was true."

When Lou came marching home again, he went back to work at NBC. Soon afterward, he was offered the position of Music Director for Channel 11, WPIX, the television news station. This was a key position then, because all the music was live. An interesting side note is that a couple years after he put Channel 11 on the air as Program Director in 1948, Lou was looking for someone to produce a daily women's program and came across a smart, ambitious young woman…and gave Barbara Walters her first job in TV. Lou returned to NBC as Associate Producer of the *Today Show,* with Dave Garroway. "I helped invent J. Fredd Muggs, remember him?" Lou said. "Then I went to the *Home Show* with Hugh Downs and Arlene Francis, as Feature Editor." And when NBC's David Sarnoff decided that the network needed an opera company, it was Lou who took charge. Sarnoff insisted on having all the operas done in English, to make them more approachable to the average American, and a lot of interesting people, including W.H. Auden, wrote the libretti. "Then," says Lou, "we commissioned Gian-Carlo Menotti to do an opera, and I was in charge of that production, including building the scenery in Rome, and shipping it from there to Brussels. The production started during the first year of the Spoleto Festival…" Jetti laughed, "When they were getting ready to leave Spoleto to go to Brussels, Menotti was still working on the last few pages of the opera, and everything had to be copied, so I was left behind to run to Rome to do that…and then I had to deliver them to Brussels, plus the costumes, which I had to pass off as my clothes! I was thinking, 'If I lose any of this opera before I get there, I will really go out and drown myself!'"

Jetti was also involved in television. It was live in those days, which made for an excitement and immediacy that's missing from a lot of television today. "First of all, we did *Angel Street,"* said Jetti. "No taping, no correcting—you had to do it right the first time. Then I got into the wonderful new acting group Sidney Lumet had started—he was young in the theatre then…Dick Kiley was in it, and Lee Grant. Yul Brynner and his wife had a television program then, and we did a whole series of acting improvisations in different styles. I also did commercials, and whatever came along. I was still doing live theatre; I went out on the road with Kay Francis. It was wonderful playing the same role for over two years in New York…I learned a lot about keeping a role fresh, and I was playing with and learning a lot from very fine actors. But the one thing against playing so long like that is that agents and directors typecast you…'Oh, young Cockney—oh, Jetti Preminger…' (that was my stage name then) and you have to live that down, so I would do anything that came along. Meanwhile, I was studying with Boris Marshalova, and going to Humphrey and Weidman Studio for modern dance…"

Jetti looks like a dancer—small and very graceful—and one of her pursuits in Tucson during the winters is not only regular aquarobics but also tapdancing! Another skill she's developed along the way is singing. "Lou said to me early in our acquaintance, 'You dance, you act, but you should sing too, or you might miss out on a role.'" Lou: "She's a baritone, you know." Jetti: "So I started going to Keith Davis, a wonderful singing coach—and got a part in a show called *Burlesque* at the Westchester Playhouse, in which I had to sing a solo and it was OK. When I played *Agnes of God* I had to sing a little bit, and the young girl in it was to join me; she had a beautiful soprano voice, but she could only go so low and I could only go so high…and I'd say every night, 'Oh please dear God, let me start in the right place.' So I get nervous about it but I can do it, thanks to the coaching."

Lou too has had a multifaceted career. At eighteen, he became the pianist in a five-man group that played for dinner dancing on the Cunard Line to and from Europe. In college, he and classmate A.E. Hochner wrote original shows, and in 1947 collaborated on a musical, *Pinwheels*. "But we never got it off the ground," said Lou, "and I got involved with other things…as did Hochner, writing *Papa Hemingway*, for one thing." Lou has never really stopped composing; several years ago Nantucket's Paulette Allemande sponsored an evening of his music, including art songs, piano duets, and a sonatina. They'd met Paulette just when Jetti was studying for a role that required an accent…and Paulette's accent was just perfect. Now, Lou continues his painting, which has become ever more important to him.

Has Jetti ever regretted becoming an actress? "Oh heavens, no!" she said. But, I wondered, how did you two manage children during all those demanding career moves? Jetti said, "Before we had the children, I went out on the road with Kay Francis in *Windy Hill*, and Kay and Lou and I became very close friends. One day she said to me, 'You know, you will always be able to play roles that are at least ten years younger than you are. I don't think you have anything against having children, and I think you should do it now!' and so that's when we decided to start our family. And it worked out very well." There have been some surprising turns in this versatile woman's career. "When we moved to Norwood, New Jersey, after Jonathan was born," Jetti said, "I was asked to be a substitute teacher…it was a tiny town and they desperately needed substitute teachers. I had a degree to teach speech and drama in high school, but I didn't have anything for elementary. And I was still going in to New York to do odd jobs in television, so I said, 'Don't expect me to say yes all the time.' So I landed in the kindergarten one day, and to shorten that story, the teacher never really got well that year, so I kept going back, and in May they asked if I would take the kindergarten for the next year. Lou said, 'You're not the garden club type, and certainly not the housekeeping type,' and I said 'Yes, I have to find something, if I'm not going to be acting all the time. If I hadn't substituted in the kindergarten I would have said that this was the last thing on earth I would ever do. But I said to Lou, 'You know, there's something really creative about this that I never thought about…and maybe I can give it a whirl. I don't have to stay. I'll see how it works out for a year.' So I took the job and went back to college for courses in music and what have you for the lower grades…and I discovered that I could use everything I had learned in theatre with these children, because they are a source of creativity right there and I could utilize it and help them develop it. So I ended up writing a whole new curriculum for the kindergarten and staying twenty years!

"I limited the acting to the little theatre in Norwood, but one day I realized I'd done everything I needed to do there and decided to go back to the theatre." Lou: "I was ready to retire at that point, and it was perfect timing." Jetti: "We said that he was graduating—because he was not going to sit down—now he could work on his music and paint, and I could go back to theatre fulltime if anybody would have me. We'd been coming to Nantucket every summer and we had a chance to buy the house we'd been renting. So now I do at least one play a year here and one in Tucson."

Lou: "We're a peripatetic pair, aren't we?" Yes, I said, but you seem very happy. Jetti said, "Well, we are!" Has Lou, with all his talents, ever acted? "No," he chuckled. "One in the family is enough!" Jetti reminded him that he'd done one play in a little theatre in New Jersey, and Lou laughed, "I was the oldest juvenile in northern New Jersey." Jetti takes on a major role every year while in Tucson *(The Exact Center of the Universe, Love Letters, I Am a Camera,* and many more) and on the island. The first play she did here was *Glass Menagerie,* and since she's starred in plays such as *Lost in Yonkers, Crossing Delancey, Driving Miss Daisy, Three Tall Women,* and more.

Knowing Solitude & Beauty

What keeps Jetti and Lou Ames coming back every year to the Faraway Isle? Jetti says: "We have so many happy memories here, and a lot of good friends, but aside from that, there is a feeling we get here of serenity…especially out here in Wauwinet. In spite of all the building and all the changes and more people and everything, there are still spots on the island where you can find solitude…and there's a beauty here that's hard to find elsewhere." Lou added, "The early years of our marriage were here, and I think a lot of that helps bring us back. We've been married 59 years." Jetti spoke up: "I was twelve and he was fifteen."

One more question: How did Jetti get her unusual name? "Well," she explained, "my mother was tired of Mary Louises, Dorothy Anns, etc., and she knew twins from Alabama who were named Jetti and Aline. So she asked their mother if she'd mind if I combined those to become Jetaline. I was called Jetaline when I was being admonished, and Jetti the rest of the time…I thought Jetaline was too long to be up in lights, so I decided on Jetti.

May Jetti and Lou be up in lights for a long time to come!

Left—Jetti Preminger Ames, 2003. Photo by Beverly Hall. Right—Contemporary photo of Lou and Jetti Ames on Nantucket.

Living with Miracles Every Day
Nancy Nelson, 1999

*N*ancy Nelson, minister of the United Methodist Church and known as "Rev Nancy" to her friends, visited me for our interview accompanied by her golden retriever, Xubie (pronounced "Zoobie," which is short for "Exuberant"). Xubie, it might be mentioned, goes almost everywhere with Nancy, and is a regular member of the Methodist congregation, where, no doubt, she reminds the parishioners that in every animal there is indeed divinity.

Nancy's history on Nantucket Island is a lifelong one. "I was born in 1950," she said (hard to believe, because despite her silver hair, she is remarkably youthful looking), "and my parents had a house on the Cliff. I wasn't born here, so I can never can be a native. I came here in utero, though…because I was born in January, so I was already in the oven, so to speak. We came here every summer, all summer, after school; I learned to swim here before I could walk…as soon as I was able to go in the surf, that was it for me—I had found my element.

"My father is no longer living, and my mom is 89 and doesn't get around too well any more, but I see her often." Nancy said. "I was the youngest of three children; I have a brother and a sister, and I was thirteen when my parents divorced…it was a hard divorce, and I really went haywire for the next fifteen years, what you might call the wild years." She showed me a picture taken during that period—it shows a beautiful dark-haired young woman resembling actress Claire Bloom, with that same serene, inner-directed look that belied the chaotic life she was experiencing. "I got kicked out of my first boarding school, after which I was sent to a finishing school in Switzerland, where I just continued to get into heavier and heavier trouble, and then I went to Briarcliff and almost got kicked out there. And then I dropped out of college…because [with a rueful laugh] it was getting in the way of my partying. At that point I went to California with the Hippies, and there I stayed for twenty years. The wild years lasted until I was 28. A lot of my friends are dead from what we were doing then, and…here I am. It is a miracle." That elicited a bunch of questions for this very together, self-assured woman of the cloth: Was that tough on you? Were you enjoying yourself? Learning anything? Were those wasted years? I asked. "No," Nancy answered firmly. "I don't think anything's wasted. I wouldn't subtract even the most painful times I had, because they made me who I am. And you know, when I'm counseling, I've been there…I've been very lost. So I really understand people's problems because I used to have so many myself. That's probably one of the best dossiers you can have to be a good counselor, to have suffered and to have screwed up a lot yourself."

QUITE A TRANSITION

How did Nancy manage to segué into her next life? After all, the transition from Haight-Ashbury Hippie to Methodist minister makes for a pretty startling story. She answered with her characteristic frankness: "I had been involved with Buddhism for ten years, but was still partying fairly heavily. Then I started having grand mal seizures, and the neurologist said I was likely going to die because I had done so much damage to myself in those years. He said, 'It looks to me like you're just going to keep on having seizures till you have a brain hemorrhage and die.' Pretty shocking." Then, something amazing happened to Nancy…she told me about it matter-of-factly, without an iota of dramatization. "Christ came to me in a dream—he called me by name. I knew who it was, and he said, 'Nancy, I love you. If you follow me, everything will be all right.' I woke up remembering it vividly. I can still see the face. And that was it—that was the difference. It was like being in a new current, pulling me to a different place. I know how very blessed I am to have had such a clear experience. That happened on October 1st, 1978. And it absolutely changed my life.

"So then I finished college—I found a place where I could do my life experience and get credit…Antioch. I wrote up a bunch of ten-page papers on what I'd learned in my life, and got credits, and was able to do two and a half years of college in one year, so that I could go to seminary, where I'd already been accepted." Did she ever have any doubts about the decision to embark on this extraordinarily changed life? "Not one," she answered. "I became literally a different person. I went to San Francisco Theological Seminary. I was a Presbyterian then, so I had to take Hebrew the first year." She laughed: "Instead of rehab, I went to seminary." Afterward, I went right into chaplaincy—I knew that was my calling. Actually, right around the time I was doing my year's internship as an oncology chaplain was when AIDS hit San Francisco. I had gay friends, and there was nobody to help them—no one famous had it yet—this was before Halston and Rock Hudson died of AIDS—nobody was helping those guys. And in fact I left the Presbyterian Church over it, because I said, 'This is my calling, this is what I do sixty hours a week…' and they said, 'No, it's not an ordainable call. Are these people ever going to be Presbyterians?' I said, 'No, probably not…' That attitude seemed to me so uncaring. So then I went to a nondenominational church, just for the connections…it was one of those storefront churches.

"I didn't have a seizure for ten years. It seems like every ten years I have seizures, because it seems to be the only way God can get my attention to change my direction. For example, as an AIDS chaplain I was working an insane amount of time, and that involved a lot of high stress, of course. After seven years of AIDS chaplaincy, I had a personal tragedy that hit me really hard, and I started having seizures again. I'm not epileptic, and I've always thought that the seizures were triggered by emotions…I had them at high stress points, so I always thought they were stress—and it wasn't until I saw the blessed Dr. Birbiglia from the Cape that I found out what was causing them. He determined that more exactly, the seizures were caused by lack of sleep. And so taking care of them is doable, workable. And thank God, because otherwise I'd have to give up ministry, because there's no such thing as a no-stress ministry that's worth anything. If you're involved with people, it's going to be stressful. Well, I can handle stress, but I have to really watch my sleep. Seizures are scary. Dr. Birbiglia has kept me seizure-free, by identifying that sleep trigger."

AMAZING GRACE

You saw a doctor on the Cape, I said, so at some point had you come back to Nantucket? "Yes," Nancy said. "In 1989 or '90, I came here to regroup. I'd been so immersed in AIDS ministry for seven years that I

Left—Nancy Nelson, already a regular summer islander, enjoying a day at Cliffside Beach Club at about age 2. Right—Nancy, a first-grader, looks as if she enjoys school.

hadn't come back, because I couldn't leave those guys, you know? I had a huge caseload, people who were at death's door, so I didn't take vacations. When my best friend died suddenly, I had to stop; I came here to heal and say, 'God, what's next?' I never wanted to be a parish minister, and boy, was I surprised when I had another mystical vision to serve the Methodist Church. My first day of ministry here was January 1st, 1995, so that must have been October of '94. At that time I was Nutrition Coordinator for Elder Services," she continued. "I did that for three and a half years—managing Meals on Wheels and Congregate Lunches. One Wednesday I was at my morning prayers, and I kept getting this kind of vision of pillars…I said, 'God, what is it? Do you want me to be a librarian? What is it? Be more specific, please God. Methodist or librarian?' And no answer was forthcoming from God on that. But that same day I served lunch at Saltmarsh and Barbara Dezalduando, who is a Methodist trustee, always came on Wednesdays, and I said, 'Barbara, I'm feeling this strange pull to the Methodist Church. I could teach Bible study, I could visit the homebound, I guess I could help your minister in some way…I'm a minister, you know, and I'm feeling this pull to your church.' Well, Barbara's jaw dropped and she said, 'I just found out that our minister quit this morning!' That morning, when I'd had my vision!" Nancy grinned somewhat gleefully—she is so direct and unassuming about these amazing things that happen to her, and clearly all of it brings her great joy. "So," she said, "it was obviously the Methodist Church. And I didn't want to be a parish minister, but God had to get my attention in this strong way or I never would have gone for it, because I hated getting up in front of people. I'd be physically ill on Sunday mornings, real stagefright…and I still get it from time to time, but now I'm more relaxed with it. I can't believe how things have worked out. I mean, it should be illegal to be having this much fun! I've just been loving it. I had a peak experience last Sunday—I mean, I was just cruising at 30,000 feet, you know? I stayed in that state all that day. And being a religious person, I call this a state of grace. I had no idea the side effects of being a minister would be this wonderful!"

A Congregation Like a Family

We talked a bit about the changes that are occurring on Nantucket Island, and Nancy said that her congregation at the beautiful, historical Methodist Church is quite small. Is there a choir? "No, they are the choir…and they are the size of a choir. The congregation is tiny…it's like a family…and there's no power to fight over. Everybody does everything. We have the wonderful Gary Trainor—he plays the piano and sings for us, and he's just great. My congregation members are not on the high end of the economic scale, so I've had eleven who've had to leave because of housing, and in a small congregation that hurts. And I'll probably lose more…they're all renters. I don't have the answer to that, but I wish I did. I do see positive changes happening here…I see them because I'm a spiritual director. I see people who, because of the stress, are having to turn to God more. You know, as in the African-American experience, some of the people with the strongest faith are those who have nothing. And that's a good thing, to be God-dependent. It is not a good thing that there is such injustice in the world, that there are the have-nots. The disparity of wealth here is really stunning. But I see people walking their faith walk and being happy even though they are overworked and underpaid." There are, I commented, easier ways to go when the chips are down than to God, so these people must be very strong. "Yes," Nancy answered, "they are." Even so, doubt, she maintained, is not always bad. "When it was time to be confirmed, I was doubting," she said, "and I told the minister, and he said, 'Keep doubting…because when you do find your faith it'll be all the stronger. I have been very fortunate that somehow I have had help in choosing the right path, because I think it's a miracle that I am who I am and where I am now, from where I came."

What's your plan for the next twenty years? I asked Nancy. The answer was quick. "To continue being open to God's guidance and healing." Do you think you'll stay on the island? "Oh yes!" What holds you here? "Well, I belong here—it's my niche." What do you do for relaxation...any time for that? "When there's time, I body-surf; and I walk a lot around the moors with Xubie, and on the beach. I also read fantasy fiction, science fiction—I love to immerse myself in an imaginary world." Do you do a lot of counseling? "Oh yes...all kinds, and a lot of people needing it come from outside the church. It seems to take just the right amount of time. Because of my seizure disorder, I have learned boundaries; I need my rest...and my congregation works with me on this. It doesn't always work out that I have free time, but when I do I really do, and I know how to use it."

As happy and satisfied with your calling as you are, I said, being a clergyperson must be an immensely difficult and demanding vocation. You have a vibrancy and an attractiveness about you that must exert a pull in both positive and negative ways…"Yup," she said, "and as in many professions, there are people who want to feed off that." But somehow, one gets the feeling that this is a woman who can handle everyone with strength, tact, and dignity, from the confused and the seeking and the ill to the "religious delusional," as she calls them. Nancy says she occasionally feels slight regret that she hasn't married ("though I've come close a couple of times") and had children. But she does have a family, a flock, and it takes lots of time and energy to "grow" and tend a congregation. Does this ever get her down? "No," she said. "I have God, and the spiritual tools, to deal with whatever happens now."

Rev Nancy is living proof that people can become strong and whole, even having lived an extremely fractured life.

Left—Today's Nancy Nelson, AKA "Rev Nancy," looking resplendent in her pastoral robes at the famous old United Methodist Church on Centre Street. Right—This is Xubie, short for "Exuberant," as a mere pup. She's as cute and fetching today, and accompanies Nancy everywhere she goes.

224

"Mrs. K," a Bawn Islander

Winifred Kittila, 2001

*W*ell, she is a bona fide born-and-bred New England islander. But not a Nantucket native. Actually, Winifred Kittila was born on Martha's Vineyard. Even so, "Mrs. K" (as she's been known for years at the Jared Coffin House, where she's been concierge, making island visitors happy enough to come back time and again) has chosen to live on Nantucket…her home of the heart.

Now to explain that word "bawn" in the title. Winifred Kittila has a deep New England accent, and I'm not making fun when I point out that Mrs. K says bawn for born, of cawss for of course, cahn't for can't, and drops many of her g's. She even told a story about livin' for a while in Bah Hahbuh, Maine. She truly has, even in the honest light of day, the hair, skin, and bearing of a woman years younger, abetted by amazingly clear, twinkling blueberry-blue eyes, as well as a hahty laugh that exhibits her obvious great enjoyment of life.

A NATURAL FOR THE HOTEL BUSINESS

How did Mrs. K end up on the Faraway Isle? "Well," she explained, "in 1938, my dad owned the Tashmoo Inn at West Chop in Viney'd Haven. And of cawss growing up I always had to work for my father, summers. So I knew the hotel business from the time I was bawn, practically. Well, to make a long story shawt, in my first year of college, my father said that if I did good I could go to any place to work for the summer except for the Viney'd. I was going to Bryant, in RI, which was then a small business school…and of course in those days, you never heard of girls taking business courses." Was she, I asked, intending to get into the hotel business? "No!" she replied, "I didn't want anything to do with it." Nevertheless, she fell into the business anyway and has been a natural at it during the last three decades. And being the wife of an officer in the Coast Guard for many years helped—"An officer's wife, you know, is with the public a lot." But that's getting a bit ahead of our story.

At the time her father made Winifred his offer, she said, "Edward Maloney owned the Ocean House on Nantucket, and my father was president of the Hotel Association for the Cape & Islands, so that's how I got to work at what is now the Jared Coffin House on Nantucket in the summer of 1938, after my first year of college." She sighed and said, "'Course Nantucket isn't like it used to be…but that's life, you know—they say every quarter of a century things change. Well, to make a long story short, I met my husband John here that summer. At that time he was just out of the Coast Guard Academy and was stationed on Nantucket. John's father had also been in the Coast Guard. John was born on Nantucket; his mother was Bertha Norcross. Horace Norcross, her father, was one of the first of the old Lighthouse Service people, who in those days patrolled beaches. So anyway, in 1940 I came back to the island as a bride." Settling back, she said, "And that's about all I can think of right now."

Oh no! I said. That's not nearly all! What did your folks back on Martha's Vineyard think about you marrying a "Scrap Islander"? Winifred laughed and said, "Oh, they didn't mind. Before we were married John said he was going to stay in the service because it was sort of a family tradition. My husband was John Kittila, Jr., and today there's my son John III, my grandson John IV, and my great-grandson John V." John III lives in Madaket now, and early on the wintry morning Winifred and I talked, she had braved the snow and icy road to drive her son back there. It was one of those special mornings when you wake up and see three inches of snow delicately balanced on every branch, twig, dried leaf, and rooftop, but the driving was tricky. You weren't worried about the roads? I asked. "Oh no!" she answered, "and it was just beautiful. On the way out there," she continued, "I was reminiscing about my early days in Madaket. Right after I was married, we were transferred to Madaket Station, at the end of Madaket Road—that's where our cottage was. I don't think there were more than twelve men at the station, and maybe twenty families out there. At that time my husband, as a chief, earned 180 dollars…a month! I said to my son, 'You know, in 1952 we could've bought land in Madaket for $25 an acre.' My mother-and father-in-law and bought land right at the end of Madaket…in fact they eventually owned about a quarter of a mile in the ocean—that much has eroded—can you imagine? So, you see, erosion is not a new problem here. My mother-in-law and I used to drive out to 'Sconset where the bank overlooking the Atlantic is, and she pointed out where the ocean came up to when she was a little girl. It's all filled in, and then Madaket's washing out."

Is John III a Nantucket native? I asked. "No, he was born on Martha's Vineyard," Mrs. K replied, "and there's a good story about how that came about. When I was pregnant, we were stationed in Maine. Do you remember the Bah Hahbuh fire? I was carrying my son during that fire. I lived in Southwest Hahbuh, and they were dynamiting around the town to stop the fire, and we had to get off the island, and I thought, 'I'm not going to sit my fanny here!' So I went to see my doctor and asked him if he thought I could drive from there to get to Martha's Vineyard. He said, 'Promise me you'll take two days getting there.' I drove down there, stopping in Lowell, MA, to visit my husband's aunt and uncle. John was born about three and a half weeks after I got to the Viney'd. John always wanted to come back to Nantucket. Nantucket is his home. One of my great-grandchildren, Michael Anthony, was born here, so he's a Nantucket native…but John V, who should have been a native, was born in Florida."

I asked if John was her only child. "No, we had a daughter who was born in 1950, but she died at eight and a half. She had one of the first cases of meningitis in the state of Maine, where we were stationed then." A little silence. "And my husband died in 1984—it was very sudden, but I thought that was a blessing, because so many people suffer." Winifred said that after John retired from the Coast Guard, the family returned to Nantucket to live—that was in 1969. "We always came here summers, and I'd bought my first house on Main Street, in 1948, the year my son was born. That's where I live now. At the time he retired, my husband was one of the first dockmasters down here, when the Marina opened up. But he just did it one summer, and then he bought a boat and docked her out at Madaket, and from then on he went party-fishing up until he passed away.

STILL A WORKING GAL

"I get back to the Viney'd often—my family, those who remain, are there every summer, and scattered about in the winter—and I fly over mostly every Tuesd'y at night and fly back Frid'y mornin' in time for work. I started at the Jared Coffin as concierge in 1970. Now I'm the grandmother of the place…I'm the oldest one there. I used to host dinner parties and cocktail parties and different activities, but when I turned 75 I decided to go part time." I knew that had been a few years ago, but since Mrs. K, like most women, doesn't want her age advertised, I won't tell…besides, she looks and acts way younger. I did say, though, that she ought to tell people her age, because she's such a good model of not acting or looking "old" as the years pass. "Well," she allowed, "age never did mean anything to me, because I was always active as an officer's wife, as a person, even when I used to come to Nantucket in the summers; when my son got older I got a job summers, working for different places in town—the drug store and Cap'n Tobey's…I used to be cashier there, way way back then. I've always kept busy." She also found time to get involved with the Theatre Workshop group—"I sang and acted in the Theatre Workshop's *GI Review* with Roger Young and Lillian Wayne, and when John was in Sunday School at St. Paul's I sang in the choir."

I'll bet you've had a lot of interesting experiences as concierge at the Jared Coffin, I said. "Oh yes…I've met a lot of people, and seen their children grow up and get married and have children. And a lot of funny things have happened…once a couple came to stay—the husband's secretary had called and I had programmed what they were to do those five days they were here—dinner reservations, theatre, and so forth. About the third day the wife said, 'Mrs. K, my husband and I have been driving all over the island, but you know, we can't find the bridge that goes back to the mainland!'" At this point Mrs. K exploded with laughter. "I said, 'Well, you came over by boat with your car, didn't you?' And she said yes, and I said, 'You're going to have to go back that way—there's no bridge.' It turns out her friend had told her to be sure to take the car to the island, because the couple would especially enjoy the drive back over that bridge. They hadn't even bought a round-trip ticket…they only bought one-way because they wanted to go back by the bridge!"

I asked Winifred if she'd ever regretted choosing Nantucket as her home. "No, not really," she said. "When we lived in Alaska, that's when we decided that we were definitely going to come back and live the year-round in Nantucket. We were in Alaska two weeks before it became a state, in 1958; then my husband had to go to London, so I was there for two months. I loved it. I've lived in New Hampshire, Vermont, Texas—oh God, I can't remember all the places! The Coast Guard moved us around every three years. But Nantucket feels like home to me, definitely." I observed that during her lifetime, Winifred had had to get used to change, to which many people don't adapt well. "Oh, I always did," she said. "Disappointments, everything…I think it's because when I was growing up, parents taught you to accept things as they were at the time. The Depression years were difficult…and of course I can remember my father being in politics, on the Board of Selectmen in the Viney'd. He ran one of the longest terms in the state of Massachusetts…I think it was thirty-some-odd years—four or five terms—without losing an election. And then when he did lose, he was 82 years of age. But my mother, none of us, wanted him to run…he was getting on in years. Of course he lived to be 94.

"On my mother's side of the family are Daggetts, a family like the Coffins on Nantucket…and none of the Coffins married the Daggetts and none of the Daggetts married the Coffins—so," she laughed, "as far as history is concerned, there's no Nantucketers in the family. Martha's Vineyard is a beautiful island. And when I was growing up it was not any different than Nantucket…maybe they had 2000 or 3000 people on the voting list…and you depended on the tourists in the summer, which is still true today. But you know, I can remember the Depression—and I think that eventually there's going to be a standstill. The rich'll stay rich and the poor'll stay poor. There's no medium class any more, you know that as well as I do. Now, I get a

228

Left—Winnie as a youngster on Martha's Vineyard. Right—The Jared Coffin House, once the Ocean House, has long been an institution on Nantucket, as has its long-time concierge, Mrs. K.

good government pension, but I'll tell you, I'm a little worried about if I live to be 90—I mean, to live the way I'm accustomed to living."

Winifred claims she never gets tired of living on a small island. "I was born and brought up on an island, and then I went away to private boarding school, Sacred Heart Academy in Fairhaven—of course I met a lot of girls from Nantucket, some of them at Sacred Heart Academy in Fall River. But I was the only girl from Martha's Vineyard as a boarding girl. When I was in school there I played basketball. And then I came back home and graduated from my home town…"

NANTUCKET HAS A LOT TO GIVE

How do you feel about all the changes taking place on Nantucket? I asked. "Well," she answered, "I feel very strongly that it's take and not give today. That's what it is. Today there's a different type of money; this isn't family money like it was out at 'Sconset and Brant Point…it's recent money, come and go. The young people can't stay here—can't earn a living here or buy houses and raise families here. Something has to happen to let the native children of Nantucket be able to have their own home on Nantucket. And another thing—when I was growing up, everything didn't have to be new. Yes, there have been a lot of changes. But Nantucket is a very special place, a living museum, as they say. I have lots of friends here…I almost feel as if Nantucket could be my native island. I love the island very much, and I'm happy that we retired here. For young people today, this island is a goldmine—they've got scallopin', quahoggin', so much from the sea, if they just get off their fannies and go out there. When my son was in high school he used to go out and dig quahogs to make extra money."

Mrs. K has definite opinions about how to live life. "Mostly, all the girls I went to school with or knew

are living today, but they don't want to do anything. Today, anybody 65 years of age is not old, and that's why I feel that Social Security should go up to 70. I'll go on working, as Mr. Read says, as long as I can get to my desk at the Jared Coffin!" And we hope she'll be at that desk for a long, long time.

Left—This beautiful young woman, Winifred Rabbitt, became engaged to John Kittila, Jr., in 1939. Below—Winifred today.

230

Sharing the Memories
Phil & Jackie Haring, 2001

You never know what memories will be unearthed in an interview, and when I spent a Sunday afternoon recently with Phil and Jackie Haring, Phil told a story that was pretty unsettling. Both the Harings were caught up in a dramatic way in World War II. For some, that war may be a distant memory or an awful but now-toothless tale told in history books—especially considering the surfeit of violence that's going on in so many parts of the globe today. But from the December 7th, 1941 attack on Pearl Harbor to the dropping of a horrific bomb on Hiroshima on August 6th, 1945, both Jackie and Phil were involved in that conflict.

Phil said he'd been born in White Plains, NY, in his grandfather's house. "I had one brother who has now died; he was a year younger. That's important in my life because he was mentally retarded, and at a fairly early age it was made clear to me that I was responsible for him—there was no other choice. That had a considerable effect; it was difficult for me as I was growing up to understand how other boys my age could be, in my view, cruel, beating each other up, and so on. My brother Pete was gentle, a very sweet guy. In many things he was extremely bright—he was tremendously sensitive to classical music, and could imitate an entire symphony orchestra—it was amazing—and yet there were other areas of his brain that were completely knocked out, such as the ability to understand things in the abstract. So part of the world was shut off from him, but the other part was very vivid. In 1924, my father became a Harvard professor, so we moved to Massachusetts, and when I went to Harvard, where I majored in history and literature, Pete became a full-time resident of the boarding school he'd attended occasionally. He had good friends and a real life there, and it was really the only solution."

THE MOST IMPORTANT DAY IN HIS LIFE

What did you do after college? I asked. "Well," Phil answered, "I had always wanted to be a poet, but I figured out that that was beyond me, and second, I wanted to be a novelist, so I did a lot of writing. However, I found I could be an editor, but I could not be a creative artist. I graduated in '37, and taught for a year…and I also worked in bookstores, which was the perfect thing for me. I even considered starting a bookstore of my own, but it was obvious that we were going to go to war with Germany. I had always loved ships, so when the war with Germany began, I volunteered for the Navy's first '90-Day Wonder School,' where you quickly learned to be an officer. That took me to the battleship California, and we were assigned to Pearl Harbor. I was there on the day of the attack on Pearl, and this was the most important day of my life, without question."

Philip Haring has a way of saying things without fanfare, and it took a moment for that astonishing sentence to sink in. And the next sentence was equally shocking. "At that time I was in command of the anti-aircraft, and so I got into the thick of it, and at the end of the attack I got amnesia. I was completely with it during the battle, aware of what was going on, functioning well. But at the end of it, the first indication to me that I was 'loosening up' was when we got the order to abandon ship. Everybody went off but I stayed back because I wanted to make sure the man who was going to be my father-in-law, who was second in command of the ship, was safe. I was afraid he might try to stay and go down with the ship. I found his cabin full of water, so I went back up on deck. There was oil all over Pearl Harbor because of the ships that had been punctured, and the sea was flaming. I went over to the side of the ship—we were sunk, but had not capsized—and the flames seemed to me the most beautiful colors I had ever seen in my life. I found myself wanting to put my hands into this magnificent stuff...I had sort of a double awareness, because I realized who I was and that this would be a crazy thing to do, but I also desperately wanted this.

"Luckily, a small boat came along and took me aboard; we went across the harbor and I was dropped off on the opposite end of the harbor, at the Navy installation. I couldn't hear anything, because of the tremendous racket of the guns and everything else...and my memories at that point are just little vignettes. I wandered all over the place, and at some point naval personnel led me aboard a destroyer and someone suggested I rest—he could see that something was wrong. But I got up and wandered off again. The attack, which had lasted from 8 to 10 a.m., had stopped, and it was now noon. By sunset, I found myself sitting in a field with others, around a bonfire, and I felt comfortable, but then the memory fades out. The next morning I awoke in a mobile hospital that had been on its way to the Philippines and had happened to be in the harbor. I got up and went outside and told some officers I thought I ought to report back to my ship. I recognized everything, knew who I was, and knew that I'd been through this action, and I was also aware that it was the greatest defeat in the history of the American Navy, so I was seeking facts to find out what was happening. I finally got a boat that took me back out to the California, which was ruined, and there were the Captain and my father-in-law. I have never seen any two people look so crushed. It was a terrible loss. And when they saw me, they said that I'd been reported dead...no one had found me, so everyone assumed I had drowned. I guess I'd recovered my memory by that morning."

Jackie Haring during World War Two, as a Red Cross "Able-Bodied Recreation Worker" assigned to combat regiments. Her job, part of which was served in Kyoto, Japan, three weeks after the atom bomb was dropped, was to help keep the troops happy, a big job in those terrifying times.

Navy Ensign Philip Haring in 1940, before he was injured in the attack on Pearl Harbor.

It was easy to see that while Phil told the story smoothly, it was affecting him very deeply; it was not only the suddenness and horror of the surprise assault by Japanese planes that had shaken him—it was also the affect it had on others. He went on, "I realized what was going on, and I also realized something I had not expected…people were running away, failing to take command…" Jackie interjected: "But not everyone. You must say too that there were others who were doing just the opposite. Phil has told me this story: During the attack, the ship was hit by a big shell and it knocked out a system that brought ammunition from the lower part of the ship to the deck. Phil and a friend named Herb, both junior officers, were on deck, and they decided that the shells and the ammunition would have to be hand-carried up to the guns. Then there was the question of who would go below and who would stay up on deck, which was quite exposed to constant firing. Phil said he'd stay on deck—he was taking the more dangerous part. Well, it turned out that the ship took another shell, and Herb and all the others who went below were killed. So there were plenty who did their jobs, even though Phil had some experiences with some of the officers who might have done more."

"A week after Pearl," Phil said, "I was ordered to report to the hospital. I said, 'No way,' but they told me I had no choice. I said the same thing to the doctor examining me, but I did tell him, 'If I fall asleep while you have me here, I don't know what's going to happen—I don't think I'm going to be very well off.' I was having tremors, couldn't bring a glass up to my mouth. Ultimately, I was transferred to a hospital in California. A member of that staff suggested I call my parents. That hadn't occurred to me…you see, I was all right but not seeing the whole picture. My mother came out and wanted me transferred to Boston, but the head of the hospital wouldn't release me…and typically," he laughed, "my mother took a train directly to Washington and went to the Navy Department, not knowing anyone there, and told them, 'I want my son home.' So they said the person to see was Admiral So-and-So, but he was very busy; he had a war going on, but Mother demanded to speak to him. She was very persuasive, and they finally let her in. She told the Admiral what she wanted, and he said, 'Very well,' and made out an order. When the head of the hospital where I was called me in, he was absolutely furious! He said, 'Your mother has interfered with my authority!' And he was so mad he gave me one hour to get off the base!"

Phil wasn't quite through with the Navy; he was offered a desk assignment, but he refused because he thought he should be back in action. Now attached to a Boston Navy hospital, he was asked by his doctor if he thought he was subject to amnesia again, to which Phil replied, "I haven't the faintest idea." There was a chance he would be given limited service, which meant that he wouldn't be qualified for action, and he felt that at that point, he'd lost all status. He wanted to be useful, with his battle experience, but the decision was made to let him out with an Honorable Discharge. There were many, many servicemen who were in this same situation at that time, and it was exacerbated by the hard-to-believe fact that it was a whole year before the public was informed of the seriousness of the Pearl Harbor attack. "The President," Phil said, "had reported it simply as an 'action.' So before December 1942, when the whole truth was revealed, there were scads of us who were given discharges without any recognition of what sort of action we'd been in, and there was great bitterness about that." I wanted to know if he'd ever received a medal for his heroism, and Phil said he was no hero—he had just been doing his job. "It was great to be relieved from future action," he said, "but on the other hand, I kept thinking of all the other people out there fighting…"

How Nantucket Happened to Jackie

When Jackie reached over to take Phil's hand, seeing that telling this story was taking an emotional toll, it seemed a good time to switch gears, so I asked her to tell about her own beginnings. "I was born in Brooklyn," she said. "My father was working in the stock market, which he detested, so he took a job with a carpet manufacturer and traveled all over the country giving lectures on how this carpet could be used in decorating a house. My mother and I sort of tagged along and saw the whole country in the process. Then Dad became head of the decorating department and buyer of antiques for the J.L. Hudson Co. in Detroit, which meant he went to Europe every year to buy antiques for a lot of very important people countrywide, including [significant look] Nantucket. The Harrises, who summered on the island, asked him to come here, and he fell in love with the island, in particular with No-Horse Barn in Monomoy. I was about fifteen then. He bought a small house there, called Mid-Pasture, and Mother and he spent summers here. Then Dad retired and they bought this house we're living in now, and started a little antique shop here, which he'd always wanted to do. It was called 'The Shop on the Corner.'"

It was a good life, and the family loved the island, but soon it was time for Jackie to go off to college. "The only thing I really knew about boys," Jackie laughed, "was from watching them drive brass-trimmed cars around Nantucket. At Vassar, I got pinned to a boy I'd known in high school—he was at Michigan. Eventually, he got interested in somebody else, and so did I, but in the meantime, I'd moved to Michigan, much to my family's annoyance, and in 1940 I was married to a boy who'd gotten a degree from Michigan and an appointment in the Army. The summer before Pearl Harbor, he was called to active service, and we went down to Fort Benning, Georgia. We were actually driving between Columbus, Georgia and the post when the Pearl Harbor attack was announced on the car radio. When he went overseas, I decided to go into the Red Cross. I took my training in Washington, and the December before the atom bomb was dropped I went overseas too. At that time my husband was fighting in Italy, and none of the girls were assigned to where their husbands were, because, you know, it would have been distracting. I was assigned to New Guinea, which was very interesting. I was responsible for getting canteens built, and had a detail of soldiers to do the construction. In July of that year I was sent on to Leyte…and there we saw the men who had been in Santa Tomas, Manila, where they'd been prisoners of war; they didn't know what was going on in the world at all, and they were in terrible shape, had what we called the beri-beri shuffle. But we found that the Filipinos had been wonderful to the Americans as they advanced—they'd sweep the roads so that there wouldn't be any sign of people having passed through and even killed their dogs so that they wouldn't bark when the Americans were advancing.

"I was assigned to the northern part of the island, San Fernando, and the men I was with were preparing to invade Japan. And then the bomb was dropped and they were sent there right away to be in charge of the Occupation. I went separately, because I was the only girl, but I rejoined them in Kyoto, which had taken only one bomb and was relatively unscathed, and being there was a very interesting experience. I was there until the men were sent home, and then I went home and at the same time my husband came back to Detroit, and we decided we'd outgrown our marriage."

DESTINY, HELPED BY AN OLD BEAU

Jackie ultimately was assigned to a job in Chicago. It turns out that the college boy she'd once been pinned to knew where she was, and also knew Phil, having gone to Harvard for graduate school and serving as an assistant to Phil's father, who was Master of the Dunster House. Phil, also divorced, was going to Chicago to grad school. So what happened, in effect, was that Jackie's old beau fixed her up with Phil!

"We met in the fall of '51 and were married the following March, and the following January our daughter Tori was born. She was probably two when we first came to Nantucket," said Jackie. Phil added, "We'd come for a week or so at a time; the house became ours in 1970, but we came here to live full time in 1984." In between, they managed to come summers for a couple of years. Phil "retired" in 1980; he'd been teaching at Knox College in Illinois. Jackie had left the government service and become an archivist, and was also President of the Archives of the thirteen Midwestern states, and that network led her to an opening at the Nantucket Historical Association. Perfect! They just happened to have a house here. Jackie, who soon became a familiar fixture at the NHA. When she retired as Director of the Research Center she went on working at Tonkin's until about 1999, when the only thing that stopped her was a bad fall and a broken hip.

To add to their already interesting life, Jackie and Phil have managed to fit in a lot of travel during their almost fifty years together. Phil said they'd been around the world three times, twice by ship. Jackie laughed and said, "At this point it's almost easier to tell you where we haven't been." What are your favorite places? I asked. "Well," she said, "I'd always had a very strange feeling toward the Japanese, because of the men I knew who were killed by them…but when I got to Japan with the Occupation troops, I got to really think I would like to respect them. On my first trip to Japan as a tourist, I wasn't quite sure, but then I got to understand a little bit more about them…and I think probably Japan and certainly the Orient are my favorite places."

Are Phil and Jackie settling into quiet retirement? Hardly. Jackie said, "I made a list last night of the things I have to do in the next couple of days, and it was two and a half pages long!" After his formal retirement, Phil went to work for island committees, "practically one for every day of the week, and that was great until I got overwhelmed. I drove home from a meeting one night and thought I'd had a heart attack, which scared me to death. So I started dropping off many activities, and what is taking up my time now…and this sounds strange…but I grew up naturally with a tremendous desire to know things…and I'm happiest when I'm learning. So I have plenty to keep me busy. I read a lot. There's so much new science, so much is going on in the political world…so I don't begin to have time on my hands."

The Harings and all their island friends are very glad they've been able to make Nantucket their home. Jackie said, "I love the houses on Main Street, and the quietness of it, and the wonderful weather…and of course the people who have become friends." Among the things that bother her about today's island are the people who come here in the summer "who have so little respect for one another—you can see it in the way they are driving. This isn't Nantucket changing, it's the outside world coming and threatening to destroy our way of life." Phil has a slightly different slant: "From the time I came onto this island, people told me what was going wrong, the island would never be the same again, it was being destroyed, etcetera. So I listened to all this twaddle. It's not destroyed at all! We don't want the island to go to hell…and we are aware that this is something that must be taken care of." He is quite confident that Nantucketers will take care to preserve this living museum that is Nantucket.

Jackie and Phil Haring have been an important part of the Nantucket community for many years…and those smiles are worn almost all the time.

238

Apple Trees, Arrowheads, and Antiques

Peter Wilson, 2002

*T*echnically, Peter Wilson says, he's a "stranger"—that is, someone who wasn't born on the island. But he started coming to Nantucket in 1926 as a two-year-old and continued coming for long spells almost every summer until he moved here (not once, but twice). "My family stayed with cousins out in 'Sconset," he said, "and almost every year of my life when I wasn't away or in the service, I'd be out here for all or most of the summer. We never owned property, but my mother's family had started coming to Nantucket when the early 'Sconset development started on the bluff...they were one of the first families to build a house, Bluff Cottage, right in town. That was the Walker family, and they were cousins and aunts of my mother. They had a lot of bedrooms and plenty of space, so we spent almost every summer for at least a month, maybe six weeks, with those cousins.

THROWING APPLES FROM THE TRAIN

"My family didn't have much," Peter went on, "but my mother had come here in 1891 as a babe in arms, and her mother came in 1879, before she was married...so every year someone from the family has been here. My mother kept coming back whenever she could, even after she was married, around 1920. She said that in the early 1900s, when they had the railroad on the island, she would take it out to 'Sconset whenever she could. She loved the fact that they would stop if you wanted them to, to pick flowers. And do you know something? When my wife Maggie and I built on Gray Avenue, we kept coming up with railroad spikes...we discovered that the railroad bed was just along the corner of our house. Another thing that surprised us—there was a beautiful apple tree in the pine grove behind us, and we're sure that somebody must've thrown an apple core out of the train window—how else could it have gotten out there? We gave those spikes to the person who bought the house from us. And this'll kill you—when we built that house in the '70s, we were able to buy three-quarters of an acre for $1200. The whole property and the house cost us $65,000. I built it myself, although I subbed the plumbing, wiring, and masonry."

Why had that first family member come to Nantucket way back in 1879? I asked. Peter said, "My mother's grandfather was a minister in Longmeadow, MA, for forty years, and his sister married a Congregational missionary. She went overseas to Turkey and the Mesopotamia area with her husband and a child, Hattie. Sadly, her husband died shortly after she'd had another baby, so she had to come back to the United States. She and her husband had endeared themselves to the tribespeople, because they weren't brimstone missionaries, they were just trying to help people come into the newer centuries, and these people guarded her all the way out on a donkey to Istanbul. When she got back—by sailing vessel, of course—her relatives decided that they'd find a place where missionaries coming back from overseas could stay and rest after their labors, and so they set up a place out here on Nantucket, which they had visited before then—in the early 1870s a lot of people were coming down. That's when they built Bluff Cottage, and they also owned Nonantum, which was the old fishing cottage that Benjamin Franklin's mother had owned.

"So Mother's relatives had plenty of room for all of this vast family," Peter continued. "We were kind of the poor side—but they never let us know that. It was just a wonderful place to come, and all my early days were 'Sconset. I went to Camp Nickanoose, which a lot of people don't remember. It was out near the Mitchells—they had a beachfront and a camp there in the Polpis area. It was delightful; there was sailing, tennis, all kinds of activities. It was for everybody, it wasn't socially divided up into any special groups or anything." It was there, it turns out, that Peter developed his interest and skills in boating...and this served him well later on, as you'll see.

240

What did Peter Wilson and his older brother Frederic and their cousins do for fun? "Do you remember old Eddie Coffin? He had a rig, a kind of a nice carriage, and he'd take parties out into the moors…and, though I never knew this until long afterwards, he always carried a pocketful of arrowheads with him. He'd surreptitiously toss them around and then he'd pretend…'Look what I found!' and we kids would all run around and pick up the arrowheads. We'd pick beach plums and blueberries when they were in season…and sweetfern, and bayberries, too. And we made candles sometimes, just for fun. I became very attached to the Whaling Museum, because any time we came into town everyone else wanted to go shopping, and I would just go over to the museum. The man who impressed me there in those days was Captain George Grant; he was the last of the whaling men, and I remember so much that he taught me. And of course that's paying off now, because I'm an interpreter (they used to be called docents) at the Nantucket Historical Association's Whaling museum, giving lectures on whaling."

I asked Peter about those shopping trips into town and he remembered that there was a little branch of the A&P in 'Sconset for a while, but "every year we'd go to town, down to Perry Coffin's, next to the Wharf Rat Club, to get new slickers, and that was a big deal. My dad worked for a bank downtown in New York City, but the Depression knocked him out—he was one of the men in the department who didn't have a college degree; the bank cut those without degrees off completely, and it just kind of destroyed him. He didn't need what a lot of people need—he educated himself, was a very erudite, brilliant man."

Did the family ever consider coming to live on Nantucket fulltime? "Yes, they did," Peter said, "but they never could manage it. I was the first one to buy a house, and that was Heart's Ease in 'Sconset, in the '60s. We also had a house at 3 Whaler's Lane. My mother introduced a very interesting person to the island in the early '30s," Peter went on. "Her name was Enid Wilmerding, and she bought the old Flagg House, one of the first houses on the upper bluff. Every year I'd work for her. I'd have little jobs—painting, cutting lawns—but I also had plenty of time to have fun. Enid also had another house over by the water tower in 'Sconset, so we always had a place to come to. And it was always exchange—we'd always do something for her. This was all before the war. Enid was a wonderful lady. She was from a wealthy New York family and my parents had met her when they were living in Greenwich Village, before they moved up to Ossining, before I was born. She and my mother got along like sisters. Enid never married, but she had a great fondness for all the young children of her friends, and she was well established in 'Sconset with a lot of the old families there."

When Peter was a preteen, he made special friends with the Vaux family. "They were particularly dear to me," he said, "because it was a family of girls, much older than I; they lived on the bluff just north of Enid, and they would always take care of me if my mother had to go to town or something…and whenever I went down to the beach they were always there and they'd play games and treated me like one of theirs…so I was in glory, really. The Vauxes were quite a famous family in Philadelphia and Virginia, so all that was wonderful exposure for me, because I learned how people fortunate enough to have money lived; it gave me a good grounding in a part of life that we all should know something about, even though we may be living modestly ourselves.

"My father, Frederic 'Ted' Wilson, was a summer friend of Bobsy Hills, who rented small catboats down near Old North Wharf. Bobsy loaned us a boat one day because money was scarce during the early '30s and Dad had helped him repair an inboard engine earlier that week. A brisk easterly wind met us as we set off down harbor toward Wauwinet. Dad was a good sailor, trained aboard the old square-rigged *Aloha* and its small boats during his stint in the Navy during World War I. But sometimes he expected more of my older brother Tod at eight and me at six than our tender years had permitted us to learn. A few days at Camp Nickanoose on Polpis Harbor had not been sufficient for me to become an able-bodied seaman. Dad took a long northeasterly reach on a starboard tack after we cleared the inner harbor moorings. Of course, I didn't know at the time that that was what we were doing, but all became clear as we approached Second Point and Dad gave the order to come about. My brother shifted smartly to the port side. I, slow to follow, stood up just as the boom crossed to starboard and it caught me on the upper back and whacked me half over the starboard gunwale with my feet kicking air above the cockpit. Dad eased up on the tiller and rocked me back unhurt onto the floorboards, and the rest of the run was filled with much more tacking and a few more never-to-be-forgotten lessons. Our dungarees had been soaked through, but were dry and starched stiff with salt by the time we tied up opposite the grand old lady of the harbor, the *Lillian,* at the old Wauwinet pier. Tod and I struggled out of our dungarees down to our swim trunks, and after a gingerale on the porch of the Wauwinet House, Dad took a photo of us aboard the Lillian. That was one of the happiest days of a long life."

GROWING UP, GOING TO WAR

What about Peter's life off-island? "I grew up in the Hudson Valley in a rather famous old town called Sing-Sing in the early days (you know, of Sing-Sing Penitentiary fame) but was changed to Ossining later on," he said. "I spent my school years there, and then went on to Syracuse University." But World War II interrupted his college years, as well as his visits to the island he loved. "I attempted to enlist in the Navy, the Army, the Coast Guard, and the Marines, but wasn't accepted by any of them at first because I was color-blind. I was also left-handed, which seemed to bother a lot of the officers when I later succeeded in getting into the Army. And there's a funny story about the color-blindness. Once color-blind men got into

Left—A happy, tan little Peter Wilson at the beach on Nantucket Island in about 1928, with his father and brother Frederic (Tod). Right—In the very early 1930s, Peter Wilson and his brother were lucky enough to go on a jaunt aboard the famous old *Lillian.*

the service, the Army found out that they could see through camouflage…so often they would take some of us up in a reconnaissance plane and we'd look down, and we could see the guns, Howitzers and so forth, through the colored camouflage…the other fellows couldn't see this.

"When I finally did get into the Army, I had a choice…and I said, 'If it's anything to do with boats, fine.' So I wound up in the Amphibious Engineers, which was a new brigade being formed, and I was based at Devens first and then Camp Edwards. And the fact that I'd had boating experience and some navigation experience and sailing helped me, because most recruits had no such knowledge. Those of us who'd been involved in things like tugboating, tuna fishing, riverboating, and sailing kind of moved along quickly. But they wouldn't let us go to OCS. I applied about six times, and the reason for the refusal was that the Army had more invested in us because we did engineering—we built bridges and beachheads, and we operated all of the Amphibious Engineers' landing craft. So they would send us off to special schools…and ironically, we were assigned to the Navy a good deal. We had a patch with an anchor, a tommygun, and an eagle—it's a Combined Operations patch. So they would use us wherever they could; we were on detached service a lot. They put us aboard Navy PAs and KAs, cargo and personnel carriers; they were large Liberty-type ships. We'd be deck-mounted on there with our 60-foot tank lighters, LCM3s.

"When we got aboard, the Captain or the Exec Officer would always ask us to start doing their work. So our officer—we had a wonderful colonel—told us, 'You just take care of the boats; do mess duty and clean up when they ask you, but nothing else, because we have to keep the boats in shape.' Well, they weren't obeying that, so he got an unwritten commission to designate all the men in charge of the waves of landing craft that went aboard the boats, as Petty Officers Third Class. So I

Frederic and Peter Wilson sit with their mother and dog Rags in front of the family fireplace. The boys were in their teens.

Peter tried very hard to get into the service in 1943, and finally landed in the Army, in the Amphibious Engineers division.

had two ratings—both staff in the Army and Petty Officer in the Navy. It's not in my record," Peter laughed; "they never put it down—it's like many of those things that slipped through the cracks. But anyway, it was thanks to my years on Nantucket that I got into this type of duty during the war. And I was on the water most of the time during my 22 months in the southwest Pacific."

BOATS & ANTIQUES & MAGGIE

Peter was in the service for three years, but when he became a civilian again he completed university, getting a dual degree in English and Journalism. Though he had always intended to become a writer, he took a job with the National Association of Engine & Boat Manufacturers in Manhattan, which owned the National Boat Show in New York. "I started off as an administrative assistant in 1949-50, but the job was just for one show. So I started repping and writing for trade and boating magazines." Then came a stint in the '50s with a large insurance company, followed by a banking position; after which he and his brother began a business back in Ossining restoring homes and antiques: antique restoration has been a life interest of Peter's, as he'd been trained in his teens by a master cabinetmaker. Finally, Peter went back to the National Association of Engine & Boat Manufacturers and worked his way up in the next twenty years to become CEO and Managing Director of the Boat Show.

In the meantime, it was Nantucket as often and as long as he could make it during the summers. In 1972, he and his first wife and three sons—Peter, Jr., Mark, and Bruce—moved fulltime to the island, and he started restoring antiques again. His marriage ended and he met his current wife, the vivacious, energetic Maggie, divorced also, and mother of one son. "She came here with a friend in 1969 and fell in love with the island," Peter said. "This was the first time that she felt she had a home. Her growing up wasn't too great—she was from a small town in North Carolina where she was denied an opportunity to go to college. Maggie has a tremendous IQ, and an uncle would've paid for her to go to Chapel Hill, but her mother said no, girls marry and settle down. She did finally go to college, but left to get married, and that was unhappy, too. At any rate, she felt at home the minute she came here, so she rented a little unheated cottage down on Old North Wharf; then she was in Harbor Square in an apartment over Still Dock, and when we married she had a little house on Millbrook Road." Maggie had an interior decorating background and she and Peter met at the Marine Home Center, where she worked in the home decorating department. They married on Christmas Eve in 1974 and later built their house on Gray Avenue. But Maggie developed asthma, so in the mid-80s they moved way, way Off—near Nogales, Arizona where, Peter laughed ruefully, there is *no ocean*. They'd traveled around in their

Christmas Eve, 1974, on the occasion of Peter and Maggie Wilson's marriage.

244

motor home, looking for a place that was comfortable for Maggie's respiratory problems. Peter said, "We sold everything we had in the east and really started over again. But we always sort of hoped that we'd come back to Nantucket one day, and it took fifteen years, but we finally did."

In March of 2002, Maggie and Peter accepted an offer to manage the Periwinkle guest houses, but this is only one of the many occupations they've had in the past—they seem to have the typically Nantucket fortitude that makes them willing to do whatever it takes to make things work. (They've even run a restaurant/deli called The Stuffed Olive!) And they've evidently had a lot of fun along the way—they laugh a lot. They've taken on some serious challenges—cancer, Paget's Disease, that familiar condition called Lackamunny—and will even take on the corporate Goliath when necessary. Maggie (who Peter describes as "a bird dog when it comes to injustice") organized a successful class-action suit against a large western telephone company which promised them a phone, fiddled around for ages, and finally told the Wilsons it would cost them $14,000 to have a phone in the little ex-mining town where they lived!

WALKING, VOLUNTEERING, READING

"Nantucket is home to us," said Peter. And we're involved: Maggie has volunteered at the Hospital Thrift Shop and I do what I can there, but in season, I'm working four or five days a week with the NHA. I also volunteer at the Atheneum when I can, as I did at the libraries when we were out west—repairing books, preparing them for the catalog, whatever. And we both read a lot; people who know us well say we could go into a closet with a candle or a lightbulb and be happy as long as we had a book. We don't watch much TV, or follow sports much, though I used to play golf and tennis. We both have to exercise, and we eat properly." Though it's sometimes been a hard life, he concluded, it's been a good life.

Peter, as a longtime islander, history buff, and interpreter at the Whaling Museum, has a great collection of Nantucket lore. "In the 1860s, he said, "ships were sailing out of New Bedford because it was so difficult then to get in and out of Nantucket Harbor—the ships were larger and couldn't get over the sandbar. The whaling ships would sail down the African coast—and that's how so many Cape Verdeans became involved in our society, because they would pick up crew members in the Azores—and they'd go under Africa, under the Indian Ocean, and come up east of Australia. When they got there, the Captain would send two men aloft, one on each side of the crow's nest—there were body rings above the crosstrees that held them in—and the job of these fellows was to look 180 degrees port, 180 degrees starboard, watching for the sperm whale spout. It was unique—it came from the left of the whale's crown, pitched forward, and when it blew, they'd call down to their mates down below, '*THAR SHE BLOWS...BLOWS...BLOWS...*' and they'd keep yelling until they got a response from the deck, and then the Mate would call out, '*WHERE AWAY?*' And they'd point, give a bearing. Then the Captain would scramble up the shrouds and spot the whale and decide whether or not to take it. Before he even got down, if he wanted the whale, he'd order a boat over the side. People who hear our lectures tell us that whaling must have been one of the most dangerous professions that ever existed, and it's true. But they survived, because they learned how to do it safely."

THE GAMMING CHAIR

What about that interesting gamming chair at the museum that carried people from one boat to another for a visit, or "gam," when two Nantucket ships met at sea? Was the poor passenger hauled way up into the air in the chair, swinging precariously over the rolling sea on the way from one boat to the other? No, that wasn't quite the case, Peter said, although it could be a scary ride. Instead, the chair was lowered into a small boat that transported the gammers to the other boat and then back again. Were the lines attaching the ships thrown across? He said, "I don't think they used cannons for firing lines to the other boat then, but later on that would be possible for rescues. The gamming chair was put right down into the whaleboat and rowed over—it didn't get pulled across the way from boat to boat. The Captain's wife and sometimes his children often went on the voyage with him…after all, he'd be gone for up to four years."

Why would a wife and even children be allowed on a ship that was going thousands of miles away from tiny Nantucket in its quest for whales? Wouldn't they get in the way? Well, no, Peter said—they learned not to, because if they didn't, the results could be serious. Many of them kept journals and passed on memories and stories that have greatly enriched our knowledge of those days. And too, Peter said, it wasn't merely acceptable, but possibly quite beneficial, to have the Captain's wife on board…not only for bringing some feeling of home to the lonely crew, some touch of nurturing femininity, but because a wife could frequently help out in a tangible way. He explained: "That was largely due to the Quaker influence on the island. They taught their children and even the neighborhood children on the island navigation and arithmetic, mathematics, and reading. So the women learned it, too. As a result, the wives were often quite capable of doing some of the plotting of courses, keeping the logs, and so forth." But it must have been a tough life: long, boring days, hot sun, screeching winds and storms, not to mention the heat, gore, and mess when a whale was caught and carved up, its precious oil extracted, meaning slippery decks, hot trypots…Not a life for the faint of heart! These whaling wives were plucky souls.

Peter continued his explanation of gamming: "When another ship was sighted, the whalemen could identify it by its huge house flag, which flew from the main truck of the mainmast; it was usually extra-long, with a lot of bright colors so that it could be spotted at a distance. When they recognized the flag they'd heave to and have a gam. So the wife, often with the children gathered around her skirts for modesty, would get into the gamming chair, which has a sling on it, and be hoisted into one of the whaleboats, which would row her over to the other ship. Now the other ship's Captain might be her father, her uncle, her brother…and members of the crew could be cousins and nephews…so they'd have a few hours together before they sailed on to exchange news from home and information about where the whales were."

FROM GREENHORN TO CAPTAIN

Peter said that youngsters visiting the Whaling Museum particularly enjoy hearing about the very young men who went to sea. "They'd be 12, 13, or 14—they became ordinary seamen quite early. When a boy came back after a two-and-a-half-year cruise—that was the average length of a voyage—he could be 16 or 17 and be a mate, or a harpooner, or a boat-steerer. By the time he was 21 he could be a captain. And by age 28 he could be part-owner or own his own ship; and by the time he was 45 he could retire. When you read the logs and the stories of Nantucket whale captains and whalemen," he said, "you see that they had long lives. The fatality rate was quite low, really, because they learned the skill—it's all they did—they learned how to capture and harvest whales. It was a tricky business, but they learned how to avoid casualties. Those paintings you see of whales breaking up boats, coming up under them and crashing them, and taking them in their jaws…these things happened, but not as frequently as the artists liked to make it seem. Once the whale was harpooned, and swam away pulling the boat behind it (this was known as a Nantucket Sleighride), the men would carefully avoid being rocked overboard until the whale was exhausted; then a lance was thrust into the creature's heart and they'd back off and let it die. They wouldn't try to make it dead right there with hatchets and things…they'd back off and just wait, until they saw the 'fire in the chimney'—the blood that signaled the death of the whale—and that was the trick."

What about the famous harpooners' pins? "One of the key men on the ship," he said, "was the harpooner, and he'd probably have worked his way up through the ranks; he also might be a mate, or another officer of the ship, but the harpooner was a prized individual, because he could also steer the boat and as a rule navigate; he could take command of the small boats when they went out. Well, when he captured a whale, he was entitled to wear what they called a pin. In the bow of the whaleboat is a notch—it's like a chock, for a line to come through. The line the harpoon is attached to, the one that goes to the whale, comes back through that notch, and to keep that from flying out of the notch, there's a pin that goes through the two side pieces; it's a very short piece of a doweling-type pin, probably carved from oak. And the harpooners were entitled to wear one on their lapel. A young man wearing the harpooner's pin was very popular when the island had a sheep-shearing, or what they'd call the rantum scoots, picnics, and other kinds of activities." Quite a catch for gals with an eye to getting married.

RANTUM SCOOTING

"In whaling times and beyond," Peter said, "people enjoyed getting into their little two-wheel carts and venturing out into the moors for picnics or just to enjoy a nice day. That's why we have so many little sandy roads through the moors from the old days. They'd pick flowers, go berrying, and so forth." He chuckled, and added, "When Maggie was working on the island in the '70s, she had a microbus for a while, and took people for island tours. One day she was talking to the elder Mr. Levine, 'Big Sam,' they called him, and he said, 'Oh, I have something you might enjoy.' He went up into the attic over the Nobby Shop and came down with this very old quarterboard that said 'Rantum Scooter.' So Maggie put that in her microbus. It went everywhere with us—our first houses, our motorhome when we were journeying out to Arizona. And when we came back to the island to live again, the first thing she did was take it to the oldest Levine son, Reggie. He was delighted. So it's back home. And," he added with a smile, "so are we."

247

PETER WILSON

Left—Always at home on the Nantucket shore, Peter Wilson smiles at the camera in about 1997. Right—Peter and Maggie.

248

Eat Lots of Vegetables and Stay Busy!
Helen Lewis Ottison, 2002

The view from Helen and Albert Ottison's living-room window is…well, it's quintessential Nantucket. As is Helen Lewis Ottison. In this November interview, it was difficult not to keep looking out that window at meadow, grasses, bright-red stands of winterberry, the creeks, and the harbor. And believe it or not, Helen has been living in this heavenly spot for her entire life. She was born in a farmhouse you can see from the house in which she and her husband now live with their son Albert (AKA "Buster"). The Ottisons' other son, Karl, lives right next door with his wife Susan.

The first thing you have to do as a reader is to imagine all Helen's words in about as Yankee an accent as you've heard. Impossible to convey, though I'll take the liberty of spelling a few words exactly as she says them.

MOTHER MARRIED THE MILKMAN

Asked about her parents, Helen said, "My mother was from Sweden, and came to the island with a family as a cook and worked down to the Point. My father used to deliver milk down to the Point, so he asked her go to a dance, and that's how it all happened! She went to that dance the Fourth of July, and in the fall she went home with the family, but she came back and married the milkman!" Helen laughed, her bright eyes twinkling in a sun-browned face.

"My maiden name is Lewis…My mother was an Olsen. Her family emigrated to this country. And my husband is also a native. That's him, workin' with the wood down there in the yard. His folks came from Latvia. I liked the name Ottison, because my mother was Olsen, so I asked Grandfather Ottison how he got that name, and he told me his folks had come from Denmark. Albert don't look into that kind of thing, but I do; I've traced things back. They came as immigrants, just like my mother. Albert's folks didn't know each other over there, they met in this country.

"I was the baby of the family—there was Sarah and Marguerite and Andrew (he always liked Madaket, so he went and built a house there), Willie (he made that stool over there when he was at the Coffin School), and Ezra. Marguerite worked at the New Haven & Hartford Railroad for 45 years. And she rode on the Nantucket Railroad…Sarah went to nursing school, but then she got married…but later in life she went back to nursing. She did all kinds of work—took dictaphone, worked in the courthouse, but she used to say if you were a nurse you were always wanted.

"My mother and father bought a house on Prospect Street, and my sisters and brothers was all bawn there ["theyuh"], at home. I'm the only one left, and when I was bawn I was a little tiny thing—I only weighed 2—pounds…but I guess I'm all there! My mother said I was full term…and I was bawn in November…she didn't have an incubator to put me in, so she put me by the oven door…eyuh, those old black woodstoves. We have one here; I have 'lectricity, but we burn wood, and my dishwasher goes by hot water that we make from the fire in the stove downstairs. *We burn wood!*" Helen added emphatically. "All our winter heat is from wood. We make everything work for us, sure do. We have an outside shower here that's solar-heated," she added, then laughed: "Albert sometimes takes a shower out there—one year in Mahch! But I'll wait till Memorial Day!" Then she whispered a story: "You know, somebody come in the winter, and I says, 'Buster there's somebody at the woodpile!' And he went down there…with a crowbar in one hand. This was half-past two in the morning. The people said, 'We wanted some wood.' Buster said, 'Didn't your mother ever tell you that you're supposed to buy things, not come and steal 'em at night?' He says, 'You take that wood and don't you ever come back again!' And they never did."

CARROTS, PEAS, TOMATOES, SQUASH, TURNIPS...

How does Helen account for her positive attitude and good health? She said, "I'm in good condition...I'm very careful. And I never had an operation in my life. I had two babies, and that was all! I like my life. We have our own garden here...vegetables! We have carrots, potatoes, tomatoes...I have to buy lettuce off and on...I've got peas and Nantucket blueberries in the freezer. I'm not much on beachplums—we used to pick 'em, but you've got to have a lot of sugar for beachplum jelly. We eat chicken, turkey, and a lot of vegetables. The carrots are still in the ground—all you have to do is cover 'em with leaves; the turnips are just coming, and butternut squash, we had that galore...so we are gonna live on butternut squash and turnip and frozen peas this winter. Oh yes, that's my secret—vegetables!"

Helen showed me lots of pictures, including one of her Nantucket High School graduating class. "I graduated in 1940," she said, showing me her class ring, which she still wears. She went on, "You know, you look back...I'm 81 years old...I'm in good shape, though I'm a diabetic. I have taken very good care of myself." Then she hopped up, scurried into another room, and brought back more pictures and the program for the class dinner, held at the Old 'Sconset Inn on Tuesday evening, June 11th, 1940. Florida grapefruit Grenadine, fresh vegetable soup, rolls and relishes, roast turkey with dressing, snowflake potatoes, garden peas, mashed turnips, jellied tomato salad...and a strawberry sundae for dessert. Faculty and guests present were Mr. and Mrs. Charles G. Taylor, Miss Sarah Packard, Miss Phelice Andrews, Mr. and Mrs. John F. Shaw, Miss Evelyn Tiews, and Miss Lottie Elzbut.

Helen went down the list of graduates, 35 of them, and told me who was still around, who had moved off-island ("mostly the girls, when they got married"), and who had died. "Not so many at our reunions any more," she said sadly. Then, pointing at her own image, she said, "There I am...tall! And there's Arline Fisher, now Bartlett, she's still livin'; Anna Garnett just died; Kenny Legg...he's a lawyer out in Nebraska; and Trina Griek—she was very smart in school...and William "Buddy" Blair...and Katherine Cahoon. Dracia Kaufman's gone—her father ran Cy's Green Coffee Pot—and Evelyn Huyser's gone...Marion Matland is still here on the island. Heathie McMillan [Pykosz] is at the Homestead. Stanworth Nickerson is gone, Adrinette Paradis is gone, Donald Pease...he went up to Alaska on the pipeline...and then he came back. Shirley Reed...I think she raised dogs...Priscilla Swift is here on the island. Samuel Thurber was the class president." And she concluded, "Helen Lewis is still here!" She took a breath and added, "You know, I've been to Europe, I've been to Hawaii, but there's nothing like comin' back to Nantucket. Yes. My haht is in Nantucket."

GROWING UP ON THE FAHM

What, I wondered, were Helen's growing-up years like? "Oh," she said, "I lived on the fahm, right here...Mr. Mooney lives in the fahmhouse now. It was moved a long time ago right down from Union Street, with horses and logs. I was bawn in that fahmhouse. So I haven't gone too far. The fahmhouse had high ceilin's...so in the winter, all you had was two rooms goin'. There was a kitchen stove, and that was it. My school years? I went' the old South School, on Orange Street. Had to walk all the way. There was a hoss fountain down here, at the corner…and 'course it would snow in the winter—there was a lot of snow in those days, more than we have now. But on the way to school in winter, we always stopped at that old hoss fountain and played with the ice…where that fountain went, I don't know. I didn't ride a hoss to school, no, but my sister, Marguerite, was quite a rider, and played golf, everything. I played baseball, rode bicycle…I always wore overhauls, and I had a hammer, and I could do anythin'.

"I had Esther Johnson in first grade at the old South School," she continued. "You know where Ryder's Market was? There was an A&P and Ryder's Market on Orange Street, and across the way was the old South School. I stayed there until they made the Cyrus Peirce School, and I went there from the fourth to sixth grade. Then I went to junior high and high school at the 'Cademy Hill School. God, I loved school. I was good in school…*I loved math!* And I used to have to go teach some of the others math or algebra. I didn't care to read, but I liked figures.

"We went to school dances…we had more darn fun. At Cyrus Peirce School. The boys'd come out one lane, and the girls would come out the other, and whoever you got as a partner, you danced with. Leo Killen! Oh, *couldn't he dance!* And Harrison Gorman! But all the girls wanted to dance with Leo Killen. Oh, we had fun! And I used to dance with David Wood…David was one grade ahead of me, and Philip Murray and Robert Murray…" In the winters, when it was a lot colder and snowier than today, Helen said, she used to skate on the harbor. "Some of our teachers even skated…Dick Porter, the principal, used to do it, for one."

I asked how Albert, still a fit and good-looking man at 87, and Helen had met and courted. Helen laughed and said, "Well, we always knew each other. But after school, he went to Florida, and then he came back, and somehow or other we kinda went together, and well, I said, 'I think I'm goin' off to nursin' school.' 'Oh,' he said, 'why don't we get married? I knew he was good, good as anythin'; so we married. He built these houses—Karl built his house next door. We used to rent this house out…and rented the two down there, the boathouse and the lobster shack. I had about

252

Note the two boys at either end of the photo of Helen's graduating class on their visit to Monticello—same boys! The photographer had to shoot the photo in two parts, and while he was focusing the second half, the two boys raced to the other side.

25 sheets a week to do…I did the laundry for the summer renters…and hung 'em out on a line, oh yes. Still use that line; I don't have a dryer. My husband was a carpenter, a plumber, everything…and my sons work with their hands too. Susan and Karl are basket-makers…we were, too. We're a bunch of workers, all the way through. But that's been fun…we've had fun, all the time.

"My grandfather, Simeon Lewis," she went on, "owned all the way to Monomoy [pronounced MonoMOY]…they had a summer house there. And this was all the meadows," she said, pointing out the window. "The painting up there shows when my grandfather was getting' the grass up, puttin' the hay on the wagon…you can see the same meadow and creek from here. We can go out there and go sailin'. Or scallopin'. They went out the other day, right out from the creek…high water. I went with the oldest boy, and once we went all winter; we used to go when it was pretty cold weather, sometimes. Oh, we used to open some scallops, I'll tell you that. It was sometimes four or five of us went. Karl and Susan, Buster, my husband…so there was five of us to open scallops…it was fun. I've had a fun life!" she said again with relish.

I asked if Helen has a favorite scallop recipe, and she replied, "Well, if they're fresh, olive oil…olive oil. You can egg 'em, dip 'em in egg and then flour, but I don't bothuh. But use olive oil on everythin' you cook! Butter ain't good for ya. Not good. You don't cook 'em very long. I put 'em in a bag and shake 'em around…They will puff up better if you dip 'em in egg and then flour…that's all right if they're not that fresh. Scallop stew? Oh, I love scallop stew! You get the milk hot and then drop the scallops in…we're going to have that tonight, because they went scallopin' yesterday. They say they're scayuss this year."

Bouncing up and hustling to another room, Helen returned with an old book about flowers, then explained that it had been her grandmother's. "Grandmother was Julia Lewis…she married Simeon Lewis. She had a hoss and buggy, and they would go out in the moors and pick the Nantucket flowers…that's what they did for excitement then. And here in this book, Grandma listed the flowers she found, and when she found them…here's coreopsis, wood lily, and so

on…and here's some dates—1898, 1900, 1902…Yes, that's what they did for fun in those days."

TILL THE COWS COME HOME…

I wondered what Helen did after school and in summers as a child. "Oh, on the fahm, we had cows, and I had to go way the heck over there and gather up the cows…I had a job to do! The cows were down in the meadow here and all the way over to Monomoy." How, I asked, does one "gather up" cows? Helen laughed. "Gather 'em up? Well, they'd come out of the gate here and go out…and everybody loved to just stop and look at the cows! They used to feed along the edges of the road, and then I'd have to take 'em way over in the lot. That was my job in the summer." How, I asked, do you take cows someplace? Another laugh: "They go! And when you get 'em at night, you say, 'C'mon…goin' home…'; then you open the gate and they run for home, because they want to be milked. Dad was a milkman. I didn't milk the cows, my mother did. I used to throw up the hay in the big barn…there was two barns here. Albert's grandmother lived up there on that hill. There was a gate here, and the house was up there. It's in the picture, the one with his grandfather hayin'. So I used to have to go up there for the cows. And then his grandmother sold the place to Judge Poland. She was getting old. I used to have to go up there and sit on her knee and sing for her…I loved to sing. I still love to sing…I listen to Lawrence Welk, and I can sing any old song! I used to be in the Congregational choir…that's my church, but it doesn't matter what church you go to…I've been in them all. Bud Egan, he was Catholic, and he and Albert went to school together. Before he died, Bud would come over and say, 'C'mon, I'll take you for a ride!' He took us for rides right up till the day he died. Bud Egan. Good friend. I have a lot of good old friends…I mean, this is Nantucket. It's a wonderful life." But the island is changing, Helen admitted: "Everybody wants a house here. Oh my God, you see a house goin' up every day…every day there's a house comin' or goin' or movin'!"

What does this peppy octogenarian do to relax? Helen laughed, and said, "I enjoy everythin' I do. Relax? I go walkin'—I can walk pretty good, with my cane. I walk down in the meadow; there's a road there, full of scallop shells…nothing but scallop shells on that whole road, the whole length, and the scallop shells here are all the ones we picked and shucked. And I knit, and sew. My son has an iceboat, and I sewed the sail for him…and someone said, 'That's got a sunfish on it,' and I said, 'Yes, because I put it on there!' I can do anything! Gosh sakes, I even made a leather wallet for my husband on my little machine. I cut it out from a real pockeybook. I'm not ever bored, never! I like my life. I've been all over. I even sailed this summer—went out' the creek, sailed…of course, this is my stamping ground."

Well, the secrets of life may be to eat lots of vegetables and stay busy. It certainly has worked for Nantucket native Helen Lewis Ottison.

Helen Lewis in her graduation gown.

256

Dancing, Daring, Dreaming, Doing

Bee Gonnella, 2002

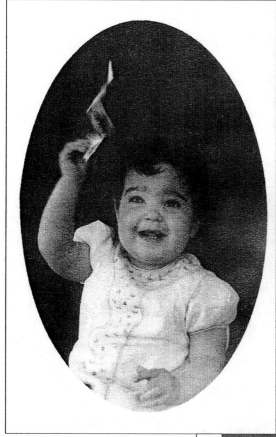

Mr. and Mrs. George Dyer of Washington, DC, got a big surprise in 1937. Their son was five, and they were eagerly awaiting the arrival of a second child. If it was a girl, they were going to name her Anne Rock Dyer, Rock being a family name. A strong heartbeat had been detected, and finally the delivery date came. And then, quite to everyone's astonishment, Mrs. Dyer gave birth to not one, but two baby girls!

Identical twins they were, and just to keep them separate, the first wore a tiny band saying "Baby A" and the second-born was tagged "Baby B." Baby A was soon named Anne; Baby B became Rock. No middle names, just Anne and Rock Dyer. And most readers on the island know Rock...only they know her as Bee (for Baby B). Bee Gonnella, who with her four children owns and runs a hotel that was established as Point Breeze in 1892, became the Gordon Folger Hotel, and was given back its original name when the Gonnellas purchased it in 1997.

That Was the Way It Was

Bee first came to the island as a baby, in 1938. "My father's family, the George Dyers, came in 1910, when Nantucket was just becoming a summer community; they lived in New Jersey," she said. "My grandfather was a major figure in advertising in New York, and I guess he heard about Nantucket and they came and bought the property at 9 Milk Street. (We have pictures of my father as a little boy, and Milk Street was still a dirt road.) They'd pack up the steamer trunks and bring the family for the summer. I don't know how long my grandfather stayed, because commuting wasn't all that easy in those days...but that tradition continued in the family. During World War II my brother, sister, and I came up and stayed with my grandmother, because Washington was not a nice place to be in the summer, particularly during the war.

"My parents stayed in Washington during the war. We children would come up on the train from Washington to Providence with the nanny and get on the boat in New Bedford, and come over from there...and the train of course was always late, so it was always a mad dash, and we invariably missed the bus and would have to take a taxi from Providence all the way to the dock. And we'd spend the whole summer. One year we stayed until November, because there was a bad polio epidemic in Washington, and my parents didn't want us back there until after the first frost, which killed the polio virus. We didn't go to school here...don't ask me why. When we got home, my mother taught us. And it was first grade—can you believe that? Children not going to school in the first grade? The next year they decided that for social as well as academic reasons we should go to school, so we started school in the third grade.

"The house that is now the Maria Mitchell little house on Vestal Street, just above the Science Museum, was my grandparents' carriage house; we always stayed in that as little kids. The iceman came every other day to deliver the ice; we had a gas stove—I guess it was Ramos who delivered the gas—and that was the way it was. My grandmother also had a beach shack down at Cliffside, and when we got to be 17 we were allowed to stay there by ourselves! Oh my goodness, we wouldn't have dreamed of violating that trust. Paragons of virtue, we were.

"Those were our innocent days of childhood, which a lot of kids don't have today. We went to the beach, we sailed...we didn't have radio, we didn't have TVs or VCRs. You didn't have any of those things, so you played with shells, the things on the beach; you made sandcastles. I was 11 before I even had a bicycle here on Nantucket, and I was allowed to ride it on the dirt road...by then my father had bought his house out in Shimmo when there were no houses, except a handful along the shore. My goodness, I've been walking those same dirt roads since 1946. It was a real quiet time during the war, and then Nantucket changed; people began coming back as a summer community. I was here as a teenager; our family belonged to the Yacht Club and I taught sailing there, and raced, and sailed day in and day out. And when I brought my children here, Gloria Dubock and Edie Ray taught the Red Cross community swimming lessons at Children's Beach, and it was a wonderful time—they were little kids then, and they made friends with the local kids and maintained those friendships, so when they came back here to school, it was an easy transition for them."

What's it like to have an identical twin? "Well," Bee said, "once upon a time we looked alike, but not so much any more. She's been a nun for forty years, and I've been married for forty years, she's a religious of the Sacred Heart, and so our different lifestyles have made some difference in our looks." (When I asked if Bee had ever considered becoming a nun, she exclaimed, "Are you *kidding?*") "Our brother lived in Hawaii for thirty-odd years; he was stationed out there in the Navy, met his wife there, came back here to Harvard Law School, and then decided to go back and raise his family in Hawaii; now he lives in Washington State."

DANCING INTO THE HOTEL BUSINESS?

I asked Bee where she'd gone to school and what she'd had in mind for a career. She laughed and answered, "Well, it was never to be a hotelier! I went to the Convent of the Sacred Heart in Washington, which is the order my sister ultimately joined, and then we went on to Wheaton College. Throughout college, you weren't allowed to major in dance; it had to be done as an extracurricular activity, but I wound

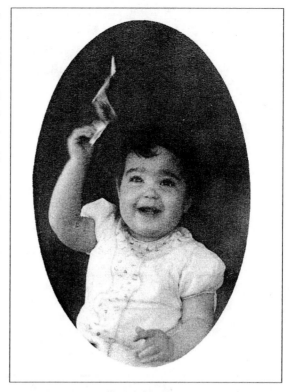

This is either Bee or her identical twin Anne—Bee says to this day they can't tell their pictures apart!

Bee and Annie—or is it Annie and Bee?—at an early age.

up putting all my time and energy into dance, and joined a professional dance company after I got out of college. And then I got married…we made choices in those days, didn't we? You know, do you go on to New York? Do you go on to Jacob's Pillow? Or do you say, 'Hmmm…I can't do both. What, ultimately, do I really want? I knew I wanted a family, and so I married…took time off to raise my family, and then went back as a dancer and started choreographing high school musicals in Winchester, where we were living then.

"I have three boys and a girl, the rose among thorns. Two of my sons are here: Paul is our general manager and Mark manages the dining room and the restaurant. John is with a major ad agency in the Boston area, and does all our advertising and graphic design work. Lisa, a CPA, is our bean-counter; she keeps our books honest. She lives in North Carolina and comes up a couple times a year to do an audit for us. Her husband is also a CPA, and he did our very first audit, when we knew our books were a shambles and we didn't know if we had any money or not! It's wonderful to have all my children involved, wonderful. Probably if you asked them, some of them think it's more wonderful than others…but we've done it now for six years and we all still love each other…so that says something. I have nine grandchildren, and five of them are on the property. It doesn't get any better!"

COMING HOME

How and when did Bee decide to come to Nantucket to live year-round? She said: "I made that decision because I was having personal problems in my marriage, and it was coming home for me— that was in 1978. My father was living here at the time and he'd given me some land, so I'd already built my own house here. We tend to come home to lick our wounds…I did that, and stayed. Had

260

Left—A 1952 photo of Bee and her twin, Anne, training their dogs. Right—Even as a mother of four, Bee couldn't stop dancing.

absolutely no desire to leave and I grew as a person, gained my independence. When I first came, I ran into Pat Hare—she and Marilyn Berthelette were doing the music at the high school, and I told them what my experience was and asked if they needed any help with their musicals. And they said they'd love help, so I started working with them.

"When we moved here, my boys were teenagers…and they were running wild. It was a very difficult time to grow up. You know, we talk about drugs on the island now, but in many ways it was worse then, because as parents and as teachers, we didn't know what drugs were! I didn't know what pot was…and I wound up literally going to the Police Department myself at one point and saying, 'What is this stuff?' I didn't know! And smoking was acceptable in the high school; there was a smoking area right under the teachers' room, and right outside the music room…and you had kids who were smoking joints out there, and teachers didn't even know what pot was. It was a bizarre time, in the late '70s and early '80s, an awful time to be a single parent. But all my kids turned out just fine. They all went to high school here except for the third one, John, who went away to boarding school after his sophomore year. The best thing that happened to him here was that the guidance counselor at the time allowed him to take private lessons with Warren Krebs, and gave him credit for it. And Warren helped him put a portfolio together, which got him into art school, and had that not happened, who knows where he'd be today? That probably never would have happened in any other school system. Paul graduated in 1981, and from where I sat—and I was working with a lot of those kids at the school—they were the greatest class of underachievers I ever saw! These were bright kids who smoked their brains out, who had no motivation, and they have gone in so many different directions. Either they've really pulled themselves together and are doing good things or else they've gone into rehab, and some have been in and out of jail… But for us it all turned out fine, and it has made us a very strong family."

And indeed, a family that works together still. When did Bee and her family decide to take over the Gordon Folger Hotel? She said, "Oh, what a joke! I had one son who was getting married and his bride-to-be had just lost her mother, so she wanted to be married on Nantucket, not in Florida without her own mother there. So we looked around at the different venues available…she of course had visions of being married on the waterfront at the White Elephant or the Wauwinet…we looked and priced, but those places were just not in the budget. So we went to look at the Gordon Folger in February of 1996. It was boarded up tight, and all you could see in the ballroom were these lime-green chairs, peeling paint everywhere, and…well, nothing shows well in January and February under the best of conditions, but this was not playing well at all. They thought it was a dump, but I kept saying 'We've had lots of junior proms and other events in here, it's gonna be great, and it's affordable. We can do this!'

A DUMP WITH POTENTIAL

"The wedding was set for October, so we started calling up to see about getting prices…and we finally got things settled…then we decided to have dinner here in June and sort of audition the chef and see how things were going to go. And the dining room was empty. I now know that that's not an unusual thing to happen in June," Bee laughed, "but Paul kept saying, 'You know, this place has such potential,' and he was itching to get his own place, so a couple of weeks later he said, 'Mom…what if we all pooled our resources and bought this place?' I said, 'Paul! Are you crazy?' Well, it was on the drums that the hotel was on the market. Paul was then assistant general manager at the Yacht Club, and previously had been a landscaper here on Nantucket, like most of the other young men, and one of his clients was Hammie Heard. So he called Hammie to see what was going on. Hammie said yes, it was on the market. I was working in the summer with Nina Hellman in the antique store, and Paul was at the Yacht Club, and we'd all get off work about 10 o'clock and start our family meeting...and Lisa and Jack would come, and they were all going 90 miles an hour and I was thinking, 'I don't know if I can keep up with these kids!' My father had passed away, and we all had some inheritance. We crunched the numbers and crunched the numbers and finally decided to make an offer. But now it was under agreement with somebody else. We said, 'It wasn't meant to be. It was a great exercise; we've had fun doing it, but...' and we all went back to work. About a month later, Hammie told us that the buyer was in jail and hadn't met the next payment and the deal was off. Were we still interested? And we looked at each other and said, 'Well, maybe it was meant to be.' Back to the drawing board. Crunched more numbers, and made the offer and it was accepted.

"My aunt was thrilled when we decided to rename it the Point Breeze. She remembered the tea dances here...and the fire on August 8, 1925, when it burned down. She was 15. She said everybody went to the fire except the girls—they weren't allowed to. It burned the earliest section of the hotel. In the attic, you can still see scars of the fire on that side where it was all attached; and you go down beneath, and it's fun, from almost an archaeological point of view, to look at the old pictures and the structure as it is today, and piece it out as to what was where then. We don't have a lot of old pictures of the old hotel and guests, but I'd love to track some of them down."

A lot of changes have taken place on the island during Bee's lifetime. "I think it's just gotten so horrifically overcrowded here," she said. "I'm grateful and fortunate to have my own place, but I have four children who can't afford to live here! (The two who live here are in hotel property.) And it may cause us serious problems in the not too distant future. I am very concerned about affordable housing. Things get built as affordable and they don't stay affordable. Our young people who have either been born here or grown up and gone to school here can't afford to stay, and they are the backbone of the island in terms of having the skills that keep it functioning. They are the tradespeople. I think back to our founding fathers: 300 years ago the island proprietors had to bring in half-share men from off-island who had the fishing, carpentry, and other skills...to make the island function. And we're right back there now! We don't have half-shares to give...but maybe we should be giving the young people what is left of this finite land, to keep them here so that we would have the trades here that we cannot operate without. I know people complain about our foreign labor...well, we couldn't function without it! Years ago, kids got out of college in early June, went back in the middle of September. Now, the kids get out in the middle of May and they go back in the middle of August. I can't run a hotel with people who are leaving in the middle of August!"

DEAD GRANDMOTHERS MONTH

Bee paused to do one of those laugh-sighs: "We call August Dead Grandmothers Month. You have summer staff, college kids, who start saying at about the end of July, 'My grandmother is really sick. 'Oh, my grandmother died—I'm going to have to leave by the second week in August.' We had one girl this summer who Paul and Elida had hired in June as a nanny; she didn't even get to July when her grandmother died. She said she had to go back to Vermont for the funeral the next Saturday...and I said, 'Oh, you know that's really too bad. Grandmothers don't usually die until August here on Nantucket.' She left (with our car keys) and that was the end of that. You get annoyed with the American college kids—they're not all like that, but unfortunately, they all get tarred with a bad brush. We are very careful now when we hire them.

"We have people who come here and say, 'I waited tables here twenty, thirty, forty years ago,' and one remembered going through the dining room with heavy trays: you'd kick the first door open, take two steps, and kick the second door open into the kitchen. And that hasn't changed…we've still got the kickplates on the doors. That woman remembered having four to a room, but now kids won't double up on their space…they have to have room for their stereos, for a monstrous wardrobe…we had one person who tried to go after us for living conditions that were 'untenable' because she didn't have her own bathroom! We respect the needs of all our help; we do the visas for the foreign help and do everything above-board, and jump through the hoops because we really value them and could not operate without them. And we have a very high rate of return every year—that's great, because they are a tremendous asset to the business. Now we have youngsters from Canada, Jamaica, Poland, Lithuania, Russia, Siberia, South Africa—they're coming from all over the world. And they all live together, and it works!"

What does Bee Gonnella see and dream for the future of the Point Breeze Hotel? "At this point, we are literally going one year at a time…but you sit here and dream about things you'd like to do. I'd love to see this place insulated, and with heat, so we could turn it into an artists' residence program in the winters. That would be a dream of mine…and you know, it stresses the building so just to close it up. We have to drain the water out of this building on the first of November because, if we have a freeze, and we have had a freeze when we turned it on too early, it is devastating! Horrific! [she shuddered] Not pretty!" The hotel business is no piece of cake.

Bee has stayed very involved in the community; she's performed with the Theatre Workshop in several plays, and currently works with Jim Patrick with his one-act play group and festival. She's co-written some plays for the Dinner Mystery Theatre she initiated for Tuesday nights with the Point Breeze Players. She plays tennis, paddle, maintains her theatre interests, does the hotel gardening, and often minds the grandkids, which is probably why she's tan and in such great shape. Attractive, determined, forthright, with snapping brown eyes and a ready laugh, she seems to have all the necessary qualities for a successful hotelier. Lucky Point Breeze!

Bee performing with Warren Krebs at the Point Breeze Hotel.

264

From a Big Island
to a Small One
Elizabeth & John Gilbert, 2002

*P*ossibly, everyone on the island knows Elizabeth and John Gilbert. They should—John was a carpenter here for many years, and now does picture framing; Elizabeth has long been known as a needlewoman supreme (she owned the Craft Center on Quaker Road and is internationally known for her needle-arts skills); and both of them have had a lengthy history with Nantucket theatre.

When we met for our interview in August of 2002, the first question I asked was whether they considered themselves coofs or washashores or something like that. Both still have a wonderful British accent, despite the fact that they've been here for almost fifty years. Elizabeth said, "I would say washashores, maybe, but back in the '50s, that wasn't the word. We were called off-islanders then…even though we came here to live. We will always be off-islanders." John, laughing, said, "There was old Willard Harvey, who came here at six months of age, and when they buried him, they buried him as a 'stranger.'" ("Stranger" is the word islanders use for people who were born on Martha's Vineyard.)

THE TASTE OF NANTUCKET

John and Elizabeth came here on their honeymoon in 1955 and not too long after that packed up their things and came back to stay. How did they happen to choose Nantucket for their honeymoon? Elizabeth explained: "My father had a house in 'Sconset, on Chapel Street. He was Dr. Miles Atkinson. We're all Mileses—I'm Elizabeth Miles, my older brother is Miles, my son is Miles…" Hmmm, I said. Me too. John laughed, saying, "At school, they used to call her Elizabeth Yards Feet and Inches." Elizabeth: "Yes, Elizabeth Yards and Yards of Atkinson, they called me."

She went on with her explanation of the Nantucket connection. "My father had left my mother and me and England in 1936, when I was ten months old. I never saw him again until 1945 when he came to a medical conference in London; he took me for lunch and disappeared again…but we kept in contact, and he used to send me Care Packages at school during the war. We kept in writing contact until I left boarding school, and he offered me a trip to the U.S. so we could get to know each other. I was here for six weeks, and he took me all over, and one of the major places he brought me was Nantucket. So that gave me the taste of Nantucket and I went home, having fallen in love with the island. But John said, 'Oh no, we're going to New Zealand,' and…John, you take it from there." John: "We'd been planning to leave England…We met when I was on leave from the RAF. Elizabeth was an evacuee during the war—she became the foster child of a family called Hallam; she was boarded out from London so she wouldn't be there during the bombing. Anyhow, I was a cyclist, used to race, and I came upon the Hallams' son Bob one day on the bridge. His bicycle was broken, so I fixed it, and he said, 'My sister's bicycle is broken too—I'll meet you back here at 2 o'clock this afternoon,' and that's how I met Elizabeth. This was after the war, 1950." That was it—they fell in love. Elizabeth was fifteen, John eighteen. John added, "I'd just done my training in the RAF; you were conscripted, drafted, when you were eighteen years old, and I'd signed on for three and a half years."

"We got married in 1955, and Elizabeth's father said, 'If we're going to get to know each other, you'd better come over here, because I'm too busy to come over for your wedding, but if you come to Nantucket you can borrow my 'Sconset cottage for six weeks. The hardest part of that was getting the time off from my work in London. I was making lasts for handmade shoes, for one of the biggest shoemakers in London; they made the Duke of Edinborough's shoes and Haile Selassie's shoes…and Greer Garson's shoes…all those people."

"After the war," said Elizabeth, "the opportunities were really very slim for young people, unless you went into a family business or had something waiting for you to start from scratch…and I just was out of college. We wanted to buy a house in England, but…" John: "Between us, we were earning ample, but the British banking arrangement was that the wife's money didn't count!" Elizabeth: "That was probably the straw that broke the camel's back, and we said, OK, we wanted to leave anyway, this is the sign that we're going. We had thought about New Zealand, because in those days if you went to one of the British colonies, like Canada or New Zealand or Australia or India, your way was paid. But you had to sign a covenant that you would stay for five years. And one of the things stopping us from going to New Zealand was that my mother and John's parents were in England, and that was 12,000 miles, should we have to go home for any reason. So we decided not to do that, and then my father came through with this offer of sponsoring us to the U.S.; we decided to do that for two years and then go to New Zealand. Well," she laughed, "that never happened. We had no idea we'd stay in Nantucket forever at that time…we stayed for two years and went back to England in 1957…and then we came back with green cards." John: "And it was 1966 when we got citizenship, because you had to wait that long."

LIFE IN WARTIME ENGLAND

John said, "I started out life living on a farm, working around the farm as a kid in the summertime and after school…and then, when my father went into the service, we moved and moved and moved—I went to thirteen schools in twelve years. I left school when I was fourteen and became a silversmith for three years, and then I went into the RAF and became a motor mechanic. I went to Yemen—it was Aden at that

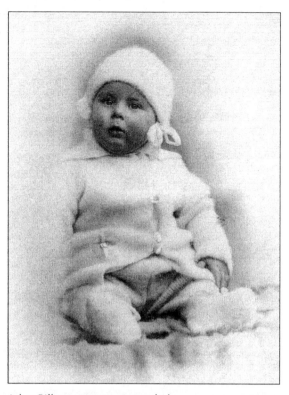

John Gilbert as a very young lad.

Elizabeth Miles Atkinson exhibits her photogenic qualities in the summer of 1938.

time—and spent two and a half years there, and when I came home I had accumulated all my leave, so I had all this time on my hands when I got home, and the gentleman for whom my father worked said, "As you've got all this time, would you like to paint my house?" So I painted his house, and he was so pleased with that he said, 'When you get through, would you like to go to work for me in London?' So that's how I became a last-maker in London."

Elizabeth didn't move around as a youngster, but she was in a boarding school outside London for twelve years. "I went to what they called a nursery boarding school when I was three," she explained, "and then at four and a half I went to a regular boarding school and stayed until I was sixteen and went to college. So that was very stabilizing in a way, but it was all through World War II, and we never slept in a bed for over six years, because all the children had to go to a shelter every night. We used to go for walks through the woods that were close by, and instead of picking up stones and leaves and flowers, we'd pick up the schrapnel—we'd have schrapnel collections…that was part of our life. We also collected ticker tape…John can explain that." John: "It was black tape, silver on one side, and they dropped it to stop the radar."

I had to wonder how these two people managed to stay so emotionally healthy under such conditions, and wondered if either of them had ever had a bomb drop close by. Elizabeth said, matter-of-factly, "Oh yes. At the very edge of the playing field at school was the railway, and of course that was a prime target for German planes. They'd drop bombs to disrupt the communications between South Hampton and London, mainly. And there were factories all along the railway on the other side, and bombs were just dropping all the time. That's why we were in shelters at night. And of course all the windows were blackened. Once a German bomber crashed in the field opposite us, and all the Germans were running around…we thought it was great fun at the time. They got captured eventually. It was exciting. Anything was exciting at a Victorian boarding school! But I don't think I was ever actually threatened. When bombs were dropping and we were doing our lessons, we used to have to carry torches, flashlights…we were all war-trained so that if there was a certain sound, like the doodlebugs—the pilotless bombs that used to come over—then you had to lie flat on the ground wherever you were, whether you were indoors or outdoors." John said, "A doodlebug sounded like an old motorcycle…and if that cut out and you lay down quick, you knew the thing was going to crash."

John said he'd had a couple of close calls. "One was when we were living at Barton-on-the-Sea; I was eight. Our street ran parallel to the shore-there was the cliff, the grass, and the street, and the street…A little friend who lived in the last house on the street came running over one morning saying. 'We have a bomb in our garden!' We hadn't heard a thing. The bomb was right in the corner of his garden—missed his house entirely. Another incident: one day early in the war, I was playing outside, and suddenly, a plane came up over the cliff, about 100 yards down—it had the swastika and the cross on it, and I could see the pilot looking at me, we were that close—and it flew over the little village, dropped the ticker tapes, missed the railway, turned around and machine-gunned the town, and then went over the Needles [three sharp rocks in the English Channel] and into the Isle of Wight, where it was shot down. And I stood on that same spot and watched all that happen." And you weren't traumatized by all this? I asked, to which John replied, "Well, it was part of life. There were machine guns placed along the cliff every 300 yards, and there were soldiers with rifles, and that's all we had defending the shore…with barbed wire all along the shore, and landmines. And the soldiers were bored stiff, because all they had to do was clean their guns…so I used to go visit them, and I learned to strip down a rifle and a machine gun. When I went into the service years later, I had no problem with that!" He laughed, and added, "A friend of mine had the biggest collection of ammunition and hand grenades which he'd picked up from the war games and crashed airplanes, and he always said if Jerry came over, we could take care of him ourselves!"

EVERY NIGHT IN AN AIR-RAID SHELTER

How Elizabeth got involved with the needle arts was a direct result of the kind of childhood she had. "I've always liked to do needlework, right from the time I was three," she said. "And all the nights we spent in air-raid shelters, to occupy the girls from 6 o'clock until bedtime, they taught us to do all sorts of things with our hands, and a lot of needlework techniques, such as lace-making and all that sort of thing. It was therapy in a way, so we wouldn't be so scared about the bombs dropping all around. Two of the teachers saw that I had a flair for it, and made it possible for me to get supplies. We used to do embroidery on all kinds of fabrics, anything that was available—sort of like the early Americans, in a way. When I came back to the States in 1957, I wanted to keep on doing it, but I couldn't find the supplies. Ultimately, I met a German lady who ran a wholesale outlet in New York City, and as we were there a lot in those days, because my father was there, I went to see her, and she set me up with all the supplies from European suppliers and American suppliers—linens, fabrics, threads, needles, and so on. So word got around that I had all this—under the bed and in the trunk of the car and in boxes and everywhere, so I sort of became the supply person for people who wanted to do good things in fine needlework. Meanwhile, I was working for Maude Dinsmore in her dress shop, and then I switched to running the Emporium for the Maurys' for quite a while...and then I went to work for the Garrison Travel Bureau for six years. But I was doing all the needlework in between, and was also the secretary of the First Congregational Church for three years, and in the theatre and all that...but needlework was getting more and more part of me because I had all these supplies...and then..." She laughed, and John said, "Well, the thing was, she kept moving boxes under the bed, and we'd already bought the Quaker Road property in 1964 for my shop, and I got so fed up with tripping over these boxes that we built her a shop on Quaker Road, and that's how the Craft Center started in 1966." Elizabeth said, "I felt if I was going to do this for the rest of my life, I needed to have an American 'signature' from somewhere; and that all started in Nantucket, actually, because, in 1961, I became involved in helping do the embroideries for the Jared Coffin House restoration. And then I was asked to teach needlework at the Bay Colony Society of Embroiderers in Boston, where I met Mildred Davis, who became my mentor. She got commissioned by Phoebe Swain to do a memorial bed—hanging set for the Hadwen House, in memory of her mother. Phoebe and I wound up doing most of the needlework for that. I commuted back and forth to the Bay Colony Society of Embroiderers...by this time, because of my wartime experiences, I had learned to do so many more techniques than almost anybody else I had met, because this country had been hung up on needlepoint, so they hadn't had the variety. Mildred sort of tucked me under her wing and had me as an instructor at the Valentine Museum in Richmond, VA. And at that time she created and offered a certification that was called Advanced Professional Studies in the Textile Arts, which basically was doing everything within the field...it covered design, color, and all manner of stitching, finishing, historical research, taking designs off historical pieces, museum restoration, museum preservation, and all that sort of thing all wrapped up into one. So I am certified as a professional artist in the textile arts. I do a lot of consulting, mostly in this country." John added proudly: "She put on a needlework show in 1979, in the Foulger Museum."

I wondered what John was doing for a living on the island during these years. "When I came here," he said, "I worked for Herman Minstrell...he was a very good carpenter. In those days you only worked in the winter on Nantucket; in the summertime people just didn't want to see their carpenters. But I always found work. I stayed in carpentry and restored, repaired, and maintained old houses; I worked on all the NHA's historical houses. But I had to stop doing carpentry in 1989—I'd had a bad fall from the third floor onto a brick sidewalk on Main Street 35 years ago, and the arthritis caught up with me and finally I couldn't go on a ladder, couldn't walk, was having a terrible time. But I couldn't keep still. I'd always helped Elizabeth with the needlework and blocking and I'd done a little bit of picture framing for us, so I went off and took some training, and that's how I became a picture framer."

The Gilberts have moved into a new house, where John has a big basement shop, and Elizabeth is very much still in business. She has taught all over the country, and received a commission in 1997 to do a Christmas tree ornament for the Blue Room, in the White House. "I did Santa coming off the island with his bag of toys," said Elizabeth, "and John filled the bag with little tiny toys. We went to the White House to present it, and received a letter afterwards from Hillary Clinton thanking me for the piece...that was kind of fun."

John's taken a crack at needlework, too. "I've always been able to draw and design," he said. "A friend had an Indian medicine bag made of beads and he wanted to do a chair seat with that pattern. So I counted the beads, made the geometric patterns, and finished that with needlepoint."

NANTUCKET IN THE '50s & '60s

270

It may surprise readers to know that Elizabeth, who people know as a needle arts expert and as a very fine actress, graduated from the London School of Pharmacy, becoming a registered pharmacist in eighteen months instead of the usual three years. "And did theatre at the same time," she laughed. Why hadn't she pursued a career as a pharmacist in the States? "Well," Elizabeth said, "my pharmacy degree didn't reciprocate in this country in those days. I'd already been a head pharmacist in the center of London for five years, so I was not about to go back to college. When we came to the island I went to Congdon's Pharmacy to ask for a job, and they said, 'You can be an assistant pharmacist as long as you run the soda fountain several days a week,' and I said, 'I don't think so!'" But this particular cloud had a silver lining...had Elizabeth become an island pharmacist, the needle arts might never have become her primary career.

"My theatre life actually started with my godfather," Elizabeth said. "The Hallams really became my family, and my godfather would take me to London on the weekends and we went to the Albert Hall, and museums, and galleries, and dance performances..." John: "Her godfather ran the wagon-lit, a railroad that ran all over Europe across Europe before the war; that was his business." Elizabeth: "It was he who introduced me to the D'Oyly Carte Opera Company, and we became very good friends with all the people in that company. So he was totally responsible for my love of the arts of any kind. I absolutely fell in love with the theatre. My first remembrance of ever walking into a theatre backstage was at the D'Oyly Carte in London, and here was this giant of a man dressed as the *Mikado*." John interjected, "And when we did The *Mikado* on Nantucket, they styled my costume from the picture of his."

Elizabeth wasn't just going to the theatre: she was in it. "All during the war I was one of what they called the ENSA [European National Servicemen's Association] kids who entertained the troops in England…a song and dance thing…and from there I went to London and did song and dance and got into the American theatre scene in London with *South Pacific,* and *Oklahoma,* and all those. I wasn't even a teenager when I began with ENSA…my first performance was when I was nine years old, tapdancing to 'Paper Doll'…so theatre has been a large part of my life."

The theatre bug bit John early, too, although the "bite" didn't really show until the couple moved to Nantucket. "When I was 13," he said, "I played Aladdin, and upset all the girls, because I was a soprano at the time…now I'm a bass-baritone. After that, I did very little theatre. Mainly church choir…" Elizabeth: "I was doing theatre partly to put myself through college. Another thing I did to help with college expenses was dance [she said "dawnce"]: I used to leave work on Saturday afternoon at half-past two and race over to the Lyceum Ballroom in Tottencourt Road and demonstrate ballroom dancing." John said, "I went off in the service to the Middle East, and when I came back, Elizabeth taught me to dance, and then we used to put on displays at church halls and things like that. She taught me to do ballroom dancing by squeezing my hand for the quick steps! We had a friend who had a combo, and the group didn't have transportation, so we'd go along as transportation, carrying some of the instruments and crew…and we'd get into all these dances for free because we were doing the demonstrations." Elizabeth added, "We went all over southern England doing that."

When John and Elizabeth bought their first house, on Vestal Street, their agent was Al Pitkin. John told the slightly roundabout story: "Al was a good friend, and we all sang in the Episcopal choir. Mac Dixon, who wanted to do Gilbert and Sullivan's *The Mikado,* asked Al if he knew anyone who sang, and Al gave him gave my name. Now, our Vestal Street house was old…built in 1805…and it had calcimine ceilings, which is a quarter-inch-thick whitewash, and to remove that, I would stand on a step-stool, put on Elizabeth's shower cap and my bathing costume, and reach up to the ceiling with a long, thin-bladed knife, slide it under the calcimine, and drop it down. Oh, what a lot of dust! And in the middle of all this, there was a knock on the door. I was expecting Al to come by, so I said [in a soprano key] 'Come in, Al,' and nothing happened. Then another knock, and I said, 'Come in, Al.' And yet again. The door opened, and a perfect stranger came in. There I was, white from head to foot, shower cap, swimming costume and all…and he said, very shyly, 'M-M-Mr. Gilbert? Mr. Pitkin said you might consider singing in *The Mikado.*' That's how I met Mac Dixon." So John was the Mikado, and to prove it he sang a few lines, but added, "I only sing in the bawthtub now." Elizabeth said that she was one of the three little maids…and Ruth Ann Flanagan was Yum Yum. And Elizabeth made a lot of the costumes, too, painting on silk fabric, taking the designs from various vases.

Soon both Gilberts became totally embroiled in Nantucket theatre. John said, "We did *The Mikado, Teahouse of the August Moon, I Remember Mama, Witness to the Prosecution…*" Elizabeth, who usually had the leads, laughed and said, "I believe I still hold the record of having been in the most plays for the Theatre Workshop…thirty-seven, I think, including *The Diary of Ann Frank, My Fair Lady, Wait Until Dark* in 1971 [which she reprised in 1988], and *Rain.*" And she claims to be able to remember a lot of her lines. She's still involved with the theatre on a consulting basis, having been on the board for nineteen years and president for seven.

Do the Gilberts ever get back to England? "We haven't been back for a long time," said Elizabeth. "We used to go back and forth, sometimes every year, because our parents became ill." John added, "Every one of our parents lived to be 84 years old, which is interesting…" Elizabeth: "Once our parents had gone, we just became so focused over here on Nantucket that there was really not the incentive to go back. And apart from that, private school and college for Allan…and then the health problems John had after falling off the house changed our lives radically. This has been the first and only home we had together. Our son Allan is a native…he's the main technician for Sears Roebuck in the southeastern region, and he does Nantucket, because he knows it inside out. He was brought up here, went to school through middle school, and then went to Tabor Academy for four years. And," she laughed, "that's what accelerated the Craft Center, because all of a sudden he said, 'I want to go away to school…'"

The conversation came around to what the island was like in the '50s and '60s. John chuckled and said, "When we first moved to Nantucket, there were 2,900 people here year-round. It's changed a lot. We're considered old-timers now. Sort of nice." "Life in those days was much simpler," Elizabeth sighed. John added, "I have three little stories of what it was like in the 1950s. (1) When we arrived, Sandy Craig and his wife Joan threw a party for us and invited all the people our age around the island…what a wonderful thing to do for new people! (2) Billy Haddon needed a new roof on his house, so he threw a shingling party on Hussey Street and invited all the people his age and our age and we all came; Charlie Davis showed up in a white suit, because he thought it was a party. And at the end of the day his white suit was black…but he worked right along. (3) There was a young man whose house burned down on Brush Road, and when he got his insurance money, a whole group of these young island carpenters went over and helped him frame it and get it up. That's how it was on Nantucket in those days. Everybody was a friend. We walked down on Main Street and people would say, 'Hi, Elizabeth and John.' We didn't know who they were, but we were the only strangers here that year, so we had to be Elizabeth and John!"

272

Elizabeth said, "Another story about how people helped people in those days: When John was building the store for me, the Congregational minister, Fred Bennett, came by and he was putting shingles on as fast as anybody!" John: "One Sunday I was trying to put up rafters and the wind was blowing, and two guys driving by in their truck saw me struggling—they came up and helped me get the first two or three rafters up and off they went. Another day we were building the cottage in the back yard, and Bill Grieder stopped by…he was on crutches…and I was having an awful struggle with the last piece of oak flooring, to get it up against the shoe of the wall of the house. He got down on the floor and put one crutch against the wall and pushed the other against the piece of oak, and pushed it in for me. I mean, that's the sort of thing that used to happen in the old days." Elizabeth said, "There was a lot more fun at home…lots of potluck suppers, and we'd play card games every Friday night, or cribbage… Also, there was a lot more satisfaction about putting a house together then…there wasn't the great expectation that it ought to be done all at once and have a beautiful garden and instant gratification—people were really supportive and you just would do a little bit at a time." John: "When we'd go off-island we'd leave the house unlocked…and when you came back someone had been in, to leave you a pie for dinner or something like that. It was so different. You could go anywhere—you always felt very comfortable." Elizabeth concluded: "All these things add up to what's kept us here, because we'd never really known that sense of community anywhere else…It's nice to go away, get into the big city once in a while, just to say, "Ah! I cawn't wait to get home!"

Even Work Is Fun

What do the very busy Gilberts do to relax? John said, "For fun, I garden, work on archaeology if I get a chance—I've been very involved in Nantucket archaeology for years. We have a Shawkemo chapter here of which I was chairman for a number of years. Hmmm…what else? Oh, I replaced the shaft of the windmill in 1977, and was involved in its restoration…" And Elizabeth? "Oh, I garden. And right now I'm trying to add to my Nantucket design collection; I don't market those pieces until I have stitched them myself, so I know they work. Also, I do a lot of wholesaling now. My work is carried at three stores here on the island and a couple off island…they keep me fairly busy." John added, "She planned and executed a 5 by 7 needlepoint rug for a client, and did a lot of the stitching while we were driving to Florida—I was at the wheel, of course," he said, laughing. "We spend the winter in Nakomis, just south of Sarasota, on the west coast," said Elizabeth, "and we're fortunate to have the same sense of community we find on Nantucket."

These two people, who have retained a great sense of humor and much gratitude for their discovery of Nantucket Island, seem to be living proof that a positive attitude and a willingness to work hard yields a happy, productive life. Carry on!

John Gilbert and Elizabeth Miles Atkinson looking blissful at their wedding on September 1, 1955.

274

Loves Nantucket,
That's All There Is to It
Don Visco, 2003

*H*e's deeply tanned, trim, has worn his signature railroad cap since he was in his teens, and says he's "supposed to be retired." But no, that tan is not from the golf links. He still keeps his hand in the businesses he started many years ago, now run by his sons. He has a nice, often-used chuckle, a great wide grin, and a Yankee accent (he says his father was a "bahbuh"), which made me, a dyed-in-the-wool, small-town New Englander, feel right at home. (Of cawss we all know that it's really everyone else who has the accent.)

Don Visco began by saying, "I am a native, born here, 1934. In 1914 my mother's whole family moved here from a farm in New Brunswick, Canada. They were poor, there was nothing in Canada for them. They came to Nantucket because my mother's uncle, Aquilla Cormie, the last blacksmith on Nantucket, was here. His shop was on Straight Wharf, where the Four Winds Gift Shop is now. Uncle Quilly had come to Nantucket years before—I'm not sure why. He was a young man then, plying his trade, and that was the days before fancy welding machines, and everything was done by smithies, including shoeing hosses. There were a lot of hosses around then. When I was a kid, people who lived out of town were still using hosses and wagons. If they had a job, they'd tie their hoss and little wagon in the little alley behind the stores on Main Street, put a feedbag on 'em, and stay there all day. I remember two: Old Man Gibby Burchell—I say 'Old Man' meaning Gibby's and Eddie's father—and Weston Esau, who lived out on Somerset Road, on the dirt part, and he used to come down every day with his horse and a little buckboard; he worked for the town.

"My mother went to school here, on Orange Street, down near the corner of Lyons Street. When her family first came they lived on the Snow Farm, on Hummock Pond Road; now there's a subdivision there, right on the big curve where you swing right. They went to school in a hoss and wagon. Eyup. I never knew my grandparents, any of them, on either my mother's or father's side. My mother met my father here in the summer of 1922, and that was it. He was a barber [pronounced "bahbuh"], and he came to do barberin' in the summer. He'd been a ship's barber in World War I. My mother's maiden name was Ross; her brothers and her father were all stonemasons.

"My schooling? I went to the first four grades at Cyrus Peirce, and then we moved…we used to live on Mill Street near Prospect Street. I grew up next to Charlie Pearl's family—Charlie was the oldest, then Carl, who had bright red hair (we called him Fuzzy) and Alfie was the youngest—he was my pal. Yup. On the corner was Mary 'Fuddy' Van Arsdale and her father Hughie Lombard, a real character—he still used his outhouse when we lived there, on Mill Street. Then we moved to Gay Street, which is right near Academy Hill. So then I went to Academy Hill School. Right next door. I finished high school right there, class of 1952. As kids, we had a lot of fun, and we raised the devil a lot…you know, on Halloween. You hear about kids today doing these awful, destructive things—we didn't do things like that. We were always busy. In the summertime, up until I had to go to work, I spent a lot of time at Children's Beach; we used to go over and dive for coins at Steamboat Whoff. We'd make two or three dollars in change, holding it in our mouths, and that was big money for us then." Wasn't that dangerous? I asked. "Yeah, and the cops were always chasin' us out, and then somebody would go up and tell my father at the barbershop, then my mother would find out that I was down there, and then I'd get the devil." Don laughed heartily at the memory.

The Barber Shop—Where Everyone Hung Out

"The barbershop was on Main Street. First my father worked for Ed Terry, who had a big barbershop down from the Hub, before you get to where Murray's Liquor Store is now. Big barbershop with a big back room and they had a bootblack there in the back, and there were tables. In those days, when there wasn't a lot doin', and if men didn't have a job or somethin', they hung around the barbershop playing cards and stuff. The barbershop was the center of activity in town. You'd go there if you wanted to know what was goin' on or which fishin' boats came in, which didn't, and so forth. All the news came out of the barbershop. That's where everybody hung out. I remember going in there—big high ceilings, no air conditioning, big ceiling fans and flypaper hanging down from the ceiling…and spittoons on the floor. You know, a lot of men chewed tobacco then. I'd go in now and then and bum a nickel off my father for an ice cream cone…it was a nickel for a single scoop, a dime for a double-decker then. I'd go up to what's now the Hub, it was Roger's then, or up to one of the drugstores farther up the street. A cup of coffee was a dime then…and I think a haircut was only 35 cents; shave was 25 cents. If they were busy in the summertime, the shop would put a sign up: 'No Shaves,' because shavin' took too much time and wasn't a moneymaker. You could hear all the town gossip there. That's where all the information flowed, in and out…the barbershop."

Did Don have to work as a youngster? "Oh yeah, we did little things like mowing lawns and cleaning people's yahds and things like that at first. I had an old bicycle—I was lucky, because some kids didn't have bicycles, and they had to walk everywhere. My tires were all worn out…you had to know how to change the chains, had to fix flats yourself. My first job as a teenager? Hmmm… Oh, I did have a job after school and on Sat'dys at Cady's food store on Main Street, which was also on that block between the Hub and Murray's Liquor Store. There were small stores everywhere—up on the corner where Congdon & Coleman is now was J.B. Ashley's Mahkit, and there was Cady's, and Doc Ryder's on Orange Street. You didn't even have to go in there and shop…you could call your order in and they'd deliver right to your house. Mr. Ashley was president of the Pacific Bank then. I can see him now. Out in front of the two big windows he had produce stands with big awnings; upstairs was a bakery, where they baked all their own stuff every day. I remember the poor guy, Ervin Chase—he's been gone for a long time now—who did all the trucking for JB. Had to lug all that stuff up those stairs on his back-sacks of potatoes and flour and all that stuff. Ice? Island Service Co. had a big ice plant on the Island Service Whoff, and people would put a cahd in their window that would tell the driver what size chunk of ice they wanted. Not many people had a fridge then, it was iceboxes. The guy who delivered had a big insulated blanket over those 300-pound cubes of ice; he had a

Here's what Don Visco looked like at 3…and without his signature railroad cap!

rubber apron on his back and a pair of tongs, and he'd sling that hunk of ice over one shoulder and then go deliver it and put it in the icebox. And we'd hang around the back of the truck waitin' till he was in the house, so we could get the chips," he laughed. "They used tongs for everything in the old days. With block and tackle and gin poles, to lift everything…these were the days before modern cranes and front-end loaders and forklifts. Everything was done by manpower.

PACKIN' OUT THE FISH

"The whoffs were very busy then…when I was in school there must have been a dozen families who either owned or captained a boat, and all based on Nantucket. They used to pack out fish here at the big ice plant, then load them on the trucks and drive them around to Steamboat Wharf and send it to market on the steamer. There was also a fella named Ed Tarvis who packed out fish on Steamboat Wharf. And I suppose before my time there were more." Did the children of the fishing-boat owners often go into that business? Don answered, "Most of them didn't, no. I know of a couple—Tobe Fleming's son Toby, who was in my class, stayed in the fishin' business. He's retired now. And also one of Jack MacDonald's sons, Robert—I think he's still fishin' to this day with his own boat."

How come Don didn't follow in his father's footsteps, become a barber? He laughed. "Everybody asks me that. I just wasn't interested. I started working in construction when I was 14 or 15 years old; worked for Walter Marlon 'Red' Rounsville, who owned and ran the Nantucket Construction Co. off the 'Sconset Road for years; for several years he also ran the big cranberry bog that belongs to the Conservation Foundation now. I worked for him during the summers, and then as soon as I was 16 and got a driver's license, I could drive a truck. In those days you didn't need a special license to drive a truck. I worked there off and on for years, and then for a couple of years one of my friends, Dick Gardner, and I also worked for Ellen Ring at Cook's Cycle Shop, which is still there on South Beach

Street." After graduating from NHS, Don said, he didn't want to go on to school—"I wanted to keep on working."

OH, THAT 1939 CHEVVIE COUPE

Despite the fact that he was working summers and after school, Don Visco managed to have a pretty satisfactory social life. Grinning, he said, "We had a lot of fun. It was so different when I was in high school; only a couple of us had automobiles. Even most of the teachers didn't have them. There was no money around then. And the season didn't start till the 4th of July, and then the day after Labor Day, boom! Everything shut down…not like it is today. But

Don Visco on his bicycle in front of his house at 11 Gay Street at the age of 15. Taken February 12, 1953.

I had a cah when I was 16, a 1939 Chevrolet Coupe—it had belonged to Walter Royal, who was cashier at Pacific Bank. He traded it in for a Jeep or something and I got his cah…I had to borrow some from my father to buy that. Ricky Lewis had a Ford station wagon, and Snook Blount had a 1934 Pontiac sedan. There were only two or three of us had a car while we were in school. And that helped my social life, definitely!" he grinned. "But I spent a lot of time as a kid on the whoff—and it was a real working waterfront. After school and after supper, I spent a lot of time openin' scallops. I got to be quite proficient at it. There were only a few old-timers who could open faster than me. They really weren't faster, they were steady. They didn't go home for supper, they didn't pause…so they ended up at the end of the evening with a few more pounds than I did. I made good money, though, and I always had a few coins in my pockets. Spent a lot of hours shuckin' scallops, yup."

Although Don was fairly young during World War II, he does remember how the island was then. "It was busy; it was a military island, practically. The Coast Gahd was everywhere, with a station at Coskata, on Muskeget, at Madaket, Surfside…they had beach patrols with dogs, everything, 24 hours a day. And the Navy was at the airport—they constructed the first two runways there, and trained the fighter pilots with bombs and rockets. That's why you go out to Tom Nevers and dig, and come up with all kinds of stuff. Yup. I don't think there's any live ammunition there now, though I think they found some ordnance not too long ago that got exposed on the beach. Of course it's washed away so much since the '40s; during the Blizzard of 1978, when New England got crippled by all that snow, we got rain, mostly…that night I saw 35 feet go at Tom Nevers. It must have been awful in the mainland cities during the war, where people had to stand in breadlines and everything, but there was none of that here—there was rationing, but everybody had a victory gahden. Everybody, I mean everybody, had a gahden…and everybody had animals. Downtown. On Orange Street, and Union Street, everywhere. People had chickens, ducks, geese, goats, and pigs, believe it or not. And it's not that long ago. There was a lot of bahter then. And there were fahms everywhere, don't forget. Nantucket was full of them, and animals everywhere…and there wasn't all this scrub pine and all this prolific brush that you see everywhere on the sides of the roads now. It's really awful, even dangerous.

FAHMS, BAHTERIN', & MORE ON THE BAHBUH SHOP

"Right up the head of Main Street, just past Caton Circle on the Madaket Road, was Charlie Thurston's fahm. And then around the corner on New Lane was Maxie Chase—they ended up swapping properties for some reason, and Maxie ended up on Madaket Road. Charlie gave up the dairy fahm and Maxie, in that big bahn, went into the chicken business. Now, Andy Lowell has chicken and fowl on New Lane…he always had them." I remembered buying eggs on the honor system from Andy's garage. Don said, "Yup—honor system—same way people would grow flowers, gladiolas and things, and put 'em in a little cart down on Main Street, and you'd put your change in, honor system, and take you a bunch of flowers…I don't know if anybody does that any more." I wondered about all the bartering. Don said, "Oh, bahtering was big, because the farmers were growing vegetables, and there was an active fishing industry here—nobody went hungry around here. Nobody. I remember my father trading for fresh fish in the barber shop.

"I want to tell you, it was rough and tumble around here with the fishermen. They'd be out at sea for ten or twelve, sometimes fourteen days—because lots of times they'd go right on to New Bedford, pack out their fish, sell them at the auction there, and then come home. And before they got to my father's barbershop to clean up, there was a place called the Spa, on the other side of Main Street—a spa and café. The café was only open in the summertime. It was kind of a rough place," he laughed. "The fishermen would stop there to have a few drinks, and then stop in the barbershop and get cleaned up and go home. (Sometimes, if they'd stayed too long at the bah, my father wouldn't let them in.) But they'd stop in and get a shave, get all dashed up. He'd crank the chair down and the fella would be back there [leaning his head way back with eyes closed] and my father would put those steamin' hot towels on him…and you know, they'd have an awful stubble after twelve or fourteen days. I can see him now, stropping those straight razors, and then shaving them all up, and then he'd splash on these tonics and aftershaves…I used to love the smell of the bay rum and that stuff. I can still smell them!"

What does Don remember about island restaurants? He said, "What's now the Atlantic Café, near the Dreamland Theatre, which was there when I was a kid, was Cy's Green Coffee Pot. That was a great place. Old Man Cy and Rose lived right next to us on Gay Street—we lived at 11, they were at number 9—and he was a great old guy." Don chuckled again: "He had an old Chevrolet truck, and when he'd leave early in the morning, I'd hear that truck start up…he'd put his foot all the way to the floor on the gas pedal, and instead of having it in first, he'd have it in high gear, and he'd go up Gay Street and around the corner, and the motor would be screamin'! I don't know how many clutches old Cy burned out on Gay Street, trying to get to work. I'll never forget that. Cy's was a popular place, and Allen's Diner, and then in the summertime next to the Spah Bah was the Spah Café, which I mentioned earlier. On Main Street were all the drugstores and the A&P branch, and then there was another little A&P branch up by the monument, and another one on Orange Street. There were stores everywhere—Doc Ryder's, and Souza's Market down at 56 Union. Where Tonkin's is now was R.G. Coffin's Drugstore; he had a soda fountain. And Toner's Drug Store was up around the corner, down Petticoat Row. Yup, they did sell a little bottle of liquor now and then. As a kid around the wharf all the time, I got an education! Oh man, the stories they told about what went on during Prohibition. As a kid around the wharf all the time, I got an education! Oh man, the stories they told about what went on. They used to fly booze in at Tom Nevers, which is full of scrub oaks now, but used to be meadow…they'd land the biplanes out there. Some of the fishermen made more money bringin' in the booze than they did catchin' fish. It was 1933 when they repealed Prohibition…but I want to tell you, there were a lot of legitimate businessmen on Nantucket who got started running booze. Oh yeah…some very prominent names." A wicked laugh.

MEETING PHYLLIS

Don met his wife, Phyllis, in the summer of 1956: "That was the year the *Andrea Doria* sank, remember that? She came here for the summer to make some money, worked at Allen's Diner, which is now the Club Car. That was a real workingman's diner. How did I meet Phyllis? Hmmm…I met her one night down to the Boathouse Restaurant. They used to have jam sessions on Sund'y afternoons in the '50s. That was before Beinecke did all the whoffs over. It was down the end of one of the whoffs…can't think of the name of it now. The Boathouse belonged to the Hutchinson family, from 'Sconset, who had the JC House too, in the '50s. It was a nice restaurant with a nice bah, and that's where I met Phyllis. [Big smile.] We went out all summer. She used to live in a

280

boardinghouse—there were a lot of boardinghouses here, where working people could come and rent a room for the summer. She paid $8 a week, at Mrs. Smalley's house on Broad Street, which is now the Land Bank Office. Yup. There were a lot of young people who'd come here to work, a lot of Irish kids, college kids…So we went kinda steady all summer, and got married the next winter at the end of January. And then I got drafted, so I went to Fort Benning in Georgia for basic training, and then to Texas, El Paso, for training in NIKE missiles. Phyllis came out and we lived in Texas for a little while, and then we went to Germany. I was in the first operational NIKE missile battalion in Europe, and we were the defense for the Frankfort, Heidelburg, and Mannheim area. 'Course that was in the days before satellites were up. It was 1957, not that long after the war-there were still whole blocks bombed out that they'd never cleaned up, just the rubble was there. We had a good time in Germany. Learned to speak just enough German to get along…we met some nice people over there, and we lived with a German family. In 1958 we bought an old cah, did a little travelin', and we went to the Brussels World Fair.

"Toward the end of my enlistment, my dad got sick and passed away suddenly, so I flew home. I only had a short time left, so I was mustered out at Fort Dix in New Jersey. I've always wanted to go back to Europe, to Italy, where I have all kinds of relatives. My father's parents were immigrants from Italy, and they came from a big family." He smiled: "Yup. That's why my name is Visco, Italian."

I wanted to know about all the "careers" Don Visco has had on the island. He said he'd run a couple of times for Selectman, "but never did get elected. I was appointed to the Right-of-Way Committee in around 1970. That had been formed back around 1950 by Town Meeting; it was supposed to be a watchdog committee to protect the public's right of access to ponds and shores. It never had any statutory authority—it was an advisory committee— we reported to the Selectmen and the County Commissioner. I've always been interested in the best things for the island and the people, and in

Donald T. and Phyllis J. Visco on their wedding day, January 26th, 1957.

1972 I was elected to the Planning Board, and was on that for ten years, and then off for eight years, and then was appointed again to fill an unexpired term, and I'm still on it.

"I started my own business, Island Excavating Co., in 1956; I said if I was gonna work this hahd, I might as well work for myself. Each of my two boys is in business for himself, and they operate here. David is our oldest; Carolyn is next; then Stephen, and then Jennifer. I have ten grandchildren." Hobbies? Clubs? "I belong to the Madaket Admiralty Club—been a member there for 35 or 40 years. It's basically a social club. And I belong to the No. 4's—that's the club over the Hub, the John B. Chase Engine Company No. 4. I like to go fishing, have a small boat in Madaket…and I have a family lobster license, so I have some pots out. Family scallopin', never miss that, oh yeah. Love that. For the last few winters, Phyllis and I have gone to Florida for a couple of months.

A TRACTOR FOR HIM; A '55 T-BIRD FOR HER?

"I've been a little bit busier than I wanted to be this year—I still have a truck that I send to the mainland for materials and stuff for the boys or different people…it keeps me active. But my real hobby is collecting antique fahm tractors. I have four of them, including a Model A in the bahn over there—just sold it yesterday. Had it for five years. Phyllis wants either a '55 or '56 T-Bird…" We talked about old cahs, and I mentioned the 1931 Model A I had in high school. Don said, "In the days before these fancy SUVs and Jeeps, that's what we went fishin' with…Model A's. We'd take the wheels off and get 15-inch tires, like on Chryslers or Lincolns or Mercurys, and those wheels would fit right over the lugs of a Model A…and that's what we used to go fishing. Yup."

I asked Don what is it that's kept him a Nantucketer. He answered, "I love Nantucket, that's all there is to it. I love it. We were lucky enough to get this land, and a little cottage on it that we rent." Had they moved that from somewhere else, as Nantucketers are wont to do? I asked. "No," he said, "but they did move houses around a lot in the old days. Horses would pull a house along the shore sometimes, and they'd slide it back on the shore on greased planks. I saw Donald MacDonald do that several times on the south shore, twenty or thirty years ago…jack the house up, set it down on greased planks, and just *psssshew*—snake it back. He was pulling them back from the eroding shore."

What, I asked, do you hope people will say about you in fifty years? Don laughed, hmmm-ed, then said, "Well! I hope they think good of me; I hope they think I was able to do somethin' for Nantucket. I got a good feeling serving on the Right-of-Way Committee; a lot of access roads to the shore were being gobbled up by property owners, and we prevented that several times…I always felt good when we could preserve access. What are my major concerns about the island? Well, Phyllis and I are fortunate enough to have worked hard and made good investments, and are able to help our kids, and I hope my grandchildren who want to live on Nantucket can afford to stay here too. But I've seen so many Nantucket families move off who inherited property from their parents or grandparents, and they couldn't afford to keep it."

Everyone knows Don and Phyllis—she was the Register of Probate for Nantucket. "She's been retired for maybe five years, and enjoys it—she doesn't so much miss the work as the interactions with people," said Don. And that railroad cap—it's a bit of a trademark for Don. He laughed: "When I was a kid, after school I started working for Al Sylva at his garage on North Beach Street, and I used to buy these caps at the Knobby Shop. They cost 50 cents. I don't think he even has 'em down there any more. We go to the State Fair in Tampa every year, and they have a big steam exhibit, so I always stop by and buy two or three, to last me through the year…they're great, because you can wash them."

TEASING THE TOWN CHARACTERS

It was difficult to find an ending for the interview; Don said, "I could go on and on with Nantucket stories. Characters, for instance. It seems like there were a lot of real characters around in those days. There was a fella who used to have a little cart with two ash barrels, and he'd sweep the street— Charlie Chase. We kids would tease him, singing: 'A rich man has a good cah and a poor man has a Ford; Charlie Chase beats 'em all with two wheels under a board.' And then there was Peter Rose, used to go around with a hoss and wagon sellin' vegetables. He painted a sign on the side of the wagon saying 'Bless the Lord Vegetables.' Well, come to find out, Peter used to go around at night stealin' the vegetables out of people's gahdens… And there was a lady named Rose, and we'd sing 'Beauty Rose, stinkin' toes, 'round the corner there she goes,' and she'd holler at us and shake her fist, and we'd run. Another fella we used to raise the devil with was the man who used to come to sharpen knives—his son still comes here summers. He walked everywhere, had his little grinding wheel on his back, and a bell, *ding ding ding,* and the housewives would come out and get their knives sharpened. We used to tease him, call him the hurdy-gurdy man. He'd holler at us, and we were a bit scared of him, because he had knives! All kid stuff—we didn't mean any hahm to any of those people.

"You know," Don concluded, "you forget about things, and when you staht talkin', they come back…"

Donald Visco in 1951.

Move Off the Island?
Never!
Joan Craig, 2003

*L*ife before Nantucket? Or off Nantucket? It hardly counts, for Joan Craig. Those who insist the term "Nantucketer" implies one was born on the island may be wrong, because Joan's a Nantucketer through and through.

When I interviewed her at her Hulbert Avenue summer home, I had to ask first about the figurehead of Richard Mitchell over the gate. "Oh," said Joan, "he had been in the yard of the old Sanford House, where the Town Building is now, and when they tore that down my husband's grandfather purchased him. At that time Sandy's grandparents owned West Brick, and they put him on a summerhouse in the back. After West Brick was sold, he was moved to his family's house farther down on Hulbert Avenue, and when that was sold we moved him here." However, she went on, the sightseeing buses would pause and the tourists would be told the figurehead was Benjamin Franklin, "and he wasn't Benjamin Franklin!" Joan said. So the Craigs asked Edouard Stackpole to research Richard Mitchell and consequently there is now a board beneath the handsome figurehead to tell people the facts.

NANTUCKET CONNECTIONS ON ALL SIDES

Joan began to spend her long summers on the island at a very early age, and came here to live fulltime with her husband, Sandy, in 1948. "I was born in Brooklyn, and lived in Brooklyn and New York City until I moved to Nantucket year-round, after the war," she said. "I was married to Sandy a year after finishing a business course at Katharine Gibbs School in New York. Both of our families came to Nantucket. My family [the Pennocks] came here when I was three, in 1923; my mother and Walter Beinecke's mother were best friends, and we moved to the island at the same time. We lived in 'Sconset at Ocean Park—now the Wade Cottages—which was leased and run by a Colonel Powers and his wife, from Foxboro, MA. There were six cottages along the bluff, called Bluff Edge #1, 2, 3, 4, 5, and 6. We rented one of those each year for the next six years. For the first two years, there was no electricity in 'Sconset. Ocean Park had a common dining room where you ate, and you had kerosene lamps and so forth. We lived there till 1929 and my mother bought her house on Sankaty Road. So I grew up in 'Sconset in the summers until I was married.

"My husband's great-grandparents came here in the 1890s," Joan continued, "and the first place they rented was Mariposa Cottage, down by Brant Point; they always stayed for the whole summer. Sandy's grandparents on both sides came to Nantucket. On the Minshall side, they were from Terre Haute, Indiana, and the grandparents built a house here on Hulbert Avenue—not this one, down a ways—in 1906. Then, in 1925, they bought West Brick and lived in it summers until my husband's grandmother died…and his mother sold West Brick to Jean Gundry in 1946. Sandy's grandparents on his mother's side lived next door to the grandparents on his father's side, and that's how his mother and father met and were married."

Was Sandy a native? I asked. "Nope—nobody in the family's a native [not quite true—Joan has a two-year-old great-granddaughter, Alexandra Grace, born and living on Nantucket]. As close as you can be to a native…I want to tell you an interesting story about how the Craig family got here. My husband's grandfather was an Army Colonel; he'd led the Signal Corps, and the Weather Bureau was part of that. The Colonel and his wife were living in Washington and wanted to find a place for the summer, so he called up a man who'd served in the Weather Bureau under him, Mr. Grimes (I think his son or grandson lives on Pleasant Street now), and said that Mrs. Craig was terrified of thunderstorms, so would Mr. Grimes tell him what place on this New England coast had the fewest thunderstorms. Mr. Grimes said, 'Well, believe it or not, Nantucket.' So that's what originally brought the Craig side of the family to the island. They came for the whole summer. My husband's grandparents on his mother's side came from Terre Haute, Indiana, as I said, and quite a few people came from there—how they ever found Nantucket or got here, I have no idea.

And then the Craigs came from Washington DC because of the lack of the thunderstorms.

Growing Up in 'Sconset

"My father, who was seventeen years older than my mother, passed away five months before I was born, so I never knew him. My mother never remarried, and my aunt came to live with us, and remained with us all my life. So we were pretty much a female family…and I had the three girls. But now," she smiled, "I have seven grandchildren, and five of them are boys…and my little great-granddaughter lives here on the island. My daughters are here all summer and each one of them has a house; they just love being here, and all my grandchildren grew up here. They're older now, but they all come back as often as they can.

"Now—my childhood in 'Sconset. We'd come up from New York or Brooklyn on the overnight boat, which I thought was the greatest experience in the world—I thought I was going to Europe each time we got on. It was quite a chore bringing the family up here for the whole summer—my aunt, my sister, my mother, and a wonderful woman who worked for us. I had a bird in a cage and we had a cat in a box and a dog on a leash…the whole kit and kaboodle. We had two trunks, always, and had to order special taxis that had trunk racks; then we'd go over to the piers and get on the boat; it was an overnight trip. If we came very early, we went to Fall River, where we got on a bus and went to New Bedford, with everything—the dog, the cat, the bird, everything! If we came at the time the schedule changed, then we went on the New England Steamship line right to New Bedford, skipping Fall River. Then we got on another boat to Woods Hole, Oak Bluffs, Nantucket. Yes, it was quite a project, but everybody did it, that's how you got here. And on the boat you had dinner, and a stateroom, and it was just wonderful. We made an ocean voyage! I was always allowed to pick out the stateroom—Mother got a little plan of the boat, and I chose the stateroom I wanted. Then you went back the same way. And oh, I hated to go back. I was in private school, so my school got out early and started late, and on several occasions we stayed into the fall because of the polio epidemic. We didn't go to school here, just stayed into the fall. Mother managed two apartment houses in Brooklyn Heights that my father had built, and during all that polio business, when she really had to go back, I moved in with the Beineckes.

"Growing up in 'Sconset was just wonderful. There were thirty or forty of us, young boys and girls, and we did everything together. 'Sconset was nowhere near as social as it is now, and it was a village to itself at that time…and you didn't go to Nantucket very often. We'd go to the Skipper sometimes for lunch; that was a big treat…I remember I always had chicken à la king. And occasionally we went to the old Chopping Bowl on Union Street, for tea and cinnamon toast. It had those big wooden benches with the high backs and the wooden table with a hole in the middle for a colored umbrella. It was owned by Mrs. Ludwig, who later owned the White Elephant. And then another time I'd come to town was on my birthday, which was in the summer. I was allowed to plan what I wanted to do, and ask a few friends. I always wanted to come to Cliffside Beach, because it was so different from the 'Sconset beach—in 'Sconset there was a lifeguard and

Left to right—Young Joan Pennock enjoying a bike ride in Siasconset. An 18-year-old Joan Pennock on the beach at Sconset. Joan with a "mess of scup," 1967.

waves and seaweed and things like that, but over here they served food, which I thought was wonderful. You got a big key and a towel and went into a locker and changed your clothes…They had swings, and there was a raft that you could swim to, and for a couple of years there was a slide on the raft… Oh, I just thought that was about the grandest thing you could do…so much better than the beach in 'Sconset. So that was my birthday every year. But really, until I was 19 or 20 and started going out with my husband, I didn't pay an awful lot of attention to Nantucket.

"We did a lot of horseback riding when I was a child; there was a stable there run by Mr. Gouin, right across from the water tower. He used to import horses. He'd come to the island and married a Nantucket woman who was a native; one of his children was Marcel, who became a rear admiral and for whom Gouin Village was named. Quite an accomplishment for a Nantucket boy. Anyway, we used to do a tremendous amount of riding over in 'Sconset. We'd often ride early in the morning and then have breakfast at the Chanticleer. It wasn't as elegant as it is now, it was just a little local restaurant, but the garden was the same and we used to sit out there.

'SCONSET HAD EVERYTHING!

"Other restaurants in 'Sconset? Where the Summer House is now was the Moby Dick. And then there was the Wander Inn Restaurant, on Broadway in what's now Liberty Hall. They had family-style meals; people would come down and buy a week's worth of meals. 'Sconset had everything—you didn't need to go to town. There were gift shops; you paid your water bill over there; there was a branch of the Electric Co.; a telegraph office, a telephone office, a gas station, a barbershop, a hairdresser, a shoeshine man…Yes, only seven miles from town, but 'Sconset was a different world. My mother, though, would go to town to play mah-jongg, which was very popular at that time. She used to play in that house that's falling apart, two doors up from us on Main Street, Mr. and Mrs. Taylor's house. She also played mah-jongg over in Surfside at a house owned by an actress named Mary Mannering. But she never drove a car, so when my sister, who was six years older than I, learned to drive she'd have to take Mother to Nantucket. Then, when I was old enough to drive, I got stuck with this duty.

"We used to spend a lot of time out at the Wauwinet beach…we'd come over with picnics, all of us, and swim on the town side of Wauwinet. One of the other things I just loved…we didn't used to have babysitters in those days, and when my mother or aunt would go somewhere for the day, they would hire Eddie Coffin—his wife's name was Tillie—they were related to all those Coffins over there. Eddie had a horse and buggy, and Mother would pack us a picnic lunch and send us out for the day with him. He was the babysitter. He used to take us out through 'Sconset down Low Beach, where the Loran Station is now, and through Tom Nevers Pond and up to the other side. It was a shallow pond and we always drove right through, up to where the Tom Nevers Inn used to be."

It's clear that Joan feels as if she grew up in 'Sconset, rather than in New York. I asked if any of her 'Sconset chums were still around. "Oh yes," she said, "several of them, and we get together. I have them over particularly on the 4th of July, so they can see the fireworks. But you know, I'm old enough so that a great many have passed away or left the island. I'm 83. I don't feel 83, and I don't particularly want to be 83, but there I am. I feel good and I feel young."

THE PERSISTENT SUITOR

How had Joan Pennock and Sandy Craig met? I asked. "Well, we met in 'Sconset as teenagers. But Sandy lived in Nantucket, and he asked me out several times but I would have no part of it, because I didn't know anybody in Nantucket and I was part of a big crowd in 'Sconset that did everything together. So for that whole year when he called me I wouldn't go out with him. And then the next summer I met him again. We always came very early, and he did too, before a lot of the summer people came, and I met him one night when I was with Leo Killen. Leo was working at the airport, and asked me if I'd like to go for a ride in the plane the next day. I said, 'Sure!' So I went out to the airport and when I got there he said, 'Go get in that plane over there.' I got in, and there was Sandy. He shut the door, took off, and said he wouldn't come down until I said I'd go out with him! Now that's a true story. And so I did, and we were together all that summer and got married the following winter. That was in 1941. War was sort of lurking in the background then, and he got a job teaching flying and ground-school classes at Princeton University—he'd been a pilot since he was 17, learned with Dave Raub out of old Nobadeer Airport. I think he was particularly interested in flying because his father had been an aviator in the First World War, in the Army; he'd been stationed in Italy, and his Commanding Officer was Fiorello LaGuardia! My husband always had a plane, all his life. I loved to fly, but I never had any desire to pilot a plane. I'm not mechanical in any way; it just didn't seem the wise thing for me to do. Anyway, Sandy started teaching at Princeton in September, and war was declared in December, so he went into the Navy as a flight instructor the first year of the war…he was sent overseas for the last two years and I remained in California at that time. You couldn't come back to Nantucket then—you had to have a good reason to travel, otherwise you didn't go anywhere.

"After the war, in 1946, my husband's mother was very ill and wanted to be on Nantucket, so we came up here for the summer—Sandy's father had already passed away. She had nurses around the clock, and she died that summer. This was where she wanted to be. She'd been here for one of the winters before the war working in the service club for the soldiers here, and living at 97 Main Street, in the West Brick. My husband and I had always been here summer, except during the war years…both of us and our families, all our lives. And in 1948 we moved here permanently. Our daughters Sherry, Haydi (Hayden), and Tina (Christina), were two months, two, and four then, so they all grew up here, and went to Academy Hill School…they'd all come home for lunch. And now they all have homes on Nantucket and stay all summer." Had Joan and Sandy deliberately planned to move to the island year-round? I asked. "No…" she said, "we just didn't have anywhere to go! I mean, we were in college, then we got the job, then the war.

"My husband started Dry Shoal Cleaners with Ernie Wheldon, where the Lobster Pot is now—we bought the land and built that—and he and a partner also started the Nantucket Distributing Co., later sold to Bill Grieder. During the first two winters we rented, but then we bought the house up on Main Street from Gladys Wood. She was the former co-owner of the Skipper Restaurant, with Miss Margaret Prentice, and was a wonderful person, very striking-looking, pure white hair, quite a lot of it. Then for two years we renovated—it had been an old barn—and my husband did every bit of the work himself, except the plastering and the wallpaper, and we moved in. In the summer we lived in the big house down on Hulbert Avenue with Sandy's sister. My husband always wanted to be on Hulbert Avenue—he loved this area, had grown up here. This house was for sale, and Gladys Wood showed it to us. We said, 'But it's so big! and she said, 'Why don't you cut it in half and make two houses out of it?' Well, we were young enough and dumb enough to think it was a nifty idea—we were still in our twenties. So we cut it in half and made two houses. We moved this part 50 feet and raised it up a foot and redid it, and so now we're fortunate enough to have the two properties. So we've been in this house since 1950."

What was it like living on a small island all year? I asked. "Well, I was busy being a mother. There were only 3000 people here then, and thanks to Ernie Wheldon, who had grown up with my husband, we met a lot of people, and they were very kind to us, and included us in everything; we became very close friends with a lot of them. So we had a wonderful life, and of course my husband was busy with business and I was busy with children and Girl Scouts and Sunday School and school and PTA and I did a lot of volunteer work at the hospital. We have so many family roots here. When my husband's uncle, Donald Craig, and his wife retired in 1945, they bought Holly Farm, out on the Polpis Road, and so they were here. And my sister-in-law was here and her family…but not all year, the way we were. We had just a lot of family ties here. You see, we didn't have any ties anywhere else.

"My husband was very involved in all sorts of things here, but I think the thing that we were most interested in was health care. We felt, living on an island, that that was probably the most important thing, and that's why my husband became very involved with the hospital. And I did a great deal of volunteer work up there. Sandy died twelve years ago, in 1991. He was a wonderful man."

I wondered if Joan and Sandy ever did any fishing? "Yes," she said. "When we first moved here we had an old Ford station wagon, and after work we would get a babysitter…we used to do a lot of beach fishing from Smith's Point, and sometimes when there were no fish there we'd drive all the way to Great Point. I remember the first fish I ever caught—it was up at the Galls, and it was in the dark. My husband had wandered down the beach, and I didn't have any more idea of what to do with this fish than the man in the moon! But a fellow by the name of Louis Ray, who worked for the Mardens and the Butlers, came over and helped me, and I was forever grateful to him. I don't recall how big it was—I thought it was a whale! As children in 'Sconset, we used to fish occasionally in Sesachacha Pond. There used to be a little place there where a man rented out little rowboats, and you could fish for little pickerel and perch and things like that. My aunt used to love to do that.

"So…" she continued, "I have learned to love Nantucket…and I think that I am just so fortunate to live in a place that I love, because so many people spend all their life waiting to move to somewhere they want to go to…I've never had any desire whatsoever to go off in the winter. I enjoy travel, and I like to get away for a couple of weeks to see something different in the world. But I love the winter here. I feel like I live two lives…a winter life and a summer life… I'm here on Hulbert Avenue about five months, but when fall comes it's time to go—you can't heat these houses, nobody is here, it gets dark early, and the boats disappear…it gets lonely here when October comes. So I go back to Main Street."

NEVER WITHOUT SOMETHING TO DO

Joan Craig has always been an active person. "There's so much to do…it's incredible. I used to play a lot of paddle tennis; can't do that now any more. I play bridge, golf; there are a lot of us who go to the 4 o'clock matinee on Sunday afternoons in the winter…and a group who have lunch together every Wednesday. We play duplicate bridge once a month; I go out to dinner with friends…I've been working very intensely for three years on Sherburne Commons, because of the need for assisted living, and that takes an awful lot of time. I have a lot of deskwork; I read a great deal…and I'm a great Red Sox fan…I'm not so sold on football. I spend some time with my granddaughter, who is a teacher here. And I have two nieces who live here on the island year-round. I'm never without something to do!

"I've seen a lot of changes on the island. When we first moved here there were only 3000 people here in the winter, and you got to know everybody…and there was nowhere to go to eat except Cy's Green Coffee Pot and Andy's Diner. One big change was when the Nantucket Historical Trust bought the Ocean House and renovated it, making it a place where you could go and have some kind of a social evening, or a party, a wedding…I remember the Ocean House was normally full of young working people from New York—there were so many bicycles parked around in front that you could hardly walk down the sidewalk!"

Has Joan ever regretted not moving back to 'Sconset? "No, because we were year-round, and when we first moved here there were very few families living there. But I do go out to 'Sconset every couple of weeks in the winter just to bring back memories and see what's going on and so forth. And I have a couple of very close friends who are living there now. Have I ever considered moving off the island? Never. *Never!*" What, I asked, does Joan consider the best and the worst things today on Nantucket? She paused, then said, "Well, I don't like seeing all these enormous houses—I don't think the people really live in them; they're not here a great deal of the time. I like Nantucket for what it is and what it represents, and some people come and try to bring what they have at home here! I don't like that at all. The best things? Nantucket is a wonderful place to live year-round now. If my children hadn't been little and I hadn't been so busy with them when we first moved here, where I wasn't a native, I think it might have been difficult. It wasn't, because we were accepted so easily. There really wasn't an awful lot to do then…but what we did do was a lot of fun, because we did it in our own homes and other people's homes…we had a wonderful time. Today there's tremendous stimulation on the island. So many interesting people have retired here, and they have so much to offer…and there are good musical groups and concerts, and the Atheneum offers a lot, and there's a great deal going on. Nantucket is the kindest place I've ever known to older people. And it's kind to single people, and there are a tremendous number of us, widows, on this island. Saltmarsh, the Island Home, Landmark…they all do a fine job. You feel safe and comfortable here.

"If Sherburne Commons eventually is built, I think that will probably be my greatest accomplishment, because I see a tremendous need for that. We're trying to do this as a Nantucket project for Nantucket people, and I have a wonderful board [Joan is president] working with me on that. I also am proud of my husband's and my work with the hospital—Sandy was president of Cottage Hospital for eighteen years; he was there from the time it was built and when the new wing was put on, and he helped bring several of the doctors to the island. So I think probably our greatest accomplishments have been in the health-care field."

Left—Joan's husband, Sandy Craig, was the Nantucket representative to the Steamship Authority for many years, and Joan was chosen to help christen the brand-new *Uncatena* in 1965. Right—Joan with her grandchildren, c. 1999.

A People Person For Sure

Gerri Stanley Price, 2003

First of all, let me say straight out that this woman does not look like a grandmother! Her youthful face, almost always wearing a broad smile, has made a lot of people feel good over the years, as has her cheery voice, the one you hear whenever you call the Nantucket Cottage Hospital. Gerri Stanley Price may know more people on the island than anyone. And it quickly became clear during our conversation that to talk about Gerri meant talking about her entire large and very close-knit family as well.

BORN ON THE RIGHT ISLAND!

And she's a native, too. How did that happen? I asked, and she responded in her typical rapid-fire manner, starting with one of her frequent chuckles, "Yes, I am a native! My grandmother Edith was born over on the Vineyard, but she came here when she was young, when my great-grandmother came to Nantucket. And my mother, Mary Perry Stanley, was born here; she was one of twelve children, all of them born here—those were the Perrys. I am one of nine, and we were all born here too. I have two children and they were born here... My son Gerry and his wife and two children live in New Bedford; and my daughter Bethany and her family live in Maryland, so my grandchildren are not natives." Gerri laughed: "We used to tease my grandmother; we'd tell her she was a traitor, because she was born on the wrong island! You know, there's this rivalry between Martha's Vineyard and Nantucket. Let's see...my mother's father was from Portugal, and my great-grandparents were also from Portugal. My father was from New Haven, Connecticut. His mother was a Madagascan Indian and his father was Caucasian, from Surrey, England. [Gerri grinned.] She had a little romance outside her marriage, and there came my dad! Dad died when he was only 36; there were eight children at that time, and my mom was pregnant with the ninth. She never remarried. I am number four. The oldest is Julian Stanley, then there's Margo Lamotta, Jay Walden, me, Vernie Peters, and, let's see, Neil, Dale, Kim, and Claudia. Vernie's husband, John Peters, was the medicine man for the Wampanoag Tribe—his Indian name was Slow Turtle. He was often on Nantucket...he was here when they found the bones in Miacomet before the housing went up. Slow Turtle passed away some years ago, but Vernie continues the traditions of the powwows; she and John did them together, but he did more educational-type things—he traveled all over the world, teaching people about Native Americans." Gerri took a breath as if to say, "There!" and then said, "So we're a melting pot, my family."

Has Gerri always lived on the island? "Always. *Always.* Once I left briefly to live in Hyannis, but I was so miserable I came home after a couple of weeks. But my other eight siblings come and go all the time. One brother's in California, one is on the Cape in Mashpee, and my last brother is between here and the Cape; my three sisters live in Chelsea, Massachusetts. They come back and forth...they'll move home for four or five years, then they'll go away for ten or twelve, then come back...but I'm the only one who's stayed here forever. I do go Off a lot, though. Just last week I went with my sister, spending money, having a good time, just the two of us, and we *laughed!* And we didn't care when we got back. I never get tired of living on an island, but if someone says, 'Oh, I'm going off-island, Gerri, wanna come?' I'll go, sure.

LIVING UP BY THE WINDMILL

"We always lived up by the windmill, on West York Street—we were number 7, but then they changed it to 38. My grandmother lived across the street at number 6, and my great-grandmother was just before that, so there were the three houses. I remember my great-grandmother very well. She didn't speak a lick of English, but I understood her! I could not speak Portuguese, but I always knew what she was telling me. We are a very close-knit family—nobody can bother us. It's wonderful…if anyone needs something, someone is there…we're always helping each other. I have a lot of nieces and nephews," Gerri laughed. "Gosh, I can't remember how many grandchildren my mother has…I think we figured out the other day she has eight great-grandchildren, but I don't know how many grandchildren!

"My real name is Geraldine, but I like Gerri because my dad was Gerald…I was named after him. Everybody called him Jerry, spelled with a *J* and a *y*. Mr. Pearl, Dr. Pearl's father, was a teacher of mine in school, but he always called me GG—even now he'll stop by the front desk and say, 'Hi, GG.' My school years? I started out first through fifth at South School…we used to call it the South School, but it was Cyrus Peirce. And then for the sixth, seventh, and eighth grades I went to Academy Hill. We used to walk over from Academy Hill to the Coffin School for classes, sewing and cooking for the girls. No school buses for us, though—I lived by the windmill, and I had to walk to school in the morning, walk home for lunch, walk back to school, then walk home again. In those days the only kids who could take the bus were really far out—'Sconset, Madaket, Wauwinet…And you could not bring your lunch to school; you had to walk home for lunch.

OH! THAT PLACE WAS POPPING!

"We didn't ride bikes; we never had them…too poor. We didn't even have a camera for pictures…that's why I don't have many pictures of me as a child. No—one parent was working, that was my dad…and my mother was working! With nine children, she was working at home! My father worked at Island Service." Gerri showed me a picture of "the Island Service gang" at the Legion Hall at a Christmas party, probably taken sometime in the 1950s (naming Billy Reis, her father Jerry Stanley, Bobby Lema, Charlie Fisher, Jimmy Duarte, Bob Caldwell, Ed Maloney, Drew Deeley, Bob McGrath, and Franklin Lamb). Then she held up a great photo of the first Thirty Acres Band, with her father at the microphone. "Do you remember Thirty Acres, the club? That

The "Island Service Gang" at the Legion Hall at a Christmas party. Left to right, standing: Billy Reis, Jerry Stanley (Gerri's father), Bobby Lema, Charlie Fisher, Jimmy Duarte, and Bob Caldwell. Sitting, left to right: Ed Maloney, Drew Deeley, Bob McGrath, and Franklin Lamb. c. late 1950s.

was my grandmother and grandfather Perry's. It was out off Bartlett Road. It started out in what was like a house, and then the business really was thriving, so my grandfather built a larger place way down in the back. Dad and that band would play every Thursday, Friday, and Saturday. I remember that so well…I'd stay in the kitchen with my grandmother and my aunt, because they were doing the cooking…and I'd peek out and watch the band when my dad was playing. They served full meals there…and then years later, after my grandfather died, they went to just burgers and fries, but for years, it was full dinners. Oh! that place was popping. People would line up outside the door…Thirty Acres was the happening place. That was before my father died in 1963…he was so young. He played guitar. He sang too, and I think my Uncle David sang. Jimmy Duarte is in that picture—he worked with the DPW for years…The other men in the band were John 'Pesky' Perry (put quotation marks around Pesky, because nobody knew his name was really John), John Gebo, Jr., and my Uncle David Perry. David Perry is the youngest of the Perry family…my mother was the oldest.

"Thirty Acres was a nice kind of nightclub—there was dancing, and it was very family-oriented. Oh, I remember Maxine and Wendell Howes, God rest their souls. He used to be the chief of police. And they loved dancing. I have wonderful memories of Thirty Acres. It was still going strong when I was a teenager and older. It was written up in the *National Geographic* years ago. They also had a picture of three kids playing in a field, with the Old Mill in the background, and Queen Anne's Lace all around. Two of the kids are my sisters, Claudia and Kim, and one is my cousin. A couple years ago I had an artist draw that picture and we framed it; I gave it to my sister for her birthday…oh, she cried!" With a big sigh, Gerri added, "Thirty Acres closed after my grandmother died."

What did Gerri and her siblings do for fun when they were young? "Not much, because with so many brothers and sisters you had to be home, helping mother. For each of the older ones my mother made up a chart…somebody had the living room to clean, someone had dishes to wash, just different things…and then when the last one was born I started taking care of her—she was 'my child.' I bathed her, combed her hair, washed her clothes, took her out in the stroller, crawled in the crib with her when she was crying (good thing I was skinny!). My first job I was ten years old; that was the summer I took care of my cousin Tommy, and I thought I was making big money—I got paid $10 a week, and back in those days, oh gosh, that was a lot!" Did Gerri get to keep her pay? I asked.

"Noooo…it went to my mother and then she would get school clothes for all of us. The older ones would work in the summer,

The first Thirty Acres band: Jimmy Duarte, Jerry Stanley at the microphone with his guitar, John "Pesky" Perry, John Gebo, Jr., and Gerri's Uncle David Perry. c. late 1950s.

and we turned in our money to my mother. But nobody minded—that's the way it was. My father died when I was 12, but we needed extra income, with nine kids. Claudia is the baby, the youngest, so she knows him only through stories, and pictures…

WORKING, WORKING, WORKING

"During high school, I worked as waitress at the old Downyflake when it was on South Water Street—I would go there after school and on Saturdays and Sundays I'd do the 6 to 2…I also waitressed at Steve Bender's restaurant on Main Street…that was the 'in' place…ohhh, can't think of the name of it now. Hmmm…what else? I worked as a chambermaid for Mrs. Reinemo's guesthouse, right across from the Town Building, on North Water Street; her husband ran the Downyflake. That was one summer…or maybe two. After high school I was secretary to the Chief of the FAA, John Betts. I didn't go on to school—Mrs. Garrabrant, the nursing administrator at the Island Home, the old Island Home, wanted to put me through nursing school, but I told her I did not want to do that. I loved being a nurse's aide, because you had one on one with the patient, and that's what I loved. That was when I was in my early twenties."

And how long has Gerri worked at Cottage Hospital, answering phones with her ever-cheerful voice and directing people to the right places? "I've been here for almost eighteen years. I started out with Home Health—I'd taken the Certified Home Health Aide course. And then I got a back injury when I was transferring a patient from her wheelchair to her bed, and so they made a job for me at the nurses' station; they called me a nursing clerk…you know, making up patient charts, transcribing the doctors' orders. And then they put me down on the phones, and I've been here the longest…since 1991, I think. I love the job, because you get to see everybody in town. I'm a people person. Lynn Pearl, who works up in dialysis, called me last week and said, 'Gerri, I just called some hospital on the Cape and they were the *rudest* people…so I just wanted to call to tell you I appreciate you!' Isn't that nice?"

When did Gerri start her own family? "My first-born, Bethany Stanley Vega, is 33; my son Gerald Stanley the second (named after my dad) is 32; he has two children—Cameron and Hailey. And

Left—Gerri and her two children, all grown up: Gerald Stanley, II (named after his grandfather) and Bethany Stanley Vega. Right—Here's Gerri, with her family: son Gerry Stanley and his wife Deanne, holding baby Hailey (who'd just been baptized); next to Gerry is grandson Jose Vega, Jr., daughter Bethany's son, next to his father Jose Sr., Bethany, and daughter Anelia. Cameron, Gerry and Deanne's son, is in front of Gerri, in the middle of the picture.

Bethany's children are Jose Vega the Third and Anelia. And they're all great kids. Grandchildren are great. When I'm going to see them, I just X each day—can't wait! After high school, Bethany got accepted to Bridgewater State College—she was the first black child in Nantucket history to get scholarships. She got three! Before that, they would not give scholarships to black kids, no matter how much they wanted to improve themselves by education…scholarships always went to the white kids. Bethany really opened the door… Fernando Esteban was her Spanish teacher in high school, and he and his wife Tinka didn't want her to go to college where she was only going to get one hour of Spanish a day…that was her major…so they took her to Maryland, enrolled her in school there. They wanted her to get an education, to become independent and learn about life. They even took her to Spain, where she spoke nothing but Spanish. She wanted to be an interpreter, but now she's working in the hospital field, and of course being able to speak Spanish is important. Today, white is not the common race in the world any more…not anywhere. Do I think there's racism on the island? It's here—it's not as prominent as it used to be…but it's definitely still here. What used to hurt me when I was a nurse's aide was that the people I was caring for were sometimes the same ones who'd called me 'nigger' as a child…oh yeah. And now that they were old and sickly, it was, 'Oh dear, you're so wonderful…what would I do without you?' That hypocrisy…it hurt."

Gerri sees overpopulation as the major problem on Nantucket. "The *housing!* You can't afford to buy a home here. And rent! It's awful—$2000 a month for a small apartment that doesn't even include utilities. It's outrageous. That's why so many Nantucketers have left the island, because they simply can't afford to live here. You go to the store…$4 for a box of cereal? And the peer pressure for kids to have name-brands of clothes! I told Bethany when she was in school, 'If you want it, you go out and get a job and buy it yourself!' So she went out and she worked! It was a good lesson. Her first job was taking care of Rafael Osona's son…and he just graduated from high school! And she also worked at the Bradts' Bake Shop—Mrs. Bradt will always hire the island children, and I think that's wonderful. My son was raised in Hyannis, so he grew up over there…but his last job before he got called to the service was working for Eldredge & Bourne, the moving company, so I got to see him a lot.

298

THE IMPORTANCE OF GRANDMA

"What's in store for the future of Nantucket?" Big sigh. "Well, unless something changes drastically, I think the prices are going to get higher. It was so different when I was a young child. I was always

with my grandmother in the summer, and she made everything…beachplum jelly, grape jelly, apple butter, blackberry jam, cranberry sauce…she did everything herself, right up until she got sick. And then Bethany helped her—my grandmother told her step by step how to make all those things. Bethany loved her great-grandmother…she was so attached…because she took us in when we

Gerri, with her grandson Cameron and son Gerry.

had nowhere to go, and we lived with her for twelve and a half years. Oh, she just spoiled Bethany!" Gerri laughed. "I couldn't even raise my voice to my own child! But she's a good girl—both my children are good, and I am so proud of them…they have both come a long way in this life. My son is into his church and is a very good family person.

"What do I see for my future? Well," Gerri laughed, "I hope I'll be at the hospital for a good long time to come." And what would she like people to say about her fifty years from now? She paused, then answered, "'Oh…I remember her…she always gave me a big smile; she always made me feel good no matter how down I might have been…' You really are a very "up" person, I commented, and Gerri responded, "Well, I love my job…I am so happy there. My family's all around me. I *like* my life!"

With a busy worklife and happily ongoing involvement with family, does Gerri Price have time for other activities or hobbies? She said, "I do a lot of babysitting, because I love kids. I also love to read…mysteries, thrillers, whatever. My sister Margo and I have the same taste in books, so we swap a lot—the thrillers, the blood-and-guts books…When I was in school I would go to the library every day to get a book…the only thing that held my interest as a kid was the mysteries…I read the Bobbsey Twin mysteries, then I went to the Nancy Drews, and anything else that was a mystery. I would read a book a night, bring it back the next day, get another one. Oh no, I'm not too young to have read the Bobbsey Twins…I am 52 years old!" Can I tell your age in the article? I asked. She laughed. "Yes! I'm a 52-year-old *NATIVE!*"

And proud of it, obviously. The conversation/interview with Gerri Stanley Price was informative and fun, full of good laughs…but most important, perhaps, it was another reminder of Nantucket Island's true wealth—its people.

299

Left—This photo was taken at a Thanksgiving reunion at Legion Hall, November 22nd, 1990. From left to right: Nana (Gerri's grandmother, Edith Perry), 82; Gran (Gerri's mother, Mary Stanley), 66; "Mami" (Gerri), 39; and "Betania" (Bethany, Gerri's daughter), 20. Right—Gerri today.

300

At Home in the "Potted Plant"

Freida Schmaltz Thurston, 2003

When I called Frieda Thurston about an interview, I asked if she is a native. "Oh, no!" she replied. "I've only been here since I was three!" Well, considering she's been here for 85 years, she fits quite well into the "islander" category.

Frieda's little house is hidden away among lots of blossoming trees, alive with birds. Little plots of flowers waved here and there, and a couple of lines of wash were flapping in the breeze this early-May day. The quarterboard above the door says "The Potted Plant," and to be sure, there are plants galore inside the house, being sung to by a cheery little cockatiel. In her comfy glassed-in sunroom, Frieda pointed to a lovely orchid in a pot on the ledge; she chuckled: "That one's a fake! My orchids only bloom in the fall, so I bought that and stuck it in a pot. Looks real, doesn't it?"

LIVING NEAR THE SHOAH

This petite, peppy woman said she began life in Wilkes-Barre, Pennsylvania, in 1915, as Frieda Schmalz, daughter of Frederick and Meta, youngest sister of Clara, Alma, and Frederick, Jr. I thought that her maiden name meant sweet, sentimental music, but it turns out that was schmaltz; *schmalz,* she said with a big grin and a wry look, means *lard* (which, like any bona fide Nantucketer, she pronounced "lahd"). So how did the family happen to come to Nantucket? "In the spring I turned three," she said, "my father was very ill. He'd had pleural pneumonia three times, so the doctor told my mother, 'You've got to get him to the shoah, and live near the water, where the atmosphere is clean.' Well, it happened that my sister had come to 'Sconset to work as a nanny the summer before, and that's all she talked about, how beautiful it was, and she'd even become engaged to a man from Nantucket, who she'd met while she was working here. So Mother came here with my sister and found a job working for two sisters who came for the summer with their parents, and they were actually from Wilkes-Barre; they made the job for her. They kept Mother busy; then Dad brought me about a month later. I was only three. Mother had found a place for us to live so we'd be all settled.

"My father and I traveled partly on the train, and then we were on a boat—I only remember what they told me. But I do remember vaguely the ride from the boat to 'Sconset in this hoss and wagon on that rutty old dirt road. My parents built a house out there in 'Sconset on Sankaty Road. It's still standing, but somebody else owns it now, and they've put a second story on it. My father recovered, and he did garden work in the summer, and in the wintertime he was a caretaker, took care of houses, made repairs and painted. And my mother ended up taking in laundry during the summer months for people who didn't want to take it to the commercial places—they wanted it hand-laundered and ironed. I do remember those days. So I grew up in 'Sconset, and went to school there till the fifth grade. I remember one teacher well: Mrs. Caton. She taught the fifth grade and later the eighth grade. I was a good student. As a matter of fact, in the third grade, if I got my work done, I'd do the fourth-grade work, so when I got to the fourth grade, it was a breeze. The first five grades were taught in one room by one teacher, and later I went to the eighth grade in the other room." What about sixth and seventh grade? "We went to those grades over in town, at the old Academy Hill School," Frieda explained, "and then of course they were building the Academy Hill School, so we had to make different arrangements, and that's why I was in the eighth grade back in the other room in the 'Sconset school. But then they finished Academy Hill, and I started as a freshman there in 1928, when it opened. We were bussed to town, and the only thing about those buses was that they weren't enclosed like they are today. They had curtains in the windows, so sometimes it was really cold and raw. But…" and here there was another prize-winning smile, "the boys were very nice and lots of times they'd get next to you and get their arm around you, and the body heat helped to keep you warm."

How were the roads then? I asked. Frieda answered, "The 'Sconset road was there, but the Polpis Road wasn't very good; they used to meet the kids from Wauwinet at the foot of the Wauwinet Road, and after school the parents would be there to drive them home. I'd known some of the other children because I used to come to town with my sister (she was fourteen years older than me). She'd come in Saturday night and visit friends with her husband, and the friends had children, though my sister didn't have any…so she'd bring me along and I'd play with them. That way I met other kids in the neighborhood, so when I went to school in town, it was 'Hi, Frieda,' you know. We 'Sconset children got acclimated well."

THE BIG JAUNT TO TOWN

Other than school and these little social visits with her sister, Frieda's family really didn't travel around the island often. "One thing we did do, though…well, let's see, I was probably around eight then. Frank Holdgate used to take us to town in his big cah every Sunday, about a dozen of us, I'd say, to go to St. Paul's Church. That was our big jaunt to town, once a week. And of course occasionally I would come with my parents, but not too often, until they got their own cah. Before that, they knew somebody in 'Sconset who had a truck and he'd take them to town to do their shopping. There was a little store in 'Sconset, though. Do know where Claudette's is? That used to be the A&P. And right next to it was Cliff Eddy's—that was like the Hub. They had ice cream and candies and newspapers, magazines, things like that…"

Since Frieda lived halfway to Sankaty, she had to get on her bicycle and ride over to 'Sconset village, to play with the other kids. Did she have chores to do when she was growing up? "Oh, well,

Below—Frieda is the baby under the umbrella; her brother Frederick, Jr. and sister Clara are at top; below, father Frederick, mother Meta holding baby. Pittsburgh, 1915.

Top left—A happy family picture: Frieda is the little girl at left, with her father, in cap, behind her. Brother Frederick is at far left; sister Alma is at right, with checkered dress. The other little girl is Fred, Jr.'s little girl Babs.

Frieda with a great old automobile.

The Dine-a-Mite, a favorite 'Sconset restaurant when Frieda was a girl.

A youthful Frieda (c. 1930) all ready to wait on tables at the Woodbox.

304

yes. I had things I had to do at home, help Mother. If she hadn't got 'round to the dishes, they were waiting for me after school, things like that. When I was 11 or somewhere around there, I used to take care of Mary Furlong's son Charles, who was about nine months old. Mary's mother, Sadie Folger (who was also my sister's mother-in-law), had the Wander Inn over near the 'Sconset pump, and she served three meals a day there. Had a pretty good business, local folks. I loved to watch them wait on tables, so one day Sadie says, 'Frieda, why don't you try it? We'll give you one table, and you ought to be able to handle that.' So she had me wait on one woman at lunchtime, and every noon then I would go over and wait on this woman. A couple years later, I became a regular waitress there. I just kept workin' and workin' after I got home from school, just because I liked to do it. Did I get paid? I got tips. And, let's see—from there I worked across the way from the Post Office at the Dine-a-Mite, which was owned by Gwendolyn Gwinn—everyone called her Pinkie. The Dine-a-Mite was a tearoom, and I waited on tables there, too. I got pretty good tips; they weren't what they are today, of course," she laughed. What did this young girl do with the money she'd earned? "I used to save it. And once in a while I'd spend it, like in the summer—I'd work all summer, and it would be hot, so I'd go to Cliff Eddy's in the early evening and buy some ice cream and take it home to my mother."

It began to sound as if Frieda was working too hard to have much of a social life, aside from having boys put their arms around her when the schoolbus was freezing. She said, "I didn't do much socializing at all. I was ill and had an operation the December before I turned 15, and the doctor said he didn't want me to do a lot of strenuous schoolwork for a month or six weeks. And I said, 'Oh no! I'll never catch up!' I really didn't want to go back, so my parents let me quit school." And then what did you do? I asked. Laughing, Frieda answered, "Well, then I met Cecil Richrod and married him! He was a native Nantucketer. We had three children—Cecil, Jr., Doris, and Frederick. Frederick died the day after Christmas last year, of cancer. His wife Mary lives next door; she's a sweetheart, and looks after me. My other two children also live on the island. Doris is now Doris Picard, and she works at Harbor Fuel. My son Cecil is retired now; he was president of the Nantucket Bank there for eighteen years. My youngest son Frederick had his own plumbing business."

Two years after Cecil, Jr. arrived, Doris came along, and Frieda said, "I went eight years and had Frederick in 1942, during the war. We had moved to town from 'Sconset after Cecil was born and lived with my mother-in-law for a year, and then we finally were able to find a house on Liberty Street. Cecil was working at the Island Service Company, at the gas station. What do I remember about the war years?" She laughed: "Standin' in line with a book! Stamp book. We got by; but you had to have stamps for shoes, and stamps for sugar, meat...just certain things that were real scarce. And of course I remember blackouts at night." With three children and still working, Frieda and Cecil still managed an active social life: "We used to play cards. I think cribbage was the big thing then; and I also belonged to the Grange, the Rebekkahs, the Eastern Star. But I kept on working. I've always worked. I've worked in the Woodbox, and at Cap'n Tobey's, and then I also worked at the hospital for 22 years, as head of the dietary department and the housekeeping. I retired in 1977." Frieda added that Cecil died in 1957, and several years later she married Harold Thurston. "He was a career man in the Coast Guard for 22 years," she said. "He's passed away too, in December of 1968. Yes, we women do have to learn to go it alone."

Hors d'Oeuvres at the Angler's Club

The Angler's Club is one place where Frieda Thurston can be found with some frequency, usually in the company of "the Golden Girls, I guess you'd call them"—sisters Irene Hardy and Ethel Dunham, and Dolores Wiszuk, to name three. "We go there pretty regularly," she said. Do you have to be a fisherwoman to belong? "No, it's social; we just go and have a couple of glasses of wine and eat hors d'oeuvres. We don't go every week, but quite a bit. We talk, and laugh...I don't pay any dues, so once a year I provide the food. That's what I was doing last week— passing around my hors d'oeuvres."

What is a typical day like for this small, peppy woman who'd already hung an impressive wash out to dry that day? "Well," she said, "I take care of my plants. That one over there with the dark red flower is a Japanese Bellflower; it has a geranium-like leaf. I saw it advertised in a catalog, and sent for it. It wasn't very expensive. It's pretty, isn't it? I used to do needlework, but I have macular degeneration and my right eye isn't very good. The other one's fine. The thing that annoys me is when I'm writing, I'm probably writing an inch above the line," she laughed. "I used to make all kinds of things. I still cook, and like to...I love making hors d'oeuvres." Does Frieda ever get off-island? "Oh yes, usually every Thanksgivin' we go up to Mary's relatives in Fitchburg. And one day about a month ago she had to go to the doctor's, and I went up with her and spent the day in the mall, and had a ball. I was there from 1 to 4, walking around—I got my exercise! I love walking, have no trouble with it.

"The only thing that really bothers me is cold weather—I don't like that. But this is a warm house; I'm snug here. I used to have another house on the corner of Pleasant and Cherry; I sold it and stayed with Fred, who had been living with my sister; but when she died I went and lived with him, and then he met Mary and got married, so I rented for a year, then built this house. I really like it here."

What does this octogenarian islander think of the changes taking place on the island? "Well," she said, "I think the problems are really all caused by building. And I'm worried about the water—what's going to happen if we haven't any water? But they keep on building and building and building...those are the things that bother me. I'm afraid that they're going to build all these great big houses, then the people are going to take off and leave 'em and they're going to be like they were years ago, all boarded up and nobody living in them. Another thing: they're killing off all the native plants...and we can't replace them. Pulling out blackberry bushes and mowing down Rosa rugosa should be considered some sort of a crime."

But things aren't all bad. Frieda pointed out that "for getting to and away from the island, we have better transportation. And we have all those services, like Cottage Care, Elder Services. I haven't had to use them yet, but the day may come. My people are pretty long-lived: my father's mother lived to be 85. We don't know anything about Mother's family, because they were in Europe. My aunts all lived to be close to 80, and Mother was almost 90 when she died.

Nantucket Is My Home

"My family's here, and this is where I've lived all my life...I did live in New Bedford for one year during the war; my husband got a job over there—but it wasn't what we wanted, and we came back. Nantucket is my home."

It had been a very enjoyable hour, and I came back a few days later to take a contemporary picture of this always-smiling lady. Pointing the camera at her, I instructed her to say "Rhubarb and soda water," which, I explained, makes the face relax for a photo. She grinned mischievously and said, "Oh, a long time ago, when nothing else worked, a photographer told me to say 'sex,' so

Left to right—(1) Frieda Schmalz Richrod, wedding picture, taken at the 'Sconset house of her parents, 1931. (2) Cecil Richrod and his bride, Frieda Schmalz, on their wedding day, 1931. (3) Cecil Richrod at the pump at Island Service, where he worked for many years.

that's what I always do." What a spirited Nantucket woman Frieda Schmalz Richrod Thurston is. With her sense of fun and "can-do" attitude, may she live for twenty more years, at least.

Frieda today.

308

Telling the Old Stories
Robert F. Mooney, 2003

*B*ob Mooney, one of the more familiar faces around town, is the real thing: a bona fide native. I knew it was going to be tough to confine the interview to under two hours, but he was ready to start at the beginning…and a bit before. "I was born on Nantucket in 1931," he began. "My father was on the police force and later became Chief, and my mother was a nurse at the Cottage Hospital. But the family goes back to 1851 when the original Robert Mooney, my great-grandfather, was shipwrecked on Nantucket on the *British Queen*. There were 226 Irish immigrants, and they were rescued off the coast of Tuckernuck and brought to Nantucket. All of them eventually went on to New York City, where they'd been headed, except for Robert Mooney and his wife Julia, who swore they'd never set foot on another boat. So that's how they came to stay. They settled down as tenant farmers on the Polpis Road. In 1900, when Robert was 80, his sons persuaded him to go to the mainland for one day to visit the Brockton Fair. And that's all he ever saw of America, after crossing the Atlantic. But Julia never left the island.

"My grandfather's name was Lawrence, my father's name was Lawrence, and I'm Robert and my son is Robert…and Robbie's little baby boy, who was born March 6th, is Robert. He is the first grandchild. (He came at a good time, too—brightened up the winter.) My grandfather had the farm on Polpis Road that is now the Slosek Farm, and raised cows and chickens and pigs and the usual stuff. When I was a kid, my father would drive me out the 'Sconset Road, and that field of Henry Coffin's, which is now mostly golf course, was covered with sheep as far as you could see; I don't know how many he had, but it looked like hundreds. I loved those sheep."

Bob's father, too, was a farmer originally, until he took a night job on the police force, where he stayed for 37 years, until his retirement as Chief in 1953. "In those days," said Bob, "it was a very simple operation; you had a five-man police force: one man on days and two on nights, and they ran the whole island that way. My mother came from Taunton to be a nurse at the old Cottage Hospital on West Chester Street, and there she met my father and they got married, and a year later I was born; I was their only child.

"The farm on the Polpis Road was a very rustic operation. There was no heat in the house, and my mother swore that she was not going to spend a winter there, so they developed a habit of moving to town for the winter; they'd rent a little house somewhere, and then we'd go back to the farm in the summers. Finally, in about 1938, they sold the farm—it was a losing proposition—and bought a house on West Chester Street. My father was very sentimental about it; he'd worked so hard on the farm that after he sold it, he didn't even like to drive out Polpis Road—he'd go around the other way to 'Sconset. So I lived mostly on West Chester Street, and went to Academy Hill School. I'd come across the Lily Pond to get there…it was dry in the summers, and it iced over in the winter, so I cut right through and came around up the little alley from Lily Street to school.

MEMORABLE TEACHERS AT ACADEMY HILL

"Yep," he said, "this is where I got my island education before I went off to college." How was island history taught? "Well, we didn't have so many Nantucket books in those days; it came mostly from veteran teachers, and most of the teachers were island people in those days. There were some wonderful teachers. There's one who's still alive—Mary P. Walker, who was the English teacher, the Dramatics teacher, and the high school principal. She's a very memorable person, and is still quite lively. We recently lost Mary Glidden, who was my seventh-grade teacher. She was Mary McCann then, and was a wonderful, very young teacher in those days. Let's see, the only other one I can think of who's still left is Edith Folger Andrews. She was the high school science teacher…that was before she married Clint Andrews. In addition, we had people like Edouard Stackpole, who used to lecture at the high school, and we got a good deal of island history that way."

"The Coffin School had a big group of young men who took carpentry and metal work. Tom McAuley, who taught the Metal-Working Department and also pitched for the baseball team, is still with us. Roy True taught woodworking, and was a very popular teacher. The girls took Home Economics, and learned cooking and sewing; they had a couple of tough women teachers, too…Lelia Ray was one of them. Boys and girls were strictly segregated. The Coffin School taught industrial arts, and turned out some wonderful craftsmen—people who are still around, like Maxie Ryder and a couple of the plumbers; my friend Mike Lamb went through that course there. Those guys became the builders of the new Nantucket…very important."

DELIVERING NEWSPAPERS FOR $1.75

Was the young Robert Mooney a straight-as-an-arrow kid in school? He laughed: "Well, I was pretty well behaved, because my father was Chief of Police, so I was always under close observation. It was a small-town environment here, and when the police cruiser pulled up in front of the school, everybody shook with apprehension. But I had a pretty good time through high school; I was one of 36 in the graduating class, and a few of my classmates are still with us. In fact, we plan a 55th reunion this summer." Asked if he had jobs during those years, he replied, "Yes, always. The first thing I ever did was deliver newspapers. Harry Turner, at the *Inquirer and Mirror*, paid $1.75 for delivering newspapers. They split the town, north and south of Main Street. I had the north part, and I don't know how many hundreds of papers we delivered, but we got $1.75, and that wasn't negotiable. We

Bob Mooney and his father, c. 1935, at their farm on Polpis Road. Looks as if someone was camping out.

picked up the big bags of papers and took off on our bicycles, and boy, you'd better get those papers there or the phone would be ringing. That was my first job. Then in the summers I started working at Cliffside Beach, which was owned by a man named Conrad, and we delivered meals on the beach from The Galley, which was sort of a lunch-counter operation; people who inhabited Cliffside rented umbrellas for the summer, and we'd deliver their meals every day. I'll always remember Old Man Conrad—he also had a very firm rule: 'Absolutely no wages will be allowed.' So you worked for tips only. You'd average three or four dollars a day, but you know, when you're 12 or 13, that's pretty good. But those were only sunny days. If you had a rainy day, you were out of luck. I worked down there with Bobby Flanagan, Charlie's brother, and he was a friend of mine.

"Then I finally got a job after school working at Nantucket Pharmacy. The pharmacist was Wally Knott, and I worked for him for three or four years. I worked on the soda fountain, and brought up the supplies and stuff from the cellar. I was working for him the night the war ended, 1945…I would've been 14 then. All the way through the war was kind of interesting, because you had all the shortages—no ice cream, no milk, no cigarettes…Oh! People would pay anything for a pack of cigarettes…of course they only sold for 25 cents then. Oh boy, if you could smuggle cigarettes out of there, you could do well. But I learned a lot from Wally. He was a very good businessperson." Didn't drugstores used to sell liquor to people, sort of quietly? I asked. Bob responded, "Oh yes, little half-pint bottles…for 'medicinal' purposes. And they took care of people on Sundays and holidays…that was always a good sideline. The co-owner of the store was Mary Mendonca, who had been a really good Nantucket schoolteacher—taught the sixth grade all her life. She was strict, but she was also very generous. Some poor soul would come in complaining about not being able to pay the rent or buy the food, and she'd open the cash register, take out some money, and say, 'Here, take it!'…and would just hand them money. It was very touching…but," Bob laughed, "Wally used to come in and say, 'I can't balance the books!' She'd say, 'don't worry, don't worry.'" Did most of them pay it back? "Oh, sure. There was a lot of personal, I guess you'd call it, loan business. In those days, you know, you couldn't walk into the bank and say 'I want to borrow $5,000.' One story I like to tell is about Esther Gibbs; she owned the North Shore Restaurant for many years. And later she was a Selectman—I think she was the second woman Selectman. Esther was a tough old girl; she'd worked for years at the Roberts House, and knew the business very well. One year she had a chance to buy the North Shore Restaurant for $5,000. So she went into the Pacific National Bank, filled out a mortgage application, and handed it to the president, who said, 'Esther, I wouldn't dare present this application to the Board of Directors.' And she said, 'Why not?' He said, 'Well…you're a woman!' She looked at him and said, 'What do you think I'm going to do—have a baby?' She was heartbroken; she went down Centre Street, where she met Cora Stevens, who had a kind of a stationery store—notions, business supplies, and everything. Cora was an old Nantucket gal. She asked Esther what was the matter—Esther was almost in tears—and she told Cora she'd been turned down. Cora said, 'Those goddamn old fools!' and then she said 'Here!', wrote out a check for $5,000, and said, 'Pay me back whenever you can.' That was what it was like then. It was personal contacts. It was a different way of life. But people got by somehow."

What about the war years? "Well, when the war started I was just 10 years old, in 1941, and I can remember that the island was blacked out at night; the streetlights were shaded, and of course there weren't many cars around, but you couldn't drive 'em anyway at night with the lights on. And my father got six new revolvers for the police department, for civil defense. Six shiny new revolvers. And of course any able-bodied guys got drafted, so there was a manpower shortage, and some pretty old guys were policemen.

Sending the A's & B's to Nantucket

"The Coast Guard was a strong force here then, with stations at Brant Point, Madaket, Surfside, 'Sconset, Sankaty, and Coskata, and they took over the Nesbitt Inn as a headquarters and a hospital. And then the Navy came down and took over the airfield; and that made a great difference around here. And you know, the servicemen reached down and made a big dent in the high school here for girlfriends." Bob paused and laughed: "There was also an Army contingent, a company of MP's, which moved into Crest Hall, at the rear of the Harbor House, on North Water Street. Louis Ayotte, who later became sheriff, was sent down here from Otis, on the Cape, and I asked him why the Army had been sent to Nantucket…it had never been down here before. And he said, 'Well, somebody decided that Nantucket would be good training for the African desert,' so they'd march the guys out to Madaket and have 'em run around in the sand dunes for a while. I asked him, 'How in hell did they ever select you guys?' and he said, 'Alphabetically. They sent all the A's and B's over to Nantucket…' Well, that's what happens in the service, you know.

"Of course we kids loved all that military stuff…we played war games and had wooden guns and all that. When I was a Boy Scout, we had a Civil Defense role to play; the famous Lookout Tower was up on Mill Hill, and we went up there and did four-hour hitches…and boy, we spotted everything—seagulls and everything! Well, the Nazis didn't dare approach Nantucket. I remember Cy's Green Coffeepot was open, and that was very busy, because it was right there next to the movies and the big USO dance hall down there where Hardy's was. The Navy Liberty Bus used to dump the guys in front of Cy's and pick them up at 10 p.m.

THE GREEN DELIVERY TRUCKS

"I did a lot of camping and hiking, mostly outdoor stuff. I built model airplanes, too, but I worked after school and weekends. I did do some sports, but they were kind of minimal. There was basketball in Bennett Hall, but no baseball or football team. Finally, the high school started to play football in 1947, and I did that for a while. Of course there was no television; it was all radio. You listened to the Red Sox—you know, they even used to broadcast those games by teletype…*click click click, tick tick tick*…That was pretty good. Other things I did? Well, mowing lawns and stuff like that. The drug store was my main event until I got to college, and then I figured I was out of the drug store business, so I went to work at Ashley's Market, where Congdon's is now. They had a fleet of green delivery trucks, and that was the thrill of a lifetime, to be able to drive a truck all day. We worked from 7 in the morning till 6 at night, and we delivered everything: meat, vegetables, bakery goods, liquor…Ashley's had a bakery upstairs. You know where Portuguese bread came from? That was just leftover dough. They'd just roll the extra stuff in a ball and throw it in the oven—it was just scraps! And it became Portuguese bread, and they couldn't make enough of it! They baked all night up there, and the policemen would come in and get hot muffins and coffee and all that. Ashley's was really quite a lively place.

"J.B. Ashley became president of the Pacific National Bank, and even then, he'd still be behind the counter with a bloody apron. Of course he went over to the bank occasionally, but normally if you wanted to see the bank president, they'd say, 'Go on over to the market.' He was a good old guy. The store was a big operation—they had about six butchers going all day long. Of course, Ashley's sold everything on credit, and you could order hundreds of dollars' worth of meat and liquor…charge liquor nowadays? Try that!" Bob laughed. "And right to your door. I delivered to big houses down on Brant Point, and Hulbert Avenue; Thursdays and Fridays were the big days, and boy, you'd take them hundreds of dollars' worth of food…SS Pierce bourbon and everything. It was really quite impressive. But I'll tell you what happened…after Ashley died, it was taken over by a fellow named Jim Brennan, who was kind of a lively Irishman, and he said to me one day: 'The days of Ashley's Market are numbered, because I just saw Mrs. Vigouroux of Brant Point pushing a wagon through the store.' And you know, ladies didn't do that in those days—they had a maid call for the food. 'But when you see a big customer pushing a wagon,' he said, 'that means the days are numbered.' Ashley got a lot of meat during the war—he had contacts, and the meat was a precious commodity then. He made a lot of money off that. And some good guys worked there. Not too many left."

COLLEGE, THE NAVY, LAW SCHOOL, & THE LEGISLATURE

Bob went to Holy Cross, in Worcester, MA. He reminisced: "Of course it's coed now, but in the old days it was very strict. The Jesuits ran it; there were no women teachers, and in fact, you couldn't even have your mother up in your bedroom—no women at all. I majored in political science, and took a lot of history. It was a pre-law course. I think I was always bent in the direction of law. My father had a great admiration for lawyers and judges…oh, of course I suppose my mother would have liked me to become a doctor, but that never appealed to me. So that's how I got going." And then, I said, you went to Harvard Law School and also became Nantucket's very youthful Representative in the General Court. Bob responded, "Well, there was a little hiatus. In 1952 I graduated from the Cross, and the Korean War was on, and so you had to make a choice: you could go to law school and probably be exempt for three years, or you could go into the service and get it over with. And I was only 21 at the time, so I figured I'd join the Navy and see the world. And I did. I joined the Navy and went into OCS at Newport, got commissioned, and

314

Left—For three years in the early 1950s, Lt. J.G. Robert Mooney served on the *U.S.S. Lowry.* Right—A 1958 photograph of Robert Mooney.

then was sent to a destroyer, the Lowry, in Norfolk. That Navy experience was important in my life, because for one thing I was still pretty young; it gave me a chance to grow up and learn about people. I had a wonderful skipper, Captain Charles B. Carroll, and he's still alive—he's 91. He was one of the great influences in my life; a very admirable gentleman.

"So I spent three years in the Navy, and then I went back to law school." And how did the opportunity to get into politics come up? "The Representative in Nantucket was Cyrus Barnes, who was quite an elderly man…I suppose he was about my age now," Bob grinned, "but he'd been there for years and years, and wasn't well. So I decided to take a chance in politics. I was in my second year. I've always been interested in politics, and I knew Nantucket pretty well, so I decided to run as a Democrat, which was unheard of in Nantucket. The island's changed completely, you know—there used to be only 200 Democrats on the island, and my father was one of those, so maybe that's why I did that. Anyhow, I ran against him, and we had a very spirited contest…except that Cy Barnes died in the middle of it…then there was real confusion, and two Republicans ran against me. And I won the thing by 130 votes!" What on earth made you think you could do that and continue law school? I asked. "Well, that's a good question; I suppose when you're young and foolish, you think you can do everything. The law school called me in and they said 'We don't have any concern with what our students do with their private lives—if you want to play baseball for the Red Sox or play in a jazz band, that's your business, as long as you keep up your marks.' I said, 'Well, I think I can try it, because the legislature meets mostly in the afternoons, and my classes are all in the mornings.' So I'd go to morning classes and then race down to Beacon Hill, and then go home and study all night. I got through it…although the day I graduated, Dean Griswold, who handed out the diplomas, said, 'I think you owe us another year.' I said, 'No thank you! I'd never make it!' I did all right." So all right, in fact, that he graduated cum laude.

A LONG LOVE AFFAIR WITH THE ATHENEUM

Bob went on: "So then I got a job in a law firm in Boston, which allowed me to work in the firm and still go to the Legislature, and that went along for a few years, and I came back to Nantucket on weekends. It was a busy time. I thought it was very exciting, and you know, I got to meet a lot of interesting people. But after six years I decided to stay with the law, because there seemed to be more future in that. I'm glad I did it. I moved back here fulltime in 1966, and that was just when things were picking up here; Beinecke was starting his development. And I was appointed Assistant District Attorney, and did that for twelve years…did a lot of criminal work. I was on the Zoning Board of Appeals when they started that in 1972, and then I got involved with the library and the Girls and Boys Club and so forth." I commented that he'd never run for Selectman, and asked why. "I never felt that urge to be a town father here. I think the Selectmen have a thankless job because they have to deal with so many minor details and personal events, and that would put a great strain on you. I just never had that urge."

Bob Mooney has been very active in the Atheneum. "I was always interested in books," he said, "and the Atheneum was a popular place for me. When I became president of the Atheneum, I thought it would be a nice, simple task. Then we got into the restoration project, and Grace Grossman talked me into heading up the campaign, and that was a very exciting time." Were there problems working with the wide variety of people involved in the Atheneum? I asked. "You always have that problem with an old institution," he observed. "There are people who don't want to change a thing; it's like trying to make changes in a church, or something—you know, 'You can't touch that statue, it's my favorite saint...' You just have to show them that it's going to better in the long run. And when I got out of the Atheneum, I was appointed to the Massachusetts State Library Commission, which sets the standards for the libraries; we go around to little town libraries everywhere, and they're very interesting. Of course the problem in Massachusetts is that every library is at least 100 years old, so they all need everything; they need rebuilding and reworking. We've had some wonderful experiences with history...and we've met all kinds of obstacles. One of the problems with libraries is that when the state gets short of money, they're the first to get the axe. I'm technically still on the Library Commission, and I'm President Emeritus of the Atheneum; and I'm active at St. Mary's church. I was involved with Bud Egan and Sam Sylvia, who chaired that reconstruction..."

When did Bob Mooney, man of many talents, start writing books? And is he working on one now? "I knew you'd ask that," he said. "Well, let's see. I wrote *The Nantucket Way* in 1980; *The Wreck of the British Queen* was 1988...then there's *Tales of Nantucket,* and *The Advent of Douglass, and The Civil War: The Nantucket Experience,* and *Nantucket Only Yesterday.* What's next? I'm always brewing ideas about new books." Does Bob ever relax? He said that he's been going to Naples, Florida in the winters lately, "to warm up"; Betty Mooney's 95-year-old mother lives in St. Petersburg. Bob and Betty have been married for nearly forty years, and, lucky people, live right next door to their new grandson. "I go over and look at him every day," said Bob.

316

IF I WERE KING

What would Bob Mooney do if he were king of Nantucket? The question brought a grin; he paused, then said, "Well, I'd like to set the clock back about twenty years. I'd like to slow down the pace of life on the island. I think we're going to be victims of our own success. I'm not all gloomy about the future, but it's going to be different. One fact that I learned when I was writing *Nantucket Only Yesterday*...I went down to find out how many automobiles are registered on Nantucket—cars that live here. And at the time the answer was 14,000. Now, if there are only 8,000 or so people on the island, that's about two to a customer. A lot of that is commercial stuff...but you drive around some of these neighborhoods and see how many cars are parked outside each house. And this is before any tourist or any summer person arrives. Something to think about.

"And if I were king, I'd also stop giving out parking tickets after Columbus Day—there's no reason to keep ticketing people in the snowdrifts down there...that's one of my pet peeves. I think the town should do is get back to basics—fix up the roads, the sidewalks...more of the basics, rather than all these far-out projects. I remember when Nantucket's town government was small and inobtrusive...the policemen and the firemen kept the lights on and the roads open, and that was about it. And now it seems the town has to get into every project anyone can dream up. It's a town of trophy houses, trophy wives, celebrities, and cellphones... But there are some good things that have happened here. The transportation is much better than it ever used to be. I can remember when there was one boat a day, and then later one plane a day. Northeast Airlines would go out in the morning, and if you missed the plane you were stuck for another day. I used to come back from Boston every weekend on Northeast Airlines, and later on, when Hyannis, Cape & Islands, and those planes were flying, it seemed more convenient to drive down to the Cape and hop over. But again, it all depends on weather and seasons. I can remember racing down to the Cape Cod Canal; you'd phone ahead and say, 'Hold that last plane—I'm coming!' and they'd hold it for you!

"Something positive happening on Nantucket is the conservation program; it's been very successful, and you have to give credit for that. And of course there's much better education and health care than there ever was in the past. People get very good service from this hospital. And the architecture of the old town is still marvelous, and hasn't changed. So I think if people just take care to preserve what should be preserved here, we'll be all right. I think that the place will always be popular, and I think that Nantucket will still be good—it will just be different. You know, resorts come and go…people can get tired of places. I wish the people who are permanent residents here took more of an interest in the community and really tried to preserve it instead of sitting back and letting everybody else do it…"

What does Bob Mooney hope people will say about him in fifty years? He laughed. "Oh, another Nantucket character! I suppose I'd just like to be thought of as carrying on some of the old traditions and bringing people up to date with some of the stories that should be preserved on the island. I like to tell the old stories; they've got to be put into print. So that's what I've tried to do."

It had been a pleasure talking with Bob Mooney. He's a man who loves Nantucket…and it shows.

Betty and Bob Mooney at the Nantucket Yacht Club.

318

Life on His "Little Old Sandbar"
Phil Grant, 2003

*P*hil Grant gets a lot of fun out of life and loves to tell stories. It's sometimes difficult to get hold of him, though, because he's a very busy guy. I'd heard he's a great golfer, playing three times a week, and he said, "At my age? Good Lord, no! I'm just a genuine hacker." Born in 1918, he looks hale, hearty, and fit. I asked about his family background on Nantucket, and he replied, "I'm a fifth-generation native. The first one here, along about 1750 or 1760—I think his name was David—was a sailmaker on a Scottish merchant ship out of Edinburgh. He was shipwrecked on the Old Man Shoal east of the island and, being a Scotsman, he decided he'd best put on his kilts before he swam ashore. It was quite a swim—10 or 12 miles—but he was a good seagoin' guy. Now this is only hearsay, but they say the Indians at Wauwinet where he landed thought he was some kind of a god! But he squared 'em away on that after a while. Then he had sons, and that's how the name was carried on.

A WHALIN' FAMILY

"There was a whole bunch of whalers in the family. Charles Grant, the Scotsman's son, was my great-grandfather; then there was George, and my father, Arthur B. Grant—oh yes, he was a fisherman and a rumrunner and an ensign in the Navy in World War I. Charles Grant was the most successful whaling master in the world, no less. Made more money and had his pick of the crews, because he was very democratic with them. His wife, Nancy Wyer Grant, got tired of waiting for him in Nantucket and she jumped a merchant ship going to New Zealand, because she knew his route, knew that in February he'd be down in New Zealand. So she was in Auckland waiting for him when he came in," Phil laughed, "and old Charles, I'll tell ya, was quite surprised! She was one of the first women to go to sea with her husband, and had all three of their children on voyages. The first one was Charles; he died in Nantucket here in his 40s; I think he went to sea too…never knew much about him. And then there was my grandfather George, who was born at Apia, in Samoa, in 1857. For good luck, the natives wrapped him in banana leaves…not banana skins, as someone said in a recent article. And then there was my great-aunt Eleanor—we called her Ellie— who lived to be 102. She became blind in the latter years, but she was a great old peach. Didn't weigh 100 pounds soakin' wet, as wiry as they could make 'em! She married into the Pierce family—pronounced 'Perse'—just outside of Fairhaven."

I asked if Phil had known his grandfather George. "Oh, good Lord, yes! When I was only 12 or 13, I used to help him down at the Whaling Museum when he was setting it up [he was curator and caretaker for some time]. After he was born in Apia, he stayed aboard the ship—in fact, he went to sea from the time he was born, you might say. They called him Captain Grant, but he was never a captain; he made first mate…and he harpooned his first whale when he was 15 or 16, when he was the boatsteerer; the boatsteerer handles the big oar back on the after end, and when they come up on the whale, he leaves and runs for'rd and grabs the harpoon and gets the honor of striking the whale. Oh yes, he talked about his whaling adventures. When he was 12, he was on the Mohawk; that was one of the biggest trips that old Charles [the great-grandfather] ever made financially. Once, George was playin' around on deck, 12 years old, you know, and usin' a dip-net to haul stuff up…and somethin' looked funny to him, looked like a bunch of old grease. He took it to his father, and his father says, 'Where'd you get that, boy?' He says, 'Right there, where they're cuttin' in the sperm whale.' And his father says, *'Good God,'* he says, *'that's ambergris!'* So to make a long story short, they got into the guts of the sperm whale and found quite a big batch of ambergris. What that is in plain English is whale puke. And it's found only in sperm whales because they eat cuttlefish, and cuttlefish have a central bone in them…and the whales swallow the darn things whole, and it gathers in the stomach. I don't know whether they ever actually upchuck it or not. But anyway, they got such a big quantity of it that everybody got quite a bonus that trip. They used ambergris for making perfume; it was very valuable, worth more than gold in those days, actually, $30 or $40 an ounce.

"I'll tell you another story about my grandfather George. He was out on the stage once, on the side of the ship, cutting out the blubber on a whale, and he missed and cut his big toe with the blade, which was very sharp. The only thing left on his toe was a little piece of skin hangin' on the bottom. So he went in, took out a sail needle, and sewed his toe back on—packed it in Stockholm tar, and let it go. A year or two before he died he showed me the scar—you could see every stitch mark right over the top of that big toe! Yep—he also used to haul out his own teeth! He'd take a sort of corkscrew out of the medicine chest down at the Whaling Museum, put the thing in, and twist the rotted teeth out—when they got bad, of course. He died in 1942, just before I went in the Navy.

DEAR OLD GOLDEN-RULE DAYS

"Growing up on Nantucket? It was a great place…I came up in the Depression days. Nobody had a sou. But we were too proud to take alms from anybody. When I was very young I lived on Orange Street—72, I think, somewhere in that neighborhood. 'Twas the old Barrett house. He was one of the veterans who came back from the Civil War, and he'd lost one eye. He and his wife lived on the first floor and we lived on the second. Then my family moved to North Liberty Street and we also spent a year or so in New Bedford. Came back, and I went to the first three grades on Orange Street, then went up to Academy Hill. I remember my teachers very vividly. And that first grade I'll never forget," he laughed. "I'm left-handed, and in those days everybody was supposed to use the right hand. Helen Bartlett was a teacher's assistant at the time, to Esther Johnson, who was the regular first-grade teacher. Well, it was a drawing of a little rabbit on

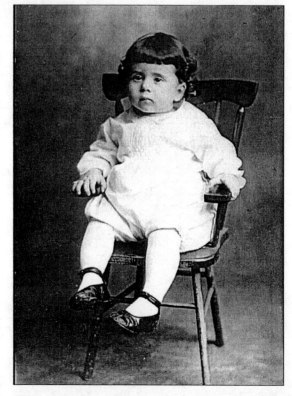

grey paper, and you were supposed to color it with white chalk, and I was doin' a pretty good job. Helen came along, snapped the chalk out of my hand, and put it in the right hand. I didn't think much of it, and soon's she turned around I put it back in my left. She came back a second time and yanked it out of my hand and put it in my right. The third time she rapped me with a ruler, and I called her a name. So then they put a dunce cap on my head and stuck me in the corner!" So, I said, I gather you were not a conformist-type child. "No—I've always been independent. But anyway, during recess I jumped out the window—it was on the first floor—and run down the street; in three or four minutes I was home, and my mother wanted to know what I was doin' there. I told her, and she gave me a backhander, grabbed me by the neck, and waltzed me right back up to the school! And

Young Philip Grant, c. 1919.

you know, that's the only time they ever bothered me about using my left hand. I never did learn to use my right—I'm 'skwy-paw,' write upside-down."

Any other high-jinks? I asked. "Oh, yuh…nothin' bad or anything. We went down to the Crest Hall for the fifth grade, and then in 1929 Academy Hill School opened, and we went into the sixth grade there. Mary Mendonca taught the sixth grade, Marie Kay Swayze taught the seventh grade, and Harriet—we called her Hattie—Williams taught the eighth grade. From there on we went upstairs to the high school. Now, everything went along pretty smoothly in the sixth and seventh grades, but I got into Hattie Williams's class and I started cutting up. She had me right down front, right next to her desk, after I got actin' up…she says, 'Philip Grant, I changed your diapers many a time when you were bawn, and I think I can still handle ya!' Well, I guess you know I shut right down…and the whole class laughed! Yep. I pretty much behaved for her after that—didn't want another taste of that! We did pull one on her once—caught a little fieldmouse after a rain; I put it in my pocket, took it in, and put it in the middle drawer of her desk. She opened the drawer, looked: 'Huh!' she says, 'I hope you people appreciate what you're doin' here. All you're doin' is creatin' disease. I'm not the least bit afraid of a mouse!' Phil laughed, adding, "Picked him up and took him right outside."

Phil said that his main job as a young fellow was caddying at the golf links, "out at Sankaty and Nantucket links—there used to be an 18-holer way out on Cliff Road." I asked if he got to keep his pay, and he said, "Oh yes. We kept it. I was brought up by my Aunt Madeline Norcross, who lived on the corner of York and Orange. She took in laundry, and she made a barrel of money! Imagine washing a white shirt and doin' it all up, starchin' it, ironin' it…for 15 or 20 cents. She worked night and day." How did it happen that he'd gone from his parents' home to live with an aunt and uncle? "Well," he said, "my mother and father divorced, and neither one wanted us kids…there were three of us. So I wound up with Aunt Madeline, and my brother, Robert Swain Grant, wound up with Nancy Grant Adams—she was the head of the Historical Association at one time. My sister went to my grandmother Tracy up on 28 Milk Street, but she was getting older and it was too much for her, so Betty came to live in Uncle Ed's house. Yes, it was a hard thing to happen to young children…but we had thick hides."

Phil in Florida, dressed in his Navy duds, just before he went overseas.

THE BEST WATERING HOLE ON THE ISLAND

Phil graduated from Nantucket High School with 35 other young people. "That was considered a pretty good figure…and I think over half of us are still alive. After high school, I went fishin'. Twenty years of it. We went mostly to Georges Banks, and made pretty darn good money. Gosh, I can remember [laughing]—we'd come in and the next day, the skipper would come down with all the paychecks, and we'd go to the Spa and have a beer. There were always ten or twelve of the old bums hanging around, you know, just waiting for us to come in with our money. A beer only cost 25 cents, but you never got out of there for less than a five-dollar bill! But we didn't mind…we were doin' well. Those fellows, the clerks in the stores, were only gettin' $12 a week, for Lord's sakes, and we were making fabulous money. Really and truly, all jokin' aside—they say fishermen are all a bunch of bums, but we weren't—we didn't believe in alcohol and salt water mixin', so we never carried it with us. But," he chortled, "after five or six days offshore, we could get drunk on one bottle of beer! You'd go home talkin' to yourself. The Spa was a great old place. Two brothers, George and John Anastos, started it. When I was 12 or 13, they had an ice cream parlor and a fruit stand right where the Spa was…I guess it's some kind of an art place now. That was a fun place to go."

We spoke of the restaurants of yesteryear, and Phil said he liked to go to the Skipper when it was run by Bill Beers, for the clam chowder, and he'd go to the Opera House every now and then, but as for meals, he said, "Well, you see, I have a first-rate cook at home, and I can't find any restaurant that can come close to it, so I'm very happily fed and well taken care of at home. Annie's a great cook."

How did Phil meet this great cook? He said, "Annie's maiden name was Grande ["Grandi"], Italian…and 'course mine bein' Grant, she didn't have to change too much. In fact, she inherited the family silverware because of the G! How did we meet? Well, her sister was working here as a registered nurse at the Nantucket Cottage Hospital when it was still up on West Chester Street. Her husband, John Meilbye, was in the Coast Guard down here. Well, I finished a fishing trip one day and went into the Spa around two in the afternoon, and Old John Anastos was saying, 'Johnnie had a baby!' Now, Johnnie's wife had the baby up in Chelsea, and I said, 'Johnnie, aren't you goin' up to see your newborn baby?' and he says, 'I haven't got liberty.' Well, I says, 'That's easily taken care of…' The Nesbitt Inn was Coast Guard headquarters at the time, and I told him to go to the commanding officer and tell him he'd just had a baby and would like to go home for 24 or 48 hours. He did, and it was OK, but he came back and said he was broke. So I gave him a ten-dollar bill…'course he traveled on the boat free, and the railroad from Woods Hole to Boston was free for servicemen, and so I said 'Johnnie, when you get up there, you go and buy a pair of baby shoes and you'll have a present for your new son.' He says, 'Goddammit, Phil Grant, if you ever come up to Boston, I'm gonna introduce you to my sister-in-law. And if you meet her, you'll marry her!' Well, truer words were never spoken. I went up there when I was going to enlist in the Navy and met Annie, and we had a couple of dates. I didn't have to enlist; all fishermen were necessary food producers, but I figgered if I didn't, some poor married guy with two or three kids would have to go. That was December of '42. So all the time I was overseas we wrote letters. When I got out in '46, it took us five days and nights comin' across country on a cattle car, as they called it…these cars all rigged up for servicemen…they treated us very well…but we stopped at every siding. We were s'posed to get off at South Station, but at the last minute the news was passed out that we were going to North Station. They announced it over the speaker system at South Station…so golly, we got off and I'm walkin' out there wonderin' what happened, and all of a sudden, here comes Annie rushin' across with her girlfriend! She'd come to meet me! I got out on April 6, 1946, and we were married in May. And came right back to the island. She hated it at first, and every time I'd go out fishing, she'd take Northeast Airlines and go back to Boston. But she loves it now…wouldn't trade it for anything!"

Phil recalled the house at 55 Cliff Road where he and Annie lived for 40-odd years, raising their two daughters, Ellen and Nancy. (Nancy married Richard Ryder and lives on the island; Ellen lives in Rochester, NY, where she's a counselor for addicts.) He remembers young Deborah and Ann Beinecke coming over to watch TV with his daughters because they didn't have a set. They also got measured along with the Grant girls on the door casing. Ultimately, that house was sold and the Grants moved to what Annie feared was "the middle of nowhere, out near the golf course," but she loves it there now.

COMING HOME TO START A FISHMARKET

During World War II, Phil Grant was mostly in the South Pacific. Head of a boat division, 24 landing barges, he helped establish the first beachhead in Leyte, then went on into the Coral Sea, then Okinawa. "I turned down a commission in the Navy," he said. "Didn't want any part of that…go to school for three months…and 'course I had the jump on them, because I'd been to sea all this time, and I knew all the Morse codes and international codes and all that stuff. And then," he added, "we went on up to Japan. In fact, my daughter says that's why I'm baldheaded, because we took one of the landing craft and went up the river from the sea to Kure, south of Hiroshima; it had been the Annapolis of Japan, where all the big ships were. Our planes came in and dropped their bombs and ruined that place. We made a beachhead there and then took a landing barge and went up the river to Hiroshima; this was only about a month and a half after the bomb was dropped. Everything was in complete ruin—it was quite a sight. So Nancy swears that I got some radioactivity, because it was too soon after the A-bomb. I don't know if that's true…well, wait a minute—I'm the first baldheaded Grant—everybody else died with a head of hair!" he laughed.

I wondered when Phil had stopped fishing. "In 1952," he said, "I bought a 40-foot lobster smack from old Cap'n Arthur McCleave, and of course a shanty went with it, so I got the bright idea to open a fishmarket. Well, I tell you, it was quite successful. I thought I could go out and catch some flounders and just come in and sell 'em, but it didn't work that way. Anyway, I ran that business for fifteen years, till Bud Beinecke changed everything. I was on Island Service Whoff, where the art colony is now. You know the Angler's Club? I designed that building. Bud says, 'Phil, what would you do if you stayed right here?' I took out a sheet of fish-wrappin' paper, and I drew it right out for him. 'Beautiful,' he says, 'I'll take it up to my architect. I like that.' Anyway, after fifteen successful years, the fishmarket had to close." He chuckled: "Ran the Miller Brothers' fishmarket right out of business. They had a big sign that said, 'If It Swims, We Have It.' Great big 8-foot sign. Somebody printed in chalk underneath it, 'If It Smells, We've Had It Too Long!' Frank Miller, oh, he was mad! After the fishmarket closed, I went carpenterin'. I'd worked in the wintertime for Dick Corkish, a local contractor, so I had a pretty good base there, and I knew how to handle tools anyway through Coffin School, which had been mandatory from the eighth grade through high school…so I was pretty handy with tools."

What does this man who says his favorite place on the island is "Prob'ly home!" do nowadays? Well, once in a while he goes out Cisco way and watches the sunsets. And every Monday, Wednesday, and Friday he golfs with Paul Smith, Tony Mello, and Wes Simmons. And he says Annie's not a golf widow—"She took it up twenty years ago and is still going at it." He's a pretty happy man, and it seems he's made all the right choices in life. Any regrets? "No, he said, "no, because if I had it to do all over again, I'd do the same things."

JUST A COUPLE MORE STORIES…

Phil told me about how Rip (Ripley) Nelson ("his wife Barbara is still sharp as a razor!") dreamed up the idea of the Park and Recreation Commission, and was abetted by Phil, Paul Morris, Charlie Swain, and Phil Murray; they had their first brainstorming sessions at the Nelsons' dining room table. Then, cruising through Volume One of *Nantucket Voices*, Phil recognized everyone in the pictures, but when we came to an old NHA photo of the Bon Ton Fishmarket on Easy Street, he stopped and laughed heartily. "That fishmarket was quite famous. They sold prob'ly 25 dozen eggs a day—used to sell eggs like the devil! And they only had three chickens and a rooster! Nobody could figure it out. Got away with it for quite a few years. Railway Express was delivering them in by the case all that time, and for a long time people thought the eggs were all from his chickens!"

He came to the H. Marshall Gardiner photo of Franklin Delano Roosevelt on his yacht Amberjack, and laughed again. "Got a little story about that visit. Old George Grant, my grandfather, was invited aboard for lunch, bein' the curator of the Whalin' Museum…but he wasn't gonna go emptyhanded, so he had a carving of a whale, one that's cut in, with the blubber all the way around and showing how they cut the head casing to get the spermaceti, and he wrapped it up and had it under his arm. And 'course there were guards all around, and they took it away from him. After they unwrapped it and found out it was OK, he finally took it aboard to give FDR.

"Oh, another story. My grandfather, old George, had eighteen years of service out the Surfside Lifesaving Station, and the men used to take turns cooking. The boys were complainin'—see, they were allowed 89 cents a day food allowance, and their pay was a dollar a day—wasn't much, $30 a month plus the 89 cents a day for food. Well, the Skipper's wife kept comin' in and helpin' herself…she'd bend over and take a big scoop out of the butter firkin, and she had some bacon and eggs, and all this stuff. The guys were steamed up about it, and Old George says, 'Well, by God, when it comes my turn to cook, she won't get away with it!' He went into the kitchen one day and there she was, helpin' herself to the butter out of the butter tub, and she had some stuff on the counter. He says, 'Madam! What do you think you're doin'?' She says, 'I'm getting some butter and eggs…' He says, 'Put that down and get the hell out of my kitchen!' Well, he got court-martialed for being disrespectful to the Skipper's wife. And he had three guys who were going to speak up for him, but they didn't—they were afraid they'd lose their dollar-a-day job. On the day of the trial he was goin' down Main Street to the court, and the Cap'n of the Lifesaving Station, I won't mention his name, was comin' up the street, and he says, 'Good Morning, Grant.' George says, 'Good morning.' The Captain says, 'Grant, my name's got a handle on it' (meanin' 'Captain'), and the old boy turned around and said, 'Yes, and so's a pisspot!'" Phil laughed, saying, "This is the gospel truth!"

Now it was indeed time to stop…even though I could have listened to this cheery-spirited man's stories for hours.

Left to right—(1) A younger Phil. (2) Phil Grant golfs three times a week, which keeps him fit and trim. (3) Phil and his wife Annie.

326

When Nantucket Had Dairy Farms

Richard Brooks, 2003

*I*magine a time when there were very few houses down West Chester Street and cows were regularly driven to pasture along that road. So many older islanders have mentioned "Dickie" Brooks and his son Gene delivering milk from their dairy farm in that area that interviewing Richard Brooks, grandson of the founder of that farm and son of Eugene, seemed a must. And he had some good stories of the Nantucket of yesteryear.

We met in Richard and Susan's home, built right where the old farm was—and testament to the cow-enriched soil there were Susan's spectacular flower gardens. "This house is where the farm was, and where the cows were grazed," said Richard. "The old farmhouse and the barn which my grandfather built in 1909 were at the corner of North Liberty and West Chester. The farmhouse is still there.

"I was born in 1942," he continued. "When my grandfather, Richard Anderson Brooks, passed away, my father took it over. They leased the lot on the property west of here and grazed the cows on it. Dad met my mother, who was living just up the street, while driving the cows from the farm up West Chester. Mother was from New Bedford; she had moved here when she was thirteen to live with her sister, who was nine years older and married to a state trooper here. Her mother had died and her stepmother wasn't nice to her, so that's how she ended up here. It's interesting that I am the only son of only sons for nearly 200 years. My father was an only son, my grandfather was an only son, his father too, and so on. Just one boy in all that time, no girls. Susan and I have two girls and a boy, and my son has two boys, so we broke the string, and the name lives on.

"My father was a likeable man. He died just a few years ago, at 85. And he lived in the little house over here. Actually, Phil Bartlett, of Bartlett's Farm, took the old farmhouse that Dad had built in 1931 when the property sold; it's renovated now and it's still a farmhouse out at Bartlett Farm. And just before you get to Cisco Beach on the left-hand side, there's a big barn, and half of that—you can see where the split is—was our barn from West Chester Street. So that lives on too in another place.

"My father's family on the Brooks side goes back to the early 1700s. The Brooks who came over had been in Ireland with the British, and fell in love and married an Irish Catholic girl. The Irish wouldn't accept them, nor would the Catholics or Protestants, so they came to this country, and that's how the Brooks family arrived here. My great-grandfather on the Brooks side was a ship's chandler and provisioner on South Street in Philadelphia, and they supplied the whaling ships. His family lived here on Nantucket, and he would come up for two weeks at a time, then go back and work for a month. So the Brooks side of the family has been here since the early 1700s.

ONE BUCK & NOT EVEN A BEAVER HAT

"My grandmother found that we go back several ways to the original settlers, through the Bunkers and from Tristram Coffin in three separate ways: the Gardners, the Pinkhams, and the Macys. When I had a title search done at one point, I found that Eugene Clisby, her father, received one dollar from his father, so that whenever you see these maps showing all the Coffin or Macy land, we're not there…we were completely excluded from that by virtue of the fact that we inherited one dollar coming down on that side. We only got a buck out of the whole deal!

"My dad went to Academy Hill School, and I did too, through the eighth grade. I did my last four years where the 'new' high school is now. And my children went to Academy Hill too for a few years when it was an elementary school. My schooldays were happy; my parents kept a pretty tight rein on me, being the only child…they probably worried more than the parents who had three or four kids running around. But life was good—I walked to school, walked home or to my grandmother's for lunch and back again in the afternoon. The farm and cows were sold in 1948, when I was six, so I can remember the farm. That's when pasteurization first came in; the small farmers had no way of pasteurizing their milk, and so they were basically put out of business. A while later, a co-op dairy was formed, but by then Dad had sold the cows. He sold the barn about a year later—that's the one you can see out on Hummock Pond Road."

Had it broken his father's heart to sell the family dairy farm? Richard said, "Actually, I don't think it did. Farming is a seven-day-a-week job, especially when you've got cows. We supplied the north of Main Street area with milk, so we had a much bigger business in the summer because most of the summer people lived up on the Cliff and on the north side of town. In the winter, things quieted down. It's interesting how they did things in those days. A lot of the help was part-time, because you had to milk the cows in the morning and then again in the evening. And it was always a rush in the morning because you had to milk, then bottle the milk, get it on the truck, and deliver it. So they had a couple of part-timers who came in and milked at 4:00 in the morning and then, as pay, they had a piece of land here on West Chester Street that they could grow vegetables on, which they sold to the Breakers Hotel and the Point Breeze. So there was this trading kind of thing that went on, it wasn't a cash-type transaction. And it worked."

Richard said his Grandpa always used a horse and wagon for deliveries. He chuckled: "He never did get a driver's license. But my dad said he was always telling him how to drive the car! They went mechanized with a truck in maybe 1936 or '37, for the last ten years; before that they did everything with a workhorse."

A Character with Character

What did Eugene Brooks do after he'd sold the business? "Well, I'd never spent much time with my

Left—Richard Brooks at about four with his grandmother, Mary Clisby Brooks, who Richard says was always dressed elegantly. Her father was the keeper of the Surfside Lifesaving Station for thirty years. Right—Young Richard with his Easter basket in front of the farmhouse his father Eugene built in 1931. The truck in back is the milktruck; the pictures looks eastward toward North Liberty. Note: No trees or houses!

dad when we had the farm, because he was up in the morning at 4 and working all day, and the interesting thing is I remember the times after, because he always got a day off then. We'd go on picnics, hike out to Eel Point and Ram Pasture, go pond fishing…We didn't go surf fishing, because Dad couldn't swim—lived on Nantucket and couldn't swim! He'd visit his grandmother in Surfside as a boy; it would take about 40 minutes to get there with a horse and buggy, and he told a story of sitting on the beach at Surfside and seeing sharks swimming right along the edge of the breakers when they came in…so I don't think he really wanted to learn how to swim.

"Life was a whole lot kinder then, although I didn't realize at the time that it was a tough life being a farmer. After the farm was sold, my father worked at Hub, which was called Roger's at the time, and then he got into carpentry. He worked at that for a good number of years until he had lung surgery, and then he went to work at Hardy's, because at 58 he couldn't keep up the pace as a carpenter. He worked there till just four years before he died; at the end he was just going in at lunchtime. Ellen Nora Toombs tells a story of my dad at about 78…she went into Hardy's and he was walking along and talking to himself, and she said, 'Gene, you're talking to yourself!' and he said, 'Well, you've gotta talk to *somebody* intelligent now and then!' He was a character. And he had character, too, as Tom Richard said at his funeral. My mother passed away at age 56 from pneumonia. Was the picture of health, got pneumonia, and died. I was grown by that time, so she spent a number of very happy years with my children."

What happened to the cows? "Dad sold them; he was in his 30s then, seven years older than my mother, so he was about 31 when I was born, and 38 or 39 when he sold the cows. They were sold to an auctioneering firm that came and got them, put them on the ferry, took them to New Bedford, auctioned them off, and then four days later the whole Nantucket herd was condemned for tuberculosis. The ink was barely dry on the check to my dad…but cashed. He'd had no idea…no one did. And they had to chase that whole herd down and destroy them—some of them had to be infected, so, as they did in those days, they destroyed them all, couldn't take the chance. And every cow on Nantucket had to be destroyed, too."

Were there any "pet" cows young Richard especially loved? He answered, "I wouldn't call them pets…probably they had names, but I don't recall them. But as they were poking along the road, my grandfather, I'm told, had some names for them. He'd come along the road, swearing at the cows, telling them to get going, and then there'd be a lady standing on the side of the road, and he'd tip his hat and continue on, swearing at the cows. They had to be driven out of the barn and into the pasture here and farther up West Chester Street. There weren't many houses around, and not many people, either…and certainly not many cars.

"We also had 250 Rhode Island Reds on the farm, besides the 25 cows. I had to go out and get the eggs. I hated having chickens, because they weren't always totally confined, and they made such a mess of the grounds…so you didn't go barefoot in the yard, I can tell you! We also had 25 cats to control the rats, because of the grain and hay. You had to have cats…and we didn't feed them because they were better ratters if you didn't. So they were probably one or two notches just south of being wild. They weren't very friendly, although every now and then there'd be a nice one. I can remember a big yellow cat named Sandy that I would sneak into the house every chance I got…and even dress him up."

GOATS, BUTTER, & GUNS

Richard chuckled again. "Summer people used to have their own goats when they came to

Nantucket…and we had an upstairs loft that we kept hay in, but we'd keep those goats over the winter for the summer people. I can still remember that as a kid I was always told, 'don't ever go up that ladder, because the goats up there will ram you!' Well, you tell a kid 'don't go up that ladder,' and of course that's just what he wants to do. So we'd sneak up and stick our heads up the hole the ladder went through…and there was one goat up there that would come charging over and ram right into the side of the building to scare us out of there!

"I'm told that my grandfather and Willard Marden and two or three other old Nantucket men used to buy bits of land and trade it among themselves; it was like a little Monopoly game. But this was when land sold for ridiculously small amounts—$200, $500, for a plot of land. Maxie Chase and Charlie Thurston swapped their farms…and my dad leased land from Charlie Thurston for his cows. They would trade these parcels of land like they were Monopoly pieces.

"Since those days," Richard reminisced, "a lot of houses have sprung up around us here…but you know, it doesn't bother me. Everything changes…it would be nice if things could stay the same; even so, those were hard times. I can remember my dad being unemployed one whole winter during the recession after the Korean War. But my grandmother, who had managed to save quite a bit of money over the years with the farm, made sure that little Dickie (me) had real butter, not margarine…she'd deliver my butter and announce to my parents that if they wanted butter, they had to buy it, otherwise they had to eat margarine—she wasn't buying butter for them. No grandchild of hers was going without real butter, in spite of the hard times. She was a very stern woman. This was Mary Brooks, Mary Clisby Brooks.

"Nantucket is a lot more prosperous today, but those were good days, happy days. I have the old logbook of the farm, and during the Depression, in the late '20s and early '30s, there were notes in the account, 'Delivered milk to Mr. So and So…haven't been paid for six months…small children, he'll make it good someday.' And there was this taking care of each other that went on then. And they were just going to throw the milk away—they needed the 25 or 26 cows for their summers, so in the winter, there really was excess."

Richard said he enjoyed pheasant and rabbit hunting as a teenager, and tells a story about Mary Walker, the fabled principal of Nantucket High School. "She was at a convention of principals one time, and the others were talking about the problem of guns in school, and she described her problem with guns, which was that after the boys went hunting, she wanted the guns in the school, not left in the cars, to avoid potential accidents. So we had to turn our guns in at the principal's office, and couldn't pick them up until after school. And that was just the opposite of many other schools!

"On the Clisby side, my great-grandfather's brother was a whaler. He died in a Nantucket sleighride off Iceland, and in his deathbed will, he left his whaling camp to his brother Eugene, and left a little Eskimo village carved of ivory to his other brother to use during his lifetime; he'd bought it when he was whaling in the Aleutians. The brother he left it to was an artist—we have a couple of his paintings—and he sold it to the Smithsonian so he could buy canvas, brushes, and probably a bottle of whiskey…and other things he needed to survive as an artist in 'Sconset. I'm told it's in storage now at the Smithsonian. My grandmother told me all that, and I don't think she would have made it up. You know, the U.S. Navy in the early days collected data from many whaling captains and made charts of the world, and they used a lot of his charts on the South Pacific from his whaling days there. I guess he was a methodical man and kept good records. After all, you were on a ship for maybe two years at a time, only making landfall when you needed water and food. So you kept yourself busy making charts, baskets, scrimshaw, sailor's valentines, and so on. Now, my grandfather Clisby was the keeper of the Surfside Lifesaving Station for about thirty years…but that's a story for another time."

SUMMER JOBS, MEETING SUSAN, & COMING HOME

Richard Brooks recalled his first job as a teenager. "I caddied at Tupancy's Golf Course out on Cliff Road for a number of years." I asked him how he spelled the name of the golf course, which elicited other Nantucket names spelled in several different ways, and he said, "Well, the Bunkers are my ancestors, and 'Bunker' really came from the French Huguenot, 'Boncoeur'…and later, because they didn't want to be French, they changed it to 'Bunker.' My next job," he went on, "was pumping gas at Al Silva's Garage down on Brant Point for a couple of summers. Then I worked in the Atheneum stocking books for a summer, and I worked at Murray's Toggery Shop all during high school and college. I went to Bentley College, where I majored in public accounting, but realized during my summers back at Murray's that I liked selling more than I liked counting beans. When I got out of college, I was number one on the draft list, so I volunteered and went to the Infantry OCS at Fort Benning, became an officer, spent four years in the Army. Susan and I married, and I got sent to Alaska, and I don't know if they lost my records or what, but I sat there in Alaska for the whole time. We loved Alaska, might have stayed there if we hadn't had family down here.

"How did I meet Susan? We met when I was at a college friend's home in Barrington, RI, for a weekend. His girlfriend was a friend of Susan's—they were seniors in high school, and were putting on a play… Susan was in the chorus line, and I asked, 'Who's that third girl from the right?' and he said, 'Oh, that's Susan Greenslade.' A little later, when we were at Howard Johnson's getting sodas, Susan was there, and she said, 'Who's that guy with Fred?' And that's how we met…and five years later we were married."

After Alaska, the couple came home to Nantucket, where Richard worked for Metropolitan Life until early in 1980, when he started his own independent agency. Susan eventually returned to college to get her BA, so the family moved Off, but Richard commuted back and forth. "Susan was in Andover with the kids and going to school part time, and I'd go back to Andover on Friday and be with the family on weekends and then come back to Nantucket. After about a year of doing that, I moved the office to Boston and came to Nantucket every other week. We did that for about ten years. When my youngest was leaving the nest, I asked Susan, 'Where do you want to live? I'm kind of tired of this commuting thing.' And she said, 'Might be fun to live in Boston for a couple of years…' I said, 'Well, if I died tomorrow, where would you want to be?' Without a moment's hesitation, she said, 'Nantucket.' So I said, 'Let's go back.' We did, built this house, and here we are.

"Some interesting things have happened over the years. My mother's sister Grace was the one who took Madaket Millie in when she had to leave her house. I always spent a lot of time as a child in Madaket at Aunt Grace's house, right on the water…one side was the surf and the other was Madaket Harbor. I will always remember the hot August day that a bunch of kids had a tractor inner tube with some meshing inside it; I was floating around and vaguely heard someone yelling *'SHARK!'* I was a little slow on the uptake, daydreaming, and everyone yelled, *'Stay there! Stay there!'* The shark came between the inner tube and shore and circled the inner tube coming back around, and with that my mother ran out into the water, snatched me off the tube, and took me back to shore before the shark came back by again. Somebody said, 'We should get Millie—she'll take care of this.' So Millie went out in this old beat-up skiff with a pitchfork. The shark had apparently been injured, hit by a boat or something, which was why it was in close to shore hunting. She took care of the shark with a pitchfork, and then rode it back into the Crick and hung it next to her house.

"I had a wonderful childhood, spent a lot of time in Madaket with my aunt and my mother…but my mother also did a lot of work on the farm. They had bottles to wash and sterilize every day." He laughed. "Once I can remember getting all dressed up to go to Sunday School, and my mother took me down to the barn to say goodbye to my father. All four of the men were milking, and when I came in the door, they all had it planned—they all turned and squirted me. Absolutely soaked my Sunday-best clothes. My mother was so mad! After that she never took me in to say goodbye.

"Oh yes, I have good memories…I think your memories are as good as your parents. Parenting is a tough job, and my mom put time into it, and once he sold the farm my dad did too."

Left—Richard Anderson Brooks at left, with friend, in front of the farmhouse he built in 1909. The pictures looks toward Sunset Hill. Above—This is the workhorse that the Brooks Dairy Farm used until the late 1930s. He's in front of the original farmhouse, which still exists at the corner of West Chester and North Liberty.

334

Teaching Students
English and "Couth"
Mary Pendlebury Walker, 2003

$\mathcal{M}$ary Pendlebury Walker, at nearly 97 when we met in October of 2003, stood very straight; bright and lively eyes sparkled behind her spectacles; her hair white and wavy, she really looked remarkable for her years. She was dressed carefully and tastefully, everything coordinated, from her glistening blue earrings to her shoes. All her very witty, erudite, correctly spoken words were uttered clearly, as befits her training as an elocutionist; as well, she accompanied her stories with dramatic gestures and facial expressions (for example, sliding her eyes mischievously to the side; a look of mock surprise; a flourish of the arm). She sometimes paused as if reaching for something in her very full memory, and after such a pause, related another story, complete with expressions and gestures, with much gusto and enjoyment. Mrs. Walker remains a very spirited woman, and it quickly becomes clear why she is respected and loved by generations of Nantucket students.

We sat in the kitchen; on the nearby radiator was a small box comfortably filled by a friendly tiger cat which did that "thing" of cats, listening attentively to the conversation while maintaining a dignity, energy, and potency that seemed to mirror that possessed by Mary P. Walker. During the interview, various people entered and left the room: her nephew, Tom Bauer, on one of his frequent visits to the island, brought her some homemade pumpkin soup; Dane, her caregiver, bustled about the kitchen; son Stephen, tall and white-bearded, passed through a few times, as did his wife, Joan. The household obviously centers on Mary P. Walker, the gracious but undisputed lady of the manse.

FROM ENGLAND TO NEW ENGLAND

Mary Pendlebury was born in England. When she was about eight, she and her parents came to the United States, settling eventually in New Bedford. The family had lived near Manchester, England, and a major depression in the textile industry there created a major exodus from that city. According to her oldest son, Dr. David Walker, "There was quite an English community in south New Bedford, and the residents even had their own sports teams and a chapter of the Daughters of the British Empire. My grandfather worked for one of the textile mills there which flourished after whaling had died, harnessing the water power from the Acushnet River."

Attending school in New Bedford, Mary Pendlebury became a citizen in 1922, and then went on to Bates College in Maine, from which she graduated in 1929. By that time she and Brooks Walker were serious; he graduated from MIT two years later, and Mary did substitute teaching and settlement-house work. After he graduated in 1931, Brooks Walker thought music might be his career; he played French horn in the Paul Whiteman Orchestra and also played the piano background for silent movies in New Bedford, and as well often accompanied Mary's dramatic readings. Son David said, "He played on ocean liners for a while, but found that while it was lots of fun, you didn't get much money or sleep, so he decided to go to medical school in Kirksville, Missouri; that was the original school for osteopathic medical training. He started a small practice in Eagleville, Missouri, to this day a very rural area, and his office had the only flush toilet in town, so as many patients went there for the bathroom as for osteopathy," he chuckled.

After their marriage in 1934, the couple lived in Padanarum, a village south of New Bedford. Dr. Walker's mother was also a physician, and "a force of nature—strong-minded, verbal, vigorous," said David. "Maybe that's why my father was so quiet," he conjectured. "Grandmother Walker used to visit my mother regularly and rearrange all the furniture, after which Mother would put it all back again." Perhaps that had something to do with Mary's desire to come to Nantucket, where she'd spent the summer of 1928 as a teenager. It was June of 1938 when she announced: "We're going to Nantucket for a vacation." That vacation turned into permanent residence. First, the Walkers rented at 12 Federal Street and ultimately bought their house on Fair Street. When I asked how long she'd lived there, Mrs. Walker replied, "Oh gosh, a very long time. When 12 Federal Street changed hands, we had to find a house, and that was no easy task. I was teaching, and a number of my students' parents had rental places and so forth, so that's how we heard of this house."

DO SOMETHING, MISS PENDLEBURY!

When Mary Pendlebury was accepted at Bates College, she pretty much supported herself by doing her dramatic recitations, which she had started in high school. She said, "I had a wonderful time and got a very good education. My major was English and I 'majored myself' in dramatics. I took part in many plays...Oh! that reminds me of a story. I had a role in a Shakespeare play, can't remember which one, and the boys on the track team had gone to Bowdoin College for some event or other—a lot of them had parts in this play. On the night of the play the theatre was jammed with townspeople and parents and students. Well, eight o'clock came and the boys still weren't there. People began stamping their feet, and Dr. Wright, who was head of the English department, came to me and said, 'You've got to go on, Miss Pendlebury—the team has had a flat tire halfway between Bowdoin and Lewiston, and they won't be here on time! Will you just go on and do something for the audience?' Many of the boys, you see, were in the opening scene, and here they were, stranded on a highway between Bowdoin and Bates. I said, 'But I am not the first one to speak in the play'; however, he insisted, '*Do* something!' So I did...I was supposed to be doing Shakespeare...and I did my version. Here am I, pushed onto the stage, seeing all these people, every seat taken. To tell you the truth, I don't know what I said or did, but I kept the audience entertained, and they even applauded every so often! Finally, the team arrived; they were quickly given robes to cover their track suits...and the play went on, and the audience clapped and clapped.

"The next morning," she continued with a sparkle in her eyes, "I went to my English class, taught by Dr. Wright, and he said, 'As you all know, class, I am an authority on Shakespeare—I have written books, I have visited his home...but last night, frankly, I heard some Shakespeare that I didn't even know existed!' He was referring to my monologue, and was pulling my leg, of course."

But the story didn't end there. Mrs. Walker said, "I went back to Bates for my second reunion, for which the class had made me a representative, so I was sitting on the stage with faculty and department heads and people like that. Dr. Wright stood and said, 'I remember when Miss Pendlebury was a senior and did this monologue...' Everyone recalled that, and there was applause. He went on: 'Once, when she came to try out for a play, I asked her what she did. She eyed me up and down, looked at my socks, and said she didn't realize that Shakespeare men wore socks like that.' More laughter from the audience. I stood up and responded,

Left—Mary Pendlebury's high school graduation photograph, 1925. She went on to study at Bates College in Lewiston, ME. Right—Julia Williams and Mary P. Walker, much-loved teachers at Academy Hill School. Maurice Gibbs said Mrs. Walker scolded him at his graduation, because he was capable of more. Then, at Dr. Walker's funeral years later, she bussed him and said, "Maurice, I never thought I'd be kissing you!" Photo compliments of Maurice Gibbs.

'Well, you know, when I got to your class on Friday morning at 10 o'clock, I always looked to see that your socks matched your tie.' When the audience laughed again, I blurted out, 'Well, I just wanted to know what he had on and what he didn't have on…' Which of course brought more laughter. Oh, my *goodness!* Then someone asked if there'd been anything I'd wanted to do when I was in college, and I said, 'Well, I always wanted to call Dr. Wright 'Eddie.' You know, here was Dr. Wright, a bachelor, and very much in demand[sliding her eyes coyly to the side]! And he said, 'Well, since we're all being frank, I'll tell you what I always wished I could do every Friday morning in my English class…' and he put his arms around me and *kissed* me! *Well!* I thought the ceiling would fall in on me! The people in the audience stamped and clapped and laughed." Asked if she'd ever, in fact, enjoyed a romance with Dr. Wright, Mrs. Walker said, "Oh, no. I recognized that he was eligible, but I was seeing Brooks Walker then. He'd come up to Bates and visit…but I had a Bates man that I liked, too," she added with a twinkle.

Mary Pendlebury and Brooks Walker had both attended New Bedford High, and his mother was chairman of the school committee, so, Mrs. Walker said, "After college, I had a sure job in New Bedford…but I remembered Nantucket, had had a wonderful summer here…I came here while I was a teenager to stay with Nancy Adams, at 17 Fair Street. She rented rooms, and I helped her; we would hurry up with the work, and then go to the beach. She used to say, 'Mary, you know, I've gone to this beach off and on all my life, and I never seemed to meet anyone. Nobody came and sat down with me, but I come with you, and we have lots of friends!' Nancy was married to Tad Adams," Mrs. Walker continued. "She was a Quaker, and a very warm individual; I was very fond of her. I had put on some of my programs for the neighbors that summer—dramatic readings, poetry—so some people already knew me when I started teaching on the island some years later. You see, I was a trained elocutionist, and was accustomed to putting on such programs, and sometimes organizations would have me do programs, entertainment, after their dinner." If you hadn't become an educator, you might have become an actress, I said. Mrs. Walker answered, "Very likely, yes. I didn't sing, couldn't. But my husband, who was an osteopath, was also a talented pianist. If you asked him about a song, he'd say, 'Just sing me a few bars,' and you'd sing a few bars and he'd start vamping, and finally he was playing the whole song. I wasn't musical, but I liked dramatics.

"After I was married," Mrs. Walker continued, "I applied for a job here, and no problem." Her family arrived on the island in mid-1938, and from that day on, Mary Walker became a dominant factor in the school system. She began by teaching English and drama at Nantucket High School, in the Academy Hill building. In 1963, she succeeded Richard Porter as principal; she retired in

In the back are Mary P. and Dr. Brooks Walker; in front from left, Dr. Mary Walker holds grandson David, and Stephen Walker is next to his grandfather, Dr. Robert Walker, holding a somewhat impatient-looking cat in his lap.

the mid-70s. In the Walkers' first years here, the island was a far different place. Her son David told me, "The island had no TV, movies only on Wednesdays and Saturday nights; radio reception was abysmal. You didn't go back and forth to the mainland as people do now. And there were only about 3700 residents. In the '30s, '40s, and into the early '50s, Nantucket was a very isolated, provincial place. And here came my mother—well-traveled, sophisticated, and well-educated, so her range of experience was vast. She became the first female high school principal in New England… Do you know, at her first Boston meeting of school principals, they made her wait outside 'until her husband came.' Then, when they did acknowledge that she was indeed a principal, they made her sit with the nuns."

Many of the people I've interviewed over the last two decades have remembered Mary Walker with great fondness and admiration. Robert F. Mooney, who Mrs. Walker said was a favorite student, said that she was an excellent teacher. She'd told me she especially loved teaching the boys in the industrial arts program, and "Yes, she did help those boys," Mooney said, "and she also set a very good example for the girls; she was always perfectly dressed. When she came down the halls at the Academy Hill School, you'd hear the 'clickety-clickety-click' of her high heels."

My "Shop Boys"

Mary continued relating her memories: "I taught English to the college preparatory people—that was what Mr. Porter deemed—but I held out because I wanted the shop boys, too. I said, 'These are the young men who are going to be running the town of Nantucket, and I want to have a part in their education.' And we just had a fine time. I especially liked teaching the industrial arts boys, because I felt that they hadn't ever been given what they needed. They didn't need to know how many parts of speech there are and so forth; they should have had some of that as they came along in the lower grades. There were other, more practical things they should know. I was very strict with the college people. But I always loved to teach the industrial arts boys. Some of them were the rascals of the town, but no one was doing anything special for them, and no wonder they didn't like school and gave trouble. Nobody wanted them. Well, I did! I talked to them about just everyday life. I taught the girls too, but with them, it was a different approach, and yes, I liked the boys better. They were more receptive. The girls were still a little…withdrawn. But they warmed up. With my shop boys, there was never a curriculum—you were supposed to just give them a general background, and that I guess I tried to accomplish."

She paused, then smiled. "When the college-course girls were studying Shakespeare and we were doing Hamlet, I gave the shop boys the same copy of the play and I paraphrased, so that they were studying Shakespeare, too…it gave them a little edge, I think. I wanted them to have a nodding acquaintance with William Shakespeare, and they all had parts to read out loud. And we used to play games. I'd say, 'We're going to have grammar today.' I'd pass out paper and ask them to write down five adjectives. Blankness. I explained to them that when they said 'It's a hot day,' hot is an adjective, and so forth. 'So,' I told them, 'You write five adjectives—they can be horrible, terrible, beautiful, glorious, glamorous—any one of those, just write them down.' And then we'd play the grammar game. I'd collect and redistribute them so that everyone had a different paper, and then I asked them to write sentences using the adjectives. In one case, for example, I had them use an adjective as if they were speaking at Town Meeting, and so forth. That's the sort of thing I did with them. I made learning interesting for them.

"I taught them how to introduce a speaker, how to accept a gift…and I also taught them how to do a 1-2-3-*KICK!* 1-2-3-*KICK!*" She laughed, as she did all the motions with her hands and eyes. "For one school assembly, I had them wear their mother's skirts and a blouse and a scarf on their heads. And I got shaving curls from Island Lumber, which I gave them and asked them to have their mother attach them with glue or thread to their scarves. So all my shop boys were 'belles of Broadway'! I knew that this was something that Nantucket would remember for a long time! They stood in a long chorus line and sang: 'Why did I ever leave Broadway/To come to a place like this?/I should have stayed in the Follies…/What's life on an island without any gin?/Stay out till 10 and hooh! It's a cardinal sin!/Why did I ever leave Broadway/To come to a place like this?'" She laughed after she'd finished her rendition of this song, and she said, "Oh, I have a lot of those stories."

TEACHING "GRACIOUS LIVING" HABITS

"I had 39 of those shop boys, and there were 40 seats in my classroom on the third floor. One day, the state supervisor came to Nantucket to check on the industrial arts program. He came into my room and took the one empty seat, way up near the back door, so I didn't know he was there. And I was going great guns at the blackboard. I began to talk to the boys about everyday life, and in the process I told them what *table d'hôte* meant, and what *à la carte* meant—I thought that would be close to their stomachs!" she laughed. "I told them when the waiter came and asked which they wanted, they should know the difference. I said, 'If you take *à la carte*, you'll pay extra for every item, but if you take *table d'hôte*, you're going to have the whole dinner at one price—that's what you must remember.' I told them that when they took a girl out, they should be properly dressed…and I even told them where to go after they had taken their girls out to dinner. They were all boys who had cars, rickety old jalopies. I said, 'You have a car, so that means you will be wearing either a heavy sweater or preferably a jacket, and a shirt, and a tie.' The response? Groans! [She made a face.] 'Now listen, boys,' I said, 'before you take your girlfriend home, take her to that place out in the pines to do your smooching.' And one boy raised his hand and said, 'Mrs. Walker, how do you know about that place in the pines?' So with a big smile, I said, 'Well, I originally came to Nantucket when I was a teenager, and you'd be surprised what I know!' We just had a fine time in those classes."

Had the young Mary Pendlebury done a little smooching of her own that first summer she stayed on Nantucket? "Oh glory," she said, smiling. "Yes, I think I did. I had somebody who smooched with me; he came down to the island periodically to check that I was all right."

Mary Walker dealt with her students evenhandedly, firmly, and fairly. She knew that most of the boys would be absent on the first day of hunting season, and that after that, they'd frequently go out early in the morning to hunt, coming to school with their guns. And she solved a potential problem: "Well," she said, "I didn't want boys walking around and going to classes with a gun; they could have caused pandemonium. And I didn't think it was safe for them to leave the guns in their cars. So I thought, 'The place for those guns is right in my office.' And that's where they had to leave them till school was over."

I mentioned that more than one Nantucket man I'd interviewed had said that she had taught the boys to be gentlemen. Mary said, "Well now, that sums it up, because that's just what I did, even to the taking of their girlfriends out to that place in the pines to do their smooching. In fact, a number of years ago, when America had just gone into the war, I received a letter from London. I thought it was from someone in my family, but it was from one of my shop boys, and he wrote: 'Thank you, Mrs. Walker, for giving me couth.' I can't just now remember who that was…"

Mrs. Walker paused, remembering, then told me about Richard Porter, who many Nantucketers also recall with great respect. She said, "Mr. Porter was the high school principal and after that the superintendent—and I succeeded him as principal. He was a very quiet gentleman. He lived across the street here, and the school committee used to have meetings in his house, you see, and when I'd get to school in the morning, the teachers would ask, 'Was there another school committee meeting last night?' And I'd say, 'Look, I don't know whether Mr. Porter has one visitor or fifty! I don't keep tabs on him…it's none of my business.' And so they didn't ask me any more." She stopped to chuckle again, and said, "Mr. Porter was wonderful at financial matters, but he was tight as a drum with money…so one day I went down to his office and said, 'Mr. Porter, do you know what would please and surprise everybody? They'd be delighted if some morning when they came in, they'd find a Hershey bar in their boxes.' Mr. Porter was aghast! He said, 'Oh, Mrs. Walker…that costs *money!*' And I said, 'Mr. Porter, you'd be the best superintendent in the whole of New England.' So the next morning, hopefully, I came in. Empty. I poked my head in his office and said, 'Mr. Porter—I thought we were going to get a surprise!' And he said, 'Certainly not! The next morning, the same procedure…and by that time, Mr. Porter knew I was going to pursue it, and that he had to do something about it. It took me, I think, four times before I came in one morning…and there were the Hershey bars! [She smacked her hands together, smiling broadly.] Oh yes, he was parsimonious."

Mary Walker remembered several teachers, including Miss Levins, who taught French, and Jack Shaw, who taught science. "But my favorite," she said, "was my very dear friend Julia Williams. Julia taught typing and shorthand. She was a very bashful person, but we got along just fine. My English classroom adjoined her typing room, and in the back of my room was a door with a window at the top, so we could see into each other's classrooms. Julia had to have all her teeth out, and when she finally got false teeth, they kept slipping out…she'd pass by that window and I would push my thumb up against my top teeth…and she'd

press them back in place!" She threw her head back and laughed heartily, then added, "She and I were very dear friends. One day, she was being interviewed when the state supervisor was visiting, and suddenly, there were these horrible screams erupting from the next room—my classroom—and the man said to her, 'What in the world is that?' Julia said, 'Oh, it's Mrs. Walker—she's just teaching Shakespeare.' Oh yes, we did get very enthusiastic."

Was Mary Walker ever sorry she became a teacher? "Oh, no, never!" she said. "I loved teaching." That was obvious in the way she spoke of the boys and girls she taught…and in the way they still speak of her. It was a genuine privilege to spend time with this woman who meant so much to Nantucket students…whether they were learning adjectives, Shakespeare, or "couth." What a special person.

Dr. Brooks Walker and Mary P. Walker in front of their Fair Street home in 1998.

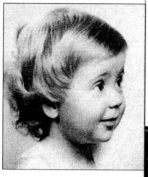

Nantucket: The Only Place She Wants to Be
Lee Rand Burne, 2003

*L*ee Rand Burne began life as Lois Lee Frances McGrady in Rochester, New York. "My father," she said, "was with Eastman Kodak, but my mother had spent much of her life in Fairhaven, and my father was born in Fall River, so they knew and loved this part of the country; they'd come to Nantucket with their parents when they were young. Eastman Kodak hired my father because he was with his father in the cotton industry in Fall River; he sold cotton linters, which are used to make cellulose. He eventually became the head of Kodak's Cellulose Products Sales Division during the early days of plastics. As a child, I lived in the country for a while, and when I was still in grammar school we moved into the city. I was an only child, and spent a great deal of time alone, very happily. I read all the books in the children's section of the library, so the librarian made me a card for the grownups' section. I read all the time now, too, and I've loved the Atheneum from the very beginning."

Lee attended Sacred Heart Academy, then Newton College of the Sacred Heart in Newton, MA, where, not surprisingly, she majored in English Literature. After graduating, she said, "My friends and I thought we should all be in publishing on Beacon Hill, but we looked for our first jobs at the telephone company. They said I was underqualified in mathematics—I really couldn't add fast enough, that's what it was. At one point in my young life, my father had showed me a Christmas card and said, 'Remember this name.' It was Edwin Land, who was the founder of Polaroid Corporation. And eventually, I did get a job with Dr. Land. He said to me, 'I hope you are very proficient in mathematics,' and I smiled. I didn't say a *word*.

TEN HEAVENLY JULYS ON NANTUCKET

"Every summer from the time I was 8 until I was about 16," said Lee, "we would leave Rochester on the last day of June and take a train to Grand Central Station, arriving at about 9 p.m. We'd walk around, and then get on the Cape Codder; its last stop was Woods Hole and the boat. We'd go to sleep, wake up in the morning and go into the dining car to have breakfast, and just as we were finishing, the door to the car would open and the conductor would say, 'WareHAM, Buzzard's BAY, OnSET,' and we'd smell salt air for the first time in a year. At each stop, more salt air would come in…and that began paradise for me for the month of July every year. Of course, before my time, everybody used to get on the Fall River Line, from New York to Nantucket—but for me, it was still very romantic and wonderful to get on a train at night in the middle of New York and wake up to the smell of salt air. And all I thought about all the time for all the rest of the year was Nantucket. It meant the world to me. The first year, we stayed at Mrs. Marks' house on Easton Street and had our meals at the Breakers; the other years we had the Breakers cottage that's still the first one on Willard Street. My family would go to Cliffside every day and I'd lie there and listen to all the people and what they were planning…I loved that. I didn't play with a lot of other children, but I rode my bicycle a lot. Nobody asked me questions at all, I just went to Young's and got my bicycle and then for one month I was on my own. The worst day of the year was the day that I had to return the bicycle.

"When my parents and I came for the month of July, starting in 1942, we put our clothes in trunks and sent them Railway Express. Why, I don't know. You didn't carry your luggage back then, there were porters—but this is what one did. The problem was that it was wartime and the trains were carrying troops, so our clothes were off on a siding somewhere, and we didn't get them until much later. We were wearing our pajama jackets, and we had to keep going down to the boat, wondering if our trunks had come. The Gurleys, on Brant Point, let us borrow clothes, and my mother went to Buttner's and bought me blue and white seersucker shorts to wear for my swimming lessons with Howard Laundry at the Children's Beach. Oh, those swimming lessons! We all would stand in a row, walk into the water and put our faces in; Howard would hold his hand under the water and we had to count how many fingers he'd hold up…

A Brant Point Mirage

"In those days I would take a book and ride my bicycle to Brant Point and sit on a rock, leaning my back up against the lighthouse, and read and read. Sometimes a friend would happen by in a boat, and I'd jump in and ride around. Once in a while, I'd get into town and find that I'd left my shoes on the rock at the lighthouse. One day while I was reading, I looked up, and suddenly, there was a house coming toward me, in between the Jetties! It came closer and closer, and I got on my bike and left, frightened. But I found later that it was the boathouse for the Coast Guard Station, which is still there, and which was being floated from Madaket to Brant Point. But there wasn't anybody else out there, and I was terrified!

"Then I started sailing, and loved that. I hung out at Sterling Yerxa's Boat Shop. David Walker, Dr. and Mary Walker's son, was there, and Carl England, and Flint Ranney…and Ben Perkins, too. He married Shirley Yerxa, and Ben later ran the Madaket Boatyard. There were two Yerxa girls, Betty Jane and Shirley. Shirley was the actress, and performed in a lot of Margaret Fawcett Wilson Barnes' plays. I saw all those plays. But Yerxa's was the center of my life then. Many years later, Ben Perkins was afraid that the people who were taking over the Madaket Boatyard wouldn't care about the old wooden boats the way I did, so he gave me the Flash, which was a Butler catboat, built in Nantucket.

"I was out sailing in about 1949 with a friend, Johnny Loengard, when we saw a black cloud over Shimmo that got bigger and bigger. (I took a picture from the water, which sat on the wall at Yerxa's boat shop for many years.) We left the boat, got on our bicycles, and rode out to Old South Road, and it was all blocked off because the fire was out there. It was terrible. I went back to the Breakers and sat out on an Adirondack chair after dinner, watching the fire across the water, and my parents said that if the wind changed, we'd probably all have to be evacuated. But the wind didn't change, and the town was spared, as we know; however, for days afterwards, embers would flare up and the fire siren would sound and we'd all think it was going to happen again. Scary.

"Back in the 1940s, there was a tall, white-haired gentleman [Billie Fitzgerald, who was sometimes called the Mayor of Nantucket] who used to run the singalongs on Main Street, in front of Mac's Drugstore, now the Nantucket Pharmacy. Everybody would gather around and he'd go into the drug store to borrow two glass toothbrush-holders—remember when toothbrushes came in glass tubes?—and he'd use those as castanets. Well, in 1941, when my father came to Nantucket, he wanted to photograph that singalong. He used to go to H. Marshall Gardiner's store, where the Looms is now—that was Kodak's central dealer here—because he loved to talk to Mrs. Gardiner, and she would put some of his laminated photographs in that wonderful long glass display case. Anyway, he went there and got what he needed, and found a young

Left to right—(1) Lois Lee Frances McGrady, at about two. (2) At about five, Lee with a toy dog. (3) In her early twenties, sitting on piling in front of the fishing vessel *Carl Henry*.

345

LEE RAND BURNE

Filipino man to help him with the flash equipment. The man went up in a tree to trigger the flash at the same time my father was taking the photograph… Well, it went off, and made a big bang, and everybody looked up in the tree and thought that it was a Japanese soldier! They were absolutely sure that the war had come to Nantucket!

"One year, I'd been away for eleven months, and I was arriving on the boat after my long trip from Rochester; that summer I had a boyfriend here. I'd thought about him all winter, so I'd put my hair up in pincurls, with many bobbypins, and had a scarf tied under my chin. As we passed the entrance to the Jetties, I went to the ladies' room of the Nobska, tore off the scarf, took out all the bobbypins; this was so that as I stepped down from the gangplank, my hair would be curly. Well, of course, there was thick fog that day, and by the time I got off the boat, my hair had gone completely straight. And for one year, I had practiced pincurls! Those restrooms were big, and nice, there was a matron…and there were staterooms, which cost all of $2. My father thought it was very clever that he could speak to someone on the crew, and order what my mother called Elephant Ear Sandwiches—overdone thin sliced roast beef—in our stateroom.

Not a Real Opera House?

"During World War II, there were no bars or cocktail lounges on Nantucket whatsoever. However, you could go to the Mad Hatter or to the lawn of the White Elephant, which was owned by Bessie Ludwig at that time. She'd sit in a huge wicker fan chair and feed her dog hors d'oeuvres, and people could sit around on the lawn and have a drink there. Or they could go to someone's house, which certainly was done, for cocktails. The first cocktail lounge opened in July of 1946 after the war, and that was the Opera House. The day it opened, my father, who loved to walk and bicycle around Nantucket, came home and told my mother that an opera house had opened on Nantucket, knowing she'd be thrilled. He said, 'We must all go down and look.' So at 4:30 that afternoon, we walked down and looked in the windows; the walls were covered with opera posters, and it was then that we realized that it was not an opera house, but a restaurant!

"I don't know about the first decade of the Opera House, because I was too young. Later, when I became engaged, my fiancé was working at Worth's Package Store on the corner of Cambridge and South Water Streets. I would fly to Nantucket from Boston on Northeast Airlines—I'd save my quarters so that I could go, believe it or not. And I'd sit on the counter at the package store under those big fluorescent lights until the store closed, and listen to the music coming from the Opera House. In the '60s, when I was older, I'd go all the time, with lots of friends. There were such wonderful people, and the atmosphere was marvelous; it was almost a club, and everybody knew everybody. Dinner was wonderful there.

"I missed seeing Frank Sinatra at the Opera House because I was sitting out on the patio. (Marjorie Benchley and Sinatra were good friends—she always called him Francis—and he'd take Carol Nickerson's cab out to see Marjorie when he was here.) I missed Judy Garland, too, unfortunately. But Harold Gaillard used to love to be asked to sing; he'd starred here in *The Fantasticks* as El Gallo. Oh my, he would sing 'Try to Remember,' with that straw hat he wore in the production. There was a piano that was eventually moved to the corner next to the big sedan chair that was the telephone booth. Wonderful people sang and played there—Carl Norman played the piano there for years. One night, Frank Conroy came in and the two of them played four-hand jazz, and it was a night that's never been equaled. One pianist there always played the theme song from Company every time I came in. It was that sort of thing. I was young and thin and blonde…those were wonderful times. And Gwen Gaillard was the queen of Nantucket. It still thrills me that I'm her friend, because she was just the most amazing person.

"We came here for the month of July every year until my father died, in 1952. So I spent ten Julys here.

And then I was in college. But I always came back to Nantucket, every year, though not always for a long time. I was dating a native Nantucketer and would come here to see him when he was on leave from the Navy. That was in 1954, '55, and we married in 1956. My father had met his father, the chief of police, in 1941, and he thought the chief was grand, and Chief Mooney was very proud of his son, so he introduced my father to his son, Bob. The first year we'd come to Nantucket, when I was eight, my father bribed me with a lemon Coke and took me to the Nantucket Pharmacy to introduce me to this very bright young man working behind the counter as a soda jerk—he was a freckle-faced, nice little boy—but I wasn't very interested then. My father rented Bob's car to drive in the daytime, and in the evening Bob would pick it up. My father would say, 'Got a date tonight?' and Bob would assure him that he had, and I'd think, 'Wow, it must be nice to be so grown up.' And I'd sit in the big Adirondack chairs in front of the Breakers and look out across the water and hear the music coming from the Boathouse, and sing 'Full Moon and Empty Arms' to myself at age 16, and think, 'Oh, if only I were old enough to go to a place like that!'

WHERE'S THE BUTTER?

"When we married in December, 1956, Bob was at Harvard Law School and he was about to become Nantucket's Representative in the General Court. The Law School was afraid that he wouldn't be able to handle the responsibilities of the General Court as well as his studies, but they worked out a schedule and later, Dean Griswold sent him a letter commending him because he not only finished but graduated cum laude. I was working at Polaroid then, and of course we both had very consuming careers. We were coming back and forth all the time. We never knew which refrigerator had the butter in it! They were fascinating times.

"At Polaroid, I became the head of the Photographic Evaluation Department. I was a photographic editor of films, rather than pictures—in other words, I tested the combinations that made the films and decided which would sell. I coordinated Project 60, which was the first pack film, and went to Europe when we introduced our color film, and also to Florida, where we sold the first Polaroid color film in this country. But the best part of the job was knowing Dr. Land, which was an extraordinary experience. I also worked with people like Maxfield Parrish, Jr.—he was a love—and I knew the photographer Ansel Adams well; he was a consultant for the company. When he came, I was sort of his 'babysitter.' That meant going out for dinner and sometimes getting up early to photograph gravestones in the fog! Oh, did we have fun! We had such a wonderful time one evening that I couldn't remember where I'd parked my car on Beacon Hill, and had to hire a cab to drive me around to find it!

"In 1957, my husband and I were invited to an Academy of Arts & Sciences breakfast meeting at the Seacliff Inn. We led a bicycle ride for the members in the early afternoon, out to Surfside—we were photographed with Dr. Paul Dudley White. As I remember, I was barefoot, and the picture, I believe, was in *Life Magazine*. Bob had to go back to town for a meeting, and he left me to lead the group back to Maria Mitchell for tea. The problem was, I didn't know where it was—I guess in all my bicycle-riding around the island as a child I'd never discovered Vestal Street. So there I was, with the National Academy of Arts & Sciences behind me, not really knowing where to take them. But halfway back, trucks with big apparatus on the top came toward us; they were from radio stations. The Russians had sent Sputnik up, and all the people who knew anything about what space was were behind me on their bicycles! So they stopped the group and interviewed everyone, and in the meantime I found out how to get to Maria Mitchell, and finally led them back. The next weekend, I was back at Polaroid; I went in on a Saturday, and all the telephones in the lab were guarded and Dr. Land was in his office in conference with Eisenhower's Scientific Advisory Committee. They were writing a Space Primer for the *Sunday New York Times* which would explain to the American public what Russia had done and what Sputnik was about. On Monday, Dr. Land showed me pages from his desk pad on which they'd all been doodling pictures of what they thought the back side of the moon might look like—because in those days, nobody knew! I wish I had those doodles!

THE SONS & DAUGHTERS OF NANTUCKET

"Back when there were few flights to the mainland, Nantucket people liked to go to the mainland to shop in October. There really weren't many stores in Hyannis then, so they'd take the boat and then go up to Boston, and it was a good time for Boston people who knew Nantucket people to get together. That's how the Sons and Daughters of Nantucket got started. Their motto was that you could be a son or daughter of Nantucket by 'birth, adoption, or affection.' For years, the group had the fall dinner meetings at the Crime Commission Building on Joy Street in Boston, and the dinner was always exactly the same: chicken pot pie. The food for the meetings always came in a white truck that said 'Witham the Caterer of Lynn.' The menus were published in the Nantucket paper, and they got funnier and funnier in retrospect. Here's one from 1960, each item listed separately: 'Fruit Cocktail, Hot Baked Chicken Pie, Creamed Mashed Potato, Green Beans, Cranberry Sauce, Assorted Rolls, Sweet Mixed Pickles, Creamery Butter.' One year, they had 'Wrigley's Chewing Gum' on the menu! That was the new thing, I guess—maybe it was dessert…

"We were always given labels that said 'Hello—my name is…' and then a glass of cranberry juice. In the program, that was called 'The Social Hour.' After the speaker, we'd sing the songs we used to sing on Main Street, like 'Old Oaken Bucket,' and things like that. Somebody somewhere has a great big scrapbook about those meetings…wish I knew where it is now. Later, we moved the meetings to the Harvard Club…and graduated from cranberry-juice cocktails to real ones. When I was president in 1956, Walter Beinecke was our speaker and first introduced his plans for the Marina.

"The speakers and members of the Sons and Daughters were very distinguished people. The vice presidents listed on the 1960 program were Lila Folger, the Hon. Philip Bowker, Frank P. Brooks, Rev. Richard H. Gurley, Col. Laurence E. Bunker, Rev. Clinton T. Macy, Marjorie Folger Drake, George E. O'Neil. The Rev. Gurley had a house at Brant Point; and his family still comes to Nantucket. The group is still going. Eventually, it formed a New York chapter, a Philadelphia chapter, and very often there'd be a summer meeting on the island.

"The 1959 Main Street Fête was the celebration of Nantucket's 300th birthday, quite wonderful. Bob, who was the Representative in the General Court, invited the entire Massachusetts legislature, and much to our horror, they came—with their children and their families and everybody—and what's more, Joe Martin, the Speaker of the House in Washington, came too, and we had to handle it! And we really hadn't prepared for them. We took Speaker

While she was working at Polaroid, Lee (right) visited Amsterdam to introduce color film.

Martin to lunch at some little place on what is now the Strip, had quahog chowder, and there wasn't a quahog in it!

"At one point, a New York crowd used to come every weekend on Northeast Airlines on the Yellow Bird airplane. And they came in hordes, sometimes not knowing where they were! It had become the 'in' thing…after work they'd get on the plane and get here at 9 p.m. They stayed at various rooming houses, and they went to the Jetties every day and stood in a crowd all day on the right side of the boardwalk. There were many very zaftig females, gorgeous; the men seemed to me to be balding at that point…and if you had a date for that evening, you sat down. In the evening they all went to the Ropewalk, which was at the corner of Union and Main, and they mainly stood outside, or sat on the curb. There'd be a group of summer people standing in a ring watching them, and then there'd be a group of the local people watching the summer people watching these people. It was a very socially interesting phenomenon. And then they'd all go back to New York on the Yellow Bird early Monday morning. Once I was in a phone booth at the airport, calling Polaroid to say that it was foggy and I wasn't going to be able to get there until the fog cleared, and there was a young woman having hysterics. She had no idea that she'd been on an island—many of them didn't, because they'd come at night—and she couldn't get back to work. So she had hysterics; they had to take her to the hospital!

BECOMING "MRS. CIVIC"

Holding an absorbing and challenging job, traveling back and forth to Nantucket, watching politics, Lee led a demanding and heady life. Her marriage to Bob Mooney ended, although they have remained good friends, and Lee married a "summer Nantucketer," Carlie Rand, in 1965. "At first we lived in Boston, then came back to Nantucket with our young son, Adam. Both my boys, Adam and Greg, went to kindergarten at the Coffin School and first grade at Academy Hill. Their father was a colonel in the Air Force in the National Guard. In time that marriage ended. It was very painful, and eventually, the boys and I couldn't live here any longer because our rent went from $75 to $125 a month. That's right! Rents were much different then, but that was a big jump! My aunts in Sharon, Connecticut, were going into a nursing home, and their little 1740 house was available to me, so we moved there. Adam is now living in Salisbury, CT, and Greg lives here; he has Island Landscape. He married Cindy Moran, and they have three children—Olivia, Max, and Sam. Adam and his wife Nancy have Samantha and Jack, and the cousins match in age almost perfectly. They are all about as wonderful as anyone could imagine."

In 1977, Lee Rand married John Burne, and also became exceedingly involved in state and community doings. "I worked for Folk Legacy Records for a while," she said. "That was pure unaccompanied folk music. They'd record at night when the tractors wouldn't be noisily going by on Sharon Mountain. It was a wonderful experience. And then I worked as a volunteer for the Sharon Creative Arts Foundation in the foothills of the Berkshire community. (In the meantime we were coming back to Nantucket, always.) Eventually, I decided I was tired of ladies' lunches and that sort of thing. I became a member of the Planning and Zoning Board in Sharon, and then a member of the Regional Planning Agency for the Northwest Corridor of Connecticut, and from there I went into planning with the Area Agency on Aging, the Emergency Medical Service for the 41 towns in the northwest part of the state. Eventually I became chairman of the Regional Planning Association of Connecticut. I also chaired committees of the Health Systems Agency; we approved nursing homes and hospital expansions, and the first MRIs and the first helicopter in Connecticut, things like that. I spent a lot of time in the Capitol building, where I represented regional planning—a marvelous experience—and I learned and learned! And that's what I love doing. I would drive east into the sun in the morning to Hartford and to the capitol building—I don't know how I walked in those heels!—and then I'd get into my car and drive back into the sunset, back up the mountain and down into the valley, and Sharon, and stop on the way to get something for dinner, and then cook dinner.

"But I literally burned out. I'd pick up a different tote bag every day for one of these agencies and go to meetings and meetings and meetings—people called me Mrs. Civic—and I just thought about the island all the time. I wanted to go back to Nantucket and do research of some kind—maybe they'd let me read a ship's log or something. Finally, I couldn't bear to go to another meeting. The boys were out of school by then, so I came here to this house as I could and spent more and more time here until finally, I seemed to be here year-round. The plan was that my husband was going to retire from his job at the bank, and join me. John loved to do little bits of carpentry, and he thought it was wonderful, because jobs here could be finished in a short time. But just after he retired, in 1995, he died of lung cancer.

"I eventually bought the house from Florence Rand, who'd added a kitchen and bathroom—it had originally been a little hermit's shack. Miss Rand taught voice to opera singers out here, because it was quiet and nobody would be bothered. In the wintertime, she lived in New York, but she saw Jane Wallach and Mac Dixon all the time—they all lived here during Nantucket summers. Do you know how Janie 'discovered' Mac Dixon? She put an ad in the paper for someone to walk her dogs, and Mac had been starring in The Emperor's New Clothes, but that was during the Depression, and he needed money very badly, so he walked her dogs, and that's how they became friends. And they eventually came here in the summers and lived with Miss Rand, and finally decided to live here year-round. Anyway, that's where I wanted to stay…and eventually I added to the house.

350

UNDERTAKING A MAMMOTH TASK

"So I came back here and painted in oils for a year—I never had painted before in my life." Why only a year? Lee laughed. "Because Bob Mooney, who was president of the Atheneum then, asked me if I wanted 'the job,' which was to organize all the newspapers at the Atheneum, from 1816 to the present, which was 1989. He showed me the Kynett Room, entirely full of newspapers, and Great Hall, also full of newspapers, and all the closets and the staircases and everything…because not only did the Atheneum have its collection, but the NHA had donated all of its historical newspapers, and there they were, covering every square inch of the Atheneum." It was a mammoth task, but with the help of Chris Tolley, she organized all of Nantucket's historic newspapers. Said Lee, "Chris and I both worked on Old South Wharf—she was at Patina and I was at Barbara Van Winkelen's—and we'd walk out the doors, each with a book, and talk. We discovered our mutual love of books, and I knew that she would be wonderful for this project. So we organized 24,000 newspapers chronologically. We chose the best one for each year, stored them in archival boxes, and eventually worked our way through the first floor and up to the second floor, through the Great Hall and all the newspapers on the stage, and all the ones up the stairs, piles and piles. This was all done through a grant, under the auspices of the Boston Public Library and the American Newspaper Project. The papers went away in huge trucks to Spaulding, a microfilming facility. The master microfilms are in the possession of the BPL. A part of the deal was that if we allowed it to have these, a copy would be made of everything for the Atheneum, and another copy for the historical association of the Inquirer and Mirror."

After that major accomplishment, did Lee Rand Burne get to rest on her laurels? Nope. The proposed renovation of the Atheneum required a feasibility study, and, said Lee, "they got a quote for what it would cost to have a professional coordinate this project, and Grace Grossman said no, she thought Lee Rand Burne could do that. So I established an office and coordinated the building campaign for the Atheneum. I loved doing that—it was organizing—it's what I did for Dr. Land for years!"

STILL THE BEST PLACE TO BE

We swung from one subject to another, and naturally began to talk about the changes on today's Nantucket. Lee sighed, saying, "One thing that's negative, and I feel so sorry about it, is that everybody seems to have a fortress mentality—people seem to need to mark off their property with fences or hedges or walls. You know, even though the earliest Nantucketers talked about parcels, there wasn't a 'parcel mentality' here—everybody was happy together, and it was lovely, and you walked from one place to another without feeling this. I can't bear it—the attitude is that this land is *mine!* and I think it's because people are fearful. And there's an element of greed in it, too. The other thing that bothers me is that there are people here who do not know Nantucket, and make no effort to know it. They want to change it into something they bring from somewhere else. I feel very sad that the Nantucket I knew and loved, the original historic Nantucket, has almost disappeared—you can hardly see it any more except on the little streets in the middle of town…"

Despite her determination to stay out of active politics (though she watches from a distance with keen interest and says, "I am a political animal…very much a Democrat"), and despite the fact that she has "retired" from major projects, Lee Rand Burne still stays busy. She loves her privacy and her little house and reading her seemingly numberless books and cooking for friends. Like many people at a certain point in life, she frets about the future—there are very few, even on wonderful Nantucket, who don't worry about how long health and money will hold out. But her attitude is positive, even ebullient, and she has her network of close friends. She has fun with her life, a real accomplishment.

Proof of her love for this community? When asked if she ever felt a need to get away, if only for a little while, Lee declared: "I never get 'stir-crazy' here—it's the most wonderful place to be. I have loved Nantucket ever since I first came in 1942. It's the only place I want to be…and I am totally and utterly content right now." Then she added, quite fervently, "The best thing about my life is Nantucket."

A 25-year-old Lee, posing in costume at Nantucket's Tricentennial Celebration.

352

Work and Laughter— R$_x$ for a Good Life

Jane Ray Richmond, 2003

On a sunny August day, Jane Ray Richmond and her little friend Ian, a West Highland Terrier, welcomed me with enthusiasm; Ian then settled down on the couch, paws crossed, ears and eyes alert, as if he were preparing to contribute a tale or two. Jane is one of those people who's a native and then some: "I am an 11th-generation Coffin," she said. "My mother was Lelia Williams, and she grew up here and taught at the Coffin School. She married my dad, Earl Ray, who was also a native, in 1924. It's through my mother's side that I get the generations count. My father was a cabinetmaker; he started out as a contractor, and when the war came along he went into the service. He'd been in the Army in World War I when he was about 18, and for World War II he just got in—he was around 41.

"During WWII, he was in the Navy as a drill instructor, which he loved. He taught marching and all that to black soldiers; they were segregating blacks then. They had flying squadrons then that were nothing but black, too…but you never hear about that, and it's a shame. He finally got sent to the Pacific, and told us, 'Before you could put your boots on, you had to sling 'em across the room because of scorpions!' He didn't see any action directly…he was in the SeaBees, and they were building a landing strip on the island of Cebu. When he came back he built a church in Rhode Island that had a rotating altar, so it could serve all denominations. Isn't that a good idea? He was a very interesting man; he loved history and would read and tell you stories about what he read… Oh, I tell you, there was never any trouble finding a subject to discuss at the dinner table with a father like that," Jane laughed.

"My mother didn't work when my brother and I were babies, but she'd trained as a teacher at what they called the Normal School, in Framingham. When the war came along, she was asked by the Coffin School if she'd go back because everybody who was teaching was leaving, so she did. I don't know exactly what year she retired, but she'd gotten to the point where she couldn't stand the girls and their giggles…and she'd say, 'If I have to listen to junior high people any more, I will *fly!*' I said, 'Well, Mother, you could retire, you know…' Mother lived to be almost 80. Dad died from what you don't hear much of any more—he had a melanoma, from being a redhead and being in the south marching and then going to where it was even hotter. I have one brother, and he has given up the island. He moved to Texas about four years ago. Before that he worked for Harry Gordon for years, and then he worked at the airport." Have you ever been tempted to leave the island? I asked. Jane answered, "Not really, no. My first husband died young, and the second fellow I married, Fred Richmond, had a hankering for Florida, so we bought a mobile home there which we kept for five years, and then we suddenly woke up and realized we did not enjoy the drive down, and Boynton Beach was building up a lot…so we stopped going.

The Last of the Best of Nantucket?

"I had an excellent childhood. We had the best, the last of the best of Nantucket in my age group, I think, though I hate to say that. I'm in my seventies—and I'm not ashamed of it! You're right, we're not finished being young yet…though there are times I realize I can't do something physically that I used to…" She chuckled, and admitted that she'd bought her comfy little house with two floors so she'd get the exercise of doing stairs every day.

What had it been like, having her mother as a teacher? Jane said, "It was difficult. She would never call on me. I asked her about it once, and she said, 'I don't want to show favoritism.' But she was very fair. We lived in the wintertime on the corner opposite the Woodbox, 27 Fair Street, and in the summers we went to Madaket—up from the Grieders. We have a cottage which my brother still comes to every summer, on the very top of that hill, right where the boats turn to go out into the channel to get into the harbor…and what a view we have! I go out every summer Sunday and sit on the deck if the weather is permissible, and I say, 'This is God's spot on earth for me.' It's my favorite spot on Nantucket; the view from there is spectacular, and so are the sunsets.

"I think I was a pretty well-behaved child, although I got the window stick a couple of times—you know, the notched stick that holds the windows up? I didn't get it at school, that was at home, in Madaket. I can see it now: my mother's got me by one arm with the stick in the other, and she's trying to whack me with it. She was strict. You didn't do certain things, and that was all there was to it. But you learned. My brother, who's older, used to tell me, 'Do what she tells you and do it her way, because there are only two ways—Lelia's way and the wrong way!' Mother taught all grades, from junior high up, at the Coffin School…her subject was Home Economics. Most people don't realize it, but Home Ec had about 22 associated subjects…it wasn't just cooking and sewing. You had to go over to the Coffin School in junior high, and you also had to take French or Latin to help you decide, when you became a freshman, what way you wanted to go with your courses…college, business, you know. I chose Civic Arts, which was a little bit of everything…and not much of anything," she laughed. "I wanted to stay away from math, which I loathed! I said—and I wish somebody would listen to me—if they would set the multiplication tables to music like the alphabet [she sings "A-B-C-D"], we would learn it in a wink!

EIGHTEEN & INVINCIBLE

"I became a hairdresser. Had my own shop on India Street. I went off to school for that, at Banford Academy in Boston. That was very scary the first week or so, but then I got into it…I loved Boston. Frances Visco (Larrabee) and I went together and shared a room. We took the subway in to school, because it was right on Boylston Street, and it worked out fine. It was a whole school year. And we weren't afraid…of course, when you're 18, you're invincible. It was exciting being on my own, and I liked it. I didn't have a boyfriend during that time…and I ended up marrying the boy down the street anyway! His name was Byron Stewart Mooney, but everybody called him Stewart. His father had come

Left—This is a photo from a 1945 Nantucket High School yearbook. The teacher, Lelia Ray (Jane Ray Richmond's mother), is instructing the girls in Home Ec skills. From left, Lelia Ray, Frances Visco (Larrabee), Marian Davis, Grace Lowell, Jane Ray, and Theresa Davis. Right—Jane Ray in front of her beauty shop at 10 India Street, 1948.

here from Rhode Island to fish. Stewart died in 1966 of cancer. He was just forty, and our two girls were nine and twelve—terrible ages for that to happen. They both live here; I'm very lucky. The oldest is Susan Clay and she works as a dental hygienist for Dr. Roberts, who is my son-in-law. My second daughter, Margaret, is married to Dr. Roberts. She's a school nurse at the moment. He is a good dentist…and I have an awful thing about dentists. You know where the Camera Shop is? My dentist, Dr. Wescott, had his office there, and I can remember climbing those stairs, dreading every moment, every step. I wore braces for three years…I hated going to the dentist!

"When I was growing up," Jane went on, "I was very into Girl Scouts, and we had quite a clique—Carol Powell was a grade ahead of me, but I was in that bunch, and we had a ball. When we were younger we even had Carol Powell's mother [Estelle Pickett Coggins] as a leader. Another leader was Mrs. McKinstry; her husband was the Unitarian minister then. I was also in the choir at the North Church. We had dances every Friday night at Cyrus Peirce School starting in the seventh grade. It was fun, though I have two left feet. Only a few boys had cars in high school. None of us had a lot of money in those days—everybody worked in the summer, soon as they were old enough. We didn't think anything about it, because everybody was the same! And families ate together—there was no television. You did your own amusements. Before high school we played a lot of games like Simon Says, Hide and Go Seek—all those games the kids don't even know about today." At that moment, we were both inspired to sing *ALLY-ALLY-IN-FREE!"*

Jane recalled all sorts of games she used to play in Madaket. "The garage had a dirt floor," she said, "and we used to have a lot of fun picking up stones with our toes in there—got pretty good at it, too. We also played marbles and jacks in there. Some of the kids who played with us were Richard and Robert Wheldon, Joe Swain, Sr., Mary and Ruthie Chapel, and Bertha Manter. Bertha had curly red hair…her father used to run the Island Service Wharf. She and I used to lie out between our garage and the one next door at night, and watch the falling stars in August…didn't have sleeping bags or anything, just slept out all night.

"We spent long summers in Madaket. And Mother didn't drive, either. When we were in Madaket, we were in Madaket, pretty much, unless Dad was around to take us somewhere. Bertha Manter [Arnold] lived two houses over from us, and when we were older, we'd go to town to the movies at the Dreamland sometimes, because her dad was fishing all the time, so she had the car. When my father was in the service, my uncle had to jitney my mother around." Jane had a sudden memory that made her laugh. "Mother used to kid me, saying, 'The minute you're in that back door, you say, *"MOOOOOM!"* Why do you do that?' I'd say, 'I want to know if you're home or not!'"

Jane went on: "Behind our house at Fair Street, where there are now two houses, were five garages which belonged to my folks—they used one and rented the rest—and one day my brother and his cronies and I were throwing stones over the garages and I put one right through the window of the garage door! My father never said a word; my brother gave me the business, though, and I thought, 'Oh gosh, I'm going to have a lesson in learning how to set glass,' which in fact I did many years later, but my father was pretty easygoing. My mother was the disciplinarian…unless you did something big. Then Dad would get into the act. As I said, we always had plenty to do; you did your chores on Saturday, and I went out with these girls who were Girl Scouters…" Jane stopped and laughed. "We were supposed to be pure as anything, and we were pretty good. I think Carol was the wildest one. She talked a big game. I said to another friend once, 'How come she can go on that darn boat and get a ride to Boston every darn time, and I could go 50 million times and never find a free ride to Boston?' My friend said, 'It's because you don't go around and ask everybody you know on the boat if they are going to Boston and could you go with 'em!'"

THE "BRAT SISTER"

How did Jane come to marry Stewart Mooney? She answered with a smile: "He was the boy down the street; I didn't pay any attention to him and he didn't pay any attention to me. I was just the brat sister. So when did she and Stewart "discover" each other romantically? "Well," she said, "a friend had a party and invited the two of us, and it just took off from there…I was 19 or 20 by then, and we married when I was 21. But when we were kids, my brother played with the two Soverino boys and Stewart, and they used to sit in our kitchen and paint models. I can remember the thrill we got when we were having a whippin' snowstorm once and didn't have to go to school; Stewart had brought his little radio and they announced that Nantucket was snowed in, no school, and all that. And of course now they talk about Nantucket all the time, but in those days it was a big thrill!

"My brother learned to knit, and he could use my mother's sewing machine. Once he made a couple of Daniel Boone hats with a tail made out of some fur my mother had from a collar or something." Did the boys go hunting in those days? "Yes, but I never had any desire to go with them. We did shoot, though. And we learned to make bullets, down in Dad's shop. He had a mold and you melted lead and poured that in. Yes, people did hunt for food in those days. The first year Stewart and I were married, we lived on rabbits and pheasants and quahogs…a lot. We tried to fool his mother, who'd come to this country from the north of Ireland when she was sixteen. She would eat pheasant, but didn't want rabbit. We told her it was chicken," Jane chortled, "but she knew…

"My mother did a lot of canning out in Madaket, and we grew all kinds of things. I remember her remarking to my father: 'I'm going to try Chinese cabbage this year.' And she did. One of my favorite things, though, was that when she didn't have any lettuce, she'd pick tiny new leaves of spinach and put them in our sandwiches. We took our lunches to school, and I loved meatloaf sandwiches with spinach instead of lettuce. Mother was big on food value, because she'd studied all that stuff.

LIVING ON FISH LOT #19

"We knew how to make things go a long way then. I learned not to go into Buttner's, because if I saw something and wanted it, I might buy it. And you know something else? We could put our kids in the baby carriage and go downtown and

Jane in the spring of 1951, in Boston Garden.

pay every bill—light company, water company, phone company—think about it. It was so different then. Mother never locked the front door, except at night. We used to rent rooms before she went back to teaching. She rented the whole house in the summer if she could, and we'd go to Madaket, because she learned early on that it was very hard to rent rooms if you had children around. We stayed in Madaket until it got too cold, and take the bus to school. Then we'd move back to town."

When Jane and "the boy down the street" married, they didn't move too far away. "We just went down the road," she said, "to Tattle Court. We bought that house in 1949 with my father's encouragement, and it was just a shell, really, with no wiring, no plumbing, no central chimney. It took us two years to fix up that house—we did it all ourselves except the wiring and the plumbing. At the time, Stewart was house-painting and doing odd jobs like all Nantucketers, who had three or four jobs. My dad would go over every day and do some carpentry work, and he also built the chimney. It was a Macy house, and had been moved from Sherburne in 1717, and the only street that was laid out in what is now town was Fair Street. Then, it was the Fish Lots, and we had Fish Lot #19. Thomas Macy owned all those houses that are in that area now...and Alice Wilson—remember her?—looked her house up and found that where that house sits today had been Thomas Macy's vegetable garden. I used to stand in the yard and try to visualize what it must've looked like when they set our house down. We faced south, as all those houses did, for warmth, they thought. Yes, in those days they moved houses all the time—still do. They took 'em apart, put 'em on wagons, and hauled 'em elsewhere. Once, Anita Stackpole Dougan showed us exactly where the Tattle Court house came from; it had been right by Reed Pond, which is no longer a pond, it's all grown in. Anita did a marvelous search on her family genealogy... She was a lovely person. It was awful to lose her. Now, what was I talking about? Oh, that house on Tattle Court. I lived in that house 52 years. Bought it in 1949 and I moved out in 2001.

"We were married on Memorial Day weekend, because then everybody could come...and I had a pretty good-sized extended family. We got married in the house I was raised in, 27 Fair, where my mother and father got married. My father and I came down the front stairs into the living room, and Stewart and I were married in front of the fireplace. We flew to Boston in the late afternoon for the weekend. We'd put all our money into the house, which we'd worked on for two years—we didn't have any left over for a honeymoon!

"As I said, I had my own hairdressing shop on India Street for five years, where Black-Eyed Susan's is now. After I had my girls, I didn't work for a while, then I worked part-time for Katherine Ellershaw. My mother-in-law and my mother would take care of the girls in the summer, and when Mother went back to school, my sister-in-law and I would shift off and take care of all the children. My husband worked in the Fire Department, did painting on the side, and delivered summonses and things for the Sheriff. Of course he worked shifts. And he dearly loved to fish. The first few years we were married we rented rooms and stayed downstairs at Tattle Court. This was hard with children, so we decided to rent the house for the summer and built our own place in Madaket. We stayed there in the summers, and then we saw each other once in a while, in passing. I finally said, 'This is crazy, it's not good for us or the girls,' so I decided not to work again till they were older. And then Stewart got esophageal cancer. And it was fast...

Getting Along Without Her Math

"After he died, I had to go back to work, but didn't have any patience any longer with doing hairdos...I was angry at the world. Probably a week after he was buried, I went to work at the Beachside Motel, chambermaiding. My mother had rented rooms while I was growing up, so I knew the routine…but there was a sense of urgency all the time now…'Get it done! Get it done!' And I didn't care for that. Then, out of the blue, I went to see Dr. Voorhees about Stewart's papers or something—he'd been wonderful when Stewart was sick—and he asked me if I'd like to work for him, doing bills. I said, 'I'm terrible at math!' And he said, 'Well, you know what 5 and 5 makes, don't you? That's all you need to know.' Because then it was $5 a visit. That was 1966. Five dollars! I worked for him almost twelve years, and loved it. Ruthie Grieder came to work there too, and when Goldie Howe joined us, well, the three of us had a ball! I stopped working when I married Fred Richmond. After I'd been a widow for a few years, I went on the Shenandoah, on a trip…and that's how I met Fred. He passed away several years ago."

So what does this vivacious woman do now that she's retired? She said, "I read…historical novels are my great love, but I read all kinds of things…even cheap novels sometimes," she grinned. "I also needlepoint, though I've had cataracts and all that happy stuff…no more cross-stitching at all because I get buggy-eyed. And I do a little gardening. I have four grandchildren; each daughter has a boy and a girl. My oldest granddaughter just got married this summer…she says, 'I can remember you teaching me to make cookies, and you always had a little bouquet on the kitchen counter.' You know, that kind of memory is important.

"We had some hard times on Nantucket, but it was OK. I'm from a very do-it-yourself family—we Nantucketers always seem to find a way. As children, my brother and I had to do chores; every Saturday we had to go around the floor with a damp cloth on our hands and knees…you didn't go out to play till you'd done all your jobs. And you had to make your bed every day. We didn't get an allowance, we were expected to do these things. I did give my daughters a whole quarter for allowance, to teach them how to value money—you know, so much for the *Weekly Reader*, so much for the church, and so on. My mother didn't approve, but I said, 'I'm not paying them…they are learning about money.' I think the kids today have too much, get away with too much, and that's not good."

Jane Ray Richmond is a real Nantucketer, one who has always worked hard and enjoyed life—and her contentedness shows in her face and in her frequent laughter.

Above—Two 5-year-olds, Jane Ray and Bertha Manter (later Arnold) inspect their toes in Madaket, 1935. Left—Three lifelong chums enjoy a good laugh: from left, Ruthie Grieder, the late Carol Powell, and Jane Ray Richmond.

Bertha's Old Photo Album
Bertha Manter Arnold, 2003

*B*ertha Manter Arnold isn't a talker, so our initial interview was somewhat short...however, when we looked through her childhood photo album, she really opened up, telling delightful stories about every picture. Hence, we have a piece that is mostly composed of old photos and captions.

Bertha said she was born in the old West Chester Hospital, attended school at Academy Hill and took Home Ec classes at the Coffin School, and has lived on Nantucket Island almost all her life. After she graduated from NHS, she went off to Boston to learn how to become a lab technician, came back to the island and got a job, then took a position in Rhode Island, where she soon met Harold Arnold. "We married in 1950, and the agreement was that we'd come back to Nantucket," Bertha said. "He wanted a better job, and luckily, my father offered him one here at Island Service Company—maybe my parents wanted me back home," she said, smiling. "We had three sons, but Harold died within ten years of complications of diabetes. My oldest son, Lloyd, is a carpenter and builder on the island; Bradley lives in Colorado, and Robert, who is hoping to open his own restaurant, lives in Ohio. He started working at the Downyflake during school vacations, doing the baking, and became a chef after going to Johnson & Wales."

Bertha's father, Gilbert, traced his Nantucket roots back to 1733, she said. Her mother was from Nova Scotia, so she has visited that part of the world a lot during her lifetime. In the past, she has worked for the Historical Association and a gift shop; then the Emporium till it closed, and she retired from Murray's not so long ago after working there for about fifteen years.

A somewhat shy woman, Bertha opened up when she showed me the old photo album encapsulating the years of her childhood—mostly the 1930s. So many pictures of a happy, simple family life, complete with pets, a skiff to row around, Girl Scouting activities, exciting overnight train trips to Nova Scotia to visit her Grandma Fleming, a thrilling jaunt to see Tony Sarg's monster on the beach, Madaket games with chum Jane Ray (Richmond)...

Even though the sepia-toned photos are not new and shiny or in color, they all seem to show quite clearly that Bertha's growing-up years were full of smiling, loving friends, grownups, and pets. The young curly-haired, very red-headed Bertha Manter surely had a childhood to be envied, and it shows in her photographs from a somewhat tattered, well-thumbed family album.

Perhaps Bertha Manter's best friend in her Madaket summers was Jane Ray. This photo show them giggling together on the porch. "Don't know why we had our feet in a box," said Bertha, "but we were having great fun, apparently." She was a true redhead, with beautiful curls.

The Bartletts had a teahouse called the Drift Inn, which Bertha Manter Arnold said was "out on Bartlett Farm Road—you could see the ocean from there, because it was on a bluff...but that land's long gone." Bertha's mother, Carrie Fleming Manter, was from Nova Scotia, born in what Bertha called "a little whistle-stop town near Halifax," and when Carrie's sister, Minnie Fleming Rushton, came from there to visit the island, they always made it a point to visit with the Bartletts, old friends. Early 1930s.

Buddy was young Bertha Manter's dog, and had a great personality. Her album even contains pictures of him looking quite dignified, wearing a baseball cap and spectacles. Bertha says that Buddy loved to go for rides in the boat, and stood up in the prow like a ship's figurehead. "He used to go over to the little boatyard, where there was a small bridge over the ditch, and get to the other side of the Crick. Then he'd bark for his taxi—that was me—and I'd have to row over in the skiff and bring him back. If I didn't, he'd just swim."

The Manter family spent happy summers in Madaket, winters in town with Grandma Manter. "My doll's name was Marjorie Ann," said Bertha. "I still have her somewhere. A woman who came to room with my grandmother every summer fixed that doll up for me. It took about size 1 in baby clothes. Marjorie Ann usually stayed in town in the summer, and when my grandmother's friend came to stay, we'd sit in the living room and I'd change Marjorie Ann's clothes and play with her. But sometimes I did take her to Madaket…took her out for a ride in the skiff that day on the Crick." c. 1934.

"This is my father, in back of the Island Service Company, with a big fish he caught," said Bertha Manter Arnold. "He looks pretty proud of it doesn't he?"

Bertha Manter was always surrounded by animals; there are pictures in her album in which she's holding or admiring baby chicks, dogs, kittens. Here she is holding a new puppy; her mother is behind her holding a kitten or two. Bertha had two pet cats she remembers well, Smoky and Boots, and they appear in many photos in her album. She said, "When we had Smoky, we couldn't take him to town with us in the winter, because my grandmother had a canary. So he stayed out in Madaket with one of the neighbors. He didn't seem to mind. We'd go out and visit him once a month at least, and he always seemed glad to see us." Not shown here are two funny photos of a cat: in the first, kitty is peering into a bowl in which Bertha had captured minnows; in the picture following, the cat is looking out at the photographer as if it had just been soundly reprimanded. Bertha said, "She loved to fish out those minnows I caught…and sometimes we'd see her scouting along the Crick, trying to catch some on her own."

This description isn't for the faint of heart, but really, most Nantucketers once knew how to catch, skin, and cook eels, which Bertha says were delicious. Here, Bertha's mother and a friend do the job. How do you skin an eel, anyway? Said Bertha, "First you had to cut its throat, then slit down the middle to take out the intestines, as you would when cleaning a fish. Then you very carefully slit through the spine, just to the skin, and then…just turn the eel inside out. You had to use paper towels or rags so you could hang onto it. And you'd think they were dead, but their nerves still kept them going, and they'd tie knots right around your wrists while they were being skinned! And any eel, if you put it in a pan of water and then sprinkled salt on it, would roll and thrash around like anything. Not alive, just the nerves. Oh yes, I skinned them, too. In the winter my father would spear them through the ice. We usually just chopped them in pieces and then fried them up in a little oil. They don't taste like fish at all—they're good!"

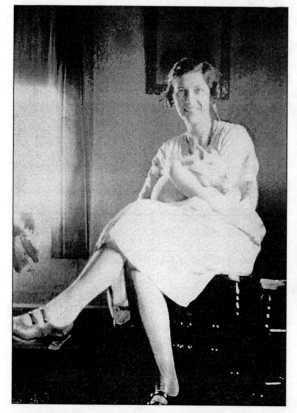

All Nantucket kids…and many parents…got around town on their bicycles. Bertha said, "During the war, the school athletic instructor used to give out points for bicycle riding. I didn't win, but since we lived in Madaket much of the year, I did log quite a few miles. I often rode from Madaket to town, or my friends there would bike out to Madaket."

This is either Bertha's mother, Carrie Fleming Manter, or her aunt, Minnie Fleming Rushton—"They looked a lot alike," said Bertha—holding a pet piglet.

366

Left—Here are two challenges: (1) Are you in this picture somewhere, and/or can you identify any of those many children? (2) Can you spot the boy in the shadows, mining the contents of his nasal passages? (AND, do you know who he is?) Right—When Tony Sarg's "monster" showed up on the beach in 1937, hordes of islanders came to take a look. Here is Bertha with cousins Chester and Robert Barrett in front of the huge creature, not looking too scared. Sarg was a world-famous puppeteer, and it was he who was responsible for the huge floats in the earliest Macy's parades.

Here, Bertha's father, Gilbert, Grandma Manter, Bertha, and her mother, Carrie Fleming Manter, are ready to go on the long road trip to Nova Scotia for a visit. "That trip took a couple of days by car," said Bertha. "I liked the train ride better, because that was overnight, and it was fun. When Grandmother Fleming was alive, my mother and I used to go to Nova Scotia fairly often on the train. You'd leave the island early, then get on the train in Boston about 7:00 at night. Of course, then you had most of the day to hang around in Boston. We'd windowshop, mostly; sometimes we went to the movies at North Station, to kill time. I don't know the make of the car, but I do remember my once had a Willis Knight."

Doesn't everyone over a certain age claim there was much more snow in the winters of their childhood? Well, it just may be true…here's Bertha by the family car on the just-plowed road to Siasconset. She said that snow must have been light, because it didn't last long, but it was probably quite a job to plow it.

Two Natives,
Mother and Son
Margaret & Herbert Crowell, 2003

*I*t all started on a chilly 26th of February, with a visit to Island Home to talk with Margaret Crowell. Later, I interviewed her son, Herbert. Margaret was ready for me, shooing off a teenager offering hot chocolate with "Later! I'm being interviewed!" I pushed her wheelchair down the hall to a sitting area in sight of the harbor, and we began. Asked when she'd first moved into the Academy Hill Apartments, where she'd lived for many years, she replied, "Oh, now you've got me stuck—I can't remember exactly. I moved in shortly after it opened up as an apartment building. I went from there to the Homestead, where I lived for five years, but then I got sick—they don't keep you if you need medical attention, so that's how I got here to the Island Home. It's very nice—they treat you very well here."

THE REAL THING—A NANTUCKET NATIVE

When I asked if Margaret is a native, she replied vehemently, "Yes, I am! I was born here on Nantucket at 29 Pleasant Street in 1907—the house is still there. My birthday is on November 17th; I'll be 96. I was born at home. They didn't have a hospital then. After a while they had a hospital on West Chester, and that was where I worked for a while. My maiden name was Backus." I asked Margaret to tell me about her early years, and she answered, "Well, I think the way we lived was good. Went to school here. I'm the youngest of five children, and there's only two of us left. My brother George was captain of the old steam-wheeler, the *Nobska*. My very oldest sister died when she was twelve years old. The one that's left is three years older than I am, and she lives in Pennsylvania." How was it being the youngest of five? "Terrible!"

370   When I commented that I thought Margaret used to be a redhead, she sat up straight and exclaimed, *"I'm still a redhead!* [And in fact there are still traces of red in her hair.] When I was a youngster, I had long braids hanging down my back. My mother used to braid them every morning before I went to school." What did children do for fun back in the teens of the 1900s? "Oh, we played like kids do. We went sliding when we had snow—we used to have lots more snow then. I do remember the harbor freezing in." What about school? "There was a building that had four grades in it on Orange Street…that's long gone now. You went there for four years, and then you went up to Academy Hill. I never got into much mischief at school, not really. Minded my P's and Q's. I remember some of my teachers, oh yes. I had a teacher whose father was our family doctor, Eda Coleman, she was. In those days, when kids got sick, they stayed at home and the doctor came to them. He was a nice old feller. I had measles and mumps and everything goin'.

"My family moved off the island when I was ten years old, so I never did go to school at Academy Hill," Margaret added. "They moved to Abington, Massachusetts, which is a small town outside of Brockton, if you know where that is. Why did we move? My mother. She wasn't a Nantucketer—she came here as a young girl, was originally from Canada…that's where she was born, on Prince Edward Island. As a young girl she went to Providence with friends, and worked. And in the summer, she and a friend came to Nantucket to work, as I did myself as a teenager, during the summer. In the fall she was goin' back to Providence, which was where she wanted to live. Well anyhow, she went to a dance with some of her friends, and she met my father, so she never went back to Providence. The dance was upstairs at the No. 4 Headquarters on Federal Street. I used to go there to dances too, when I was growing up. They also had dancing classes there. My mother's maiden name was Currie. She and my father were married in 18…somethin' or other, in February. In fact, I think either today or tomorrow was their anniversary. My father's first name was John. He was related to the Wauwinet Backuses; he and Jim Backus were brothers. He was a farmer. My Grandfather Backus was in the Civil War, and when he come home he started farming and he did it till he wasn't able to work any more, so my father and another brother took it over, and they did it for years. The farm wasn't very far away—it was on Dover Street, down in that vicinity. Cows and a hoss...I don't know how many cows...

"We moved because my mother thought the mainland would be better for the children, the schools and so forth. But it didn't do me any good, because I wasn't a scholar...I just got by, and that was it. Then my father worked wherever he could find a job. See, it was during the First World War when we moved away. I went to school in Abington, but I didn't finish. I went to work. What did I do? Oh, whatever I could find. Then in the summertime I'd come down here and work. I took care of children—babysitting. I worked for one family from Abington for the whole summer, and stayed with them. I liked coming back to the island; I wanted to come back, to begin with."

TAKING CARE OF FAMILY

Finally, Margaret said, she fulfilled her wish and came back to her island to stay. When was that? "In about 1930. Then I met up with somebody and got married. He was a fellow from Cape Cod. And it was the biggest mistake I ever made. Not good. 'Course, everybody told me, but you know, you don't listen to people. The marriage lasted two years. I have a son who lives on the island...Herbert. And he married Carol Magee, a girl who was working down here for the summer. He has stayed on the island. He was born here, so he's a native too. By then my parents had come back—'course my father was a Nantucketer, and he wanted to come back, so they did." Did he go back into farming? "Yes, same idea, but not same place. And my parents died here in 1940, both of them. My mother died in June and my father died in the following November. I was the only one home then, because the rest of the family were off the island, married. I had my son to take care of, and I took care of my parents, until they died."

I wondered about if Margaret, always a hard worker, found time to relax in those days. "Well, I always worked, of course. I had to support my child. I had housekeeping jobs, babysitting... But I had a social life, oh yes... I never played cards, but I did other things—went to dances, went out to the movies, to parties, and things like that. Not really a social butterfly. The movies were where they are now, down on Water Street. Never even considered getting married again.

Margaret Backus Crowell in 1931.

Never. You know, when I left the hospital with my son, the nurses said, 'Well, you'll be back here next year,' and I said 'Not so you'd notice it! Once is enough!' I made up my mind that I was just going to stay home and take care of my child and bring him up. And I hope I did a good job.

"Herbert was born in the hospital at West Chester Street. He went to school here, graduated from Nantucket High School. He likes being an islander—wouldn't live anywhere else. When I used to go away to visit my sisters, and we'd be up there a few days, he'd say, 'Let's go home.' You know, he had a lot of friends here. When he graduated from high school, he went into the service for four years [during the Korean conflict]. Did I worry about him? Lord, yes, I worried…when he came home I never was so glad to see anybody in my life. So then he went to work right away; he was a plumber. Now he's retired from that, and sometimes works summers, but not like he used to, in the winter.

MORE JOBS THAN YOU CAN COUNT

"When Herbert was in school, I started work in the hospital, and I was a nurse's aide, housekeeper, or whatever. They didn't pay very heavy, but it helped. I worked for the hospital for fifteen years, and then I worked for the Jared Coffin House for five or ten years, and then I got a job working for the Historical Association. I worked there for fifteen years…and that's where I retired from…another job I retired from! I have retired out of more jobs than you can count!" I asked Margaret if she remembered refusing to let me into the Foulger one day because I'd forgotten my card. "But you *know* me," I'd said, "and you know I'm a *member*…" But Margaret was adamant: "You can't come in without your card!" She laughed at the memory, and said, "Well, they were strict about that." (And so was she!) Of all the jobs, she said she'd like the one at the NHA best. "They paid you pretty good

372

money, and you could learn a lot about the island. The last of the jobs I had there, I worked up at the Oldest House…it was interesting. I liked it. You had to tell people about the history of the Oldest House and the island…or whatever they wanted to know. But people do ask silly questions sometimes."

Margaret's a longtime member of St. Paul's Church, and says, "and when my boy went to Sunday School, I used to sing in the choir…I don't remember the minister at that time. We've got a good one now, Joel Ives; he's a very nice fella. I haven't been to church for over a year, but they bring communion to us here." How does Margaret Crowell keep busy these days" Plainly, her memory and mind are still pretty sharp. She said, "I still have my hearing, but my eyes aren't

Margaret Crowell and her son Herbert, who was just about two years old. They are standing in front of the old Steamship terminal. 1935.

so good. But I read, watch TV, then they have parties here for us at Christmas, Valentine's Day, and so forth. My son and his wife come to see me most every day." Asked what her favorite years were, she smiled broadly and said, "Well, right now, I guess. I'm enjoying my life."

<hr />

HERBERT CROWELL

When I interviewed Herbert, he began by showing me a painting of the old steam-wheeler *Nobska,* which his uncle George Crowell had captained. He also pointed out that there was an anachronism in the picture: it showed radar equipment, and "that was not on the boat in the year the painting says," he said. I asked if he'd ever aspired to be a ferryboat captain, and he said, laughing, "No, I didn't."

Concerning his early years, Herbert said, "I was born on May 6th, 1932, and went to Academy Hill School and the Coffin School. The first three grades were on the first floor at Academy Hill; grade four was on the second floor in back and the fifth was in front; sixth grade was also in the back. Half of the second floor was junior high, and the third floor was the high school. We had to go home for lunch, you know—I lived over on North Liberty Street then. I remember my teachers: Miss Johnson in first grade—I believe she was an aunt of Johnny McLaughlin; in second grade, Rita Hull; and in third her sister Marjorie Hull. Their father was a state representative. I remember being let out of school when the war started, but not much more—there was rationing, of course." Herbert then took a mental walk on Main Street: "The First National and the A&P were side by side, as were the two drugstores, eventually. I think Nantucket Pharmacy was called Mac's…and now of course there are two insurance companies next to each other on that side of Main Street. The A&P was where Arno's is now, next to what is now Nantucket Pharmacy; then, going up, there was Coffin's Gifts, and a store that I knew as Coffin's Hardware—it used to be Brown's. Then on the corner of Centre Street and Main, still on that side (where the insurance companies are now) was Ashley's Market." Did all

Roy Egan, Jack Fee, Jack Dempsey, Maurice Gibbs, and Herb Crowell at "Dempsey's." The legend under the picture, furnished by Maurice Gibbs, says "Who's ready for a fight?"

those stores do OK side by side? "Well, Ashley's must've…its owner was also president of the Pacific National Bank. He was a meat-cutter, and I can still see him with his straw hat and his white long apron. He'd go across to the bank…His store carried fancy stuff like S.S. Pierce…Ashley's had a bakery on the second floor, and Aime Poirier was the baker; he later had his own bakery where Cumberland Farm is now, and lived next door."

Hard Work Runs in the Family

Herb Crowell is a chip off the old block; like his mother, Margaret, he's been a hard worker from an early age. "I had to work in the summers when I was a kid," he said. "My first job was at the Nantucket Golf Club, working for Elwyn Francis. Then I worked at Young's Bicycle Shop. And I worked at the Hub, when it was Rogers'…I was a soda jerk. Yes, on that wall with the mirror they had a soda fountain, served ice cream sodas, frappes, cokes, and so forth. Then later I worked for Bill Grieder's Nantucket Distributing Co., delivering. And I also worked for Miller's Fish Market, driving the truck. When I got out of high school I went to work for Austin Tyrer, who was a plumber. I did that for six months and then joined the SeaBees, the Navy, during the Korean War. The SeaBees were construction. I never saw action, but I went to Newfoundland, North Africa, Guantanamo Bay, and then went to what they called UT School compliments of the Navy, for four years in Port Hueneme, California, where I learned plumbing. When I came back to Nantucket I first worked for W.B. Marden and Company, then worked for the Water Company for nine years as a meter reader, laying water mains, and so forth. Then I worked for Franklin Bartlett Plumbing. Finally, I went to work for the Beinecke family in jobs around the Marina, his hotels and properties. I retired at 62. Then I took a year off," he smiled, "but my wife finally said, 'No more of this! No more staying around the house!' so I drove a cab for a summer, and hated every minute of it. Then for three years I worked at the Lifesaving Museum. I've worked part-time at the car wash by D&B for three years.

"I met my wife, Carol Magee, when she came here to waitress one summer—she was going to Boston State Teachers College. She worked in a restaurant that's where Tonkin's is now—first it was called Haskell's, then The Quahog. Carol was born in Stoughton, Massachusetts. We married in 1960, and have been married almost 43 years. Carol taught math at Nantucket High School for three years, and ultimately became Vice Principal. She retired about eight years ago. She stays very busy; for one thing, she knits sweaters—she uses a knitting machine to make the body of the sweaters, then hand-knits the cuffs, waistband, and collar. Carol does a lot of needlework," he added proudly, then took me around the house to see some of her beautiful handiwork, among which were quilts, pillows, and a fabulous collage of lighthouses done in needlepoint so perfect that it looks like a painting. Herbert went on: "My son John lives on the island; he is a carpenter, and he's into boats—he had a tuna-fishing boat, and now he scallops. His wife is the business manager at that expensive new golf course. And I have a daughter who is a nurse at Mass General."

At that point the phone rang; Herbert answered and when he hung up, explained the call was about the skiff Carol had just bought. "Carol's the captain," he said, "and I'm the mate. She's a big-time fisherman, fishes in all the ponds on the island. She won last year's year-round Esther Barlow Tournament at the Angler's Club. Myself, I like surf fishing, for blues and bass; I go out to Surfside…Great Point's just too far." What else does Herb Crowell do to relax? "Well, I read…and I've always been a Nantucket history and World War II history buff, read anything I can about them." I wondered if he accessed the Internet for information on that war, and he laughed, "Oh no—the agreement here is that I don't touch the computer, the checkbook, or the VCR."

Herb Crowell seems quite happy with his busy life, and is, of course, proud to be a bona fide native. Have you ever considered living anywhere else? I asked. His answer was a direct and forceful as his mother's responses: "No! This is my home…I've never wanted to be anywhere else. And my wife has blended well into the community…she still calls herself an off-islander, though…knows about this 'native' business. You can't call yourself a native unless you're born here." He paused a moment, then laughed and said, "There was a feller called Butler Folger who was a professor at Dartmouth; he and his family summered here. He and I were talking one day, and he said, 'Well, you're related to half the town and I'm related to the other.' Then I asked him if he was a native…and I found that while he let people think he was (and was probably perturbed that I asked him), he finally admitted he'd been born in San Francisco. I said, 'Butler, old boy, then I'm one up on you!'"

The apple doesn't fall far from the tree, they say…and both Margaret Crowell and her son Herbert are good apples…finest kind, Cap'n.

Margaret Backus Crowell at Academy Hill, in 1998, with Robert F. Mooney, Lee Cahoon, and Bob Gotto, who are attending a NHS Class of 1948 reunion.